AF540484

AAKAR BOOKS CLASSICS

THE INDIAN CAPITALIST CLASS

AAKAR BOOKS CLASSICS

THE INDIAN CAPITALIST CLASS

A Historical Study

V.I. Pavlov

The Indian Capitalist Class
V.I. Pavlov

© Aakar Books

First Aakar Edition 2016
Reprinted 2023

ISBN 978-93-5002-406-5

All rights reserved. No part of this book may be reproduced or transmitted, in any form or by any means, without the prior permission of the publisher.

Published by
AAKAR BOOKS
28 E Pocket IV, Mayur Vihar Phase I
Delhi 110 091, India
www.aakarbooks.com

Printed at
D.K. Fine Art Press, Delhi

CONTENTS

PREFACE

The principal aim of this book is to throw light on the basic laws governing the origin and the development of capitalist enterprise in the national industry of India. The author had neither the intention, nor the means, to paint a complete picture covering all aspects of industrial development in India during modern times. The reader will, undoubtedly, notice the lack of statistical data regarding a number of important phenomena, as also the fact that a purely economic analysis has not been attempted in these cases. The specific features of the development of the Indian bourgeoisie up to the general crisis of capitalism is the problem which has attracted the special attention of the author and has been examined by him in greater detail.

The Indian bourgeoisie was composed of numerous national groups, communities and castes whose uneven development was due to a variety of factors including the different stages reached by the social and economic forces in the various Indian feudal states at the time they were conquered by the colonial invaders, the uneven development of capitalist relations in individual provinces of colonial India, the diverse conditions of collaboration and the various kinds of contradictions existing between the Indian propertied classes and the colonial government in separate parts of the country. The complexity of the problem has been described by D.R. Gadgil, the outstanding Indian economist, in his very interesting and valuable *Interim Report on the Origins of the Modern Indian Business Class*, from which the following passage has been taken:

> It became clear as one looked into the historical material that, though a number of monographs on particular periods or aspects had appeared during recent decades, a comprehensive view of modern Indian economic history, especially in relation to growth of modern business, had not been taken. This part of the task appeared, therefore, to be that of writing serious economic history even though based on secondary sources. As the field was almost uncharted, it became necessary to organise bit by bit the total data in some sort of meaningful sequence. The basic geographical characteristics of different regions, the changing political situation

and policies of various regimes, the qualities and the degree of adaptability displayed by particular business communities, the pervasive influence of British power and British business interests operating against the background of a technological and industrial revolution—all these had to be taken into account for an understanding of the situation.[1]

Up to the beginning of the general crisis of capitalism, i.e. up to the First World War, the only Indian section that brought forth a large group of factory owners was the Gujarati bourgeoisie. Marwari capitalists too played an important role among the Indian bourgeoisie, and in recent times many of the biggest Indian monopolists rose from their ranks. The formation process of the Gujarati and the Marwari bourgeoisie displays the general laws of development of the big Indian bourgeoisie in a most comprehensive way. For this reason we have concentrated our attention on these two groups when analysing the rise of the upper strata of the Indian bourgeoisie. The development of small-scale capitalist industry and the genesis of the lower and middle strata of the Indian bourgeoisie can be best illustrated on the example of the middle classes in Maharashtra and Bengal. The specific features and fundamental laws that are common to the Indian bourgeoisie as a whole are most clearly revealed in the economic and political development of these four sections of the Indian bourgeoisie.

The events of the last decade have unambiguously shown that some of Stalin's views regarding the national bourgeoisie in the Eastern countries were rather dogmatic. The scientific exploration of the past and present activity of the hourgeoisic in the Asian countries is, therefore, a problem set by life itself.

Fundamental methodological propositions regarding the nature of the bourgeoisie of the oppressed countries have been already enunciated in Lenin's works which were written either during the first years of the general crisis of capitalism or even on the eve of it. Lenin stressed that Asia, in contrast to Europe, still had a bourgeoisie capable of championing sincere, militant, consistent democracy, and willing to advance together with the people against reaction. At the same time he noted the danger inherent in the nationalist ideology for the working people of all nations. For that reason Lenin came out, on the one hand, for the resolute support of the fight of the bourgeoisie of the oppressed nation against the bourgeoisie of the oppressing nation, and on the other, against narrow nationalism and the aspirations of the bourgeoisie of the oppressed nations to obtain privileges for itself.

In the analysis of the political course followed by the national

---

1 D.R. Gadgil, *Origins of the Modern Indian Business Class, An Interim Report*, New York, 1959, p. iii.

bourgeoisie, which Lenin made in his report at the Second Congress of the Communist International, he took the two trends discernible in the policy of the national bourgeoisie as his starting point. On the one hand be observed that in the years immediately following the First World War and the October Revolution the bourgeoisie of the oppressed nations in most cases joined the imperialists in fighting against the revolutionary movements and the revolutionary classes; but on the other hand, Lenin pointed out that it supported national movements, and he considered a really revolutionary bourgeois liberation movement possible. How attentively Lenin studies the changing attitudes of the bourgeoisie of the colonial and semi-colonial countries, is evident from the fact that already two months after the Second Congress of the Communist International he noted as a matter of utmost importance that the bourgeoisie in the countries oppressed by the Entente, whose population made up about 70 per cent of the world population, was favourably inclined to Soviet Russia.[2]

The dual character of the national bourgeoisie was accentuated because it exploited the working people of its own country—the industrial capitalist exploited the proletariat, the merchant and the moneylender exploited the peasants and craftsmen. A correct dialectical approach to the study of the national bourgeoisie has to take the two contradictory aspects of its economic and political existence equally into account and to analyse both. If one disregards one of these aspects, investigations tend to become metaphysical, and the conclusions are likely to show either sectarian dogmatism, or revisionism.

Soviet works on colonial and semi-colonial countries written in the period preceding the 20th Congress of the Communist Party of the Soviet Union often under-estimated the intensity and depth of the contradictions that existed between the national bourgeoisie of these countries and imperialism. The analysis of the inter-relations of national capital and imperialism was divorced from the examination of the relations obtaining between the national bourgeoisie and the colonial regime. Moreover, the fact that the national bourgeoisie was the personification of national capital was not taken into account. Stalin's methods of approach led to a dogmatic appraisal of many political phenomena and events in post-war India.

It should not be overlooked that the two aspects of the

2 See V.I. Lenin, *Selected Works*, Vol. IV—*Democracy and Narodism in China*, Moscow, Leningrad, 1935, p. 307; Vol. X—*The Report of the Commission on the National and Colonial Question at the Second Congress of the Communist International*, p. 241; V.I. Lenin, *The National Liberation Movement in the East*, Moscow, 1962—*Backward Europe and Advanced Asia*, p. 62; V.I. Lenin, *Questions of National Policy and Proletarian Internationalism*, M., 1960.—*The Right of Nations to Self-Determination*, p. 81.

contradictions inherent in the national bourgeoisie (in relation to imperialism and to the working class) arise and take shape during the capitalist development of the country, and reach maturity and their greatest intensity only in modern times. In this study we will endeavour to trace the evolution of these two contradictory sides of the Indian bourgeoisie within the historical framework of this investigation.

× × × ×

It will be recalled that the fundamental laws governing the formation process of the bourgeoisie have been defined by the founders of Marxism-Leninism.

A general outline of how the European bourgeoisie arose from the ranks of the free burghers has been given by Karl Marx and Frederick Engels in the *Manifesto of the Communist Party*. The discovery of the sea-routes to India and South-East Asia and to America opened up fresh ground for the activities of the rising bourgeoisie. The feudal system of urban industry, under which industrial production was monopolised by closed guilds, no longer sufficed for the growing requirements of the developing society. The handicrafts of the medieval town were replaced by capitalist manufactories where the division of labour was applied to single operations. The establishments of manufactories heralded the rise of the bourgeoisie. The guild-masters (here the term denotes a full member of a guild, a master within, not a head of a guild) were pushed on one side by the manufacturing middle class. The European bourgeoisie evolved within the feudal system; because it was the feudal society in Europe that created the means of production and of exchange on which the development of the bourgeoisie depended. Already within the feudal society did more or less advanced forms of the capitalist mode of production come into being and mature in the European countries. As a result of the further development of capitalism "the place of manufacture was taken by the giant, Modern Industry, the place of the industrial middle class, by industrial millionaires, the leaders of whole industrial armies, the modern bourgeoisie. We see, therefore, how the modern bourgeoisie is itself the product of a long course of development, of a series of revolutions in the modes of production and of exchange."[3]

The passages quoted from the *Communist Manifesto* indicate that the founders of Marxism considered the formation process of the bourgeoisie as an integral part of the general development of the capitalism mode of production. Ten years after the publication of the *Manifesto*, Marx wrote: "Capitalists and wage-workers are therefore one

3 K. Marx and F. Engels, *Manifesto of the Communist Party*. In : K. Marx and F. Engels, *Selected Works in Two Volumes*, Moscow, 1958, Vol. I, p. 35; see also p. 39.

of the chief products created by capital in the process of self-expansion."[4] Marx and Engels established the very important fact that each step in the development of the bourgeoisie was directly linked to the corresponding stage of capitalism : guild organisation and guild-masters (according to the *Manifesto* the first elements of the bourgeoisie'); the manufacturing system and the manufacturing middle class; large-scale industry and the industrial millionaires, the modern (pre-monopoly) bourgeoisie.

Lenin wrote that the rise of the Russian bourgeoisie—which he analysed in his work *The Development of Capitalism in Russia*—provided "perhaps one of the most striking manifestations of the intimate and direct connection between the consecutive forms of industry".[5] This is an extremely concise and exact definition of the fundamental law advanced by Marx and Engels namely that each step in the development of the bourgeoisie depended on the corresponding stage of capitalist production. We will attempt to outline the action of this general law in respect to the rise of the Indian bourgeoisie and to determine the specific features of this process.

The bourgeoisie had not yet come into being in the feudal states of India when they were conquered by Britain. The colonial subjugation of the country began before Indian feudalism had given rise to any well-developed forms of capitalism. Only the first elements of capitalist relations existed in individual regions of India; in industry they appeared in the shape of simple capitalist co-operation, with a division of labour which exhibited a certain feature characteristic of manufactories; while in agriculture one can discern the beginning differentiation of the peasantry, a typical sign of fully developed feudalism. The formation process begain in earnest during the second half of the 19th century, when the country was already subjected to methods of colonial exploitation—including the export of capital—which are characteristic of imperialism. The fact that up to the British conquest, only merchant's and moneylender's capital had been generated in India largely determined the specific course of development and the distinctive feature of the Indian bourgeoisie. It is, therefore, necessary to begin with a brief review of the business activities of the Indian traders and moneylenders up to the middle of the 19th century.

4 K. Marx, *Grundrisse der Kritik der Politischen Okonomie (Rohentwurf), 1857-1858*, Moskau, Verlag fur Fremdsprachige Literature, 1939, S. 412.

5 V.I. Lenin, *The Development of Capitalism in Russia*, In : V.I. Lenin, Collected Works, Vol. III, Moscow, 1960, p. 541.

PART I

First Beginnings of Indian Capitalism

CHAPTER I

THE FIRST BEGINNINGS

The origin of the Indian bourgeoisie is to be traced in the process of primitive accumulation of capital and the formation of a capitalist social structure. These fundamental changes were taking place in India during the colonial period. But research work carried out recently by orientalists including Soviet scholars, gives reason to believe that already in the pre-colonial period certain phenomena appeared in India's economy whose further development might have prepared the ground for the rise of the bourgeoisie. We must, therefore, begin our work with a brief analysis of the level of social and economic development which India had reached prior to its colonial subjugation and the position of those strata of feudal society that subsequently gave rise to the bourgeoisie. This question is of great interest, for it enables us to determine clearly the part which British conquest played in India's historical development.

The works of Marx and Engels contain observations on the specific features of Indian feudalism which are of basic methodological importance. Taking these as their point of departure, Soviet orientalists have investigated the social and economic conditions existing in India just before it was conquered by the British. Their research work enables us to form an idea of the level of development attained by feudalism, the social division of labour and economic organisation of artisan production.[1]

Any analysis of the social and economic structure of a feudal country must begin with the relations of landownership. The study of this problem, which presents great difficulties in any country, is particularly complicated in feudal India owing to the variety of forms

1 Cf. I. M. Reisner, *Nekotorye dannye o razlozhenii derevenskoi obshchiny u maratkhov v XVII—nachale XIX veka* (Data Regarding Differentiation in the Maratha Village Community from the 17th to the Early 18th Century) in *Uchenye sapiski Instituta vostokovedeniya Akademii Nauk SSSR*, t. 5, Moskva, 1953; E. N. Komarov, *Agrarnye otnosheniya i zemelno-nalogovaya politika angliiskikh kolonisatorov v Bengalii v seredine—vtoroi polovin XVIII v* (Agrarian Relations and the Land-Tax Policy of the British Colonialists in Bengal in the Middle and the Latter Half of the Eighteenth Century) *dissertatsiya na soiskanie uchenoi*

of landownership and land tenure existing there and the original differences in the level of social and economic progress, and finally the paucity of available documentary sources in this country. We will, therefore, now merely record the general laws governing the development of Indian feudalism that were already set forth by the founders of Marxism and investigated by Soviet orientalists.

Soviet researchers have described three important elements of the social and economic structure of feudal India—namely, ownership of land and irrigation works vested in the state, feudal land property held by individuals which existed under the supreme state ownership, and the village communities composed of peasants who enjoyed hereditary tenure and use of the land and have examined their mutual relationship and inter-dependence.

Ownership of land vested in the feudal state was the economic basis of the Great Mogul Empire, the last oriental despotism in India. The product taken from the peasant by right of this ownership appears as rent-tax. The concentration of enormous material values received in the form of rent or tax in the state was the chief material prerequisite for the existence of a powerful centralised despotism. Absence of private property in land was, as Marx remarked, the key even to the oriental heaven.[2] Regarding feudal India Marx wrote: "Sovereignty here consists in the ownership of land concentrated on a national scale. But, on the other hand, no private ownership of land exists, although there is both private and common possession and use of land."[3]

---

stepeni kandidata istoricheskikh nauk, Instituta vostokovedeniya Akademii Nauk SSSR, 1953; E N. Komarov, *K voprosu ob ustanovlenii postoyannogo oblozheniya po sisteme zamindari v Bengalii* (The Problem of the Zamindari System of Permanent Settlement in Bengal) in: *Uchenye zapiski Instituta vostokovedeniya Akademii Nauk SSSR*; t. 12, 1955; E. N. Komarov, V. Ya. Grashe (V. I. Pavlov). *Nekotorye dannye ob obshchestvennom razdelenii truda i ekonomicheskoi organizatsii remesla v Indii na rubezhe XVIII i XIX vekov* (Data on the Social Division of Labour and the Economic Organization of Handicrafts in India at the Close of the Eighteenth Century and the Beginning of the Nineteenth, in: *Kratkie soobshcheniya Instituta vostokovedeniya Akademii Nauk SSSR*, t. XV, Moscow, 1955; K. A. Antonova, *Agrarnye otnosheniya v Indii nakanune angliskogo zavoevaniya* (Agrarian Relations in India on the Eve of the British Conquest) in: *Izv. Akademii Nauk SSSR, Seriya istori i filosofii*, t. VI, No. 5, 1949, K. A. Antonova, *Osnovnye formy feodalnogo zemlevladeniya v Mogolskoi Indii XVI v.* (The Principal forms of Feudal Landownership in Mogul India during the Sixteenth Century) in: *Uchenye zapiski Instituta vostokovedeniya Akademii Nauk SSSR*, t. 5; K. A. Antonova, *Ocherki obshechestvennykh otnosheny i politicheskogo stroya Mogolskoi Indii vremen Akbara 1556-1605* (Essays on the Social Relations and the Political Structure in Mogul India during Akbar's Reign 1556-1605), Moscow, 1952.

2 Karl Marx and Frederick Engels, *Selected Correspondence*, (Moscow,) 99.

3 Karl Marx, *Capital*, (Moscow, 1959,) 111, 772.

Under certain historical conditions, chiefly in the early Middle Ages, state property formed the economic basis of a relative political centralisation in the East, and thus played a progressive role by countervailing feudal anarchy and internal dissension, and furthering the early development of medieval towns. At the same time the immaturity or absence of the forms of private ownership of land was a serious impediment to the emergence of new, capitalist relations within the feudal society. The particular form of capitalist development which Marx described in the first volume of *Capital* was historically inevitable only in the west European countries. Where, however, in contrast to west Europe, the transformation of one form of private property into another form did not take place; or where, for instance, common ownership of the means of production predominated in agriculture or the land was state property, the social and economic development might be different from that of west Europe, and had in reality its own specific features. The dialectics of historical development manifested itself, in particular, in the fact that at a certain stage state property in land began to impede the rise of the new economic enterprise of the urban population; in short, it became an obstacle to economic progress.

During the golden age of the Mogul Empire the sovereignty of this centralised despotism was powerfully expressed in the state ownership of land, although feudal land property held by individuals continued to exist even at that time. Very significant changes occurred, however, in the sphere of land relations when the Mogul Empire began to disintegrate. State ownership of land and water, which up to then had fairly adequately reflected the real economic relations, was being transformed into various forms of private feudal property. The political decentralisation of the Mogul state and its disintegration were, undoubtedly, caused by economic processes taking place within the Indian society, which had already made use of all available possibilities of feudal development based on state ownership of land. It was the tragedy of the country that precisely at this crucial point the expanding west European powers entered the arena, and thereby for a long time determined the further development of India, a development which subsequently was to proceed under colonial conditions.

The contradiction between state ownership of land and private possession and use of land (by both feudal lord and peasant) became one of the cardinal contradictions of Mogul society in the period of its decline. As long as the Mogul state continued to bring under its dominion new regions by waging successful wars, the feudal lords who served the Moguls received new conditional holdings of land in the conquered territories. Therefore, they generally accepted a situation where a considerable part of the rent they collected had to be handed over to the state treasury in the form of tax. But in the latter half of the

17th century, when the Great Mogul Empire had almost every where (except in the south) reached the natural boundaries of India, the Mogul nobility was no longer able to increase their revenues by conquering new territories and incorporating them into the empire. Subsequently they could enlarge their income either by intensifying the exploitation of the peasants or by changing the principles according to which revenue was divided between the feudal state and individual feudal landowners.[4]

Efforts to increase the absolute volume of rent were resisted by the peasantry. The most powerful and best organised peasant movement was that of the Sikhs in the Punjab. The Sikhs, with the support of urban artisans and traders, first undermined and later in the second half of the 18th century abolished Mogul rule in this rich province. Warned by the uprising of the Sikhs and other actions of the peasantry, the feudal landowners were forced to seek, in addition to intensified exploitation, other means to augment their income. They tried particularly in outlying districts, to increase their share of the common feudal rent at the expense of the state rent-tax. The fight for their share of the rent was, in our view, the basis of separatist, anti-Mogul movements headed by the local feudal lords. Whether these movements gradually led to virtual defection while formally preserving vassalage (as for instance in Bengal) or developed into armed uprisings (as for example, in Maharashtra) depended on a number of factors, among which the religious and communal affiliation of the majority of the population occupied an important place. Researches carried out by I. M. Reisner and later by his former pupil E. N. Komarov enable us to form an opinion regarding the level of development which feudal society reached in these provinces at the end of the 17th century and the first half of the 18th.

By the middle of the 18th century, the feudal institution of state ownership of land had reached an advanced stage of decline in Bengal. Conditional holdings that were granted in return for services tended to be converted into hereditary feudal estates. The rent appropriated

4 The class of feudal lords can be subdivided into three principal groups: the Mogul nobility, in the main Muslims, who held the largest feudal (conditional) tenures—jagirs; big and medium feudal lords, mainly Hindu, who retained hereditary rights to their lands; small feudals who rose from the village communities during the differentiation process and added waste land allotments held by members of the community to their own official holdings of land. The relations of these feudal landowners to each other and to the central authority were very complicated. The works of Soviet orientalists show that private feudal property in land continued to exist in Mogul India side by side with conditional feudal tenure (the prevailing form of feudal ownership of land), and this means that the Moguls were, in fact, unable to convert all the lands of the empire into full state property.

by the feudal lords was separated from the rent-tax, the individual feudal lord (zamindar) usually receiving a bigger share of the surplus product than that taken by the government as tax.[5] All this indicated that feudal land property held by individuals was actually emerging in place of feudal state ownership of land.

The formation of private feudal property and the disappearance of state property passed through several stages in Maharashtra, where, in the 17th century, feudal relations had not yet reached such mature forms as in Bengal. The victory of the Maratha liberation movement naturally led to the abolition of the state property in land existing in the Mogul Empire. But the continuing fierce struggle against the Moguls demanded a strong centralised state. Only state ownership of land, the basic means of production, could serve as the material foundation for such a state. Shivaji therefore created vast state domains from the holdings of the Mogul feudal lords, who were either driven out or exterminated. Separatist rebellions of hereditary feudal lords were mercilessly suppressed. The feudal groups on whose support Shivaji relied consisted of the military and civil nobility maintained by the treasury and the holders of military fiefs *(sarinjams).*

But under the subsequent rulers of Maharashtra (the Peshwas) medium and small feudal lords extended their landholdings by seizing the lands of village communities. This, as well as the farming of the rent-tax practised by the state, undermined state ownership of land. Tax collectors were usually small feudals risen from the ranks of Patels (the Patel is the chief official of the village community).[6] Thus feudal land property held by individuals was, in Maharashtra too, superseding state property.

The structure of the Maratha village community, its nature and the consequences of its disintegration have been studied by I. M. Reisner, the prominent Soviet orientalist. In his work on the Maratha community from the 17th to 19th centuries Reisner stated that the holdings of the Maratha *mirasdars,* their hereditary lands, were purchased and sold and also mortgaged in the 17th and 18th centuries. The question whether the *mirasdars* were the owners or the hereditary holders of their land has been raised by Reisner, who has also tried to find the answer. He writes:

> The Maratha *mirasdar* was a typical feudal peasant, a hereditary holder of the land, which he tilled with his own implements and draught-animals, and ran his farm on the basis of his own labour. The peasantry, which the *mirasdar* represented, was an oppressed class tied down to the tax burden and subjected by the owner of

---

5 E. N. Komarov, *K voprosu ob ustanovlenii postoyannogo oblozheniya,* 3-11.

6 I. M. Reisner, n. 1, 234-36

the land, the feudal lord or the feudal state to serve non-economic coercion.[7]

Reisner stresses that the personal property rights of the peasant and the handicraftsman to his individual peasant farm and to his agricultural implements based on his own labour were curbed by feudal property which predominated and formed the foundation of the feudal order.[8]

On the basis of the researches carried out by Reisner we can, for instance, assert that on the whole the village community in India retained its old organisation. Although it is true that allodial property in land was coming into being as well as private property in implements and means of production, and that various social groups were arising in the village community—in particular a top layer which formed the lower strata of the feudal class—and free peasants, whose lands held in perpetual tenure tended to become their property. But a number of factors delayed the feudalisation process of the top layer of the village community as well as the generation of peasant property and, consequently, the emergence of the peasantry as a class. State ownership of land appears to have impeded the rise of feudals within the village community, and the development of the peasant allodium was slowed down by the fact that the village community did everything in its power to maintain its ownership of the land, the principal means of production.

Historically seen, the consolidation of private property in land gave the countries of the East the possibility to transform feudal private property into capitalist private property. The intervention of the European colonialists, however, has left its impress on the processes which were taking shape in the feudal society of the East, hastening, on the one hand, the disintegration of the old relations and, on the other hand, strengthening the worst aspects of the domination of the feudal landowner while at the same time furthering the expropriation of the peasants from their property.

The development of feudal relations was accompanied by an increasing social division of labour. A serious obstacle to the further development of the division of labour and of trade between town and country in medieval India was the preservation of the village community and its peculiar organisation which was "based on possession in common of the land, on the blending of agriculture and handicrafts, and on an unalterable division of labour."[9] Marx points out that this blending of agriculture and handicrafts in Indian village communities of the simplest form shows itself in the fact that "spinning

7 *Ibid.*, 196.

8 *Ibid.*

9 Marx, *Capital* (Moscow, 1956) I, 357.

and weaving are carried on in each family as subsidiary industries."[10] The division of labour firmly established within the community led to the institution of village artisans, who specialised in a particular craft and catered to the needs of the members of the community. In return the artisans received a portion of the harvest from the agriculturists of the commune and were also given a small plot of land. Thus the division of labour within the community, which was based on a natural economy, made the community a compact self-sufficient unit, where production was "independent of that division of labour brought about, in Indian society as a whole, by means of the exchange of commodities."[11] The economic isolation of the simplest type of Indian community prevented the development of division of labour within the workshop. "The whole mechanism (of the village community) discloses a systematic division of labour; but a division like that in manufactures is impossible, since the smith and the carpenter, etc., find an unchanging market"...[12]

But the economic organisation of the village communities deteriorated during the 17th and 18th centuries, as the researches of Soviet orientalists show. While in earlier times the members of the community nominated and removed the Patel and the other village officials, these posts now became hereditary and the officers received land for the performance of their official duties which was separated from the land of the community and exempt from taxation. As a result of such grants officials of the village community gradually became feudal landowners.[13] The transformation of community lands into feudal land property held by individuals undermined one of the basic principles of the community, namely common possession and use of land, and consequently state property in land.

Another essential element of the Indian village community—the fusion of agriculture and handicrafts and the firmly established division of labour—was also weakened by the further development of feudalism. We will examine this question closer, since it is directly pertinent to our subject.

Which processes helped to breach the natural self-sufficiency of the village community, and led to the development of simple commodity production in agriculture? The well-known Soviet orientalist K. A. Antonova holds that as early as the 17th century, when Akbar began to levy taxes in money, the Indian peasants "established connections with the market since they had to sell their products to pay the land tax; they did not, however, appear in the market as

10 *Ibid.*

11 *Ibid.*

12 *Ibid.*, 358.

13 Reisner, n. 1, 220.

buyers."[14] In reply to this point of view one must say that the money rent-tax could, of course, bring peasants from surrounding villages to the urban markets, but the peasants' connections with the market remained incidental and did not become widespread. For otherwise commodity production in the peasant economy would have reached a considerable degree in the 150 to 200 years that elapsed between the introduction of the money tax by Akbar and the British conquest. This, however, did not happen. The notion, moreover, that the system of taxation played a leading role in the disintegration of the natural self-sufficient peasant economy seems rather doubtful. It will be recalled that even "the brutal interference of the British tax collector", as Marx wrote, did not lead to the destruction of the village community. Is it, therefore, likely that the fiscal apparatus of the Mogul Empire should have been able to destroy it?

Source material indicates that the conversion of the land tax into a money tax need not have noticeably affected the natural self-sufficiency of either the village community as a whole or individual peasant households.[15] Even during the 18th century and at the beginning of the 19th century the peasants in Gujarat, Mysore and Rajasthan—that is, in the regions which had comparatively well developed commodity-money relations—as a rule paid their taxes either in kind direct to the tax farmer, or in money which they borrowed from the moneylender, to whom they later handed over part of their harvest.[16] It is obvious that in either case the peasant did not have to sell his produce on the market in order to pay his taxes, and did not become a commodity producer.

The Soviet orientalist I. B. Alaev has advanced a different opinion about the causes leading to the disintegration of the natural self-sufficient village community. Recalling Marx's statement that the extremely ancient, small Indian communities were based on possession in common of the land, on the blending of agriculture and handicrafts, and on an unalterable division of labour.[17] Alaev asserts that "the blending of agriculture and handicrafts in the form of domestic industry was the most important of the features distinguishing the Eastern village community".[18] He quotes

14 See *Sovetskoe vostokovedenie*, (1957) No. 6, 54.

15 D. R. Gadgil is quite justified in writing that "The export or sale of produce helped in paying the dues owed to the state or landlord by the agriculturist but did not usually give him resources in exchange with which he could buy significant quantities of the products of urban industry" D. R. Gadgil, *Origins of the Modern Indian Business Class*, 5.

16 A. K. Forbes, *Ras Mala, Hindoo Annals of the Provinces of Goozerat in Western India* (London, 1856.) II, 247; F. Buchanan, *A Journey from Madras through the Countries of Mysore, Canara and Malabar...* (London, 1807) I, 265; J. Todd, *Antiquities and Annals of Rajasthan* (London,1832) II, 282.

17 Marx, n. 9, 357.

18 *Sovetskoe vostokovedenie*, 1957, No. 3, 96.

numerous sources showing that weavers became separated from the body of the village community. These weavers formed independent corporations (*shreni*) and, declares Alaev, entered into commercial relations with the village community. "This process undermined the basis of the stagnant Indian village community".[19]

Alaev, unfortunately, divorces the study of such important and closely related processes as the evolution of the forms of landownership and land tenure from the analysis of the separation process of the handicrafts from agriculture. In examining the common possession of land he completely disregards the handicrafts in the village community,[20] while in his analysis of the natural self-sufficiency of the village community the relations of production are left out of account. Naturally, such a method of research prevents L. B. Alaev, just as it prevents K. A. Antonova, from making a comprehensive investigation of the causes leading to the breakdown of the old economic system in the Indian village communities.

The proposition put forward by L. B. Alaev does, indeed, contain several points that are open to criticism. First, although the fact that individual groups of weavers detached themselves from the village community can be considered as proved, it is up to now uncertain how far-reaching a process this was and, in particular, whether weaving ceased to be a domestic industry of the peasants. Alaev himself chiefly adduces evidence about weavers in the coastal regions of south India where the handicrafts were associated with foreign trade. It still remains to be demonstrated that weaving became completely separated from the system of communal handicrafts in the interior regions of the country, and supposing it were demonstrated, one would still have to ascertain whether the weavers entered into commodity-money relations with the peasants by way of the market, or worked on orders from individual customers and were paid in kind. The existence of isolated fairs does not prove conclusively that commodity-money relations between weavers and agriculturists were widespread. Even if this should be proved, it would merely establish the fact without, however, explaining it.

It is not possible to give an explanation without analysing the principal elements of the communal system obtaining in medieval India and examining all processes, their mutual relations and interactions. Marx attached the greatest importance to the specific forms of landownership as one of the factors determining the concrete pattern

19 *Ibid.*, 104.

20 L. B. Alaev, *Formy obshchinnogo semlevladeniya v Yuzhnoi Indii v XIV-XVIII vv.* (Forms of Communal Landownership in Southern India in the Fourteenth to Eighteenth Centuries) in *Indiya i Afganistan, Ocherki istorii i ekonomiki* (India and Afganistan, Historical and Economic Essays) Moscow, 1958.)

of the transition from one mode of production to another. Probably the most comprehensive of the definitions which Marx has given of the "national" mode of production in the East is contained in the following passage :

> The broad basis of the mode of production here is formed by the unity of small-scale agriculture and home industry, to which in India we should add the form of village communities built upon the common ownership of land, which, incidentally, was the original form in China as well.[21]

It was precisely the circumstance that the Indian village community was based on the common ownership of land, which, in our view, formed the greatest obstacle to the separation of the handicrafts from agriculture, the extension of the social division of labour and the emergence, first, of simple commodity production and, later, of the capitalist mode of production.

The influence exerted by feudal property in land was similar. Marx wrote that the form of landownership in Asia explained the existence of huge cities, or military camps,[22] which served as military and administrative headquarters, and maintained only weak commercial relations with the countryside. Commerce and handicrafts in these cities were almost exclusively engaged in catering to the needs of the court, army, administration and individual feudal chiefs or they worked for the foreign market, and this aspect of their activity was—just as the handicrafts in the village communities—virtually independent of the social division of labour obtaining in the country as a whole.

In the regions of India where vast areas were solely inhabited by an agricultural population that had no economic contacts with cattle-breeders, and where as a matter of fact the social division of labour began with the separation of the handicrafts from agriculture, the initial stimulus seems to have come from the feudalisation of the top layer of the village community which gravely upset the natural self-sufficiency of the community. It appears that the first owner of commodities to emerge from among the full and equal members of the village community was the landowner who was turning into a feudal. His appearance in the market had, undoubtedly, considerably greater consequences for the structure of the village community than the activities of the moneylender who was also dealing in commodities and money for the village landowner could use the income he received from commerce to acquire land on an increasing scale, to enslave at first, villagers who did not enjoy full rights, and later also full and equal members of the community, and even to hire labour. I. M.

21 Marx, n. 3, 328.

22 Karl Marx, *Theorien urban den Mehrwert,* Teil 3, Berlin.

Reisner's and L. B. Alaev's studies of the Indian village community during the later period show that the first stages of this process could be observed in India.[23]

Although one has to take into consideration the part which feudal land property held by individuals played in disintegration of the early form of the village community and the overcoming of its natural self-sufficiency, it would be wrong to overestimate the impetus and scope of these processes, which remained within the framework of feudalism and were based on the natural economy. In particular, the emergence of big private landed property did not by itself lead to radical changes in the social division of labour which had earlier taken shape. As long as the communal organisation and state property in land predominated, the bulk of the surplus produced could become a commodity only in the hands of the state; under conditions of big private landed property, however, part of the agricultural surplus-product in the shape of tribute or rent of land was used by the big feudal lords in the natural form they received it, while another part was transformed into luxury articles or other consumer goods for them, and the rest was turned into wages paid to the handicraftsmen.[24]

The consolidation of private feudal property, therefore, did not by itself destroy the natural foundation of the economy; this is quite understandable, if one considers that the development had not yet exceeded the limits of the feudal mode of production, a distinguishing feature of which was the predominance of the natural economy. At the same time, feudal land property held by individuals which to an increasing extent, was not merely infringing upon the rights of the village community to distribute part of the agricultural surplus-product but also the necessary product—disrupted the division of labour which existed in the village whose whole mechanism disclosed a systematic division of labour; but, as Marx wrote, a division like that in manufactures was impossible.[25]

James Forbes's description of the village communities in Gujarat contains interesting information regarding the influence which the growing private landed property of the zamindars exerted on the division of labour within these communities. In 1765, when Forbes was 16 years old, he arrived in Bombay, where he entered the service of the East India Company. For approximately four years he stayed in Gujarat working as a tax collector and trading in cotton in Broach. After his return to England in 1784 Forbes began to revise his records and notes about India. His *Oriental Memoirs*, the result of this work, provides quite

23 Reisner, n. 1, 176-244; Alaev, n. 20.

24 *Ibid.*, 604.

25 Marx, n. 9, 358.

a number of useful data if one reads it critically.[26]

In his account of how the land in the Gujarat village community was used, he writes:

> Some particular fields called *pysita* and *vajeefa* lands, are set apart in each village for public purposes; *varying, perhaps, as to the mode of application in different districts;* but in most cases, the produce of these lands is appropriated to the maintenance of the Brahmins, the caree, washerman, smith, barber, and the lame, blind and helpless, as also to the support of a few vertunnees, or armed men, who are kept for the defence of the village, and to conduct travellers in safety from one village to another.[27]

The assigning of certain fields for their use was, however, as we will see, not the only way of maintaining the officials and craftsmen of the village community. A different method of recompensing the craftsmen was, for instance, used in the Maratha and Mysore village communities.

In any case, however, the consolidation of feudal land property held by individuals gradually weakened the natural links between agriculture and the handicrafts in the village community. Forbes remarks that the zamindars appropriated the harvest of the fields, called *pysita* earmarked for the Brahmins and craftsmen in the Gujarati village, and thereby caused great harm to the peasants.[28] It is obvious that one cannot place the losses of the Brahmins and of the craftsmen on the same level. The former, who became small feudal landed proprietors, made good their losses at the expense of the peasants; while the craftsmen were compelled to enter into commercial; relations with the agriculturists.

As, therefore, feudal land property held by individuals developed and became widespread, the direct relation of agriculture and the handicrafts was broken and both agricultural and handicraft production became dependent on "that division of labour brought about, in Indian society as a whole, by means of the exchange of commodities".[29] On this foundation arose some of the conditions necessary for the emergence of, first, petty commodity production and, later, the capitalist mode of production, including manufacture, which no longer came into being merely locally and sporadically but in the form of permanent centres, that were—through commerce—more or less closely linked with agriculture.

---

26 James Forbes, *Oriental Mermoirs: A Narrative of Seventeen Years Residence in India,* (Second Edition, London 1834) I, II.

27 *Ibid.*, 42.

28 *Ibid.*, 604.

29 Marx, n. 9, 357.

F. Buchanan's investigations[30] provide a greater amount of factual information on the social division of labour and the economic organisation of Indian handicrafts than any other source at our disposal. From 1801 to 1808 Buchanan, an employee of the East India Company, travelled through Bengal, Bihar, Mysore and the Karnataka on the directions of the Company's administration to study, in the main, agricultural production, commerce and the handicrafts. The British bourgeoisie, having carried through the industrial revolution, needed information about these branches of India's economy to organise the systematic exploitation of the Indian population not only by non-economic means (i.e. taxation and the imposition of military contributions) but also by way of a big expansion of trade. Buchanan's works are one of the earliest attempts of the British colonialists to produce a district by district account of the conqured Indian territories. In compiling his report Buchanan mainly used material provided by the local colonial administration, especially communications of the Company's so-called "commercial residents", he also questioned various "well-informed persons": landowners, traders, artisans, and so on. This, as well as the comparatively systematic arrangements of the material, makes Buchanan's works a most valuable source of information for the student of Indian economy at the end of the 18th century and the beginning of the 19th.

The political and to a certain extent also the economic situation in the districts enumerated earlier was, at that time, far from uniform. While the English colonialists subjugated Bengal and Bihar as early as the 1750s and 60s, placing them under the direct government of the East India Company, Mysore was conquered only in 1799, barely two years before Buchanan made his journey there. Mysore remained a native principality but the British greatly reduced its territory and turned its ruler into a vassal.

At the beginning of the 19th century, Bengal and Bihar experienced in a greater measure than Mysore the disastrous effects of colonial robbery, which manifested themselves in the sharp increase of feudal exploitation, the extensive destruction of productive forces and the

30 The description of a number of regions in southern India was published in 1807 under the title: F. Buchanan, *A Journey from Madras through the Countries of Mysore, Canara and Malabar, Performed under the Order of the Most Noble the Marquis Wellesley Governor-General of India, for the Express Purpose of Investigating the State of Agriculture, Arts, and Commerce, History . . in Dominions of the Raja of Mysore,* (London, 1807) I, II, III Montgomery Martin, *The History, Antiquities, Topography and Statistics of Eastern India, Comprising Districts of Behar, Shahabad and Bhagulpoor, Goruckpoor, Dinajpoor, Purniya, Rangpoor and Assam* (London, 1832) I, II and III, is a description of five districts of Bihar, two districts of Bengal, and of Assam, which was published, after Buchanan's death, by Montgomery Martin.

rapid decline of the whole economy in these provinces. During the latter half of the 18th century, no appreciable social or economic advances were made in the provinces subjugated by the British invaders. The colonial exploitation did not change the country's economic structure during this period. Marx referred to this fact when he wrote that India's "social condition has remained unaltered.... until the first decennium of the 19th century." He considered that the "constructive work" of the English only began in the following period. As late as 1853 Marx pointed out that "the work of regeneration hardly transpires through a heap of ruins".[31]

The level, therefore, of the social division of labour in India traced on the basis of information relating to the end of the 18th century and the beginning of the 19th, and the particular forms of the economic organisation of the handicrafts existing at that time are not the result of the British conquest, but arose out of the development of the country preceding the conquest.[32] When appraising data regarding the handicrafts, one must keep in mind the general economic ruin and in particular the decline of the handicrafts, especially in towns, brought about by ruthless colonial robbery.

It is worth remembering that at the beginning of the 19th century the economic relations existing in feudal India were preserved in Mysore in a purer form than in Bengal and Bihar, where they were bound to be distorted by five decades of colonial rule. We will, therefore, examine in greater detail the material collected by F. Buchanan in south India, and recall the principal conclusions arrived at by Soviet orientalists who studied documentary sources relating to Bengal and Bihar.

The system by which a number of village artisans received payment in kind from the members of the community who tilled the soil was still in existence as late as the second half of the 18th century and the beginning of the 19th. In the villages of Mysore, for instance, the cultivators of the village community would give the barber 30 seers from each heap of grain (apparently a traditional measure of capacity); the potter's share was 20-30 seers. The portion of the harvest given to other craftsmen depended on the amount of labour spent by them, the smith received for each plough 20 seers from every heap of grain, the washerman was given from 50 to 150 seers by each family, in accordance with the number of persons it contained.[33] The last two examples show that a direct, personal exchange of labour took place between the individual cultivators and the

31 Karl Marx and Frederick Engels, *The First Indian War of Independence 1857-1859*, (Moscow) 17, 33.

32 The methods used in British factories to exploit artisans were not basically new. It will be shown later that the system of exploitation applied there had been evolved in the coastal regions of feudal India.

33 Buchanan, n. 30, I, 267, 337.

individual artisan. This exchange, which did not yet break the close combination of handicraft and agriculture, prepared however the ground for commodity-money relations between the cultivator and artisan.

These relations undoubtedly became increasingly widespread. It is significant that so far it has not been possible to find evidence showing that the weaver received the whole of his remuneration in kind, and, after all, the weaver was the most important craftsman. Even in the remotest parts of Gorakhpur—a district in the eastern part of modern Uttar Pradesh—the remuneration of the village weaver consisted not only of grain and yarn but money too. "The greater part of the thread is purchased" by the village weavers of the Purani district "and the weaver sells at the market what he makes every week."[34] In a number of cases, therefore, the village artisan became a small commodity producer.[35]

According to the information we have in regard to village weavers in Mysore, they can be described as craftsmen who use their customer's material (yarn) to manufacture cloth for a fixed monetary payment. They did either no agricultural work at all, or they were hired by rich peasants as seasonal workers. Buchanan records:

> The Toogotaru are a class of weavers (probably a caste) that make a coarse, thick, white cotton cloth with red borders, which among the poorer class of inhabitants is used as the common waist-cloths of all ages and sexes. . . The weavers of this class are poor, and say that they cannot afford to make the cloth on their own account. They in general receive the thread from the women in the neighbourhood, and work it up into cloth for hire. For weaving a piece that is worth 8 anams, or 5s. 4½d., they get 2½ anams, or 1s. 8d. This occupies a workman four or five days; so that his daily gains are from four to five pence. They never, cultivate the ground.[36]

Weavers of the Walliaru caste, who produced coarse cloth for the poor, lived in the countryside and were often employed as day-labourers by farmers and others prepared to hire them. These weavers bought yarn from women of all castes who spun it at home.[37] We do not, so far, possess sufficient data to determine to what extent the natural relations between handicrafts and agriculture obtaining within the village community were supplanted by individual commodity-money relations between the craftsman and cultivator. It is however clear that the old manner in which the community remunerated the artisan in kind, that is by allotting him a share of the harvest or a plot of land, was beginning

34 Martin, n. 30, III, 324-28.
35 *Ibid.*, II, 252, 261.
36 Buchanan, n. 30, I, 217-18.
37 *Ibid.*

to give way to commodity money relationships between the craftsman and the consumer or customer.

Not only the economic self-sufficiency of the village community hampered the development of commodity exchange between the town and the countryside in feudal India, but also the fact that the bulk of the surplus product appeared in the form of a rent-tax paid in kind. Economic relations between town and country amounted, in fact, to a one-way flow of agricultural products to the town, products taken from the peasant in the shape of a feudal rent. Craftsman in medieval towns, especially in big cities, worked mainly to orders received from the court, the administration, the army and individual feudal lords. The feudal rent was the chief source of revenue of these customers. Marx wrote that in feudal India:

> It is the surplus alone that becomes a commodity, and a portion of even that, not until it has reached the hands of the State, into whose hands from time immemorial a certain quantity of these products has found its way in the shape of rent in kind.[38]

Marx stressed particularly that archaic relations between the feudal lords and the craftsmen were still maintained in the backward provinces of colonial India; the non-agricultural labourers there are ....

> directly employed by the magnates, to whom a portion of the agricultural surplus-product is rendered in the shape of tribute or rent. One portion of this product is consumed by the magnates in kind, another is converted for their use by the labourers, into articles of luxury and such like things; while the rest forms the wages of the labourers, who own their implements of labour.[39] Not only the political but also the economic subjection of the Indian town to the feudal lords was due to the fact that both the urban handicrafts and commerce and finance catered primarily for the needs of the feudal class.

Another important circumstance should be taken into consideration, namely, that feudal state ownership of land in India extended to the towns as well. The feudal chiefs levied not only taxes on the commercial transactions of the merchants, craftsmen and other urban inhabitants, but received also a kind of ground-rent payable on the land occupied by houses and shops. That was why the land and air of the Indian towns—in contradistinction to that of the West European towns—could not free their inhabitants from the arbitrary actions of the feudal lords.

---

38 Marx, n. 9, 357.
39 *Ibid.*, 598.

It was quite consistent that the leaders of the local communities of merchants and artisans were frequently appointed by the feudal ruler of the town. K. A. Antonova quotes in her monograph a very interesting extract from *Ain-i-Akbar* (Akbar's Regulations), a work written by Abul Fazl, Akbar's historiographer. This passage shows that the Mogul governor of the town had the right to appoint the heads of the craft guilds and the officials whose duty it was to supervise the commercial affairs of the artisans and to inform the urban authorities daily about all transactions.[40] That the commercial operations of the craftsmen could be controlled by the feudal state testifies to the economic dependence of the handicrafts on the goodwill of the state administration. Such control was, obviously, impracticable in regard to the European guilds, which maintained commercial links with the burghers and peasants of whom their clientele consisted.

The headmen of the local artisan communities in feudal Gujarat collected taxes from the members of their caste, and handed the money over to the public treasury, either direct or through the head of the merchants' guild who was responsible for the tax payments of all merchants and craftsmen in the town. An important official of the local administration could order the head of a craft guild, to manufacture for him, any article he required at the guild's expense. In return, the official would give his support to the guild.[41] In other words, the craftsmen had to pay for their political importance in their native town.

But the guilds of merchants or artisans were themselves feudal organisations monopolising a particular type of commerce or handicraft. Only members of a particular caste could join them, and a person who had recently settled in the town had to pay the guild a big entrance fee (from 20 to 500 rupees in Ahmedabad). The caste monopoly in a particular trade made the institution of apprentices and journeymen, which existed in west Europe, superfluous. The young craftsman learned his trade in his father's workshop, after finishing his training he would give a dinner to which he invited the members of the guild. The head of the caste saw to it that the traditional methods and standards of production were observed.[42] Thus, we find the principal reactionary features of the West European guilds and corporations also in the Indian merchants' and artisans' organisation, which lacked, however, the chief progressive quality of their European counterparts, the ability to defend their rights against arbitrary actions of the feudal lords.

Available data on the commercial relations of industries in various towns of feudal India suggest that artisans, in a number of towns—

40 K. A. Antonova, *Ocherki obshchestvennykh otnosheny*, (Moscow, 1952) 135-36.
41 *Bombay Gazetteer* (Bombay, 1879) IV, 107.
42 *Ibid.*, 106–09.

and especially in big military and administrative centres—continued to work for the court, the army and nobility as well as the foreign market, during the latter half of the 18th century. This, for example, was the case in Dacca, the famous weaving centre, and in Bangalore where the weavers mostly fulfilled orders received from the court of the Sultan of Mysore in Seringapattam.[43]

But a number of towns catered mainly to peasant consumers as early as the 18th century. According to available information, urban artisans manufactured coarse cloth and a considerable inland trade in this cloth was carried in Bengal and Bihar. A great variety of textiles was produced in the towns and handicraft communities of Dacca region during the 18th century ranging from the finest muslins, which adorned the inmates of *Zenankhanas* (women's quarters) of native noblemen, to the coarse fabrics used as garments by the poor ryots.[44] Taylor mentioned five towns in various districts of East Bengal that were well known for the manufacture of the cheaper kinds of coarse cloth.[45] S. Master, a Dutch merchant who lived in India in 1675-80, related that a factory of the British East India Company sent ilach[46] and coarse cloth worth Rs. 300,000 from Malda to Dacca, and small traders from Rajmahal, Murshidabad and other places along the Ganges, i.e., in Bengal proper, bought a similar amount of these goods.[47] Patna, the biggest handicraft centre in Bihar, was well-known for its production of woollen blankets, an article of mass consumption in great demand in Bengal. But at the beginning of the 19th century, the export of blankets from Patna rapidly declined.

In Waluru, one of the bigger towns of Mysore, where the chief industry was the manufacture of cotton cloth, the weavers worked both

43 According to Taylor, the export of cloth from Dacca amounted to Rs. 2,650,000-2,850,000 in 1753. The East India Companies (i.e. the English, French and Dutch Campanies) and individual European traders exported cloth worth Rs. 850,000 from there. In the same year, merchants trading in Asia and northern India bought for Rs. 1,050,000=1,150,000 cloth in Dacca. In addition cloth worth Rs. 400,000 was sent to Delhi, the capital of the Great Moguls, and Murshidabad, capital of the Nawab of Bengal; Indian merchants trading in Bengal bought cloth for only Rs. 200,000 to 300,000; and the Jegat Seth ordered cloth worth Rs. 150,000. See J. C. Sinha, *Economic Annals of Bengal*, (London, 1927) 32-33. As Buchanan wrote there was little hope that the industrial output of Seringapattam would ever reach the level existing in the reign of Hydar Ali, unless a foreign market was found for its goods. See Buchanan, n. 30, I, 221.

44 K. Datta, *Studies in the History of Bengal Subah*, Part I, (Calcutta, 1936) 425.

45 *Ibid.*, 425.

46 *Ilach*—a kind of coloured silk, a whole length of which is used as a garment by women in India.

47 S. Master, *The Diaries of Streinsham Master, 1675-1680*, ed. by R. Temple, (London, 1911), I, 40.

for local consumption and for export. The coarse cloth they manufactured was sold at weekly fairs. The following rather significant incident shows that firm commercial links existed between Waluru and the neighbouring areas. During the British-Mysore war, when Tippu Sultan, the ruler of Mysore, prohibited trade with the Lower Karnataka seized by the British, cheap cloth from Waluru was smuggled there.[48] Other towns of Mysore also produced cloth for mass consumption. For instance, Sirjapur, a small handicraft centre near Bangalore, manufactured besides expensive fabrics cheap cloth, a part of which was sent to Bangalore.

The fact that merchants from Bellary, Adoni, Hoobly, Gooty and other places situated hundreds of kilometres from Bangalore maintained permanent agents in that town showed the extent of commerce even between distant regions of south India. Goods sold by these agents included cotton, coarse yarn, blankets and wheat. In exchange Bangalore exported dyed cotton fabrics. In one year, a total of 1,500 bullockloads of cotton wool was brought to Bangalore, 50 bullockloads of cotton thread and 230 of raw silk.[49] There is some evidence relating to Bengal and Bihar which testifies to an increasing differentiation of town and countryside and a developing commodity exchange between them.[50] One can assume that the merging of small local markets into one common market covering a large area for instance, pre-British Bengal or Mysore, began in the 18th century. Although commodity exchange in 18th century India was in the main restricted to the satisfaction of the needs of the feudal class, it created at the same time, some of the preconditions for the rise of the capitalist mode of production. The formation of a home market took place simultaneously with an increasing division of labour between town and country and, in its further development, might have led to the sporadic appearance of new capitalist relations within the feudal system. The study of the activities of merchant's capital in industry and of the first manifestations of industrial capital in the late 18th and the early 19th century is particularly important for an understanding of the specific features distinguishing the economic organisation of urban handicrafts.

Up to the beginning of the 19th century, the independent producer who sold his goods himself to the consumer or merchant prevailed in the urban industries of India. The Dutch merchant W. Bolts, who stayed in Bengal in the 1760s, wrote:

In the time of the Mogul government, and even in that of the Nabob

48 Buchanan, n. 30, I, 40.

49 *Ibid.*, 185, 207.

50 Seek E. N. Komarov, V. Ya. Grashe, *Nekotorye dannye obshchestvennom razdelenii truda*, 8–9.

Allaverdy Khawn[51] the weavers manufactured their goods freely, and without oppression; and though there is no such thing at present, it was then a common practice for reputable families of the Tanty, or weaver caste, to employ their own capitals, in manufacturing goods, which they sold freely on their own accounts.[52]

Bolts followed this up by an example showing that during the reign of the nawab—i.e., in independent Bengal—a certain English merchant bought on his own doorstep in Dacca 800 pieces of muslin from the weavers who brought them there.[53] The English author of *Remarks on the Husbandry and Internal Commerce of Bengal,* writing at the end of the 18th century, states that, because the Indian artisan "is unable to wait the market or to anticipate its demand, he can only follow his regular occupation, as immediately called to it by the wants of his neighbours. In the intervals, he must apply to some other employment which is in present request and the labours of agriculture, ever wanted, are the general resource.[54]

Side by side with this there are a number of facts which indicate that merchant's capital penetrated industry to a very considerable extent. The simplest primary form in which merchant's capital manifests itself in small industries—the purchase of wares by the merchant from the independent, small commodity producers—was widespread in the weaving industry of so large a weaving centre as Dacca. S. Master, who described the methods used by the Company to acquire cloth in Dacca, related as early as the 1670s that comparatively big merchantbrokers *(dallals)* who had experience in the cloth trade received loans from the Company. They then distributed the money among their *paikars* (retail traders) who travelled from town to town making advances to weavers.[55] It will be shown later that a similar practice evolved in Bombay at the beginning of the 18th century. During the first decade a resident of the East India Company at Salem ordered cloth from the weavers of Coimbatore and advanced money to them, which they took eagerly in spite of the fact that they were often cheated when accounts were settled.[56]

It is hardly likely that the factories of the European East India Companies could have acquired cloth in the way described if it had

51 Aliverdi was Nawab of Bengal from 1740 to 1756.

52 W. Bolts, *Considerations on India Affairs,* (London, 1772), 194.

53 *Ibid.*

54 H. T. Colebrooke, *Remarks on the Husbandry and Internal Commerce of Bengal,* (London, 1806), 48. According to the author's preface, "the original treatise was written in 1794, and was corrected for this edition in 1803." It was first published in Calcutta in 1804.

55 Master, n. 47, II, 14.

56 Buchanan, n. 30, II, 264.

not already been customary for Indian buyers to advance money to artisans. In fact, an examination of the economic structure of various Indian regions reveals that, in a number of cases, handicraftsmen were enslaved by local merchant's capital. F. Buchanan's investigation into the economy of Mysore contains the most detailed information with regard to the methods employed by moneylenders to enslave artisans.

For instance, he relates, that in the town of Nalarayanapalliam, near Coimbatore:

> 'Native merchants frequently make advances for the cloth intended for country use. These persons endeavour to keep the weavers constantly in their debt; for, so long as that is the case, they can work for no other merchant, and must give their goods at a low rate. When a merchant wishes to engage a new weaver, he must advance the sum owing to the former employer. With this the weaver buys goods to fulfil his old contract; but then he becomes equally bound to the persons who has advanced the money. A few weavers are rich enough to be able to make cloth on their own account, and in consequence sell it to the best advantage . . . . Those who once get into the debt of a native merchant are ever afterwards little better than slaves, and must work for him at a very low rate.[57]

This example illustrates vividly the combination of merchant's and usurer's capital, where "the relations of the creditor to the debtor inevitably lead to the personal dependence of the latter, to bodage."[58]

Traders in Nalarayanapalliam advanced money against the manufacture not only of cloth earmarked for distant markets but also of cloth for local use, which indicates that merchant's capital strengthened its domination over the handicraft industries. It was, however, usual for traders to make advances to artisans against manufactures intended for distant markets. Merchants from the "Nagarit" (probably, *nagarthar*) caste, questioned by Buchanan, said that as a rule advances were not made upon the production of the common types of cloth unless the demand originated in a very remote place. In that case, and also when ordering more expensive fabrics, it was usual to advance half the value of the commodity so that the producer could buy raw material. The loan was made for three months and no interest was paid during this period, but if the order was not fulfilled on time 0.75 per cent was charged for every additional month beyond the contracted date.[59]

57 *Ibid.*, 239-40, 264.

58 V. I. Lenin, *The Development of Capitalism in Russia*, in *Collected Works*, III, 368.

59 Buchanan, n. 30, I, 218.

A consequence of the extremely extensive development of moneylending was that the creditor of the artisan—especially when the latter worked for the local market—frequently was a professional moneylender and not the buyer-up or merchant. Describing the whole organisation of the weaving industry, Buchanan writes:

> When the goods are in much demand, it is customary for the merchant to advance one half, or even the whole, of the price of the goods which he commissioned; but when the demand is small the manufacturers borrow money from the bankers at two per cent a month, and make goods, which they sell to the merchant of the place. They never carry them to the public market.

If the weaver manufactured cloth for his own account, he sold a part of his product to traders and a part at the weekly bazaar, but having received an advance the weaver could not sell any cloth until he had fulfilled his contract.[60] Buchanan's descriptions of various districts of Bihar and Bengal contain similar information with regard to the development of merchant's and moneylender's capital in the weaving industry.

Buchanan's detailed report contains, however, indication that the dealer handed out raw materials to the weavers.[61] It is as yet difficult to tell whether the absence of such evidence is accidental, or reflects the fact that such practices were rare in the weaving industry. That the enslavement of the craftsman weaver by merchant's capital often reached a stage when the weaver was no longer able to manufacture his wares independently, for his own account, is beyond any doubt, and in this respect it makes hardly any difference whether money is advanced to the weaver for which he buys raw materials, or raw materials in kind are handed out to him by the buyer. Information relating to the same period indicates that raw materials were distributed by the buyer in other industries. On the basis of the data gathered by Buchanan during his journey, E. N. Komarov showed that the handing out of raw material to certain handicraftsmen, i.e., shoemakers, jewellers, smiths and butter makers, was widely practiced in Bengal and Bihar at the beginning of the 19th century.[62]

The data cited indicate that, at the end of the 18th century and the beginning of the 19th almost all principal forms of merchant's capital existed in the small industries of feudal India, which is a characteristic feature of the handicrafts during the advanced stages of feudalism.

---

60 *Ibid.*, 212, 217-18.

61 There is, indeed, evidence that peasant women received cotton from traders, spun it into yarn and, for a payment, returned it to the trader. But one cannot regard these spinners as home workers, because for them spinning was only a subsidiary occupation. It is not known on what terms the merchant sold the yarn to the weavers. See Buchanan, n. 30, III, 317–18.

62 Martin, n. 30, I, 337; II-265, 958.

An examination of economic relations in handicrafts leads to the conclusion that the form of merchant's capital prevalent in the handicraft industries of Bengal, Bihar and Mysore was that for which combination with moneylender's capital is typical. In the weaving industry, moreover, the artisan often bought all his raw material with money that had been advanced to him by the dealer. This form of merchant's capital in small industries is already very close to the highest form under which raw materials are handed out to the handicraftsmen to be worked up for a definite payment.

Analysing the transition from the feudal mode of production to the capitalist, Marx pointed to the great historical importance of the path along which "the merchant establishes direct sway over production." At the same time Marx stressed that "it does not by itself attain the transformation of the old mode of production, but tends rather to preserve and retain it as its precondition. . . This system" continued Marx, "presents everywhere an obstacle to the real capitalist mode of production and goes under with its development."[63]

One can get an idea of the influence which the dealer exerted on the Indian handicrafts from the description of the panchayats in the agate industry and trade in Cambay. In this industry the Karkhanas in each separate process such as polishing and drilling were organised in separate panchayats, but at the head of the whole organisation stood the panchayat of the agate dealers. It was the dealer who bought the rough stones, had them sawn and chiselled in his own Karkhana and then had them appropriately processed by others.[64] Thus, the self-governing caste organisation of the craftsmen in Gujarat was controlled not only by the feudal administration but also by the merchant's capital of the dealers. There was, however, a definite connection between these two powers, for the dealer, or buyer-up, catered to the needs of the very same feudal chiefs by selling them the products of the agate industry. Hence, the control exercised by the dealer over the craftsmen did, in the last analysis, represent the feudal lords' general domination over the mode of life in the Indian towns.

The highest form of merchant's capital was, as a rule, not fully developed in the principal branches of Indian handicrafts, including weaving, and the exploitation of the craftsmen was greatly aggravated by the fact that the latter were enslaved by the usurer. This position heightened the preserving role of merchant's capital in Indian handicrafts, delayed extended reproduction and worsened the position of the producers.[65]

---

63 Karl Marx, *Kapital*, (Berlin, 1959) III, 366-7.

64 The source of this passage, which we quote from Gadgil, n. 15, 26, is the *Gazetteer of the Bombay Presidency, Statistical Account of Cambay*, (1877) 30-32.

65 "Accumulation of capital, innovation, etc. were much more possible and were

There is indeed a good deal evidence showing the poverty and cruel exploitation of the craftsmen in the late Middle Ages. For example J. A. de Mandelslo, a Holstein diplomat who visited India as early as 1638, wrote about the artisans of Surat:

> All they can do is to get five or six pence a day. They must accordingly fare very poorly, their ordinary diet being only *Kitsery*, which they make of beans pounded, and rice, which they boil together in water till the water be consumed. Then they put thereto a little butter melted, and this is their supper for all day they eat only rice and wheat in the grain.[66]

The Englishman John Frayer relates at the close of the 17th century that the Indian handicraftsmen "can hardly live for those, who will grind their faces to fill their own hords, as much as the Desies do."[67] The great skill of the Indian craftsmen as well as their exceedingly low living standard were also stressed in a work of the English Merchantile School published towards the end of the 17th century.[68] In general one can say that the "Golden Age" of the handicrafts, if this term is to include the prosperity of the artisans, never existed in feudal India, but the craftsman had at least his work and a piece of bread of which he was deprived by colonialism.

The relations of production in handicrafts which were discussed earlier corresponded on the whole to the level of development of the instruments and methods of labour. The productive forces in handicrafts during the period under consideration were, as a rule, characterised by primitive implements on the one hand and a very high degree of productive experience and craftsmanship attained by the individual producer on the other. Marx wrote about the Indian weaver: "It is only the special skill accumulated from generation to generation, and transmitted from father to son, that gives to the Hindu . . . this proficiency".[69]

As an example of such proficiency one may refer to the enthusiastic

---

likely to be more evidenced among the trading and financing classes rather than among the large numbers of scattered tradition-bound and relatively poor artisans". See Gadgil, n. 15, 16.

66 [J. Albert de Mandelslo] *The Voyages and Travels of J. Albert Mandelslo (A Gentleman belonging to the Embassy, sent by the Duke of Holstein to the great Duke of Muscovy, and the King of Persia) into the East-Indies*, (London, 1669), 64.

67 J. Fryer, *A New Account of East India and Persia being nine Years' Travels 1672-1681*, (London, 1912,) II, 108.

68 The author of the work stated that the countries usually called East Indies abounded in valuable commodities, good and cheap industrial raw materials and the people inhabiting it were skilled artisans accustomed to process these materials who, in some places, worked for a penny a day. There were, continued the author, spices in large quantity, for many species were harvested twice a year and others even four times; a variety of diamonds and other precious stones; several kinds of medicines and diverse useful and costly

account which was given by an eyewitness after observing the skill of the Bengali silk-winders in the 18th century. Although the yarn was classified, according to its fineness into 20 grades and the thread moved through the fingers of the winders so fast that the eye was unable to discern it, their sense of touch was so perfectly developed that the winders managed to break the thread as soon as the fineness changed.[70] Describing the extremely simple tools of the Gujarati craftsmen, Forbes relates that jewellers using nothing but an iron nail were able to produce the most magnificent articles.[71] According to J. Dubois, a Frenchman, who visited India early in the 19th century, the carpenter's only instruments were one or two axes, a few saws and planes, "all of them so rudely fashioned that a European workman would be able to do nothing with them."[72]

The usually very limited division of labour within the production process itself is the most important indication that in general a low level of development of the productive forces prevailed in the handicrafts of medieval India. The producer often carried through the whole production process, from beginning to end, without any assistance. "Subdivision of labour" was, according to Buchanan, "very unusual in India".[73] The author of the *Remarks on the Husbandry and Internal Commerce of Bengal* has given the following description of the organisation of Indian handicraft production at the close of the 18th century : "The want of capital in manufactures and agriculture prevents the division of labour. Every manufacturer, every artisan working for his own account, conducts the whole process of his art, from the formation of his tools to the sale of his production."[74]

Nevertheless, signs of a detailed division of labour appeared in a number of handicrafts as early as the 17th and 18th centuries indicating that a certain progress in the development of the productive forces had been made. Lenin pointed out that "on the basis of hand production no other progress in technique was possible except by division of labour.[75] Even in the 1660s Mandelslo noticed that 'a piece of work must pass through three or four hands before it be finished".[76] Although

articles that attracted the eyes and hearts of all merchant nations of Europe, see, *A Discourse of Trade, Corn and Paper Credit and of Ways and Means to Gain, to retain Riches* (London, 1697) 96.

69 Marx, n. 9, 340

70 Forbes, n. 26, II. 95-96.

71 *Ibid.*, I, 465.

72 The passage has been quoted by A. Sarada Raju, in *Economic Conditions in the Madras Presidency 1800-1850,* (Madras, 1941) 148.

73 Martin, n. 30, III, 320; Antonova, n. 40, 136.

74 Colebrook, n. 54, 48.

75 Lenin, n. 58, 428.

76 de Mandelslo, n. 66, 64.

Mandelslo wrote about the handicraft industries of Surat in general without giving any further details, one can hardly doubt that he had specific instances in mind which he had observed himself.

Buchanan gave some information about division of labour into separate operations practised in the production of articles from bidry and in the manufacture of table-cloths in East India.[77]

As a result of the further development of the productive forces and the division of labour in feudal India, the capitalist mode of production was engendered also in a revolutionising way, in this case "the producer becomes merchant and capitalist".[78] Such an evolution is necessarily accompanied by the expropriation of the immediate producers. The presence of simple capitalist co-operation and of manufacture—which was however still in its early stages that is of the first forms of capitalist organisation of production showed that capitalist relations were arising in the small Indian industries at the end of the 18th century and the beginning of the 19th.

It is quiet certain that a differentiation process was taking place among the weavers and that simple capitalist co-operation and rudiments of capitalist manufacture existed in the weaving industry. The employment of wage workers was rather common in the weaving industry of Mysore. The master weavers had from two to five servants who were paid by the piece. Records of the weaver's average daily earnings have been preserved, showing that he received from six to eight pence according to his qualification and the difficulty of the work. It was such a common occurrence that a petty proprietor owned several looms that this was taken into account in the tax laws of Mysore. The owner of one loom had to pay a tax of 3.75 fanams (2s.6¼ d.), the owner of two looms, five fanams, the owner of three and more looms paid only two fanams per loom.[79] The fiscal policy of Mysore, thus, encouraged the expansion of weaving establishments. The small master weaver who employed workers borrowed money from the merchants or bankers at an interest rate of 2 per cent per month.[80] Similar relations existed also in the weaving industry of Bengal. Well-to-do weavers employing hired workers often served merely as middlemen between the latter and the traders. Such relations retarded the advance towards higher forms of capitalist organisation of production.

The differentiation of the artisans led to the separation of a well-to-do group that exploited hired labour, at one end of the scale, and of workers devoid of the means of production who had to seek paid work at the other end. It was precisely the beginning of expropriation process

77 Martin, n. 30, I, 354; III, 320-21.

78 Marx, n. 3, 329.

79 Buchanan, n. 30, I, 121, 216, 222; II, 264.

80 Martin, n. 30, II, 973.

of the direct producer which indicated that primitive forms of capitalist relations were arising in Indian society.

A distinctive type of small-producers' co-operation which had already some elements of capitalist manufacturers existed in the iron foundries and iron works of Mysore. Establishments of this kind had from 13 to 22 workers. The proceeds from the sale of their products were divided into a fixed number of parts (42 parts in the example quoted). The share of each producer was calculated according to his role in the production process and the amount he spent on equipment that was used in the enterprise. The owner received a quarter of the value of the output, and often more. In a metallurgical establishment in North Mysore the product was divided in the following manner: the proprietor received 11 parts; the smith 3.5: the carter of the ore 2.5: four blacksmith's strikers 7; six workers who operated the bellows 8; nine coalshippers and one miner 10 parts.[81]

The greater shares of the smith and carter were due to the fact that the former owned the tools and the latter the cart and buffaloes. Pre-capitalist features of small-producers co-operation were, thus, preserved both in the distribution of the revenue (or more accurately, of the product) according to the metayage system and in the plural ownership of the means of production. The workers themselves lived in the countryside and when seasonal interruptions in the work of the establishment occurred they sought employment with the rich peasants. But the great difference between the share of the owner and those of the ordinary workers and the primitive division of labour are indications of new rudimentary capitalist relations, and in particular show traits of an advance towards capital.

These rudimentary pre-capitalist relations were interwoven with bondage, the master lent 70 to 100 fanams to the workers to enable them to exist until they sold the iron they had received for their work. Until the workers paid their debts they were obliged work for one and the same proprietor.

Simultaneously manufactories appeared in India which were less encumbered with the pre-capitalist relations we have described earlier, although they still retained a primitive division of labour. Buchanan has described several iron-works in Mysore with a highly developed division of labour, where the workers' wages were paid in money, the rates varying...from 6 to 12 fanams for a season, approximately 8 months... according to the type of work performed. For instance, one of these establishments employed 20 workers, four of these collected ore, six made charcoal, four operated the smelting furnace and six worked in the smithy. The sum total paid in wages amounted to 1200 fanams per season (8 months). In addition, the owner paid 100 fanams

81 See Buchanan, n. 30, I, 17-18, 35-36; II, 1[illegible], 21, 36-38; III, 362.

in taxes and rent. Buchanan gives also particulars of similar smithies employing from 11 to 22 workers.[82]

Historical sources contain extremely interesting data regarding capitalist manufactories producing sugar from the sap of the sugar-cane in Bengal at the beginning of the 19th century.[83]

In the famous shipyards of Gujarat the production process was, undoubtedly, organised on the lines of manufacture. How, indeed could handicraft production have solved the technical problems that the Gujarat shipbuilding industry was able to take in its stride? Ovington relates that

> the very Ship-Carpenters at Suratt will take the Model of any English Vessel, in all the Curiosity of its Building, and the most artificial Instances of Workmanship about it, whether they are proper for Convenience of Burthen, or of quick Sailing, as-exactly as if they had been the first Contrivers. The Wood with which they build their Ships would be very proper for our Men of War in Europe; for it has this Excellence, that it never splinters by the Force of a Bullet, nor is injur'd by those violent Impressions, beyond the just Bore of the Shot.[84]

The Surat shipyards built vessels with a displacement of up to 500-1000 tons able to sail to China and Europe.

It is very likely that enterprises organised on the lines of capitalist manufactories also existed in other branches of industry based on manual labour.[85] Nevertheless, the data quoted earlier certainly produce the impression that manufacture was only beginning to develop, and was not yet wide spread, on the eve of India's colonial subjugation. Feudal India had not yet entered the manufacturing period. Simple capitalist cooperation was fairly highly developed, but it does not, in itself, present a fixed form characteristic of a particular epoch in the development of the capitalist mode of production.[86] Hence, while on the one hand the development of simple capitalist cooperation and the appearance of the first manufactories entitle us to speak of the growth of capitalist relations in Indian feudal society, these relations, on the other hand, did not yet amount to a capitalist structure of society. The

82 *Ibid.*, I, 175, 177; II, 439-40.

83 Martin, n. 30, II, 957, 978-85; W. Hunter, A *Statistical Account of Bengal*, (London, 1876) VIII, 95.

84 J. Ovington, *A Voyage to Surat in the Year 1689*, (Oxford, 1929), 166.

85 The hiring of workers was a common occurrence in big Indian towns. This is illustrated, for instance, by the following remark of Ovington's: "For Herbs (which are the common Food of the Poor) are here in plenty, and bought at very low Rates, which encourages the daily Labourers to work for very low Wages." See *Ibid.*, 189.

86 Marx. n. 9, 335.

capitalist relations arising in India existed at that time only in isolated local centres which were deeply embedded within the feudal society.

Investigations carried out by Indian and Soviet orientalists lead to the conclusion that the forms of land ownership and land tenure, the social division of labour and the relations of production in the handicrafts in the advanced regions of India had, in the 18th century, reached a level characteristic of a developed feudal society which showed already signs of a transition to late feudalism.

In his book *The Discovery of India* Jawaharlal Nehru gave a brilliant sketch of the state of the productive forces in India on the eve of its colonial enslavement. With patriotic pride he referred to the skill of the Indian craftsmen and the magnificent articles they manufactured, the highly-developed organisation of commerce and finance and the beautiful and rich cities.[87] Nehru was fully justified in stressing that foreign political rule "led to a rapid destruction of the economy India had built up, without anything positive or constructive taking its place."[88] But one cannot possibly agree with his assertion that at the time of the British conquest "the economy of India had thus advanced to as high a stage as it could reach prior to the industrial revolution."[89] The point is that India had no developed capitalist manufacture, the basic prerequisite for the transition to factory production (and in our view the term industrial revolution means precisely this).

The complete or partial elimination in the course of the colonial conquest of the traditional consumers of handicraft products—the feudal rulers, their administration, and court—and the interruption of old-established commercial relations with foreign countries caused a serious decline of the big handicraft centres in the presidencies of British India, for instance Dacca, as early as the beginning of the 19th century. Local handicraft centres that were more closely linked to the home market for consumer goods, which was developed in feudal India, suffered less. But the destruction and general economic disorganisation resulting from the colonial plunder, carried on with methods of primitive accumulation, dealt a heavy blow also at these handicraft industries. The transformation of India into an outlet for English industrial products, which began in the first half of the 19th century, led to a further decline of the principal centres of Indian handicraft production, especially weaving.

Thus, the colonial conquest delayed the development of capitalist relations in the country and frequently even destroyed the rudiments of such relations in feudal India. The establishment of capitalist relations in the handicraft industries was only resumed in the last three decades

87 Jawaharlal Nahru, *The Discovery of India,* London, 1951,) 261-63.

88 *Ibid.*, 263.

89 *Ibid.*, 262.

of the 19th century, and then it was taking place under quite different social and economic conditions. Colonial exploitation strengthened those forms of transition to capitalist relations prevalent in the Indian handicrafts which tended to preserve and protract the harassing exploitation of the producer by pre-capitalist methods.

CHAPTER II

MERCHANTS AND MONEYLENDERS IN FEUDAL INDIA

Commerce and moneylending in feudal India were to a considerable extent concentrated in the hands of special castes and constituted the traditional occupation of the members of these castes. Trading and moneylending castes, which existed in almost all Indian nationalities, attained their greatest development in Gujarat and Rajputana, through which lay the famous trade route from the Gujarat ports to the historical centre of the Great Mogul state. The Gujarati, Marwari[1] and other castes of merchants and moneylenders served the feudal aristocracy in many ways: they were tax-collectors (especially collectors of the land tax), they supplied the feudal lords with goods and gave them credit, and acted as army purveyors and money-changers. Moreover, they exploited the peasants directly through commerce and usury.

The important role which the trading and moneylending castes played in the collection of the feudal revenue-tax—the basic form of surplus-product in Mogul India—and hence in the feudal exploitation system of the peasantry accounts, first and foremost, for the close ties linking the Marwari and Gujarati traders and moneylenders to feudal aristocracy. For instance, the feudal rent-tax in the Rajput principalities was paid in kind by the peasants and converted into money by the Marwari or Gujarati, tax-collectors.[2] Merchants who undertook to collect tax in a given area paid the treasury a sum of money fixed in advance and collected the tax in kind from the agricultural population, then they sold the products for a profit in the towns and army camps. Tax-collecting and the conversion of the land tax which was paid in kind into money was, for example, in the principality of Jaisalmer, in the

---

1 The inhabitant of Marwar (or Jodhpur), the north-eastern district of Rajputana, are known as Marwaris. The name is also applied to trading and moneylending castes originating not only in Marwar, but in other parts of Rajputana.

2 J. Tod, *Antiquities and Annals of Rajasthan* (London, 1832) II, 282.

hands of Brahmins of the Palliwal subcaste that had become a trading and moneylending caste.[3]

The tax-collecting activities of the Marwari moneylenders reached a particularly wide scope after the formation of the huge Mogul Empire in the middle of the 16th century. The great distances separating provincial centres (viceregencies) from the capital and the frequent replacement of the big feudal landowners, the jagirdars—who superintended the collection of taxes—were factors conducive to the development of the system of revenue. The decay of the feudal state ownership of land and of the central fiscal bodies, which set in the 17th and 18th centuries, provided the tax farmers with new opportunities to extend their activities in the various provinces of the disintegrating Great Mogul Empire.[4]

How far the peasantry of feudal India was directly exploited by moneylending capital through loans granted to small producers who owned their means of production, is a problem that has hardly been investigated. K. A. Antonova stresses the part played by Akbar's introduction of a tax to be paid in money—thus sharply increasing the peasant's need for money—in intensifying the exploitation of the peasantry by usurers.[5] But the data, we will quote later, regarding revenue collectors who converted into money the tax they had received in kind show that the peasants of Mogul India did not always and everywhere pay their taxes in money.

The village usurer was a sufficiently important figure in the village community of feudal Gujarat to claim a share of the harvest of the agriculturists of the community. It was the usurer who weighed the harvest after it was gathered and marked the part due to the officials and artisans of the community, then he divided the rest equally between the feudal lord and the peasant. Nominally the usurer received his share of the harvest for his "labours" in dividing it.[6] But it is much more

3 *Ibid.*

4 "The Bania communities.... (such as Aggarwal, Oswals, Meshris, etc.) were all trading communities also of U. P. and Bihar. It is possible that the migration of these, especially into U. P. and Central India took place at an early period. However, their migration to regions other than the U. P. and Central India cannot have taken place much earlier than the 17th century, and most probably, occurred in substantial numbers only in the 18th century. This migration took place, in the main, to the East and to the South. To the North and the West, there were predominantly Muslim areas in which important Hindu trading communities with capital resources and high skill already operated. To the southwest (in Gujarat and Saurashtra) also there already existed highly organised expert business communities" (D. R. Gadgil, *Origins of the Modern Indian Business Class.* 18).

5 K. A. Antonova, *Ocherki obshchestvennykh otnosheny* (Moscow, 1952) 128.

6 A. K. Forbes, *Ras Mala, Hindoo Annals of the Provinces of Goozerat in Western India,* (London, 1856) II, 247.

convincing to associate this fact with the role which moneylending played in the life of the Indian village during advanced feudalism. It must be noted, however that the communal ownership of land prevented the transfer of the land from the peasant-debtor into the hands of the moneylender.[7] Members of the trading and moneylending castes owned hardly any land appertaining to peasant allotments when India was conquered by the English.

The difficulties that the peasants encountered when they had to pay their taxes and rents were utilised by the moneylender as a means of enslaving them. Buchanan writes that after he has assembled the village officers and principal farmers, '. . . they informed me, that the merchants of Bangalore frequently advance them money to pay their rents, and are afterwards contented to take one half of the crop for the advance, and for interest. These advances are sometimes made six months before the crop is reaped.[8]

As a result of the tax-collecting in which the Marwari trading and moneylending castes engaged, members of these castes frequently occupied high positions in the state machinery of Rajputana.[9] It is well known that the ancestors of the biggest Marwari capitalist, Gopaldas Mohta, many times headed the administrative apparatus of Bikaner and were granted jagirs and various privileges for their military and administrative services.[10]

Tax-farming also helped many members of the trading and moneylending castes to advance to high posts in the administration of the Mogul state. Todar Mal—a member of Agarwal, a Marwari caste—organised and headed the financial department of Akbar at the end of the 16th century. A Jain,[11] Kharsukhrai, was treasurer of the Moguls and responsible for paying the troops. His successor P. D. Ramchander was in charge of remitting revenue payments to Delhi.[12] In the beginning of the 18th century the Gujarati shroff (banker) Anandrai Mashraf was minister of the last Mogul viceroy in Gujarat.[13]

---

7 A. Sarada Raju, *Economic Conditions in the Madras Presidency 1800-1850* (Madras, 1941) 134.

8 F. Buchanan, *A Journey from Madras* (London, 1804) I, 265.

9 *Ibid.*, 240, 360; R. V. Russels, *Tribes and Castes of the Central Provinces of India* (London, 1916) II, 118-9, 157.

10 *The Rajputana Gazetteer*, (Shimla, 1880) III, 27; *Indian Year-Book 1947* (Calcutta, 1947) 1449.

11 The Jains formed a religious community in north-east India consisting in the main of Marwari traders and moneylenders.

12 B. Bhargava, *Indigenous Banking in Ancient and Medieval India* (Bombay, 1934) 29-32.

13 *Indian Textile Journal* (Bombay, January 1934). Among the outstanding Marwari merchant houses who had the honour of serving various rulers were such well-known firms as Tarachand Ghanshamdas and Bansilal Abirchand, *Ibid.*, 31.

As the private feudal landowners grew stronger, they tried to increase their share of the rent by restricting the tax-farming activities of the shroffs. The zamindars even encroached upon the moneylender's sphere pushing aside the bankers and moneylenders. Describing the situation in the Gujarati countryside as he saw it in the 1770s Forbes relates that between the patels and the government tax-farmers stood venal men, called zamindars, who derived benefit from both sides.[14] When the sowing was about to begin the zamindars lent money at 3¾ per cent a month (that is at a rate of 45 per cent per annum) to the patel and the peasants to buy cattle, seed, etc. As security for the loan the zamindars took the future harvest; when the time came to pay taxes they were therefore called "minutedars". Although by right this title belonged to the shroffs (bankers) and financiers of the district who in accordance with the agreement and after a thorough examination undertook to pay the amount fixed by the government tax-collector.[15]

As we see, the representative of the East India Company is rather ill-disposed towards the Gujarati feudal chiefs. This is quite understandable, since they were the direct political antagonists of the Company, which was preparing for the conquest of Gujarat. But we are here more interested in the fact that the feudal lords were obviously trying to oust the tax-farmer and banker as the agent who helped the feudal state to exploit the peasantry. But they did not always succeed. The zamindars in Bengal, for instance, became themselves dependent on the banking house of the Jagat Seths.

Provisioning of the troops and the resale of plunder amassed during the campaigns were the most important services rendered by the traders and moneylenders of the feudal class. A banker in Mogul India grew rich if he received the office of "modi,"[16] i.e. that of a supplier of victuals to the army.[17] The banker purveyors had agents in various centres of the country along the roads used by the army, whose job it was to supply the army on the move. The well-known French traveller, J.B. Tavernier, who visited India towards the end of the 17th century, wrote:

> A great part of the money belonging to the state is always in the hands of the shroffs, who derive from it considerable profits. According to the rules of the country the troops are paid monthly,

---

14 J. Forbes, *Oriental Memoirs*, (London, 1834) II, 44.

15 *Ibid.*, 75.

16 Many big Indian capitalists have the surname "Modi", which indicates that they are descendants of army purveyors.

17 Bhargava, n. 12, 29.

18 J. B. Tavernier, *Les six voyages de M. Jean-Baptiste Tavernier, chevalier-baron d'Aubonne, qu'il a fait en Turquie, en Perse et Indes... Seconde partie, ou il est parle des Indes, et des Isles voisines* (Paris, 1681) 12. The army, especially during military campaigns, created many opportunities enabling merchant's capital to carry out lucrative operations. As D. R. Gadgil remarks, "The prevalence of general

but the majority of soldiers as well as many captains and other officers do not wait till the end of the month but borrow money from the shroffs who take 18-20 per cent interest per annum.[18]

The Marathas employed a similar system to finance and provision the army on the march. Predatory raids were for the Maratha states one of the principal sources of revenue; but the organisation of such a raid largely depended on whether the local bankers were prepared to advance the money necessary for the maintenance of the army. In 1760 when Marathas marched north for the decisive fight against the Afghans, the Peshwa Balaji Baji Rao was able to give only 200 thousand rupees in cash to Sadasheo Bhao, who commanded the army, while the expenses of the campaign exceeded 500-600 thousand rupees per month.[19] One of the chief functions of the big moneylenders and bankers charged with supplying the Maratha troops during campaigns was to advance money to the so-called banjaras with which the latter were to purchase grain and bring it to the camp. Accounts of British eyewitnesses confirm that big moneylenders and merchants helped to provision the Maratha troops.[20]

The bankers were instrumental in plundering by means of taxation the regions seized by the Maratha feudals, for whom the phrases "to wage war" and "to collect taxes" were synonymous.[21] It was seldom possible to collect the taxes in cash. The Marathas, therefore, sought the help of the local banker who gave them a bill of exchange (apparently, the local authorities undertook to repay with interest the sum for which the bill was drawn). The conqueror could present the bill for payment in any part of India.[22] The highly developed system of bills of exchange was thus used by the Marathas during their forays to obtain the greatest possible amount of tribute in the shortest time.

> Transactions connected with the issuing and discounting of bills of exchange were an important source of the bankers' wealth. One "function" of the bankers. . . was that of providing bills of exchange.

---

self-sufficiency in products of agriculture did not mean that there were no specialised products and that sometimes these were not traded over long distances. Even the carriage of grain for large distances overland in considerable volume was absolutely essential for all military operations of the time. As a result, we see growing in importance the special business of big pack-animal carriers who satisfied the needs of the military, on the march. Apart from the carriage of produce for the military, there were also specialised products in which long-distance trade took place." Gadgil, n. 4, 6.

19 J. Sarkar, *Fall of the Mughal Empire,* (Calcutta, 1949) II, 243.

20 T. Broughton, *Letters Written in a Mahratta Camp during the Year 1809* (London, 1813) 54; Sir C. W. Malet's *Memoranda on the Maratha Army 1795* see Sarkar, n. 19, II, 293-94.

21 Forbes, n. 6, II, 50.

22 *Ibid.*

> These usually arose out of commodity trade and were the means by which trade was financed or money remitted for purposes of trading. These operations depended on the existence of a system of banking houses with either branches or correspondents all over the trading area. Such a system was in fully developed operation in India before the beginning of the 18th century. The system obviated the need for carriage of large amounts of coins over long distances, which in view of contemporary transport and political conditions would have been both risky and costly. Highly developed forms of bills of exchange had been evolved with elaborate security practices and a number of banking houses in important centres of trade in India were in position to provide bills drawn on branches or correspondents throughout the country. The resources of the largest among these banking houses were very large and some of them maintained independent courier services of their own.

To this description given by an Indian scholar we would merely like to add that the circulation of bills of exchange could develop so successfully only because the corresponding bankers as members of the same caste maintained close relations with each other. Very valuable too is D. R. Gadgil's observation regarding the use of bills of exchange and the function of the bankers to remit revenue payments.

> Banking houses might be authorised to receive payments made either by local officials or functionaries and remit them to headquarters. Even where they were not so directly authorised, exchange business would arise out of needs of remittance.[23]

The supply of luxury articles, weapons, horses and other imported goods to the nobility was the third, and final form in which the trading and moneylending castes (i.e. the trading and moneylending capital) served the feudals. Trade in these goods helped to spread the business connections of the Indian merchants far beyond the borders of the country. Later we will enlarge upon their commerce with the countries of the Near East and Southeast Asia. Here we will merely refer to the fact, thoroughly examined in our literature, that Indian merchants including Marwari traders made their way through Central Asia, Iran and Transcaucasia to Astrakhan, where they established a permanent colony. N. M. Goldberg ascertained that a Muslim merchant from Bengal sent as early as the middle of the 16th century three ships with a cargo of silk to Russia; they were however shipwrecked in the Persian Gulf. Indian merchants played an active role in the trade along the Volga and were frequent guests not only in Nizhni Novgorod and Yaroslavl

23 Gadgil, n. 4, 32-30.

but also in Moscow during the 17th and early 18th centuries.[24]

The French traveller De Thevenot, who visited India in 1666, gave the following description of the Banias[25] and their relations with the feudal aristocracy:

> No service whether low or noble, is repugnant to them; they are always prepared to serve those who wish to use them. Everyone in India has therefore his Bania. There are distinguished persons here who entrust them with everything they have, although they don't forget that the Bania is mendacious and grasping. Some of the richest Indian merchants are Banias.[26]

The Englishman A. Hamilton wrote about the Banias of Surat, the greatest port in Gujarat: "The Banyas are most numerous in this City, and are either Merchants, Bankers, Brokers, or Pen-men, as Accountants, Collectors and Surveyors, but few or none Handycraftsmen, except Tailors and Barbers."[27] He also noted the dependence of the rich Mussalmans, apparently feudal lords, on Bania brokers.[28]

While big merchant's capital was in the main serving the feudal lords and participating in foreign trade, its poorer representatives pursued their occupation in the small industries and retail trade. Travelling from Surat to Agra, Tavernier counted in one of the small towns on his route "five or six shops belonging to Banias which sell butter, rice, straw and vegetables". In describing one of them, Tavernier remarked that "by its side stood a large warehouse filled with sacks of rice and grain".[29] The expansion of these activities of merchant's capital were connected with the changes which took place in the social division of labour in feudal India during the 17th and 18th centuries. It seems that with the further advance of this development, trading and moneylending capital would have acquired a greater independence

24 Cf. the manuscripts kept at the Central State Archives of Ancient Documents and the works of A.F. Malinovskii (*Trudy i letopisi Imp. obshchestva istory idrevnostei rossiiskikh*, ch. VII, 1837), V.A. Ulyanitzky (*Chteniya v Imp. obshchestve istory i drevnostei rossiiskikh*, kn. 3, 1888), and *N.M.* Goldberg (*Uchenye zapiski Tikhookeanskogo instituta AN SSSR*, t. II, M., 1950).

25 Bania, in the narrow sense, is the common name of a number of Hindu and Jain trading and moneylending subcastes in Gujarat (altogether there were 84 of them), but since the Europeans came first into contact with this group of merchants they, subsequently, applied the term also to other traders and moneylenders in India.

26 De Thevenot, *Voyages de M. De Thevenot, contenant la relation de l'Indostan des nouveax Mogols, èt des autres peuples et pays des Indes*, (Paris, 1684) 162.

27 A. Hamilton, *A New Account of the East Indies, Being the Observations and Remarks*, (Edinburgh, 1727) II, 150.

28 *Ibid.*, 163.

29 Tavernier, n. 18, 34.

with regard to feudal production.

Money-changing finally, was an important source of revenue for the mercantile and moneylending castes.[30] It is no mere chance that "shroff"—the name of the Indian banker—is a distorted form of the Arabic word "Sarraf" (money-changer). The fact that coins from a variety of mints circulated in the country provided the shroffs with many opportunities to enrich themselves by changing coins and assessing their value in terms of the leading currency.[31] According to Tavernier's description, the shroff would, after having evaluated a certain quantity of coins, sew them up in a bag, indicate their value on it and affix his personal seal. When the bag passed from hand to hand the shroff confirmed the value of its contents and received for this a fixed interest.[32]

Because commercial and financial operations were conducted on an enormous scale, both according to their volume and the territory they covered, the Indian merchants and bankers had to create a complicated and at the same time reliable credit and information system.[33] This system, which was based on caste organisation, will be explained later; we will now merely quote Jawaharlal Nehru's description of it: India's

> banking system was efficient and well organized throughout the country, and the *hundis* or bills of exchange issued by the great business or financial houses were honoured everywhere in India,

30 Coining was not highly centralised and there were large number of local mints. The variety of coins put into circulation was thus large. Moreover, coins were liable to deteriorate and new issues of even the same mint were usually at a premium. Large transactions, therefore, involved operations with a variety of coins and the fixing of their mutual values in exchange. This led to creation of agencies ready to accept payment in a variety of coins or ready to exchange one type of coinage into another. Sometimes the money-changers were specialised as such, but usually money-changing was combined with other financial or banking business." D. R. Gadgil, *Origins of the Modern Indian Business Class*, p. 32.

31 N. Downton, *The Voyage of Nicolas Downton to the East Indies* 1614-1615, ed. by W. Foster, (London, 1939) I, 146-47.

32 Tavernier n. 18, 11.

33 As indicated above, the castes among the trader merchant group were not based on particular specialised economic activity. Hence at all times trader-merchants group in the larger centres would include members of more than one caste or community. The long distance over which trader merchants often travelled and the existence of correspondents of branches of big indigenous financial houses in all main trading centres made for a somewhat mixed caste composition of the merchant group in central locations. Thus in the case of merchant-traders congregated in large centres of trade the problem of a group organisation for economic purposes would necessarily arise. Gadgil. n. 4, 26.

as well as in Iran, and Kabul and Herat and Tashkent and other places in central Asia . . . there was an elaborate network of agents, jobbers, brokers, and middlemen . . . a very rapid and ingenuous system of communicating news and market prices had been evolved.[34]

The methods used in commerce and monetary operations, which were handed down from generation to generation and further developed by each of them, had produced excellent business abilities among the members of trading and moneylending castes. The Portuguese seafarer Tome Pires, who visited Cambay, the Gujarat port in the beginning of the 16th century, compared the commercial skill displayed by the local Banias with that of Italian merchants, who were at that time famous for their resourcefulness. In his view the Banias of Gujarat far surpassed the Arabian and Central Asian merchants. Pires even considered that Portuguese wishing to become salesmen should go there to study commerce, "because", he says, "the business of trade is a science in itself".[35]

The big trading and moneylending capital of tax-farmers became particularly influential early in the 18th century when the fiscal affairs of the Mogul Empire were to a considerable extent concentrated in their hands. We will explain the activities of big trading and moneylending capital during this period on the example of the Jagat Seths great banking house. At the close of the 17th century, the forefather of the Jagat Seths, Hiranand Saho, came to Bihar as banker-purveyor to the Mogul war-lord Man Singh, Maharaja of Jaipur, a principality in Rajputana. Hiranand Saho was a banker from Amber, the capital of Jaipur, and belonged to the Oswals, a Marwari mercantile and moneylending caste.[36] His son Manik Chand was, in the beginning of the 18th century, the banker of Murshid Kuli Khan—the practically independent Nawab of Bengal—and his right hand regarding financial (taxation) matters in Bengal, Bihar and Orissa. Manik Chand enjoyed also great influence at the court of the Shah in Delhi. Using his influence and money, Manik Chand helped Murshid to retain his position as nawab and secured his independence in the administration of Bengal. In return for these services Murshid Kuli Khan fully supported Manik Chand when the latter solicited the title of Jagat Seth (World Banker). The title, which was granted by the Mogul Shah Farrukhshiar in 1715[37] became the proper name of Manik Chand and of his heirs Fathi Chand

34 Jawaharlal Nehru, *The Discovery of India* (London, 1951) 262.

35 *The Suma Oriental of Tome Pires (An Account of the East from the Red Sea to Japan, Written in Malakka and India in 1512-1515) and the Book of Francisco Rodrigues,* (London, 1944) I, 42.

36 Bhargava, n. 12, 29.

37 H. Sinha, *Early European Banking in India* (London, 1927) p. 1.

and Maktab Rai, who enjoyed an enormous influence at the court of the Bengal Nawabs during the first half of the 18th century.[38]

It was no mere chance that Bengal and Bihar became the principal field for the activities of the Jagat Seths. Huge revenues were collected every year in these rich provinces of the Mogul Empire and sent to Delhi. Bengal was one of the most important centres of handicraft (especially weaving) and commerce not only in India but in the whole Middle East.

The tax returns of Bengal were remitted to Delhi by means of the banking house of the Jagat Seths, who had their branches and *gomashthas* (agents) for the collection of taxes and the transmission of the money raised in all important commercial towns of the country.[39] Their duties included also the conversion into money of the tax levied in kind from the population.[40] The Jagat Seths granted credits to the hereditary feudal landowners, the zamindars, who needed money to pay the land tax and, then taking advantage of the zamindars' liabilities seized many of their estates.[41]

The Jagat Seths conducted an extensive trade, especially, in Bengal cloth, and carried out big financial operations in the commercial centres of Bengal with merchants from various Asian and European countries. During the first half of the 18th century the English and other European trading organisations in Bengal were granted credit by the Jagat Seths.[42]

Currency speculations, too, were an important source of the riches amassed by the Jagat Seths, who also controlled the mint in Murshidabad. Using their position in the treasury of Bengal, the Seths fixed a compulsory rate of exchange for the sikka rupee (i.e. the rupee of the latest issue) in terms of rupees coined earlier. Transactions involving the exchange of sikkas were, according to Bolts, "a fund of infinite wealth to the family of the Seths".[43]

The vast fortune of the Jagat Seths was estimated by their contemporaries to have reached 100 million rupees. This is, perhaps,

---

38 W. Hunter, A *Statistical Account of Bengal* (London 1878), IX 258-90.

39 W. Bolts, *Considerations on Indian Affairs* (London, 1772), 194.

40 R. Mukerji, *The Foundations of Indian Economics* (London, 1916), 276.

41 "The Zamindars, who generally are in want of large sums of ready cash, as well as of security to be given for the payment of their rents according to agreement, have been usually necessitated to call in the Shroffs, or bankers and money-changers, to their assistance. Juggut Seat, the head of a Centoo family of the weaver tribe of caste (Bolts was probably mistaken) in the time of the Nabob Jaffer Khan, availed himself of this circumstance, which the succeeding times of confusion in the empire enabled him to improve, to the introduction of new customs at the Durbar, in the department of the revenues, and to the raising and enriching of himself and his family". Bolts, n. 39, 156-57.

42 *Ibid.*

43 *Ibid.*, 157-58.

an exaggeration and in any case merely an approximation. But it is known that even after losing more than 20 million rupees as a result of a Maratha raid, the Jagat Seths continued to grant loans of 10 million rupees to the Nawab of Bengal.[44] Relying on their economic strength, the Jagat Seths were able to exert considerable political influence in feudal Bengal. Bolts asserts that Jagat Seth "acquired an influence at the Durbar little inferior to that of the Nabab himself: for instance he was the chief instrument in the acquisition of Lord Clive's famous jageer."[45]

Although the most important, the Jagat Seths were not the only Marwari bankers in feudal Bengal. During the reign of the last Moguls there were seven rich bankers, called *kothiwalla* (the owner of the firm) in Murshidabad who had their own agents in important towns. All of them were members of the Oswal caste from Western India who had settled in Bengal. They imported European woollen cloth, cotton and cotton goods as well as pepper and other spices, and exported ginger; their main business, however, was the provision of bills of exchange. Taxes collected in various localities were, during the Muslim rule, remitted by these bankers to Murshidabad.[46] The close relations usually maintained within their caste helped the Marwari moneylenders and bankers in Bengal to consolidate their position. In 1748, for instance, the Jagat Seths dismissed a number of employees who were not members of their caste.[47]

Trading and moneylending capital in the Maratha country developed in the main on similar lines. Maharashtra was a comparatively backward region of India up to the 18th century. The Maratha towns were not so much independent centres of commerce and the handicrafts as the headquarters of Mogul viceroys or local

---

44 The Sair-ul-Mutaharin relates that the wealth of the Jagat Seths was so great that no banker could compare with them either in Hindustan or the Deccan. It is quite obvious that at that time all bankers in Bengal were either associates of the Jagat Seths or members of their family. The following incident gives an idea of the size of their fortune: during the first Maratha invasion, when Murshidabad was not yet surrounded by walls, Mir Habib with a detachment of his best cavalry managed to take the city before Aliverdi was able to come to its aid, and removed 20 million rupees in coins of the Arcot mint alone from the house of the Jagat Seths. The loss of so huge a sum seems to have affected the brothers no more than might have the loss of two sheaves of straw. They continued to draw bills amounting to 10 million rupees for the government. See *Murshidabad, Eastern Bengal District Gazetteers* (Calcutta, 1909) 60-61.

45 Bolts, n. 39, 158.

46 *Report of Bengal Provincial Banking Enquiry Committee* (Calcutta, 1930) I, 183.

47 J. Long, ed., *Selections from Unpublished Records of Government for the Years 1748 to 1767 Inclusive Relating Mainly to the Social Conditions of Bengal* (Calcutta, 1869) I, 9.

feudal lords and stopping points for transit trade. In the 18th century, the formation of a federation of Maratha feudal states centred on Maharashtra and the rapid development of feudal relations created new conditions for urban life.[48] The vast amount of riches that the Maratha army amassed by robbing the conquered regions and the intensified exploitation of the local peasantry, caused an increased flow of orders from the local feudal chiefs and the feudal state, which spent enormous sums on the maintenance of the army, administration and court. It should be stressed, that the means available to pay the artisans consisted of the rent-tax and war booty, i.e., the demand had a natural basis and greatly depended on the prosperity of the feudal state.

As a result of an increased flow of orders from the state and from individual Maratha feudal lords urban handicrafts flourished in Maharashtra during the 18th century. The artisans' dependence on state orders was, in particular, reflected in the fact that to a certain extent the state regulated the handicraft industries by means of an ordering system and by granting individuals the monopoly of manufacturing a given article. As far back as the early 18th century for example, Radho Naik granted the monopoly of silk production in Yeola to the Gujarati Bania Shamdas Balji.[49]

The local artisans were unable to satisfy fully all the requirements of the feudal towns and skilled weavers and other craftsmen from Hindustan, Bihar and Andhradesha settled in Maharashtra and above all in Poona, the capital of the Peshwas. The immigrating handicraftsmen preserved their religious, communal and caste isolation forming separate groups

48. "Maharashtra, during the 18th century experienced some respite from the extremely troubled time of the 17th century. This was a period of comparative peace and prosperity for this region of India. Within the region two comparatively new cities (Poona and Nagpur) rose to considerable importance in the decades immediately after 1750. Nagpur, in the east of Maharashtra, developed because of its central position into an important trading centre, being connected with routes in all directions except the south-east which was largely tribal country. Nagpur became the centre of trade in raw cotton and also rose rapidly to importance as a weaving centre. Poona in the west grew in size and activity chiefly as a very influential political capital. Poona through its political relations became for sometime an important centre of financial transactions, though not trade or industry "Detailed examination of contemporary records regarding the number of houses, etc. in Poona led to estimating the population of that city at about 40,000 in 1760; it had reached over 100,000 before the end of the century. At the beginning of the 18th century, Poona probably could not have contained more than 10,000 persons. These figures indicate the growth of a city which during the 18th century rose very rapidly to great political importance, but was not originally, and did not become in the process of growth, an important industrial or commercial centre". Gadgil, n. 4, 15.

49 *Nasik, Bombay Gazetteer* (Bombay, 1883) XVI, 155.

within the Partisan population of Maharashtra. The urban castes of both Maratha and newly arrived craftsmen were a kind of guild organisation.[50]

The consolidation of the feudal Maratha state and, as a result of conquests, the extension of its territorial limits far beyond Maharashtra proper created extremely favourable conditions for the activity of big merchant's capital. Such transactions as collecting and remitting the rent-tax, buying up war booty, granting loans to the feudal lords and supplying goods to them and to the army, and the growth of maritime commerce provided traders and moneylenders with many opportunities to enrich themselves. The route of the important transit trade in salt ran across West Maharashtra. At the beginning of the 19th century, up to one hundred thousand vehicles passed annually through Poona alone.[51] When the harvest was bad Maharashtra needed great quantities of imported grain.

Money-changing and determining the value of coins from diverse mints, which circulated in the country was an important source of profit for bankers and moneylenders in feudal Maharashtra. As R. D. Choksey says:

> There was, under the late government (that of the Peshwas) so large a number of siccas, with such variation in their value when they were brought for exchange to the markets, that the surrafs, sawkars, and merchants defrauded the public at will.[52] Bankers often resorted to forging and counterfeiting money.[53]

I. M. Reisner's monograph which was published posthumously contains much interesting material regarding the activities of the Gujarati and Marwari bankers at the courts of the Maratha states. I. M. Reisner writes:

> One can say without exaggeration, that merchant's and money-lender's capital played an important role in financing the predatory military campaigns of the Maratha feudal chiefs, and that it appropriated a handsome slice of the spoils. One has to remember

50 "In Poona during the latter half of the 18th century there was considerable immigration of artisans like cobblers, potters, carpenters, etc. from regions outside Maharashtra. The local artisans in these occupations continued also to ply their crafts. The immigrants came and established themselves chiefly because they either specialised in certain products which member of the indigenous castes did not ordinarily produce or because they brought in greater skill. There is no evidence, contemporary or later, to indicate that the two caste groups engaged in the same craft were brought under one craft or trade association." Gadgil n. 4, 25.

51 R. D. Choksey, *Economic History of the Bombay Deccan and Carnatak (1818-1868)* (Poona, 1945) 51.

52 *Ibid.*, 53.

53 *Ibid.*

that these wars were carried on with hired troops who had to be paid all the time, and that the Maratha peshwas were chronically short of funds with which to pay the mercenaries.[54]

Beginning with Peshwa Baji Rao I, the government in Poona had constantly to seek the help of the local moneylenders and bankers who granted loans on enslaving conditions. The outstanding debts which remained after Baji Rao's death amounted to 1,450,000 rupees. The money had been borrowed from 30 different persons at rates varying from 12-30 per cent per annum. The biggest creditors were Raghunath Patvardhan (who had lent 300,000 rupees), Gorakh Mandrawani (105,000 rupees) and Balaji Jomi (36,000 rupees).[55] In 1736 Baji Rao was greatly encumbered with debts, and all his efforts to obtain new loans failed because the moneylenders in Poona considered the Peshwa insolvent.[56]

But the principal source of profit for moneylenders in Maharashtra, and also in many other regions of feudal India, was the collection of the rent-tax. Usually the ryot gave a promissory note to the moneylender, who paid the patel the tax that had fallen due. When the patel had to remit the tax to the treasury offices of the district he, in turn, gave a promissory note (havalla) to a bigger moneylender who then paid the tax in cash. This "mode was most prevalent, so much so that it is estimated that scarcely 25 per cent of the revenue was paid directly in money."[57]

Just as the growing demand for handicraft products drew artisans from other parts of India to Maharashtra, so the rapid expansion of commercial and financial activities caused an immigration of merchants and bankers from adjoining regions of India into the towns of Maharashtra. Moreover, while a considerable part of urban artisans always were Marathas, the position was quite different among the merchants. During the formation period of the Maratha feudal state, the village community was only beginning to overcome its economic

---

54 I. M. Reisner, *Narodnye dvizheniya v Indii v XVII-XVIII vv.* IVL (Moscow, 1961) 302.

55 C. A. Kincaid and D. B. Parasnis, *A History of the Maratha People* (London, 1818) II, 272

56 S. Sen observes that the Peshwa was quite unable to finance military expeditions, and that the feudal chiefs themselves had to find the money. It seems that only very few of the Maratha leaders had any surplus or reserve funds at their disposal, which they could have used for this purpose; on such occasions they were, therefore, compelled to turn to the moneylenders. It was precisely for this reason that rich bankers, like Gokul Parekh, could rise to the position of chief minister under Daulat Rao Sindhia.—S. Sen, *Administrative System of the Marathas* (Calcutta, 1925) 469.

57 Choksey, n. 51, 84-85.

self-sufficiency,[58] and the social division of labour between town and country lagged behind the level reached in the advanced regions of India. That was the reason why no such powerful trading and moneylending castes developed in Maharashtra as, for example, in Gujarat or in Rajputana—Hindustan. The majority of big local merchants and tax-farmers in the Maratha state were Brahmins.[59] But the leading positions in large-scale commerce and banking continued to be occupied, as previously, by Gujarati and Marwari Banias, who had began to immigrate into the country[60] when it was still under Mogul rule.

As early as the 18th century Maharashtra was in a way divided into spheres of influence by the Gujarati and Marwari communities of merchants and moneylenders. The former predominated in the West, in the Peshwa state, the latter in the East, in Nagpur. D. R. Gadgil writes:

> In Poona, the earliest migrant elements appear to have been Gujarati Banias and Bohras, and it is likely that both of these came to Poona through Burhanpur and Aurangabad. In Nagpur, on the other hand, the trading immigrants were Bania castes from Rajasthan, which had spread into central and north India. With the rise of cotton exports from the Berar-Nagpur tract, it was these elements that came to control this trade.[61]

The mint privileges in Poona were held by the Gujarati banker Dullabh Das Govindhji, the head of the local community of merchants.[62]

In the 1820s, J. Malcolm met "princely bankers" of Gujarati descent in the principalities of Central India ruled by the Marathas. Some of

---

58 Cf. I. M. Reisner, *Nekotorye dannye o raslozheny derevenskoi obshchiny v maratkhov v XVII-nachale XIX veka.*

59 J. Malcolm writes about the Brahmins from the Deccan: "a very small proportion of..[them] are devoted to religious duties, at the utmost not more than one thousand, and the remaining seven thousand constitute that active and abstemious body of men of business who carry on all the duties of the Mahratta government, and are the most industrious and intelligent, both of the higher and lower classes of merchants and clerks" (J. Malcolm, *Memoir of Central India Including Malwa and Adjoining Provinces*, (London, 1832) II, 115-6). D. R. Gadgil remarks that "an entry relating to the year 1797-98 in the Selection from the Peshwa's Diaries gives names of nearly 175 persons (all apparently Brahmins from Konkan employed in the administrative offices of the Peshwa who were exempted from payment of transit excise through the passes of the Ghats, etc., on the imports made by them of rice and other products from the Konkan. The imports would mostly represent bulk purchases made in the Konkan but might also partly represent receipts of rent. They point to streams of internal trade set up by important migration movements. *Selections*, Bajirao II, pp. 201-207". Gadgil, n. 4, 4 n.

60 *Imperial Gazetteer of India* (London, 1885-1886) I, 104.

61 Gadgil, *n.* 4, 19-20.

62 *Ibid.*, 28.

these bankers' families had already settled in this region at the time when independent Rajput states existed there. For instance, the ancestor of the principal banker in Ujjain, who hailed from Gujarat, had come there 300 years ago.[63] Many of them occupied high positions in the Maratha principalities. The dispatches, for example, of the English resident at Sindhia's court in Gwalior written between 1811 and 1818, contain references to the great influence exerted upon state affairs by the banker Gopal Parekh, who headed the financial administration of the principality. The banker's nationality is not indicated. But from his typically Gujarati name and, above all his surname, which is the same as that of the biggest mill owner in Gujarat at the end of the 19th century, we can safely assume that Gopal Parekh was a shroff from Gujarat. He made his way up by granting a loan to the princely treasury which was about to go bankrupt, for the taxes had been collected for several years in advance.[64] Out of gratitude the prince entrusted Parekh with the treasury. Later on, however, Parekh's position became rather shaky.

It was quite natural that the Banias always headed the financial and fiscal administrations in the principalities of Gujarat, their native country. Evidence of this can be found even in records from the nineteenth century.[65]

J. Malcolm asserts that in the 1820s "almost the whole of the Soucars and Shroffs (bankers and money-brokers), and a great proportion of Bunnias (or retail dealers), in Central India (Western Hindustan), are either from Gujarat or Marwar, and generally not very old settlers".[66] "The number (of immigrants) from Marwar is greater than from Gujarat, but this is only since the Mahrattas governed Central India".[67]

Up to the English conquest the bankers in Western Hindustan served in the Maratha feudal lords, their main occupation being tax-farming in the Maratha principalities. Having got hold of tax-collecting, the Marwaris began to exert influence in the state administration of the principalities. J. Malcolm writes:

> As many of the renters are either bankers, or men supported by that class, they have acquired, and maintain an influence both in the councils of the State, and the local administration of the provinces, that gives them great power, which they solely direct to the object of accumulation. The richest bankers mix in the petty revenue details of the smallest village.[68]

---

63 Malcolm, n. 59, 115-16.

64 *Daulat Rao Sindhia and North Indian Affairs, English Records of Maratha History, Poona Residency Correspondence* (Bombay, 1951) XIV, 70, 106.

65 Forbes, n. 6, II, 113, 208.

66 Malcolm, n. 59, II, 159.

67 *Ibid.*, 162.

68 *Ibid.*, 38.

Taking advantage of the heavy tax burden the starving peasants had to shoulder, the usurer or tax-collector would "help" the peasants by granting them a loan in kind for which he charged interest at a rate of 50 per cent per annum.[69] Under the conditions of semi-natural peasant economy, tax-farming therefore was a means employed by moneylending capital to enslave the peasants.

Not only did the Marwari emigrants in the first half of the 19th century remain in touch with Marwar, their native land, but they usually returned there in their old age, handing over the share they held in the small shops to their young compatriots who were arriving every year from Marwar to scrape up a fortune in Central India or the Deccan.[70]

Moneylending capital in feudal India thus existed in the two forms that are characteristic for the period preceding capitalist production. Marx writes:

> These two forms are: first, usury by lending money to extravagant members of the upper classes, particularly landowners; secondly, usury by lending money to small producers who possess their own conditions of labour—this includes the artisan, but mainly the peasant, since particularly under pre-capitalist conditions, in so far as they permit of small independent individual producers, the peasant class necessarily constitutes the overwhelming majority of them. Both the ruin of rich landowners through usury and the improvement of the small producers lead to the formation and concentration of large amounts of money-capital.[71]

Anticipating later development we would like to mention here that this definition of Marx remains also valid in regard to the activity of usurers in colonial India, although of course the peasant had to bear a far heavier burden of debt, than the big landowner.

Only as an exception did merchant's capital in feudal India take on productive forms. While D. R. Gadgil mentions the fact that buyers-up financed handicraft production, he stresses at the same time that

> they would provide loan capital and not risk capital. Therefore, accumulation of capital in the hands of trader-merchants did not augment in any way resources invested in capital equipment for industrial production. The unit of industrial artisan production was the small individual workshop.[72]

In the 17th and 18th centuries trading and moneylending capital in India, which participated in the feudal exploitation of the peasants

69 *Ibid.*, 383,

70 *Ibid.*, 162-63,

71 Karl Marx, *Capital* (Moscow, 1959) III, 581.

72 Gadgil, n: 4, 34-35.

and the enslavement of the craftsmen, piled up enormous accumulations. But the development towards the following, historically higher form of capital was to a considerable extent hampered by the existing state structure. Engels writes:

> In point of fact, Turkish, like all Oriental rule, is incompatible with Capitalist Society; the appropriated surplus-value is not safe from the hands of rapacious Satraps and Pachas; the first fundamental condition of profitable trading is wanting—security for the person and property of the merchant. [73]

This remark of Engels, made in regard to the Ottoman Empire, helps to understand the position of traders and moneylenders in Mogul India as well. Mandelslo writes about the Gujarati merchants:

> Merchants are infinitely more happy than Tradesmen; but they also have this inconvenience, that as soon as they have gotten any wealth together, they are exposed to the envy of the Grandees, who find out ways to fleece them, as soon as they make any shew of it. And whereas they cannot do it with Justice, they many times make use of such pretences as cost those their lives who have acquired excessive riches.[74]

Mandelslo also remarks upon the low social position occupied by Hindu and Jain castes of merchants and moneylenders in feudal Indian society:

> The Men (Banias) are very civilly apparell'd, and live without any scandal among the *Mahomedans,* who being imperious and insolent (this is, undoubtedly, a reference to Muslim feudal chiefs) treat the *Banias,* as if they were their slaves, with great contempt, much after the manner the Jews are treated in Europe, in those places where they are permitted to live.[75]

To get hold of the wealth accumulated by the merchants and moneylenders the feudal rulers did not hesitate to use the most savage tortures. James Forbes speaks of the cruelty exhibited by a prince of Sind, a Muslim, at whose court in Tatta only Hindus—members of the trading and moneylending castes—were employed in the revenue administration. The vezier and his retinue subjected a rich bania, who was a customs officer, to the most brutal tortures for two days. But only the threat to kill his only son forced the rich banker to disclose where his treasures were hidden.[76]

---

73 F. Engels, *The Foreign Policy of Russian Tsardom* (Time, London June, 1890) 526.

74 J. A. de Mandelslo, *The Voyages and Travels* (London, 1669) 65.

75 *Ibid.*, 51.

76 Forbes, n. 6, II, 54.

In 1798, the wealthiest shroffs of Poona were tortured to death. One of them, the richest and most influential one, died on the scorching hot muzzle of a cannon.[77] Such atrocities conflict with the legal declarations of the Peshwa state. Here is a free translation of the extract (devoted to traders and bankers) from the *Agnyapatra* an old Marathi treatise on statecraft:

> The Savkars are ornaments of royalty and of the kingdom. They make the realm prosperous. Unobtainable commodities enter the territory. The kingdom becomes wealthy. When contingencies arise they provide loans. By their aid, calamities are averted. There is much profit in extending protection to them. For this they should be accorded status. They should be protected from arbitrary acts and insults. Shops and markets should be established in various localities of the city for elephants, horses, silk clothes, cloth of gold, wool, jewellery, weapons etc., so that they can conduct trade. Leading merchants should be encouraged to reside in the aristocratic quarter.[78]

The fact, incidentally, that such principles are advanced is in itself significant; for, as every historian knows, in a way laws represent the negative side of reality.

The position of the rich Muslim merchants was not adequately safeguarded either.[79] A. Hamilton, an Englishman, who traded with India and the countries of the Near East from 1688 to 1723, writes about a merchant in Surat:

> *Abdul Gafour, a Mahometan* that I was acquainted with, drove a Trade equal to the *English East-India Company,* for I have known him fit out in a Year, above twenty Sail of Ships, between 300 and 600 Tuns, and none of them had less of his own Stock than 10,000 Pounds, and some of them had 25,000; and after that foreign Stock was sent away, he behoved to have as much more of an Indian Stock for the following Year's Market. When he died, he left his Estate to two Grandsons, his own Son, who was his only child, dying before him. But the Court had a Fling at them, and got above a Million Sterling of their Estate.[80]

---

77 James Douglas, *Bombay and Western India, A Series of Stray Papers* (London, 1893) I, 107.

78 Gadgil, n. 4, 22 n.

79 "The traders do not seem to have wielded much political influence. The position of Hindu trading communities under Muslim rule would obviously not be strong, but even Muslim traders or trading interests, wherever they existed, do not seem to have exercised influence on administration". *Ibid.*, 31.

80 Hamilton, n. 27, I, 147-48.

The famous French traveller F. Bernier asserted that both Hindu and Muslim merchants were often even afraid to make too great advances in commerce, because they were under the apprehension that people might consider them rich and think up a way of ruining them.[81] Bernier, moreover, was in India at the beginning of Aurangzeb's reign when feudal anarchy was still kept in check by the central power. It appears, however, that the position of the rich Mussalman merchants was nevertheless better than that of the Hindu merchants. J. Fryer, in any case, notes "There are some great merchants among them (the Muslims) that are buoy'd up more by the Authority of their Religion and Cast, than Cunning, the Banyas being forced to flee to them for Patronage".[82] The Muslim trader's greater personal security also showed itself in his outward appearance and his habits; in contrast to the Hindu Bania, who dressed like an ascetic, the Mussalman merchant wore rich garments. The comparatively privileged position which the Muslim merchants occupied in Mogul India, undoubtedly, slowed down their defection to the side of the colonialists. Incidentally the restraint with regard to the satisfaction of their requirements, which was a distinguishing feature of the Hindu trading and moneylending castes, was due to the necessity to conceal their wealth from the grasping emirs and rajas. Ovington relates that the constant fear of 'expropriation' caused the rich merchants in Surat, brokers of the East India Company, who owned one and a half to three million rupees to spend as little as 3,000-4,000 rupees per annum on their personal requirements.[83]

It is obvious that wealth in the form of money, bills of exchange and precious stones can be easier preserved (or rather hidden) than land, buildings or enterprises.[84] That is why the fact that the merchant's property was constantly threatened by the feudals did not simply slow down the accumulation of capital but also, and that is very important, hampered the transition of capital from the money form to the productive form, that is its manifestation as means of production. If, however the Indian merchant possessed any immovable property it was, as a rule, for the personal use of the owner and his family (e.g., a

81 *Voyages de Francais Bernier. Doeteur en Medecine de la Faculte de Montpellier. Contenant le Description des Etats du grand Mogol, de l'Hindustan du Royaume de Kachemire..*, Tome Premier (Amsterdam, 1710), 309-10.

82 J. Fryer, *A New Account of East India and Persia* (London, 1912) II, 112.

83 J. Ovington, *A Voyage to Surat, in the year 1689,* (Oxford, 1929) 118.

84 "It is not surprising that bullion and jewellery should play a very important part in the economic life of these centuries. They had advantages of easy concealment (which was important in times of political insecurity), of comparatively little risk of depreciation of value, and of being easy to transport. In the absence of avenues of capital investment for productive or development activities accumulation of resources in these times logically became tantamount to hoards of bullion and jewellery." Gadgil, n. 4, 35.

dwelling-house).[85] Ovington made very interesting observations confirming this.

He writes about the Surat Banias at the close of the 17th century:

> Their Wealth consists only in Cash and Jewels, the distinction of personal and real Estate is not heard in *India,* and that they preserve as close and private as they can, lest the *Mogul's* Exchequer should be made their Treasury. This curbs them in their Expenses, and awes them to great secrecy in their Commerce, especially in their receiving, or Payments of Money, for which they either make use of the darkness of the Night, or of the obscurity of the Morning, in conveying it to the place of Payment.[86]

In the first half of the 18th century when the Mogul Empire was disintegrating, while, as Marx wrote, "all were struggling against all,"[87] the traders' and moneylenders' position became still more precarious in many parts of the country. The merchant and his property were constantly threatened not only by foreign enemies (the robbery of the Jagat Seths' property),[88] but also by their "own" feudal lord who was always in need of money for internecine wars. It was the necessity to protect themselves and their property against the feudal club-law which drove a number of the big Indian merchants into the arms of the European invaders.

One has to remember that the information, we quoted, about discrimination against merchants mainly relates to Mogul India in the latter half of the 17th century, when Aurangzeb persued a policy of religious intolerance and persecuted the non-Muslim population of the Great Mogul Empire. He introduced in particular a special capitation tax levied on all non-Muslims. Aurangzeb's action antagonised influential groups of Indian merchants, mainly consisting of Hindus,

---

85 "Apart from commercial and financial capital, investment by the merchant-traders would be chiefly in houses and gardens etc. and other real estate or property round the city. Thus mercantile accumulation did not affect productive activity either in agriculture or in handicraft industry. The growing fortunes of merchants of cities would be exhibited outwardly, where such outward exhibition was not considered unsafe, in such features as the rich carved frontages of merchants' houses as in Gujarat cities; or they would be exhibited in acts of religion or charity by way of building temples, tanks, dharmashalas, etc." *Ibid.*, 35.

86 Ovington, n. 83, 187.

87 Karl Marx and Frederick Engels, *The First Indian War of Independence 1857-1859*, (Moscow), 32.

88 De Thevenot reports that after the raid on Surat in 1666, Shivaji carried away valuables worth 30 million (apparently pound sterling). He seized 22 pounds of precious stones in the house of one Bania alone (De Thevenot, n. 26, 84). These figures are of course, only estimates but they confirm once more that merchants in feudal India were enormously rich.

Jains and Parsis, and was, in fact, conducive to their reconciliation with the English.

The precarious position of the merchant and his property was not a universal phenomenon in feudal India. Even in the 18th century there were times in Mysore, the Punjab or Bengal when the merchant received specific guarantees safeguarding him against the outrages of the feudal lords. In these conditions (for example, in Mysore) the merchants supported the fight of their rulers against the colonial intruders. In other words, the extreme feudal reaction, that advanced under the banner of religious intolerance split the forces resisting the English and paved the way for the colonial conquest.

CHAPTER III

TRADING AND MONEYLENDING CAPITAL IN THE PERIOD OF PRIMITIVE ACCUMULATION

The bearing of the English colonialists varied according to the historical conditions they encountered. In the 17th century they were merchants—(by Indian standards not very rich ones)—who tried, by flattery and bribes, to secure the right to trade and to establish their factories in coastal districts.[1] Before gaining political supremacy the colonialists, obviously, could not bend to their will the system of commerce and banking which had arisen. They were moreover forced to adapt themselves to this system when entering into relations with Indian merchants on more or less equal terms. Especially firm and close economic links between the big Indian merchants and European traders existed in Gujarat.

When European vessels first appeared on the western shores of the country, Gujarat was economically one of the most highly developed states of India. Gujarat, the western-most part of the country, was naturally the centre of India's trade with the Middle East and East Africa.

The transit trade from the Middle East to Southeast Asia passed through the ports of Gujarat. Already Pires gave an excellent description of the important role which the Gujarat ports played in regard to through traffic: Both Gujaratis and merchants who had settled in Cambay sent many ships to every part of the world, to Aden, Ormuz, the Deccan kingdom, Goa, Bhatcal, to the whole Malabar Coast, to Ceylon, Bengal, Siam, Pedir, Pase and Malacca. They carried one cargo of goods there and returned with another, enriching and aggrandising Cambay. This town spread out its arms towards the most important points along the shipping lines, touching Aden with its right and

1. J. Douglas records that the Emperor Jahangir told Sir Thomas Roe, our ambassador in 1615, after he had delivered his gifts from the King of England, "Your presents have been inferior to those a merchant you have seen here has brought" (J. Douglas, *Bombay and Western India*, London, 1893, I, 115).

Malacca with its left; the other places are less important.[2]

Permanent colonies of Gujaratis existed in the ports of the Red Sea and the Persian Gulf already at the end of the 17th century. Houses in Surat had windows made of Venetian glass imported by way of the Ottoman Empire. A lively trade was carried on with the countries of Southeast Asia. J. Fryer mentioned a Parsi in Surat who, acting as broker for the kingdom of Bantam (Java) became so rich that he built a magnificent house.[3] John Ovington, who visited Surat in 1690, writes about this port—the chief one in Gujarat which had forced Cambay to take second place in the 17th century : "*Suratt* is reckon'd the most fam'd Emporium of the *Indian Empire,* where all commodities are vendible, though they never were there seen before".[4]

The development of foreign trade brought prosperity to the handicraft industries, especially weaving. The numerous and rich towns of Gujarat were famous for the skill of their craftsmen. Trade with the adjacent regions of India was stimulated by the fact that Gujarat's agriculture could not satisfy the needs of the urban population. Grain, in particular, was imported from other parts of India.

The arrival of the Europeans did not, right away, affect the economic position of the towns in Gujarat, although the Mussalman merchants, in whose hands maritime commerce was concentrated, became very soon aware of the fact that the European merchant-pirates dominated the sea-lanes. But commerce did not come to a standstill because the Europeans pushed the Muslim traders aside. The establishment of direct trade links with Europe, even stimulated to a certain degree artisan production in Gujarat. In 1690 Ovington wrote that Surat craftsmen manufacturing silk fabrics exactly reproduced the finest and most beautiful specimens imported from Europe.[5]

Ahmedabad flourished during the 17th century. As the *Gazetteer* relates:

> Ahmedabad was formerly celebrated for its commerce and manufactures in cloths of gold and silver, fine silk and cotton fabrics,

---

2 *The Suma Oriental of Tome Pires* (London, 1944), I, 42. Pires then lists the goods sold in Gujarat (cotton cloth, indigo, opium, hides, as well as wheat and rice, which were either grown in Cambay or imported from the neighbouring states), and refers to the great number of Gujaratis in the main ports on the coast of the Indian Ocean and the adjoining seas; he says, for example, "the Cambay merchants make Malacca their chief trading centre. There used to be a thousand Gujarat merchants in Malacca, besides four or five thousand Gujarat seamen, who came and went. Malacca cannot live without Cambay, nor Cambay without Malacca, if they are to be very rich and very prosperous." (*Ibid,* 45).

3 J. Fryer, *A New Account of East India and Persia,* I, 231.

4 J. Ovington, *A Voyage to Surat,* 131.

5 *Ibid.,* 166.

articles of gold, silver, steel, enamel, mother-of-pearl, lacquered ware and fine wood-work. Excellent paper was also made here, and there were many artists in portait-painting and miniatures. The trade in indigo, cotton, and opium was very great.[6]

The list of articles produced in Ahmedabad shows that its craftsmen worked for the feudal lords and foreign markets. At the beginning of the seventeenth century, 200 carts loaded with goods were sent from Ahmedabad to the ports every ten days.[7]

Commerce and moneylending in Gujaraṭ had been in the hands of a few Muslim (Bohra, Khoja) and Hindu (Bania and Bhattia sub-castes) castes, long before the boats of European merchant-pirates appeared at the shores of India. The Bohras and Khojas were in the main engaged in foreign, maritime trade with the Muslim countries of the Near and Middle East and with East Africa. The Hindu castes mainly specialised in monetary, banking and moneylending operations and internal trade.

Early in the 17th century, the richest shroff of Gujarat, Shantidas, received the hereditary title "Nagar Seth", i.e. Head of the Town, from Shah Jahangir for commercial services rendered to the Mogul court. In addition, the treasury redeemed all his bills of exchange. From this time onwards the head of the banking family of Nagar Seth also became the chief of the Ahmedabad trading community and represented its interests in relation to the Mogul administration.[8]

The territory through which the trade routes from the ports of Gujarat and Bombay passed was at first in the hands of Mogul viceroys and later the Marathas, the strongest enemies of the British East India Company. As long as a considerable part of Gujarat and Maharashtra remained under Maratha rule, that is up to 1818,[9] the chief method employed by the English colonialists to enrich themselves in these regions was, naturally, their monopoly of foreign trade, and not military plunder or taxation. The English, therefore, required the services of the

6 E. Thornton, *Gazetteer of the Territories under the Government of the East India Company* (London, 1854) I, 430.

7 *Ahmadabad, Bombay Gazeteer*, IV, 88.

8 B. Bhargava, *Indigenous Banking*, 32. "In 1725 the then Nagar Seth of Ahmedabad saved the city from plunder by the Marathas and, in recognition of this, the combined guilds of the city assigned to him the perpetual right to levy a quarter per cent on all goods stamped in the municipal weighing yard" (D. R. Gadgil, *Origins of the Modern Indian Business Class*, 27).

9 During the first half of the eighteenth century Gujarat was the object of a fierce struggle between the Marathas and the Mogul feudal lords. Only in 1757 did Ahmedabad finally pass into the hands of the Marathas. Later on the English invaders made raids into Gujarat, which formed part of the Gaikwar's territory. In 1780 General Goddard took Ahmedabad by storm. But the colonialists finally succeeded in capturing Gujarat and its capital only in 1818.

local merchants. The opposition of the Marathas thus forced the East India Company to grant the leading Gujarati traders and moneylenders more advantageous terms for their collaboration than they offered for example, to the Bengali merchants.

While methods of primitive accumulation were used to exploit India, that is up to the beginning of the 19th century, the Gujarati merchants, on the whole, acted as agents of the British foreign trade monopoly. N. Downton, one of the first Englishmen to set forth his impressions of a voyage to India, 1614-15, relates that already at that time the British East India Company had long established regular contacts among the Gujarati Banias to whom it sold swords, knives, telescopes and other articles. The Mogul viceroys of Gujarat communicated with the English through the Bania Lakhandas. In the beginning, business contacts of the English merchants with the local population were apparently restricted to Banias, for the Englishmen believed that all Gujarati Hindus were Banias.[10] Records belonging to a later period also confirm that local merchants acted as intermediaries between Indian feudal lords and the European traders.[11]

As early as the 1670s J. Fryer found that a system had developed in Surat according to which Englishmen traded through the mediation of Indian merchants. For every transaction they concluded the Indian merchants who acted as intermediaries received a commission of 2 per cent.[12] In addition, they secretly appropriated according to Fryer's assertion, part of the value of the goods they sold. It was difficult to check up the intermediary, for the Englishmen's knowledge of Gujarati was poor. Moreover, declares Fryer, "Ignorance is safer, than to hazard being poysoned for prying too nearly into their (the middlemen's) actions".[13]

The first contradictions between British capital and the ancestors of the Gujarati merchants who were collaborating with the British were, thus, easily solved, if one is to believe Fryer.

J. Fryer paints a very colourful picture of how the European merchant is received by the Banias of Surat, and their subsequent relationship:

10 N. Downton, *The Voyage of Nicolas Downton*, 13, 24, 133. A hundred years before Downton, T. Pires writes: "The Heathen (i.e. Hindus.—*V. P.*) of Cambay are called Banias' (N. 2, I, 39).

11 According to the *Discourse of Trade* treaties and agreements with the Indian princes could be concluded through their ministers, for the rules were always prepared to conduct negotiations with any merchant and there was no need to approach the prince himself. (*A Discourse of Trade*, 122).

12 Ovington, who visited Surat a few years after Fryer, mentions a commission of 3 per cent (n. 4, 233).

13 Fryer, n. 3, I, 218.

> As soon as you have set your Foot on Shore, they crowd in their Service, interposing between you and all Civil Respect, as if you had no other Business but to be gull'd; so that unless you have some to make your way through them, they will interrupt your going, and never leave till they have drawn out something for their Advantage. At this time of Shipping they Present the Governor of *Surat*, to license them to keep a Mart here, which they make the *Europeans* pay dearly for:
>
> Yet such is their Policy, that without these, neither you nor the Natives themselves shall do any Business, though they are worse Brokers than *Jews;* if they be not the Spawn of them, the *Rechabites* that would drink no Wine. These generally are the Poorer sort, and set on by the Richer to Trade with the Seamen for the meanest things they bring; and notwithstanding they take them at their own rates, get well enough in exchange of Goods with them. They are the absolute Map of Sordidness, fareing hardly, and professing fairly, to entrap the unwary; enduring servily foul Words, Affronts and Injuries, for a future hope of Gain; expert in all the studied arts of Thriving and Insinuation; so that, Lying, Dissembling, Cheating, are their Masterpiece: Their whole desire is to have Money pass through their Fingers, to which a great part is sure to stick: For they well understand the constant turning of Cash amounts both to the Credit and Profit of him that is so occupied; which these *Banyas* are sensible of, otherwise they would not be so industrious to enslave themselves.[14]

As we see, the English merchant, driven to distraction by the resourcefulness of the Gujarat traders, nevertheless tries to find a sort of economic explanation for the enterprise of his Indian associate. For the time being, the European "champions of primitive accumulation" accepted the fact that the Indian merchant was, unlike the native inhabitant of the West Indies or South America, a first class business man whose commercial shrewdness was not inferior to his own. But having conquered India the colonialists endeavoured to get rid of the Indian merchant middleman who traded on equal terms. How far they succeeded we shall see later.

Almost all European travellers were unanimous in their admiration of the efficiency of the Indian traders, but opinions diverged regarding their moral qualities.

> They (the Indian merchants) are all cunning folk, and owe nothing to the people of the West, themselves endued with a keener intelligence than is usual with us, and hands as subtle as ours: to see or

14 *Ibid.*, 212.

hear a thing but once, is with them to know it. A cunning and crafty race: not, however, fraudulent, nor easy to defraud. And what is to be observed of all their manufacture is this, that they are both of good workmanship and cheap. I have never seen men of wit so fine and polished as are the Indians; they have nothing barbarous or savage about them, as we are apt to suppose. . . .In fact the Portuguese take and learn more from them than they from the Portuguese; and they that come fresh to Goa are very simpletons till they have acquired the airs and graces of the Indies.[15]

Mandelslo writes about the Gujarati Banias:

They never drive any bargain, but they endeavour to surprise and circumvent those they are to deal with. The *Dutch* and *English* know this by experience; whence it comes, that they make use of these people, as their Brokers and Interpreters, that they may discover the Impostures and cheats of others. There is no Trade which they apply not themselves to; and there is no Commodity but they sell it, unless it be Flesh, Fish, or any other thing that hath had life.[16]

English traders greatly appreciated the services of the Bania Virjee Vora, the biggest merchant broker engaged in commerce with the Europeans in Gujarat,[17] who at the beginning of the 17th century captured the wholesale trade in English goods brought into Surat harbour. At the height of the hostilities between the Mogul authorities and the Englishmen, Virjee Vora granted the latter a loan of Rs 200,000 for trade purposes.[18] This British agent was executed by the Mogul viceroy in Gujarat.

---

15 *The Voyage of Pyrard de Laval* (1608-1611) ed. Albert Gray, Pt. I, II, 298-99. The passage is taken from D. Pant, *The Commercial Policy of the Moguls*, (Bombay, 1930), 148. Pant quotes William Finch opinion of the Banias, who said "they are as subtle as the devil, whose limbs I certainly persuade myself they are". (*Ibid*, 147). De Thevenot wrote that the fourth caste in the Hindu hierarchy of castes were ouens or Banias, who were all merchants, bankers or brokers and their purpose in life seemed to be the extraction of every possible kind of profit. (De Thevenot, *Voyages de M. De Thevenot* (Paris, 1684, 184). Fryer notes how strictly the Banias observed the religious ceremonial and adds "in cases of trade they are not so hidebound, giving their consciences more scope, and boggle at no villany for an emolument" (Fryer, n. 3, II, 107-08),

16 J. A. de Mandeleslo, *The Voyage and Travels of J. Albert Mandelslo* (London, 1669), 51.

17 De Thevenot writes: "There are many rich people in Surat; a Bania called Vargivora, a friend of mine, possesses according to estimates not less than eight million" (apparently rupees—*V. P.*) (De Thevenot, n. 15, 44). An English contemporary considered Virjee Vora the richest merchant in the world, and estimated that his fortune amounted to eight million rupees (Douglas, n. 1, 114).

18 Cf. D. Pant, n. 15, 190.

Virjee Vora was not the only creditor of the English merchants. A documentary source dating from the close of the 17th century refers to the practice of Surat bankers to finance English trading expeditions to to China. Employees of the Company borrowed money from a Bania at a rate of 25 per cent, but if the expedition was shipwrecked on the way interest was not paid.[19] In the 1680s, the East India Company raised big loans from Indian bankers for the purchase of goods intended for Europe.[20]

Up to the end of the 18th century the main aim, which the East India Company pursued in its commerce with India, was to use its import monopoly to make a profit from the sale of Indian goods on the British and other European markets by exploiting the difference between commodity prices in India and Europe. According to the custom-house records Britain received from India medicines, saltpetre, silk fabrics and yarn, diamonds, spices, calico, indigo, skins, cabinets, Chinese goods, cotton yarn and wool, gloves, muslin and Persian silk.[21] The fashion for Indian manufactures proved very stable. A source from the end of the 17th century stated that no one—from the most distinguished gentlemen to the poorest cook—considered it fitting to wear anything but Indian manufactures.[22] Swift made fun of the dandy who very nearly clothed himself in Indian carpets.

Had the East India Company confined itself to selling Indian goods in England, the Company's stockholders would, as a result of this trade, have become rich at the expense of the Indian artisans and English consumers, and the English industry would have greatly suffered from the competition of Indian imports. But matters developed quite differently. Even the mercantilist treatise we mentioned, which on the whole described unfavourably the activity of the East India Company, admitted that half the goods—in terms of value—that arrived from India were re-exported from England to other European markets.[23] Warren Hastings declares:

> The foreigner must desist from the trade, and leave to the Company not only a national but an *universal* monopoly; from which the nation, not less than the Company, would be gainers in proportion as England would become the emporium for supplying all the other countries of Europe with the productions and manufactures of India.[24]

---

19 Ovington. n. 4, 391.
20 A. Hamilton, *A New Account of the East Indies,* I, 199-200.
21 N. II, 97, 98. The goods are listed in the same order as in this document.
22 *Ibid.,* 99.
23 *Ibid.,* 98.
24 Warren Hastings, *Memoirs Relative to the State of India,* (London, 1784), 149.

The re-export of Indian goods to the European continent was necessitated, as Marx pointed out, by the English prohibitive duties.[25] The monopoly of commerce with India, held by the East India Company, was for the British bourgeoisie a means of enriching itself not only at the expense of the Indian artisants but also at the expense of the European nations.

Indian merchants acted as intermediaries with regard to the export of goods manufactured by the Indian handicraft industries. S. Master relates in his diary that the manufactures of the Bengal weavers were bought through merchants connected with the weavers in the Hooghly region or through Banias who travelled to the distant weaving centres of the country. These Banias received from the English passes freeing them from the payment of duties. The biggest merchants of Bengal acted as wholesale dealers and buyers-up for the East India Company. Omichand, for instance, received advances of 100 thousand rupees a time to buy goods (1748).[26]

Especially firm commercial ties between the Indian merchants and the English developed in the middle of the 18th century, when Bombay became the commercial and political centre of the East India Company in the western part of India. In 1661, Charles II of England, who married a Portuguese princess, Catherine of Braganza, received the small island of Bombay as part of the dowry. Seven years later he handed over the island to the East India Company for a token rent of £10. This was a very timely acquisition for the Company, since their factories in the coastal towns of Gujarat, including the main factory in Surat, were threatened by the Marathas. Bombay's insular position facilitated its defence and made it possible to raid with impunity the neighbouring districts of Maharashtra. It possessed, in addition, an excellent harbour. That was why in 1687, the main factory of the English East India Company was transferred from Surat to Bombay, although the latter had an unhealthy climate.

In the 18th century the Gujarat ports lost their importance.[27] The decline in foreign trade and the feudal anarchy also undermined the economic position of towns situated in the interior of Gujarat, first of all of Ahmedabad. Numerous transit duties and plundering raids undertaken by feudal chiefs paralysed commerce.[28] In 1789 Forbes wrote about Ahmedabad, that formerly everything had favoured the development of trade in this town. It had been the meeting place for a

25 K. Marx and F. Engels, *The First Indian War of Independence*, 28.

26 *Selections from Unpulished Records of Government for the Years 1748 to 1767*, I, 15.

27 For example, only very few boats carrying salt or cargoes of cotton and other local agricultural products called at Cambay at the end of the 18th century.

28 N. 7, (IV) 89.

multitude of merchants, artisans and travellers from diverse countries, but it was now a picture of devastation, poverty and neglect. A British administrator reported in 1810 that on his arrival Ahmedabad presented a sad spectacle of desolation.[29] Local merchants began to move to Bombay. Because Bombay traded with districts which were in the hands of the Marathas it was absolutely necessary to use local traders as intermediaries. The East India Company was, therefore, compelled to offer merchants taking up residence in Bombay relatively favourable conditions. As early as 1671 when Surat Banias were asked by the Company to move to Bombay, they stipulated that the Company should grant them a number of privileges.[30]

Especially close collaboration developed between the English and Parsi merchants. The Parsis are descendants of Zoroastrians who fled from Mohammedan persecution in Iran. The first of them landed in Sanjan, 94 miles north of Bombay, in the middle of the 8th century. At the close the 17th century the Parsis lived near Surat on the southern seaboard of Gujarat, in a district which stretched for forty miles along the coast and twenty miles inland.[31] They preserved the religion of their ancestors and did not intermarry with other communities. But having lived in Gujarat for over a thousand years, the Parsis have established close connections with the economic, political and cultural life of the Gujaratis, and Gujarati has become their mother tongue. Only the caste system and religion have prevented their complete assimilation.[32] Phenomena of this kind—that individual castes or ethnical groups preserved their isolation—were rather frequent in India.

It would be incorrect to think that commerce has always been the only occupation of the Parsis. They had been agriculturists rather than merchants, although they also supplied the sailors with timber and water. The Parsis raised the famous Gujarat strain of cattle.[33] Among them were many skilful weavers.[34] Mandelslo asserted that in his time the Parsis were growing tobacco, preparing palm wine, they were engaged in commerce, money-changing and the handicrafts, with the exception of smithery for their religion forbids them to follow that trade.[35] The forefathers of Peston Jahangir, the Bombay capitalist (born

29 *Ibid.*, 90.

30 *Materials towards a Statistical Account of the Town and Island of Bombay*, Pt. I, History *(Bombay Gazetteer, XXVI*, Bombay, 1893), 64.

31 Fryer, n. 3, I, 239.

32 "Religion or a change of religion made no difference. The Parsees, who originally settled in Gujarat thirteen hundred years ago, may be considered as Gujaratis for this purpose (Their language has long been Gujarati)." Jawaharlal Nehru, *The Discovery of India*, 310.

33 Fryer, n. 3, I, 295.

34 Ovington, n. 4, 219.

35 J. A. de Mandelslo, n. 16. 59.

in 1831), received from the Great Moguls a jagir near Surat and the titles Nekshant-Khan and Jabiar-Khan.[36] Prominent representatives of the Indian bourgeoisie such as Dadabhai Naorojee and Tata are descendants of landowners. Landowning Parsis had, of course, little in common with the soldiers of the Muslim nobility. Chand Kamdin, an ancester of Naorojee nine generations removed, won by his skill as perfumer, the favour of the beautiful Nur Jahan the wife of Jahangir and in 1618 was granted 100 bighas of land free of tax. The Parsis were, therefore, not restricted in the choice of their profession by religious prohibitions in feudal India.[37] J. Fryer notes the low social position of the Parsis in Mogul Gujarat, who "having been curbed formerly by the *Gentiles*, and now by the *Moors* used as perfect Slaves".

After the European merchants came to India, brokerage became the main occupation of rich Parsis. During the 17th century, the centre of the Parsi community was transferred to the English factory in Surat. When Surat's importance declined in the beginning of the 18th century, the Parsis began to move to Bombay. According to tradition, the first Parsi, Dorajee Nanabhoy, settled in Bombay in 1640 while it was still in Portuguese hands. Among those who took up residence in Bombay in the 1840s were Kuwarjee Cama, the forefather of the well-known magnates, Lowjee Nushirvanjee Wadia the founder of the ship-building industry in Bombay, and Rustamjee Dorabjee whom the English later appointed patel of Bombay.[38] As early as 1773, the Parsis from Gujarat who had settled in Bombay were allotted a separate district in the centre of the town on the Malabar Hill.[39] About 3,000 Parsis lived in Bombay in 1780; a decade later, fleeing from starvation, many more Parsis moved from Gujarat to Bombay.

According to J. Forbes, in the 70s and 80s of the 18th century, a considerable part of the land in Bombay belonged to Parsis, and also many beautiful houses, which they had either built themselves or bought from Englishmen who had gone home. Forbes, incidentally, notes the excellent knowledge of political affairs displayed by the Parsis, and the absence of those caste prejudices which are characteristic of

---

36 C. H. Rao, *Indian Biographical Dictionary* (Madras, 1915) 325.

37 " From early times, Parsis established connections as brokers with European traders. A remarkable feature to be noted about the Parsis is that their traditional occupations were not connected with trading or finance. In the accounts of the 17th century travellers, they are noticed chiefly as artisans, carpenters, weavers, etc. Their prominence in Bombay was also established, in the first instance, through their ship-building activity. Though they later became a dominant trading and financing community like other Gujrat communities, their original artisan background is an important feature that deserves notice" D. R. Gadgil, *Origins of the Modern Indian Business Class*, 20.

38 *Gazetteer of Bombay City and Island*, (Bombay, 1909) I, 152, 154.

39 Ch. Fawcett, *English Factories in India* (Oxford, 1936) I, 79.

the Hindu and Muslim merchants.[40]

Muslim merchants in Gujarat, who had been trading since long with the Middle East, were, in the beginning, political and commercial opponents of the East India Company. They were, therefore, at first unable to benefit fully from the developing trade. But from the beginning of the 18th century onwards, the ties between the Musalman merchants and the English grew stronger. Their commercial activity in the service of the foreigners compensated the Muslim traders for the loss of so profitable a customer as the big Musalman feudal lord. The links between the East India Company and the Muslim merchants were, however, never as close as those with the Parsis or Hindus. The Muslims continued to trade along the old established lines with the Middle East and East Africa. Two Gujarati castes, the Bohras and Khojas, occupied a dominant position among Muslim merchants.

The following figures give an idea of the national and religious-communal composition of the big merchant houses in Bombay at the beginning of the 19th century: Nine leading private European firms were registered in Bombay in 1805; 16 Parsi firms and 2 Parsi-Chinese agencies; 15 Hindu firms; 4 Muslim (Bohra); 3 Portuguese and 4 American firms.[41] Thus, 37 of the 53 Bombay firms belonged to Indians. But in spite of the numerical predominance of Indian firms, their commercial transactions were controlled by British merchant capital, which relied on the political power and the greater concentration of its capital.

Let us now examine the activities of the merchants in Bombay during the 18th century. Their profit was in the main derived from commercial operations conducted in the service of foreigners. The Bombay traders appear as junior partners of British merchant's capital. The "cooperation" between Bombay merchant and the English took on diverse forms.

At the beginning of the 18th century, the East India Company traded in Bombay through its official brokers[42] The brokers not only acted as commercial agents but collected taxes as well. When, however, the English established closer relations with local merchants, the privileged intermediary or broker became an impediment. In 1737, therefore, the system of brokers was abolished. Justifying this decision the Bombay Court of Directors declared:

We are satisfied our investment may be carried on better by con-

40 J. Forbes, *Oriental Memoirs*, II, 385-86.

41 N. 38, I, 414.

42 Because of prolonged warfare between the Marathas and Moguls in the beginning of the 18th century, the Company did not permit its servants to sell commodities on the internal markets of the country and entrusted local and other independent merchants with these operations. It employed agents for the purchase of goods (*Ibid.*, 408).

tracting direct with the merchants, and that our duties and the consulage at Surat may be collected equally well by a proper person appointed for that purpose... This we hope will also restore to "our servants" trading from all parts of India to Surat, that perfect freedom of trade we would have them enjoy, which they have made such continual complaints they have hitherto "not been able to obtain" being always obstructed by the power, interest, and influence of the broker.

Many Bombay traders were simply partners of British firms. According to one source (of 1828), every European trading establishment had a Parsi partner, who usually provided most of the capital.[43] The colonial position of the country forced the Indian merchant to pay a kind of tribute to the powers represented by his British "partner". That English firms valued the services of their Indian "associates" can be seen from the following well-known incident. When, as a result of speculations, the Parsi Hormuz lost the huge sum of £ 200,000 (it is quite possible that the amount has been greatly exaggerated), the firm of Charles Forbes, with whom he had close business ties, helped to set him again on his legs.[44]

At the time when methods of primitive accumulation were used to exploit India, Bombay traders were engaged in exporting goods, selling English manufactures in India, and provisioning Bombay's population, garrison and fleet. In 1731 "Landas, the Surat broker, having bought all the woollen goods, lead, copper and iron received by the ships last arrived from England" was as a sign of appreciation, presented by the East India Company with a horse worth Rs 800.[45]

Bombay merchants were trading with the Middle East. A. Hamilton met Indian Bania and Muslim merchants in the ports of the Persian Gulf early in the 18th century.[46] This trade, which always showed a balance favourable to India, helped the English to cushion the constant foreign exchange deficit in their commerce with India.[47] A petition sent by three Hindu merchants in 1741 to the authorities in Bombay is interesting in this connection. The merchants complained that the recent decision of the council abolishing the escort of warships for convoys sailing to the Arabian coast would seriously affect their old-established

43 W. Hamilton, *East-India Gazetteer* (London, 1828) I, 261.

44 *Handbook for India*, (Bombay, 1859) II, 283.

45 N. 30, I, 263.

46 Hamilton, n. 20, I, 41, 91.

47 Between 1710 and 1759 the Company exported from England to the Orient goods worth £ 9,240,000; while its foreign currency and bullion exports amounted to £26,833,000 (H. B. Morse, *The Chronicles of the East India Company Trading to China 1635-1834*, Oxford, 1926, I, 8).

commercial relations. Realising, however, that the English administrators would not be moved by complaints about the cruel lot of their households, but by commercial reasons the merchants continue: "By the loss of this beneficial trade from the north the Honourable Company would lose imports which contribute no trifling sum to the customs. To your petitioners the failure of the north trade will be fatal, as it is mainly with this money and from the profits of this trade that we are able to carry on our business and maintain ourselves and families". The Company could not withstand such arguments and reversed its decision.[48]

Commerce with China carried on by Gujarat merchants was very important for the East India Company. Indian opium and cotton were the chief items exported to China.

During the latter half of the 18th century large consignments of cotton were exported from Gujarat to Bengal and China. This commerce was in the hands of Bombay merchants both Englishmen and Gujaratis, who signed agreements with local traders whose job it was to buy up cotton in the villages.[49] The fact that in 1801 seven merchants of Bombay purchased a quantity of cotton for export to China amounting to 850 thousand rupees already shows the size of these operations. Three of the merchants concerned in this deal were British and four Parsis (Hormud Borman and Peston Borman, Ardashir Dadi Shet and Sokar Muncher Readymoney).[50]

At the beginning of the 19th century commerce with China was the principal item in the turnover of Bombay. For example, in 1805 the export to China reached Rs 6,473,600 while the export to Britain amounted only to Rs 588,700.[51] But this does not mean that the China trade was an end in itself. In fact, the export of cotton, and later of opium, to China was the principal source from which the East India Company obtained foreign currency enabling it to purchase Indian commodities to be sent overseas.

Maritime commerce with China and the other Asian countries contributed to the rise of Bombay's shipping. The Parsis began to take an interest in navigation in 1735. Readymoney was the first Parsi to reach China in 1756. By 1792 the Parsis owned more than twenty big ships—mainly built in Bombay—two of them, moreover, had a displacement of more than 1000 tons. The biggest shipowners were

48 N. 30, I, 274. The escort was necessary to protect the ships mainly against European pirates, among whom the British predominated. Hamilton confirms that the principal pirate in the Bab-el-Mandeb was the English captain Evory.

49 Forbes, n. 40, II, 65.

50 Douglas, n. 1, I, 241-42.

51 J.M. Maclean, *A Guide to Bombay: Historical, Statistical and Descriptive* (Bombay, 1880) 105.

members of the Wadia family, possessing six vessels, and members of the Readymoney family, who held three vessels. The richest shipowner in Bombay was also a Parsi, Rustomjee Kavasjee Banajee. Members of the Davar family—apparently the ancestors of K. N. Davar, the first factory owner of Bombay[52]—were also among the first shipowners of Bombay. During the second half of the 18th century and the beginning of the 19th century the principal source of the wealth the merchants of Bombay were amassing was shipping revenue.

These are some of the aspects of the collaboration between the Gujarati merchants and the British colonialists. Helping the East India Company to fleece India, the Gujarati traders acquired considerable wealth. The Englishman John Burnell, who visited India in 1711, wrote:

> The Banias or merchants are not only rich and wealthy, but like the rest of the world are covetous after more, placing the height of their happiness in riches, which they will scrape together by mean and petty offices, some of them amassing prodigious sums of money, being accounted worth 90 or 100 lakhs, or so many times a Rs 100,000.[53]

Evidence regarding the enormous riches accumulated by the Gujarati merchants cooperating with the English is confirmed by documentary materials. For example, in 1721, after the death of the well-known broker of the Company, the Parsi Rustam Manek, his heirs demanded the return of a loan, amounting to Rs 690,000 from the East India Company. After the Bombay council of the Company refused to pay back the money, one of Manek's sons obtained the agreement of the chief Board of Directors to reconsider the matter. As a result, Manek's heirs received Rs 564,000.[54]

Up to the end of the 18th century, the British energetically propagated handloom weaving in Bombay as well as in other factories throughout India.[55] "By 1676 a regular industry had been established. The Company imported silk and cotton and distributed it to the weavers who worked under a *Mukadam* and were paid partly in money and partly in rice."[56] The *Bombay Gazetteer* quotes factual material on the handicrafts in Bombay during the 17th and 18th centuries. These documents permit us to form an opinion of the functions which the Indian middleman, the so-called Mukadam, performed. The Mukadam recruited weavers for the Company, supplied them with raw materials,

---

52 W.H. Coates, *The Old Country Trade,* (London, 1911) 51, 90.

53 J. Burnell, *Bombay in the Days of Queen Anne,* (London, 1933), 110.

54 *Gujarat Population, Hindus (Bombay Gazetteer,* IX, I, Bombay, 1899), 196.

55 Manmohan P. Gandhi wrote in his essay on the history of the textile industry in India that in 1668 the East India Company proposed to develop calico production on a huge scale in Bombay, which was then a fisherman's settlement *(Indian Textile Journal,* 1924, July).

56 *Gazetteer of Bombay City* (Bombay, 1909) I, 462.

granted them loans, collected the finished product and paid the weavers in money and foodstuffs. The trust which the Company placed in their agent was extremely great, for at times sums amounting to several thousand rupees passed through his hands for which he did not have to account; the agent was only obliged to hand over a fixed quantity of manufactured goods.[57] Since the weavers completely depended on the Mukadam, he was able to exploit them "in his own interest". Several Mukadams are mentioned by name in various documents. In the beginning of the 18th century, the chief master of the weavers working for the East India Company in Bombay was the Parsi Manna or Manak.[58]

Handloom weaving in Bombay, apparently, catered exclusively for the European market. The Company even sent weavers, dyers, and other artisans to India in 1670 to show the Indians how to manufacture those kinds of goods that were most likely to please the Europeans and which would therefore prove most profitable for the Company.[59]

We will later examine the history of ship-building in Bombay and the part the Parsis played in it.

Thus, in the period when methods of primitive accumulation were applied in the colonial exploitation of India, the big Gujarati merchants in Bombay acted primarily as agents for British merchant's capital and received the greater part of their profits for their services as brokers in regard to the overseas trade which was a British monopoly.

Up to the beginning of the 18th century, the monopoly of foreign trade provided most of the profits for British capital carrying on primitive accumulation in western India, while in Bengal and Bihar, conquered earlier by the British, pride of place belonged to tax robbery of the peasants (based on the fact that the colonial government assumed ownership of the land), direct exploitation of artisans by British merchant's capital and open military plunder of the population. During the latter half of the 18th century, the tragic fate of Bengal confirmed that merchant's capital, when it holds a position of dominance, stands everywhere for a system of robbery.[60]

The following sentence written by Marx applies above all to Bengal and parts of South India: "During the whole course of the 18th century the treasures transported from India to England were gained much less by comparatively insignificant commerce, than by the direct exploitation of that country, and by the colossal fortunes there extorted and transmitted to England".[61] It is clear that the traders and

57 N. 30, II, Trade and Fortifications *(Bombay Gazetteer,* XXVI, Pt. 2), Bombay, 1894, 131, 132.

58 Ch. Fawcett, n. 39, I, 57.

59 N. II, 99.

60 K. Marx, *Capital,* III, 325.

61 Marx and Engels, n. 25, 29.

moneylenders of Bihar and Bengal were forced to collaborate with the East India Company along different lines and on different, less favourable, terms than the traders of Gujarat. The fact, moreover, that the tribute from these regions was transferred to Great Britain in the form of commodities—which were purchased for the money collected as tax and then exported—was of the greatest importance.[62]

The Company, which tried to increase tax receipts as much as possible, at first preserved and even extended the system of short term tax farming.[63] In 1765 when the Mogul Emperor had to hand over officially the right to collect the land tax in Bengal to the East India Company, Clive appointed an eighteen year old descendant of the Jagat Seths shroff of the Company.[64] In the same year Clive censured the Seths for ruining the zamindars. But it was the same Jagat Seth who, on the evidence of Bolts, played the major part in Lord Clive's acquisition (or appropriation) of his famous jagir. In 1773 Hastings established the Central Bank of Bengal and Bihar headed by Rai Dayal Chand, a member of the Jagat Seth family, and Huzuri Mal, a Calcutta based merchant whose business it was to remit tax payments.[65] The English continued to use the services of local bankers to transmit revenue payments to Calcutta during the 1780s.[66] In this way, shortly after the conquest of Bengal, the British enlisted the help of local big trading and moneylending capital in the exploitation of the peasantry by taxation which became the principal method of primitive accumulation employed by British capital in this part of India from the middle of the 18th century onwards.

During the first decades of British rule the bankers of Bengal retained so important an investment sphere of money capital as the granting of loans to the government (by then already a colonial government). But henceforth this took the shape of the bankers acquiring securities issued by the colonial authorities. According to Warren Hastings, there were not many Indian creditors, merely a few old Hindu families of the presidency, whereas the majority of security owners were Englishmen.[67]

62 *Minute of Lord Teignmouth 18th June 1789*, published in *Fifth Report*, 1812, 109-238. The document is taken from *British Rule in India Condemned by the British Themselves*, (London, 1915), 17.

63 "The Bengal District Records of the 18th century show that the revenue was not paid by the landowners to the revenue officers of the East India Company direct, but was collected through the agency of the indigenous bankers" (Ch. L. Jain, *Indigenous Banking in India*, London, 1929, 18).

64 W. Bolts, *Considerations*, 158.

65 P. Benerea, *Indian Finance in the Days of the Company*, (Calcutta, 1918), 67.

66 H. Sinha, *Early European Banking in India*, 169.

67 "The fact is, that our public credit, by which I mean the credit of our interest Notes and Treasury orders, never extended beyond the English servants of

After the conquest of Bengal, the East India Company brought under its control the wholesale trade, and to a certain extent also retail trade, within Bengal in addition to the monopoly of foreign trade which it already possessed. Romesh Dutt wrote about commerce in Bengal after 1757: "The Company's servants conveyed their goods from place to place duty-free, while the goods of the country merchants were heavily taxed in transit. The country traders were ruined".[68] Some merchants. however, were able to adjust themselves to the new colonial conditions; they began to serve British merchant's capital and became agents of the East India Company, so-called Gomastas. It was precisely with the help of these agents that the British laid their hands on a considerable part of retail trade in Bengal. The Nawab of Bengal Mir Kasim wrote to the Governor in 1762: "The Gomashthas and other servants in every district, in every Gunge, Perganah, and village, carry on a trade in oil, fish, straw, bamboos, rice, paddy, betelnut, and other things."[69]

The agents, especially the Banias, displayed great cunning in the treatment of their British masters. Official documents of the East India Company record that Banias employed by Englishmen countenanced the bad habits of young officials, involved them in debts and became the real masters of the situation.[70]

By resorting to brute force, the Company arrogated to itself the exclusive right to conduct foreign trade in the principal commodities. An English work written at the close of the 18th century reports that "piece-goods, silk, saltpetre, opium, sugar, and indigo, pass almost wholly through the Company's hand, excepting only what foreign commerce and the traffic to various ports in India, export of such among these articles as the Company do not monopolise".[71] In 1773 Warren Hastings established the monopoly right of the East India Company to trade in opium. Merchants holding contracts were obliged to deliver opium at prices fixed by the Company. Thus the position of opium merchants in conquered Bengal differed sharply from that of the Bombay traders who sold their opium direct to China.

The trade monopoly, especially that of foreign trade, depended on the colonial exploitation of the enslaved artisans and peasants of Bengal.

Francis wrote:

In order that the East India Company might avail themselves of

---

Company, and the European inhabitants of Calcutta; and to these may be added a few, and a very few, of the old Hindoo families of the presidency" (Warren Hastings, n. 24, 18).

68 Romesh Dutt, *The Economic History of India* (Delhi, 1960), I, *Under Early British Rule, 1757-1837*, 13-14.

69 *Ibid.*, 14.

70 N. 26, I, 462-63.

71 H. Collbrooke, *Remarks on the Husbandry*, 169.

72 J. C. Sinha, *Economic Annals of Bengal*, 80-81.

their increased revenues, it was necessary that their investment should be enlarged. . . This could not be suddenly done without a monopoly of the manufactures; a monopoly supported by the numerous servants and agents, armed with authority, which caused great oppression of the manufacturers.[72]

The Company used its extensive network of Gomastas to enslave the craftsmen. Before the conquest, there were in Bengal, as in other parts of India, side by side with independent artisans, handicraftsmen working at home who depended on the dealer. J. C. Sinha, who made a study of the economy of Bengal in the latter half of the 18th century, noted that the arrival of the English increased the power of the buyer-up.[73] Before the East India Company established its rule, it exploited the artisans through intermediaries, the Bengal merchants, who according to the contracts undertook to supply the commodities specified in the agreement at definite times and fixed prices.[74] After the conquest of Bengal, the British preferred to work through their direct agents, the Gomastas, who were given money by the Company which they advanced to the weavers[75] enslaving the latter by usurious loans.

In 1772, the Dutch merchant W. Bolts published a pamphlet against the East India Company in London. The author, who had scraped together a tidy sum £20,000 during his service in Bengal from 1760 to 1768, later quarrelled with the administration of the Company and was sent back to England. He claimed that the Gomashtas forced the weavers to sign a bond for the delivery of a certain quantity of goods, at a set time and fixed price, that is at a very low price. The weavers were given part of their wages in advance.[76]

Non-economic coercion was added to debt bondage. "The assent of the poor weaver is in general not deemed necessary; for the Gomastas, when employed on the Company's investment, frequently make them sign what they please."[77] Sinha quotes from the record of an English court sitting on 12th April 1773. According to evidence given by the weavers of Santipura—whose bona fides the judge had no reason to doubt—the weavers were forbidden to work for private traders and to manufacture any goods whatever apart from those ordered by the Company on pain of corporal punishment and confiscation of their property.[78]

Non-economic coercion and the debt slavery of the artisants secured huge monopoly profits for the East India Company. Bolts writes: "The prices which the Company's Gomastas, and, in confederacy with them

73 *Ibid*, 79.
74 *Ibid*.
75 *Ibid*., 80.
76 Bolts, n. 64, 193.
77 *Ibid*., 193.
78 Sinha, n. 72, 83.

the *Jachendars* (examiners of fabrics) fix upon the goods are in all places at least fifteen per cent and some even forty per cent less than the goods so manufactured would sell for in the public bazaar, or market, upon free sale. The weaver, therefore, desirous of obtaining the just price of his labour, frequently attempts to sell his cloth privately to others, particularly to the Dutch and French Gomastas, who are always ready to receive it. This occasions the English Company's Gomasta to set his peons over the weaver to watch him, and not infrequently to cut the piece out of the loom when nearly finished".[79] The intensification of labour of the artisans apparently brought about a certain expansion of cloth production in individual areas. James Taylor,[80] the author of a monograph on Dacca, the centre of the textile industry of former Bengal, held that in 1787 trade in fabrics reached its highest peak in Dacca.[81]

Direct coercion practised by the administrative and police organs of the East India Company and the enslavement of craftsmen through buyers-up and brokers of the Company were common phenomena also in other regions occupied by the British. The Indian economist, A. Sarada Raju, who investigated the economic position in the Madras presidency during the first half of the 19th century—on the basis of the documents of the East India Company and other sources—painted a dark picture of violence and arbitrary rule practised by the Company in relation to the Indian artisans.

In accordance with the demand on the European market the administration of the Company gave orders for the supply of goods to its commercial residents. The resident granted loans to local traders and buyers-up acting as intermediaries who distributed the money among the weavers as advance payments. The craftsmen were forced to accept these advances which enslaved them, since orders from customers, other than the Company, came in very irregularly, for the traditional commercial links of the Indian artisans had been severed. As a result, many weavers were up to their neck in debt. The traders received a commission of 5 per cent calculated on the value of the goods, but their position was not too good either, for they had to bear the transport expenses as well as any losses that might occur.[82]

"Early in the 19th century, the Committee of Reform reported that the weaver derived no gain by working for the Company, but had to supplement the meagre earnings thus obtained by producing coarse fabrics for sale in the market to maintain his family."[83]

The Company's officials admitted that the artisans had to be

79 Bolts, n. 64, 103.
80 J. Taylor, *Sketch of Topography and Statistics of Dacca* (Calcutta, 1840).
81 See Sinha n. 72, 87.
82 A. Sarada Raju, *Economic Conditions* 173.
83 *Ibid.*, 172-3.

compelled to work for them.[84] The authorities of the East India Company did not, in fact, permit the weavers to accept any private orders until they had fulfilled those of the Company. At one time they were altogether forbidden to work for the private market. Weavers trying to escape from the Company's yoke by running away were brutally punished.[85]

Let us return to the analysis of the situation in Bengal. Peasant revolts and dissatisfaction among the feudal landlords forced the East India Company at the end of the 1770s to discontinue the farming of land tax on a mass scale. From that time onwards the Company preferred to deal direct with the zamindars. The exclusion of trading and moneylending capital from the sphere of collecting tax and government loans as well as from foreign trade and, partially, from internal trade too led to the decline of the big banking houses of Bengal at the close of the 18th century.[86] According to H. Sinha the reason for this should be sought in the fact that foreign trade slipped out of the hands of the Indians while internal trade was for a considerable time also monopolised by the servants of the Company. As a result the indigenous bankers, naturally, lost their leading position. The foremost banking house, that of the Jagat Seths was but a shadow of its former name, although it still continued for some time to act as a medium for transmitting local revenue payments to Calcutta.[87]

The Jagat Seths remained bankers of the Company up to 1782.[88] They were then replaced by the Marwari banking house of Gopal.Das. Gopal Das was a member of the big Banaras firm *of* Marwari bankers from the Agarwal community. He and his brother moved to Calcutta in the 70s and acquired there a great fortune. His son Bhavani Das was the supplier of the British army that invaded Mysore in 1799. How great the 'services' were which Bhavani Das rendered to the usurpers is evident from the fact that he received the sword of Tippu Sultan after Seringapatam was taken by the British.[89] But these bankers were never able to reach the position occupied by the Jagat Seths.

Since the end of the 80s the remittance of tax revenues ceased to be the business of the shroffs. Local bankers, above all the Jagat Seths, suffered also great losses as a result of currency speculations; for the

84 According to the report made in 1802, commercial residents were constantly emphasising the fact that production for private customers was much more profitable than work for the Company, and that the craftsmen who worked for the Company did so not of their own choice but under compulsion. (Quoted in Sarada Ruju, n. 82, 173).

85 *Ibid.*, 172, 173.

86 Ch. L. Jain, n. 63, 23.

87 Sinha, n. 66, 166.

88 Ibid., 148.

89 *Benares (District Gazetteers of the United Provinces)*, (Allahabad, 1909), 119.

East India Company deprived them of the mint privileges and began to issue its own coins.[90] The descendents of the Jagat Seths lived on a pension of Rs 12,000 which they received from the British for the "services" the firm had rendered in the past.[91] By the close of the 18th century the East India Company and the British banks had completely taken over the financing of foreign trade. The British began to establish their own banks in Bengal in the 1780s. Although these banks restricted the activities of the Bengal bankers they did not eliminate them.[92] It is interesting to note that according to the rules of the "General Bank" established in 1786 anyone could be a shareholder, but only "natural born subjects of England, or naturalised subjects" could become directors.[93] In other words the money invested by the Indian shareholders was controlled by the British and employed by them for the political and economic enslavement of India.

Close credit links between the British banks and Indian bankers in Marwar existed as early as the beginning of the 19th century. Local bankers borrowed money from the banks of the presidency and acted as guarantors for Indians who were granted credit by the banks. After the establishment of English private banks, at the end of the 18th century, it became the business of the shroffs and discount brokers to stand surety.[94]

Already at the time when the permanent settlement of the land tax was introduced, the principal activity of the big moneylenders in Bengal was the granting of loans on the security of the zamindari right of tenure. The Bengali historian Romesh Dutt wrote about the situation in Bengal in the 1780s: "Descendants of old houses found their estates pass into the hands of moneylenders and speculators from Calcutta."[95]

After Indian trading and moneylending capital which was

---

90 N. 26, I, 165.

91 *Murshidabad (Eastern Bengal District Gazetteers)* 68. The Bengali Bania B. Chunder wrote in the 1860s that the descendants of the Jagat Seths still occupied their ancestral residence in Murshidabad, but were completely impoverished and lived by selling the family treasures until the British granted them a pension of 12,000 rupees per month (B. Chunder, *The Travels of a Hindoo to Various Parts of Bengal and Upper India*, (London, 1869, I, 79).

92 Sinha, n. 66, 175.

93 *Ibid., 14.* "Each system had a distinct and separate existence because each had its own particular function. The indigenous banker, concerned himself with the granting of credit to the agriculturists and the artisans and the financing of the internal trade of the country, while the early European banks confined their activities almost entirely to the three Presidency capitals, providing remittance and deposit facilities chiefly made use of by Europeans, and financing the external trade" (Ch. L. Jain, n. 63, 25).

94 Sinha, n. 66, 173. The shroffs maintained close contacts with both the European and indigenous banks. (*Ibid.*, 171).

95 Dutt, n. 68, I, 44.

engaged in commerce and tax collecting in Eastern India, had been seriously restricted and partly destroyed by English capital, it was—by way of compensation—given the opportunity to acquire with its accumulated wealth feudal landed property. But none other than Warren Hastings admitted that acquired landed property and money lent on the security of property in land was, in the 1770s, not yet sufficiently safeguarded and proved in the final account less lucrative than investments in securities issued by the colonial authorities.[96] To make landed property a safe investment, it was necessary to affirm the legal rights of the landowners and to fix the land tax, which was done by the Act of 1793.

In 1793, when Lord Cornwallis was Governor-General, the zamindars were recognised as the legal owners of the land who were obliged to pay a fixed land tax (the so-called "permanent settlement"). The old feudal nobles were unable to fulfil the enormous tax demands and, in the majority of cases, lost their estates. During the first two decades after the introduction of the permanent settlement, a third or even half of the lands belonging to zamindars were taken over by new owners, who acquired them at public auctions.[97] Marx remarked that as a result of the Act of Cornwallis a considerable part of the zamindar's estates fell "into the hands of a few city capitalists who had spare capital and readily invested it in land".[98]

Thus, during the period of primitive accumulation in England, the trading and moneylending capital of Bengal grew rich by collaborating with the British capital which robbed the country through taxation and contributions and exploited the forced labour of peasants and artisans. Having consolidated their position in the Ganges valley, the British usurpers were, by the close of the 18th century, to a considerable extent able to dispense with the services of their Indian commercial and moneylending agents. The merchant's capital of Bengal was, in the end, partly destroyed by the colonialists and partly made completely dependent on them. While under favourable conditions Bengali merchant's capital might have produced industrial enterprise as an offshoot, it now concentrated on landownership since it had been largely ousted from the towns. Merchant's capital and enterprise had been turned towards the land, wrote with satisfaction Governor-General, Lord Moira,[99] in his memorandum of 1815 on the results of the zamindar land tax system—permanent settlement—introduced in Bengal. The

96 Hastings, n. 24, 18, 19.

97 *Bengal Revenue Consultations*, cf. S. Gopal, *Permanent Settlement in Bengal and its Results* (London, 1949), 3.

98 K. Marx, *Notes on Indian History* (664-1858), (Mocow), 120.

99 *Affairs of the East India Company* 111, Pt. I, Suppl. 9, Lord Moira, *Minute of 21., IX. 1815*, (London, 1832), 83.

majority of the new zamindars were tax collectors and servants of the Company belonging to the highest Bengali landowning castes, the Brahmins and Kayasthas.[100] It is, so far difficult to explain why the other trading and moneylending castes including the Marwaris, did not participate, to any considerable extent, in the acquisition of landed property. Perhaps caste traditions, which were at that time very strong, stood in the way.

As we see, in the 18th century Marwari and other non-Bengali bankers, chiefly from the northern parts of India, predominated in local finance and banking. But while in the beginning they entered into business relations with the East India Company in Bengal as independent brokers, they gradually became agents of the Company. D. R. Gadgil writes:

> The position in Bengal is somewhat peculiar. There were in Bengal communities like the Subarna baniks, who traditionally specialised in trade and business and who corresponded to the Banias in other regions. They do not, however appear to have been important in Bengal banking or trade in 1750. In Bengal, in 1750, the situation appears already influenced in part by the advent of the British and other Europeans. An important indicator of this was the rise to importance of some elements in Indian society through association with Europeans. Here it is necessary to distinguish between relations of foreigners with Indians on the basis of businessmen to businessmen and relations of foreigners with Indians who acted as . . . agents of the foreigners.... In Bengal, from the foundation of Calcutta onwards, the Englishmen sought chiefly administrative assistants and business agents. As a result, communities such as Brahmins and Kayasthas from Bengal who had no previous footing in business make their entry into it as the assistants and agents of British businessmen.
>
> .... (During the latter half of the 18th century) Bengali names in business are relatively unimportant and where they occur are mostly of the rising professional agent class and not those from indigenous trading elements.[101]

The close economic ties existing between the Indian merchants and moneylenders and the East India Company helped to create conditions in which the colonialists were able to establish a political foothold within the country. Gujarati Banias rendered the English military and political services as far back as the 17th century. They warned English merchants

100 By the middle of the 19th century more than 90 per cent of all zamindars were members of these castes in one district of Bengal (cf. E. N. Komarov, *K voprosu ob ustanovlenii postoyannogo oblozheniya*, 13).

101 Gadgil, n. 8, 18-19, 21.

in Surat of raids which the Rajputs were preparing.[102] We have already mentioned Virjee Vora's fate who was executed by the Mogul viceroy for his connections with the English East India Company. After the Europeans fortified their factories on the Gujarat coast, rich Indian merchants began to use them as shelters during the internecine wars. In 1664, for example, during Shivaji's assault on Surat only the English and Dutch factories were, thanks to their artillery, able to withstand the attack.[103] From the end of the 17th century onwards Bombay became the safest refuge of the Gujarati Banias. J. Fryer wrote in 1674 about

> the Banyas liking it (i.e. Bombay) better than Surat, living freer, and under milder Taxations, which they put the present President in some hopes of complying with, could he open the way from hence up the country; but that depending on so many Intricacies, must be not only a work of Time, but Power to bring to pass, as afterwards may fall more properly in our way to make appear.[104]

During the struggle of the Marathas against the British usurpers, a time full of trouble for the English, the Gujarati traders behaved as the most loyal 'subjects' of the East India Company. They helped with supplies and loans the British who were fighting against the armies of the Marathas. Rich townspeople frequently appealed to the administration of the East India Company to extend its authority and jurisdiction to the town in which they lived.[105] Gujarati Banias and Parsis served the colonial administration as councillors and agents. For example, two Parsi families of officials who had served the peshwas for several generations took service with the colonialists after the conquest of Maharashtra.[106] The well-known English official M. Elphinstone, Governor of Bombay from 1818 to 1827, when he was resident at the Peshwa's court in Poona, valued highly the services of Kurshed Modi, an official of the mission. This Parsi had an excellent knowledge of local matters and served the British faithfully; and was, apparently, for this reason poisoned by the Marathas.[107]

A. Hamilton explains frankly that a certain amount of protection against plunder in war time was one of the main reasons inducing Indian traders to move to Fort St. George, around which subsequently the town of Madras arose. Hamilton writes:

---

102 Downton, n. 10, 116.
103 J. B. Tavernier, *Les six voyages*, 84.
104 Fryer, n. 3, I, 181, 182.
105 A. K. Forbes, *Ras Mala*, (London), II, 21, 80, 81.
106 *Minutes of Evidence Taken before Select Committee on the Government of Indian Territories*, (London, 1853), 294.
107 *Poona Affairs (Elphinstone's Embassy), English Records of Maratha History, Poona Residency Correspondence*, XII, Pt. I, 1811-1815. Bombay, 1950, 323, 324, 358-61.

> The War carried on at Bengal and Bombay by the English against the Mogul's Subjects, from 1685 to 1689, made Fort St. George put on a better Dress than he wore before; for the peaceable Indian Merchants, who hate Contention and War, came flocking thither, because it lay far from those Incumberers of Trade, and near the Diamond Mines of Golcondah, where there are, many Times, good Bargains to be made, and Money got by our Governors, the black Merchants' (apparently a reference to the dark-skinned Dravidians) resorting to our colony, to secure their Fortunes, and bring their Goods to a safe Market, made it populous and rich, notwithstanding its natural inconveniences.[108]

The immigration of Indian merchants helped to make Madras the largest commercial centre of south India although the port did not possess a good harbour.

During the first half of the 18th century, many Indian merchants, headed by the banker Omichand, settled in the shelter of the guns of Fort William on the territory of the future city of Calcutta.[109] They became the biggest house owners in this English factory.[110]

In the middle of the 18th century, when the East India Company began its open territorial conquests in the Ganges valley, it received extensive financial and political support from the Jagat Seths and other Marwari and Bengali bankers. The Jagat Seths granted the conquerors a loan of 1.2 million rupees in 1749.[111] When Calcutta was captured by Bengali troops in 1756 the banker Omichand remained to the end faithful to the defeated British.[112] In 1757 before the battle of Plassey which delivered Bengal into the hands of the foreign usurpers, the Seths gave large amounts of money to the British commander Colonel Clive. An English official handbook admits that the rupees of the Indian banker strengthened the sword of the British colonel who overthrew the Muslim power in Bengal.[113] After the battle of Plassey, the Jagat

108 Hamilton, n. 20, I, 360.

109 There exists some evidence indicating that Omichand was a member of the Sikh trading community. In this context it might be worth recalling D. R. Gadgil's remark about the Sikhs. "In the earlier period of Sikhism" he writes, "for example, the Khatris played a very important part and before Sikhism became a militant religion, Sikhs were reported to be important in trade both internal and external. It is natural to assume that this was due to elements such as the Khatris among the Sikhs. The presence of Omichand, described as a Sikh, in Calcutta has to be interpreted in the light of this." (Gadgil, n. 8, 18).

110 *Old Fort William in Bengal. A Selection of Official Documents, Dealing with its History (Indian Records Series)* London, 1906, I, 46, 47, 57, 102, 136.

111 B. R. Rau, *Present-Day Banking in India*, (Calcutta, 1930), 250.

112 *Old Fort William in Bengal*, II, 98.

113 *Murshidabad (Eastern Bengal District Gazetteer)*, 62.

Seths, Omichand and other bankers hampered the efforts of the nawabs of Bengal to free themselves from the British and to restore the independence of the country. On British instigation they conspired against Nawab Suraj-ud-Daula and refused to grant any loans to Nawab Mir Jafar.[114] The Jagat Seths received just punishment for their treachery; in 1763 when the British started a new war Nawab Mir Kasim immediately ordered the execution of the two senior members of the Jagat Seth family. The British sent a protest but it was already too late.[115] Omichand's behaviour was no less treacherous; in 1757 he informed the British that Suraj-ud-Daula intended to attack the British factory in Calcutta.[116]

The activities of the Jagat Seths and other Indian banking dynasties corroborated once more Marx's well-known statement that "under Asian forms usury can continue a long time, without producing anything more than economic decay and political corruption".[117]

Firm economic and political links between the East India Company and the big trading and moneylending capital of Hindustan were established in the middle of the eighteenth century. This is well illustrated by the family history of the Banaras bankers, Rai, who belonged to the Marwar caste of Aggarwals. Partab, the forefather of the Rai family, occupied various posts at Akbar's court. All his descendants served the Moguls, until one of them, Khayaliram, was appointed to a high position in Bihar. This official under the Moguls made friends with the English in Patna and, for the services Khayaliram rendered the Company, Clive (in the name of the Mogul Shah Àlam!) granted him a jagir and the title Raja Bahadur. A new system of colonial taxation was worked out under the direction of the new jagirdar. His son received from Warren Hastings further grants of land. In 1803, one of the Rai family negotiated, in the Company's name, with the Nawab of Oudh, the Maharaja of Gwalior and other feudal chiefs, and received in return still more jagirs and the title raja.[118] Many other bankers of Hindustan also served the British.

The defection of the big merchants to the side of the colonial conquerors did not merely signify that they found subordination to the feudal lords extremely burdensome. With very few exceptions, Indian towns did not become independent political centres of a popular resistance directed against the alien conquerors. The attitude of the merchants and other strata of the Indian urban population during the conquest is, in our view, an important indirect indication of the level

114 *Ibid.*, 62-66.
115 Rau, n. 111, 251.
116 N. 26, I, 77.
117 Marx, n. 60, III, 583, 584.
118 *Benares (District Gazetteers of the United Provinces)*, 118.

the economy attained in the towns of feudal India. An independent political plebeian-burgher opposition to feudalism could not, at that time, take shape, because urban commerce and industry in the principal regions of India had not yet shaken off their feudal dependence.

> Though the Indian merchant and manufacturing classes were rich and spread out all over the country and even controlled the economic structure, they had no political power. . . . Hence there was no middle class strong enough, or even consciously thinking of seizing power, as in some western countries.[119]

Because of the military and political preponderance of the feudal rulers over the town, the Indian towns were unable to organise an independent resistance movement against the usurpers after the defeat of the feudal armies.

For separate groups of merchants the colonialists created in a sense the conditions necessary for the accumulation and safety of monetary wealth. But the participation of these traders in industrial production was, in the coastal regions, restricted because the East India Company kept certain manufactures under its own control in the trading stations. The isolation of the handicrafts in the factory from the internal Indian market and the colonialists' predatory draining of the surplus product created by the artisans delayed the growth of capitalist relations in these industries. Neither the handicraftsman or producer, nor the merchant or buyer-up, who occupied a comparatively favourable position, turned into an industrial entrepreneur. The discrepancy between the accumulation process and the transformation of money-capital into productive capital, a characteristic feature of colonial India, appeared as early as the second half of the 18th century.

The flow of merchant's capital to the outlying coastal districts where it served the foreigners interfered with the development of commodity circulation within the country, which was based on the social division of labour as it existed in the 17th and 18th centuries. After the territorial conquest of Bengal, the colonialists established the Company's monopoly of commerce which was even more detrimental to the growth of the social division of labour.

Finally, with regard to the regions conquered by the British we should like to stress that it was the colonialists' agrarian policy which caused the greatest harm to the development of the economy. The assumption of the right to state ownership of land—which was, in effect, already disappearing at the time of the conquest—and the fixing of the rent-tax at a rate unprecedented even at the highest peak of Mogul despotism meant the restoration of outgrown feudal relations, in a form

---

119 Nehru, n. 32, 263.

distorted by colonialism. The excessively high rent-tax, which drained away a considerable part of the product created by the peasant households, was perhaps responsible for an even bigger retrogression in the social division of labour than the control exercised by the colonialists over commerce and industry.

During the 17th and 18th centuries the colonial expansion as a whole fettered the development of both the productive forces and the production relations in India and delayed the rise of the Indian bourgeoisie and the other classes of capitalist society.

CHAPTER IV

TRADERS AND MONEYLENDERS DURING COLONIAL EXPLOITATION BY INDUSTRIAL CAPITAL

The period of the colonial exploitation of India by the British industrial bourgeoisie began early in the 19th century, when the industrial revolution had been accomplished in Britain. The abolition of the East India Company's trading monopoly in 1813 marked the transition to the exploitation by methods characteristic of industrial capital. The process was speeded up by Napoleon's blockade which deprived Britain of a considerable part of its markets and of the sources of several raw materials like hemp, raw silk, and so on.[1] The most important of the new methods employed was the exploitation of the country as a market for English manufactured goods. But the adoption of the new methods of colonial exploitation did not mean that the older practices of robbing the country—taxation, military plunder, and the monopoly of foreign trade—were discarded. On the contrary they were further developed in the 19th century and, in a contradictory manner, combined with the new trend of colonial oppression.[2]

While the export of Indian hand-made fabrics to Europe declined during the first half of the 19th century the import of English machine-made textiles increased rapidly (Table 4.1).

1 For example, as a result of the blockade, which deprived it of Italian raw-silk, Britain was forced to accelerate the export of this raw material from Bengal. See Bholanath Chunder, *The Travels of a Hindoo to Various Parts of Bengal and Upper India*, (London, 1869 , I, 65.

2 The contradiction between the old and new methods of exploitation (the old practice of colonial plunder on the whole hampered the exploitation of India as a commodity market) were reflected in the fight of the British industrial bourgeoisie against the oligarchy of the East India Company.

TABLE 4.1
Export and Import of Cotton Cloth

Year			*Import into Great Britain (pieces)*	*British Export to India (yards)*
1814	...	...	1,266,608	818,208
1821	...	...	534,495	19,138,726
1828	...	...	422,504	42,822,077
1835	...	...	306,086	51,777,277

Source: Evidence of G.G. de H. Larpent, Director of the East India Company, before the Select Committee of the House of Commons (1840)—see R. Dutt, *The Economic History of India* II, (Delhi, 1960) *In the Victorian Age 1837-1900*, 79.

The following figures reflect, in terms of value, the increasing import of English cloth into India.[3]

1815	*1832*	*1849*	*1851*	*1857*
26	400	3,131	4,681	6,133 (In £1000s)

The transformation of India from a supplier of textiles to Europe into a consumer of English textiles was brought about first of all by the technical superiority of the English factory as compared to the Indian weaver and also by the tariff policy of the British government, which introduced customs duties of 75 per cent—amounting in fact to a prohibitive tax—on Indian cloth imported into Britain. The authorities of the East India Company went even further along the path of customs and tax discrimination against the Indian handicrafts. In the 1830s they imposed the following duties on the local weavers: 5 per cent on the raw material they used, 7.5 per cent on yarn, 2.5 per cent on cloth, and another 2.5 per cent if the cloth was dyed not in the weaver's workshop but somewhere else. The tax exacted, thus raised the cost of Indian hand-made cloth by 15-17.5 per cent. At the same time a customs duty of only 2.5 per cent *ad valorem* was levied on British factory produced textiles.[4] Such a tax policy created additional advantages for imported British machine-made textiles, which were in any case cheaper, and for the Lancashire mills in their competition against the native weavers. Moreover, this policy provided the English millowners with new super profits at the expense of the Indian consumer. (One should not forget that as a result of the tax the market prices of all textiles including British textiles, went up.) Finally the growth of manufacturing in England harmed Indian weaving also in an indirect way;

3 I. M. Reisner, *Ocherki klassovoi borby v Indii*, 52.
4 A. Sarada Raju, *Economic Conditions in Madras Presidency 1800-1850*, (Madras, 1941), 175.

since Indian cotton began to be exported to England to be worked up there, the prices of this raw material rose, thereby increasing the working expenses of the artisans.[5] The basic changes in the structure of the trade between India and Britain are illustrated by the following figures, while cloth exported by private individuals from Madras Presidency to Britain fell from Rs 1,681,000 in 1820 to Rs 459,000 in 1850, cotton exports increased from Rs 167,000 in 1811 to Rs 5,822,000 in 1850.[6]

Describing how the new methods of colonial exploitation affected the Indian economy, Marx wrote:

> It was the British intruder who broke up the Indian handloom and destroyed the spinning-wheel. England began with driving the Indian cottons from the European market; it then introduced twist into Hindustan and in the end inundated the very mother country of cotton with cottons. From 1818 to 1836 the export of twist from Great Britain to India rose in the proportion of 1 to 5,200. In 1824, the export of British muslins to India hardly amounted to 1,000,000 yards, while in 1837 it surpassed 64,000,000 of yards. But at the same time the population of Dacca decreased from 150,000 inhabitants to 20,000. This decline of Indian towns celebrated for their fabrics was by no means the worst consequence. British steam and science uprooted, over the whole surface of Hindustan, the union between agriculture and manufacturing industry.[7]

It is no mere chance that Marx refers to the weavers of Dacca as an example of the tragic fate which overtook the urban handicrafts of India in the first half of the 19th century. It will be recalled that almost all the cloth produced in Dacca was either exported to other parts of India and beyond the borders of the country or consumed by the Bengal court and the army. The weak connexions between the textile industry in towns like Dacca and the local market, especially the peasant market, made it easier for the British to gain control over the industry. By destroying the feudal state of Bengal in the middle of the 18th century and then disrupting the ancient foreign trade links of Dacca, they deprived the textile industry of its traditional markets and became the only buyers of its products. The severence of the old commercial ties of

5 A. Sarada Raju quotes the following statement made by the Board of Revenue in 1818: "Either the actual improvement that had taken place in the manufactures of Europe, or the arrangements adopted by the different states on the continent to encourage such improvement, had operated to the disadvantage of the manufacturers in this country by creating a demand for the raw instead of the manufactured material, a demand for cotton instead of cloth" (The quotation is taken from Sarada Raju, n. 4, 174).

6 *Ibid.*, 178, 302.

7 K. Marx and F. Engels, *The First Indian War of Independence 1857-1859*, 17-18.

the Bengali artisans, together with non-economic coercion, was one of the causes that brought about the complete submission of Bengal's merchant's capital to the colonialists.

Henceforth the fate of the urban handicrafts of Bengal depended entirely on the goodwill of the British bourgeoisie. Up to the beginning of the 19th century, the weaving industry of Bengal was to a certain extent compensated for the loss of its old commercial links by the increased sale of its products in Europe, in spite of all possible obstacles put up by the British industrial bourgeoisie to prevent the import of Indian cloth. But with the shrinkage of the demand on the European market early in the 19th century began the continuous deterioration of the textile industry in the towns of Bengal, which became a catastrophe when, in the twenties, the mass import of British machine-made cloth started. It was not till 1824 that cotton goods became a significant import item in Bengal.[8]

According to the data given in Thornton's *Gazetteer*, the decline of weaving in Dacca began in 1801. Up to that year the East India Company and private merchants annually bought cloth for £250,000 in Dacca, but by 1813 the amount had shrunk to £ 20,595.[9] It follows, therefore, that the reduction of the textile output began in Dacca even before the large-scale import of machine-made cloth commenced, and was caused by the severence of the traditional commercial relations. The decline of the handicrafts in Santipur, another textile centre which had apparently maintained closer links with the local market, started later than in Dacca—in 1813—and was brought about by the competition of imported cloth.[10] As late as the beginning of the nineteenth century fabrics worth £150,000 were bought there every year by the East India Company alone.[11] The loss of their former markets and later on British competition reduced the handicrafts of Dacca to a sorry state. Writes Thornton's *Gazetteer*:

> The manufactures of Dacca are at this time scarcely deserving of notice in the middle of the 19th century. A small quantity of coarse cotton, silk, and embroidered goods, constitutes the sum of them; and even this scanty remnant of skilled industry is constantly and rapidly giving way before the competition of British fabrics.[12]

The *Gazetteer* pointed that the weavers remaining in Dacca had lost the art of producing the famous muslins and manufactured nothing but coarse cloth. The position was similar in Murshidabad, Faridpur and other towns of Bengal. For having been deprived of the foreign

8 *Imperial Gazetteer of India*, II, 327.
9 E. Thornton, *Gazetteer of the Territories*, (London, 1854), II, 65.
10 *Nadia (Bengal District Gazetteer)*, (Calcutta, 1912) 96.
11 *Ibid.*, 65.
12 Thornton, n. 9, 64.

market and a considerable part of the orders from the feudal class, the weavers of these centres tried to fight the British competition on the home market, primarily the village market and produced therefore coarse, but comparatively cheap, cloth.

The other handicrafts of Bengal also experienced a decline, although not to the same extent. R. Heber, who stayed in Bengal in the middle of the 1820s, wrote that magnificent iron work, including weapons, was produced in Monghyr, a small town famous for the skill of its blacksmiths, who, it was said, "derived their art from the Indian Vulcan".[13] But B. Chunder, visiting the same town twenty years later, remarked that the former prosperity had vanished forever.

By the 1840s vessels were no longer built in the shipyards of Calcutta, although the prospects for shipbuilding in Bengal had been as favourable as in Bombay. In 1795-96 alone, six ships with a total displacement of 4,150 tons were built in Calcutta and in the following years ships continued to be launched. Calcutta's shipyards were, apparently, owned entirely by the East India Company. In any case there are no records showing that Indians took part in their administration.[14] Only ship-repair yards were maintained in Bengal during the latter half of the 19th century.

The first attempts by rich Bengalis to engage in large-scale industrial enterprise were made in the second quarter of the 19th century. For example, Dwarkanath Tagore, a member of a famous zamindar family, acquired coal fields in Raniganj the exploitation of which had been started by English capitalists in 1812. The coal output of these mines amounted to approximately 50,000 tons in 1840 and around 200,000 tons in 1860.[15] However, industrial enterprises belonging exclusively to Bengalis were as a rule shortlived. The mines in Raniganj were soon taken over by the Bengal Coal Co., in which British capital played an important part.

Similar developments were taking place in the Maratha country during the first half of the 19th century. Maharashtra was conquered by the colonialists at a time when methods of industrial capitalism were already used in the exploitation of India. The British usurpers succeeded in breaking the fierce resistance of the Marathas only in 1818, after three bitter wars. The Maratha Peshwa state, which had up to then prevented the British from using the trade routes from Bombay to the interior of the country, vanished from the map of India. Part of its territory, including Poona the former capital, was incorporated into the Bombay

13 R. Heber, *Voyage a Calcutta, Bombay et dans les provinces superieurs de l'Inde Britannique*, (Paris, 1830), I, 369.

14 R. Dutt, *India in the Victorian Age, An Economic History of the People*, (London, 1904), 114.

15 Chunder, n. 1, 170.

Presidency; the eastern districts of Maharashtra were divided between the Central Provinces of British India and the principality of Hyderabad, a loyal vassal state of the East India Company (Berar, a region of Hyderabad principality inhabited by Marathas, was later included in the Central Provinces).

For Maharashtra the first half, and especially the second quarter, of the 19th century was a period of severe economic crisis. Wars lasting many years ravaged the country. The system of feudal relations which had been evolved was undermined by the destruction of the Maratha state and the introduction of a new system of land taxes by the colonialists. The urban craftsmen, who had been fulfilling orders received from the court and the army, were deprived of their customers, and the competition of imported British commodities prevented them from strengthening their commercial ties with the countryside. In 1819, as soon as Maharashtra was conquered, British goods were freed from import duty and flooded the markets of the country. The producers of high and medium quality fabrics suffered most, while the manufacture of coarse cloth in the villages, where the weavers started to use British yarn, was less affected.[16]

The British competition led to a state of affairs where the artisans:

> were soon to leave the looms for the plough, and, like the soldier, burden the land. The land was to supply the raw material for the steel giants of Manchester; the millions of India were to be bound to the soil to cultivate for the greed of their new masters that wealth which was to make England the richest country in the world, and the Indian ryot so poverty-stricken as to make it difficult to find a parallel in the world.[17]

The drift of labour power in Maharashtra from the handicrafts to agriculture was also admitted by the English administrators. One of them wrote in 1830 that many craftsmen in search of the means of subsistence were forced to turn to agriculture, although the burden on the land was, in his opinion, already too great.[18] Thus, already in the first decade of British rule began the progressive ruralisation of the economy of Maharashtra. This development was, moreover, common to the whole of India.[19]

---

16 R.D. Choksey, *Economic History of the Bombay Deccan*, 165, 213.

17 *Ibid.*, 34.

18 *Ibid.*, 213.

19 "The compulsory back-to-the-land movement of artisans and craftsmen led to an ever-growing disproportion between agriculture and industry; agriculture became more and more the sole business of the people because of the lack of occupations and wealth-producing activities" Jawaharlal Nehru, *The Discovery of India*, 277.

The craftsmen who did not forsake the trade their forefathers were doomed to an existence of semi-starvation. According to the calculations of British administrators a weaver and his family had to spend, in the early twenties, on grain alone—usually the cheapest kind of millet.—Rs 84 per year, while their annual earnings amounted to approximately Rs 108.[20] If one takes into account that they also require other foodstuffs, clothing, fuel, household utensils, and so on, one can imagine how desperate the position of the artisans was. One should moreover remember that we are, describing the early years of the colonial rule; later on their position became even worse. For instance, an English official who examined the weaving industry in the Belgaum district in 1849 admitted that the weaver's income was reduced to half the amount it had been twenty years earlier. The weaver, in fact, only earned two annas per day, or roughly Rs 50-60 a year.[21]

We possess no reliable information regarding the economic organisation of the handicrafts in Maharashtra during the first half of the 19th century. On the basis of the scattered facts available it seems likely that craftsmen who depended on the buyer-up were prevalent in the towns. The dependence was particularly strong where the craftsmen manufactured expensive goods, because the dealer controlled the supply of raw materials and semi-finished products required for their output. From the 1820s onwards the artisans in Maharashtra, and in India as a whole, began to use imported semi-finished products (yarn, metals) which increased the hold of the buyer-up on the small industries. While the loss of the feudal customer had somewhat weakened the power of the merchant the changeover to imported semi-finished products restored it again.

But it seems that, side by side with the dependent artisan, the wage labourer made his appearance in the industries of Western India even before the colonial enslavement. An English official, for example, related in 1822 that a weaver working "by hire" received half a rupee per day. A weaver "working by contract", that is for the buyer-up, considered that he made a profit if he earned more than that and a loss if he earned less.[22] Thus the earnings of the hired worker already served as a criterion for the income of the dependent craftsman.

How destructive the consequences of the conquest were for the economy of the Peshwa state may be illustrated on the example of two towns: Bagalkot and Poona. According to an English employee, Bagalkot in the extreme north of Kanara owed its former prosperity to the native court and to the general condition of the population under the previous government when a constant demand for handicraft wares

20 Choksey, n. 16, 306.
21 *Ibid.*, 311, 312.
22 *Ibid.*, 305.

existed because the people were well-off.[23] Expensive fabrics were among the goods offered for sale on the town bazaar, and Rs 50,000 worth of them were sold during one religious festival alone. "All that had depended on the expenditure of the people of rank, was in 1822 nearly annihilated; those classes of Marathas were no longer met with. Even those who could still afford to purchase valuable goods were content with the cheaper"; as the English employee remarks, "there were no occasions of show or inducement for men without office or trade to dress well; greater number were even bereft of all means".[24]

Another stroke aimed at the handicrafts of Bagalkot was the imposition of British taxes. Eighteen manufacturing houses—apparently large workshops—had paid Rs 400 tax, and the largest of them Rs 88 under the Indian rulers. The British system of taxation extracted from the same establishments Rs 1,900 and Rs 500 respectively. As a result, trade and industry of this Maratha town began to decline.[25]

Poona suffered even more. The state of its trade and its handicrafts has been thus described by an English work published in the middle of the 19th century:

> With the exception of grain-dealers, and those who trade in the raw products of the country, the mercantile classes in Poona are said to be declining in wealth. No market is now found for jewellery and precious stones, which were much sought after when Poona was the seat of native rule. The introduction of European piece-goods has caused the disappearance of native fabrics, which could not compete with them in price, and Poona has now scarcely any manufacture except a very small one of paper.[26]

The towns of Gujarat, too, were in the throes of an extremely serious crisis after the establishment of British "law and order" in the first half of the 19th century. Of Ahmedabad, the capital, the *Gazetter* writes:

> The city was always more indebted to the Court and army, of which it was the headquarters, than to its natural advantages. When we also consider that its brocade and silk manufactures were severely affected by the depression of Native Courts who were the chief customers, and that its lower classes of textile fabrics were from the first outrivalled by imports from Europe, we may easily understand how the once splendid commerce of the city, instead of returning to its old centres, became diffused among smaller outlying towns.[27]

In Gujarat, as in other parts of India, it was the output of expensive

23 *Ibid.*, 307.
24 *Ibid.*
25 *Ibid.*
26 Thornton, n. 9, IV, 160.
27 *Ahmedabad (Bombay Gazetteer*, IV), 95.

fabrics which was reduced first of all, while craftsmen who manufactured coarse cloth were for a long time able to resist the foreign competition.[28]

The output of the handicraft industries in the Madras Presidency also declined during the first half of the 19th century. Weavers working for the foreign market were the first victims. For example, at the beginning of the 19th century the export of cloth from Masulipatam to the Persian ports amounted to five million rupees according to official data. "But Manchester", as the *Gazetter* for South India writes in 1855, "has superseded Masulipatam and the trade is now half a lack".[29] In the opinion of Gadgil and Sarada Raju one reason for the ruin of the handicrafts in South India was the shrinkage of the demand from the native feudal aristocracy.[30] A. Sarada Raju records:

> With the influx of British piecegoods into country, even those who catered to the home markets received a severe blow. Many of these were obliged to take to the manufacture of the coarse varieties which could alone withstand foreign competition. But, here the net income had always been low, and was now still further reduced owing to the depression in industry and agriculture.[31]

As a result of the reduced demand and the competition of British commodities the position of the artisans in the Madras Presidency also took a sharp turn for the worse. The prices for their manufactures dropped, in Visakhapatnam a piece of Punjum cloth cost Rs 6 in 1815, while it cost only Rs 3 and 8 annas in 1844. The weavers' earnings fell by 25-50 per cent. The Collector of the Madura district wrote in 1844 that very many of the families of the five thousand weavers living in the town of Madura could not afford to buy rice for more than one meal a day.[32]

The decline of handicraft production enabled trading and moneylending capital to strengthen its hold on the craftsmen and to consolidate the worst forms of enslavement. Sarada Raju relates that in the first half of the 19th century all types of craftsmen were to be

---

28 *Ibid.*, 131.

29 Quoted by Sarada Raju, n. 4, 174.

30 Sarada Raju quotes the following observation made by the collector of Ganjam, "the Comparative opulence of the zamindars and of private individuals at that time (previous to 1815) and their love of buying valuable cloth were sources of profit to the weavers" (*Ibid.*, 181).

The demand from the native feudal lords had greatly decreased by the 1830s (see *Ibid.*, 180). D. R. Gadgil refers to the decline of the economic life in Tanjore after the death of the last raja in 1855 (D. R. Gadgil, *The Industrial Evolution of India in Recent Times* (Madras, 1929), 9.

31 Sarada Raju, n. 4, 180.

32 *Ibid.*, 180, 181.

found in the weaving industry of the Madras Presidency, from the independent artisan who worked for his own account and sold his wares himself on the market, to the weaver who depended on the buyer-up to such an extent that he was in fact, a serf. "Once the weaver got into the clutches of a dealer, he became a slave and remained one till his dearth".[33] Weavers working on their own account usually manufactured cheap, coarse cloth for local consumption. Nevertheless they often had to obtain yarn on credit. If, however, a particular kind of cloth was in great demand, or was sold in a distant market, the weaver worked only to order. When placing the order, the buyer-up gave an advance to the weaver amounting to half the value of the goods or more. The craftsman paid 2 per cent per month on the sum advanced.[34] Sometimes rich weavers, too, made advances. The economic organisation of the weaving industry in the first half of the 19th century differed little from that described by F. Buchanan, except perhaps for the fact that the weavers' enslavement by moneylenders had gone even further. Presumably a new phenomenon was the custom to advance yarn to the weavers.[35] It was only occasionally that rich weavers hired workers, at piece or time rates.

Handicrafts in the big towns which had formerly served the feudal lords as administrative and military centres—among them Ahmedabad, Poona and Seringapatam—suffered most from the disruption of the traditional mercantile relations and the British competition. The handicrafts in smaller towns which maintained close links with the local rural market, and the domestic industry in general stood up better to the impact of the foreign imports. One should keep in mind that the

---

33 *Ibid.*, 167.

34 *Ibid.*, 168.

35 *Ibid.*, 168. Sarada Raju refers in this context to E. Hoole's work *A Mission to the South of India* (S. 1.) 1829, 156. J.A. Dubois, the French missionary, gives a vivid picture of the working and living conditions and the mode of life of the weaver in Southern India at the beginning of the 19th century:

"All these magnificent articles are produced in a miserable hut consisting of mud walls covered with straw, thirteen feet long and seven wide. The artisan carries on his trade sitting on the floor of the hut, surrounded by his family, side by side with the cow and the chicken, and operates his shuttle without hurry; the instruments he uses are extremely simple...

"As regards the artisan, his poverty matches the simplicity of his workshop. There are two or three rather numerous tribes in the country whose only occupation is weaving; most of their members are very poor and have not sufficient means to work on their own account. Merchants who need the products they manufacture, find the necessary cash and, after coming to an agreement with the weavers regarding the price, quantity and quality of the commodities, undertake to give them an advance. The weaver, then, buys yarn and other materials he requires for his work" (J. A. Dubois Moeurs, institution et ceremonies des peuple de l'Inde, [Paris, 1825] I, 98).

cotton fabrics imported by the British during the first half of the 19th century—a few dozen million yards in all—were quite insufficient to clothe 200 to 250 million Indians. Marx pointed out that although the British used their direct political power to destroy the unity of industry and agriculture in India, they succeeded only very gradually.[36] However, the general decline of the economy, the ruin of the peasantry and the interruption or disturbance of the commercial relations hampered the development of the productive forces and the relations of production in industry. It is obvious that under these conditions an industrial bourgeoisie could not possibly emerge from the ranks of either the rich handicraftsmen or even the buyers-up.

The transition to the exploitation of India as a market by no means meant, as we indicated earlier, that the colonialists renounced their old methods of oppression. As before they did not disdain even military plunder. But oppressive taxation was the most important of the old methods of exploitation employed in the first half of the 19th century. The introduction of the permanent settlement in Bengal was the first of the land-tax reforms to be imposed by the colonial authorities. The colonial land-tax legislation has been examined in detail in the Soviet literature on India. Therefore, we will here merely outline the main aspects of this legislation that influenced India's economic development.

The fact that the two reforms of the land-tax introduced by the British—the zamindari and ryotwari—combined "the most contradictory character—both made not for the people, who cultivate the soil, nor for the holder, who owns it, but for the Government that taxes it", was already stressed by Marx.[37] The property in land established by the colonial government could be nothing but a caricature of private property, if only because the land-tax reforms were based on the assumption that the colonial state was the supreme owner of the land. State ownership, moreover, was not merely a juridical statement, but an economic reality, which manifested itself in the fact that the colonial state appropriated 50-60 per cent of the harvest as land-tax in the regions where the ryotwari or "peasant" holdings prevailed. In imposing such a high land-tax the East India Company assumed the right that had belonged to the oriental despot to levy a rent-tax. Because in a number of cases the tax absorbed not only the surplus-product but also part of the necessary product, the price of land dropped and, as Marx pointed out, often the land lost all its value.[38]

The following passage demonstrates that a British official, Robert Richards, saw the connection between the excessive tax burden and the fact that the saleable value of the land shrank or disappeared

36 K. Marx, *Capital*, III, 328.

37 K. Marx and F. Engels, *On Colonialism* (Moscow), 74.

38 *Ibid*.

altogether. When he was examined by the Committee of the House of Commons on the affairs of the East India Company, he was asked:

> You have stated that the tax is equal in some cases to the produce of the land; has land then a saleable value in any part of India where the taxes take away the whole of this produce?
>
> Richard replied:
>
> I am personally acquainted with instances where the revenue assessed upon certain lands has actually exceeded the gross produce ... Land, however, has a saleable value in those parts of India where our revenue systems admit of some rent being derived from the land by the landholders or proprietor but when the whole rent is absorbed by the government tax or revenue, the land is of course destitute of saleable value.[39]

The two main systems of land taxation deprived the village communities of the right to own their land, for the previously existing traditional limitations of the feudal rent, which formed an integral part of this right, were abolished by the steep rise in the land-tax. The property rights of the peasants were also infringed upon by the colonial administration, which took away the holdings of the peasants who defaulted on their tax payments—an expedient to which the fiscal machinery of the feudal rulers of India did not resort. Even H. I. S. Cotton, who occupied a high position in the colonial civil service, stated that the Mogul system of landownership was totally different from the British system, that is the system introduced by the British in their colonies. He admitted that the revenue departments of the Mogul rulers—despite the acts of violence committed by them—never sold by auction the land of those who failed to pay their taxes, which as a rule the British did.[40] In other words, the Indian village community, whose principal basis was communal ownership of land, was undermined and afterwards—when the colonial regime dissolved the direct links that existed between the handicrafts and agriculture—completely destroyed. Only miserable remnants of the former system survived in a few districts where the British preserved the village community, or to be more precise its administrative organisations, for fiscal purposes.

When, in these conditions, the colonial government proclaimed the right of the landowner or ryot to inherit, dispose of and lease his land, it was often nothing but a legal fiction. The "landowner" did by no means cling to his plot, on the contrary he frequently tried to get rid of it. The peasants' flight from the land interfered with the collection of taxes. Having in a number of cases restored the practice of levying the

---

39 *Committee on East India Company's Affairs*, 1831, V, The quotation is taken from *British Rule in India*, (London, 1915), 22-3.

40 H. S. I. Cotton, *New India or India in Transition*, (London, 1884), 55.

rent-tax, the colonial administration proceeded—in districts where the ryotwari system prevailed—to attach the peasants to the land in order to retain the taxable population.

It should be understood that the land-tax which absorbed the whole of the surplus-product and took the place of the rent-tax did not cover all regions of British India but was a characteristic feature of certain districts, in particular Madras and to a certain extent Bombay. In regard to the other parts of the country it is more accurate to say that there was a dual ownership of land exercised by the colonial state and the landowner (the landed proprietor, the peasant or the village community). But on the whole, real private property in land, not a caricature of it, could at that time be found only in exceptional circumstances.

Despite the reactionary features of the colonial land-tax legislation the right of the private individual to own land, which it proclaimed, undoubtedly had a revolutionary effect. "The zemindari and ryotwari themselves, abominable as they are, involve two distinct forms of private property in land—the great *desideratum* of Asiatic society".[41] The land tax reforms gave the Indian zamindars and ryots the legal basis for their opposition to the arbitrary taxation imposed by colonial despotism. The struggle for the consolidation of private property was, in our opinion, progressive even when it was waged in defence of feudal property held by individuals for it helped to create the preconditions for capitalist development in India.

It is no mere coincidence that the immediate cause of the Indian national uprising was the abolition of certain property rights of the feudal landowners in Oudh by the British, and that one of the results of the uprising was a pledge to safeguard the property rights of the Indian landlords. We consider that the historical importance of the uprising of 1857-59, as far as it concerned the economic development of the country, was that it helped to bring about the progressive consolidation of property in land, although this process was not completed. Only in consequence of a consolidated system of private feudal and small-peasant landownership were the conditions created for the emergence of capitalist relations in agriculture, and therefore also for the gradual decline of these forms of property.

The colonial oppression distorted the process of primitive accumulation in India. The ruin of the Indian peasants and artisans up to the middle of the 19th century cannot be considered a consequence of this process, that is, of the expropriation of the direct producer from the means of production. The ruined peasant in the countryside was attached to the means of production (the chief one of which—land—did not in fact belong to him) both by the traditions of his community and caste, and the obligation to pay tax to the colonial government.

The urban handicraftsman was tied to his workshop as a consequence of his enslavement by the usurer and, in those districts where British factories existed, by order of the administration forbidding him to leave his place of residence. Finally, even if the peasant or craftsman attempted to abandon his work, he discovered that there was no demand for his labour power. Even after direct producer was deprived of his title to the means of production, he remained bound to them by semi-feudal conditions of enslavement. In other words, the ruin of the peasants and craftsmen during the first half of the 19th century was not accompanied by the formation of a market for free labour power.

Another precondition of capitalist development that was absent in India during the first half of the last century was a market for means of production in the modern sense. The land either lost its value or was in the hands of the feudal lords. The implements of the artisan could not serve as objects for capital investment for they suffered a kind of moral depreciation after India became one of the markets in which British manufacturers sold their products. As regards modern means of production, their supply was a British monopoly, since none was produced locally.

The absence of the conditions necessary for the development of capitalism determined the parasitic nature of the activities of merchant's capital in agriculture. In the ryotwari districts of Madras and Bombay the peasant, who was overburdened with taxation, as Marx wrote, fell a pray to the extortions of the usurer.[42] But the land in these districts had lost so much of its value that the moneylenders, at times, did not even endeavour to seize it. Only a comparatively small number of peasant holdings was taken over by moneylenders during this period.

The only aspect of primitive accumulation for which, in the first half of the 19th century, the conditions were ripe was the accumulation of money-capital. In this period the merchants continued to enrich themselves throughout colonial India, although the extent varied in different parts of the country. As before, Gujaratis serving the foreigners remained in the most favourable position.

Collaboration of Gujarati Merchants with British Capital.

During the first half of the 19th century Bombay became the centre

---

41 Marx and Engels, n. 7, 33.

42 See Marx and Engels, n. 37.

43 The value of Bombay's export and import (in million rupees):

1800-1809	*1810-1819*	*1820-1829*
56.0	46.7	56.6
1830-1839	*1840-1849*	*1850-1859*
82.2	192.4	262.0

(*Bombay City, Bombay Gazetteer* [Bombay, 1909], I, 416)

of trade routes which extended far into the interior. The rapid increase in Bombay's foreign trade began after the conquest of Maharashtra.[43] By the middle of the century, more than a third of India's overseas trade passed through the port of Bombay. The growing flow of British commodities encouraged an ever greater number of Gujarati merchants of all types, from the big wholesale dealer to the small shopkeeper, to act as middlemen. Describing the Bohra merchants from Gujarat who traded in Central India, J. Malcolm wrote: "The Bohras, who came from the sea-coast of Gujarat into Central India, have imported the improvements of European settlements, even in the construction of their houses and furniture; they are the chief medium through which the trade in European articles is carried on.[44] Maria Graham, an English traveller who visited India in 1809, thus related her encounter with the Bania merchants of Gujarat:

> In Bombay there are a good many Banyas, or travelling merchants, who come mostly from Guzerat, and roam about the country with muslins, cotton cloth, and shawls, to sell. On opening one of their bales, I was surprised to find at least half of its contents of British manufacture (she speaks here of textiles.) and such articles were much cheaper than those of equal fineness from Bengal and Madras. Excepting a particular kind of chintz made at Poonah, and painted with gold and silver, there are no fine cotton-cloths made on this side of the peninsula.

Maria Graham's further account makes it clear that the British fabrics she saw in the bale of the Gujarati trader were machine-made. She goes on to say how strange it seemed that cotton exported to England worked up there and returned as cloth to India should sell here at a lower price than the local manufactures, where labour was so cheap. She believed that this was due to the unsettled state of affairs and the difficulty of sending goods to different parts of the country, but the chief reason seemed to be the fact that England employed machinery.[45]

In the period of the exploitation of India by industrial capital, the British bourgeoisie did not merely confine itself to selling its factory-produced commodities in India. The British also exported agricultural raw materials (cotton, jute, indigo) and foodstuffs from India. Indian merchants, especially those from Gujarat, who collaborated with the colonial regime made enormous fortunes by trading in opium, and began to take part in the cotton export. In the twenties of the last century, the Gujarati compradors headed by Jeejeebhoy the richest merchant

---

44 J. Malcolm, *Memoir of Central India, including Malwa and Adjoining Provinces*, (London, 1832), II, 111-2.

45 Maria Graham, *Journal of the Residence in India*, (Edinburgh, 1813), 32-3.

started, with the backing of Maratha traders, to export cotton from Maharashtra.[46] Cotton export from Gujarat began even earlier. Cotton export trade in western India was almost entirely in the hands of Gujarati merchants up to the middle of the 19th century.[47] An English economist who studied the Indian cotton trade explained that the British traders' poor knowledge of the northwestern parts of India, the absence of a network of agents and the competition of the natives, accounted for the weak representation of British merchant's capital in these regions.[48] The real reason however was, undoubtedly, that the Marathas withstood the conquerers for so long a time.

An English eye-witness has written the following account of the organisation of the cotton trade in 1836:

> The exporters of cotton to the coast are chiefly opulent individuals and native firms of Bombay. They have Gomashtas (agents or factors) who have located themselves at Khamgaum (a cotton growing centre in Maharashtra) from whence they send out subordinates to the several pergunnahs, to make advances to patells (village headmen) and substantial ryots of villages about two months previous to the gathering, at 2 per cent, per month. Such security is taken as can be got, and they deem good, usually of mahajuns (moneylenders) or able and wealthy patells themselves. They likewise purchase cotton from the mahajuns who are settled in the kusbas, and almost every respectable village in the country, these mahajuns having made advances to the ryots in the similar way. When the cotton begins to come in, the principal talookdars and mahajuns of large towns and points meet and fix what is called a sahookar's price and receive the wool from the producers (cleared from the seed) at the kusba or the village itself. They take a discount of one rupee per nug on account of the advances made by them.[49]

The penetration of commodity relations into the Indian village caused trading and moneylending capital to expand its sphere of activities, this occurred first of all in the parts of the country which started to produce industrial raw materials. But in the first half of the 19th century, barter was still used as a means of extracting raw material even in Gujarat, a relatively advanced region. In order to obtain a small quantity of oil needed for lighting, the peasant who had no ready money gave the local shopkeeper cotton or grain in exchange, which the latter

---

46 *Buldana (Central Provinces District Gazetteer)*, (Calcutta, 1910), 276,

47 "The present commerce in cotton between Berar and Bombay was originated, and is chiefly carried on, by native merchants" (J. Chapman, *The Cotton and Commerce of India*, London, 1860, 15).

48 *Ibid.*

49 *Ibid.*, 90.

sold in the town.[50] Although the shopkeeper made use of every opportunity to enslave the peasant—such as the debt which the peasant incurred in the shop, the loss of his cattle, failure of crops, a wedding[51] and in the final resort he simply fell back on cheating and swindling his illiterate customer—the self-sufficiency of the peasant household permitted the agriculturist to retain a certain independence in relation to the trading and moneylending capital.

Only the gradual increase of elements of commodity production in the peasant household brought about a situation where the peasant was more and more frequently forced to borrow money from the usurer, not as a consumer who cannot satisfy his personal requirements by means of his own natural economy, but as a small commodity producer who has to turn to the moneylender mainly because his economy depends on the market. In both cases the loans—apart from rare exceptions—were of course intended for purposes of consumption and were not made with the intention of investing the money in production. This apparent similarity was due to the fact that the object of both the natural economy of the peasant and the small commodity producing peasant economy in colonial India always remained personal consumption, not accumulation in order to expand production (the few existing prosperous peasant households are here disregarded). Not until the sixties of the 19th century can one observe the phenomenon in India that the peasant's dependence on the moneylender increased when there was a good harvest of industrial crops—and their prices fell!—and, on the contrary, that the dependence of the peasant somewhat decreased when poor harvests caused the prices of agricultural products to rise.[52] Finally, it is only from this time onwards that the conditions prevailing in the capitalist world market began to exert a determining influence on the output of the Indian peasant economy, by way of the Indian trading and moneylending capital.

The agriculturists' dependence on the trader increased already in the twenties and thirties of the 19th century when the peasant households turned to the cultivation of export crops. The Gujarati peasants increasingly depended for their supply of grain on the merchants, who grew rich on this trade especially at times when the harvests were bad. The population in the northern provinces of west

50 A.K. Forbes, *Ras Mala*, II, 248.

51 *Ibid.*

52 Anticipating much later developments, we recall the conditions at the time of the Second World War which enabled the well-to-do and many of the middle peasants to take advantage of the sharp rise in prices for foodstuffs and raw materials which took place while agricultural output remained stagnant or even decreased to wipe out or reduce the debts they had incurred with the moneylenders. A radically different situation arose during the world economic crisis of 1929-33

India always suffered from great famines. The Bania merchants who possessed big stores of grain refused to sell them during the first famine year, in the hope that later they would make enormous profits.[53] The feudal exploitation of the peasants and their exploitation by taxation went together with their enslavement by the moneylender. As we have already seen, a whole network of middlemen and agents—consisting of landlords, urban moneylenders, the top strata of the countryside, and the village moneylenders—were employed by the Gujarati compradores to exploit the peasants. The enslaved peasants were forced to sell their cotton at a reduced price. The Indian landlords and merchants, thus, enabled British industrial capital to obtain the raw material for the British cotton industry at a cheaper rate.

The dependence of the East India Company on the services of the Gujarati merchants compelled it to admit them to the trade with China, an "exclusive monopoly", which the Company jealously guarded against all European traders.[54] The merchants of Bombay sold opium and cotton to China and brought from there tea and other commodities which were for the most part re-exported to Europe.

The Indian production of opium was concentrated in the eastern part of the country, in the Banaras and Patna areas, and in Central India, in the Malwa region, from where it was sent, via Bombay, to Canton. Although opium was produced around Banaras and Patna, the merchants of East India were unable to derive much benefit from the traffic in opium, for the East India Company completely monopolised this trade from 1799 to 1803.

The merchants of Bombay who collaborated with the colonialists were in a more favourable position since the bulk of the marketable opium passed through their hands. It would, however, be wrong to assume that the British colonialists did not control the opium trade in Western India. After the final defeat of the Maratha state in 1818, the production of opium was declared to be the exclusive privilege of the princes of Indore and Gwalior and of other native rulers. But the buying-up of opium was the monopoly of the East India Company. It brought the opium to Bombay and sold it by auction to local merchants. In 1831 the British annulled their agreement with the princes, and abolished the monopoly which Malwa had in regard to the production of opium, at the same time handing over the marketing of opium to private traders.[55] But the British imposed extremely high transit-duties on the opium exported through the port of Bombay.[56]

---

53 Postans, *Western India in 1838*, (London, 1838), II, 222-23.

54 Marx, n. 36, I, 752.

55 F. S. Turner, *British Opium Policy and its Results to India and China*, (London, 1876), 55, 56.

56 The East India Company received seven shillings six pence from each pound

The opium trade was carried on direct by the merchants of Gujarat. One of them Hathisingh, who was a member of the Nagar Seths, an old family of bankers from Ahmedabad, regularly sent large consignments of opium, containing up to two thousand chests, to China.[57]

The acknowledged "king" of the merchants of Bombay was the Parsi J. Jeejeebhoy. In the first three decades of the 19th century he managed, through his activities in the opium trade, to scrape together an enormous fortune, amounting to thirty million rupees, which he deposited in the British "Bank of Bombay".[58] It may be worthwhile to consider in greater detail the career of Jeejeebhoy. Postans, who visited Bombay in 1838, called him the wealthiest Parsi of Bombay.[59] His way to success is rather typical for the traders of Bombay.

Jamshedjee Jeejeebhoy was born in 1783 in a family of modest means; at the age of twelve he was apprenticed to his uncle, a glass merchant. But Jeejeebhoy did not remain for long in his uncle's shop. His biographer Jhabvala wrote that opium, silk and similar expensive goods opened enormous prospects to the enterprising young man, Jeejeebhoy soon went to China where he traded in cotton, but he was unsuccessful and returned poor in a pitiful state. But the failure did not discourage Jeejeebhoy; he made three more journeys to China and laid up a purse. Even the French navy, which operated along the shipping routes and, once seized a vessel with a cargo belonging to Jeejeebhoy, did not stop him. Jeejeebhoy was connected with one of the leading English firms in Bombay, Crowford and Co. In 1824 he headed a group of Bombay merchants who began to export cotton from Berar.[60] Lastly we shall mention that this gentleman had investments in the shipbuilding industry and was the biggest dock owner, employing on the average approximately 3000 workers.[61]

Many other merchants of Gujarat—the forefathers of the richest industrialists of Bombay and Ahmedabad—made their fortune by trading in opium.

The opium trade caused a revival of sailing activities in Bombay during the first half of the 19th century. By 1840, i.e. the time of the

---

of opium sold in Calcutta in the middle of the ninteenth century and transit-duties levied on opium from Malwa brought the Company five shillings eight pence per pound. (J. W. Kaye, *The Administration of the East India Company. A History of India's Progress*, London, 1853 683.) Duties imposed on opium rose from 125 rupees per chest in 1835-42 to 700 rupees in 1862.

57 *The Indian Textile Journal*, 1931, February; Turner, n. 55, 56.

58 S. H. Jhabvala, *Sir Jamshedji Jeejeebhoy. Baronet*, (Bombay) (S.a.) 20.

59 Postans, n. 53, I, 122.

60 Chapman, n. 47, 75.

61 Postans, n. 53, I, 122.

opium wars waged by the British in China, the greater part of the opium traffic was in the hands of Parsis. Dadabhoy Rustomjee alone lost, according to British estimates, up to two million rupees when the opium was confiscated by the Chinese authorities.[62] Special clippers were built in Calcutta for the illicit traffic in opium. One of these ships, the famous 'Sylph', which belonged to the Parsi Rustomjee Kovasjee, could make the journey from Calcutta to Macao in sixteen days. It is no mere coincidence that during the war with China the Parsi opium merchants placed their vessels at the disposal of the British command to be used as troop carriers. The ships of the Parsis were the principal means of transport which enabled the British to convey their soldiers to the Chinese ports. Rustomjee Kovasjee alone supplied fourteen boats for this purpose.[63]

The Wadias were the biggest shipowners in Bombay during the first half of the 19th century. Between 1786 and 1842 they owned sixteen large vessels, Readymoney had seven, Kama seven, Patel eight, and so on. After the British-Chinese war, however, many of the Parsi shipping companies disappeared. This was partly due to the fact that China started to produce and sell its own opium and partly to the development of steam navigation, from which the English excluded their Indian partners. In 1845, however, one firm was formed, the Bombay Steam Navigation Company with a capital of one million rupees, which owned one steamship making trips to Ceylon and Karachi. The management of this company consisted of Englishmen and native merchants from Bombay. But the large shipping companies that were later set up in Bombay were purely British, with the exception of shortlived companies founded during the cotton boom.[64]

Steam navigation became the principal monopoly of the colonialists, and the main instrument enabling them to control India's economy. Not till 1906 did the Muslim merchants of Bombay, headed by Adamjee Peerbhoy, form a shipping company which acquired nine old steamships. But after a number of accidents the enterprise failed.[65] The creation of a modern mercantile marine was again postponed for several decades. This difficult problem is being solved at present.

The inland trade which the Gujarati merchants carried on was mainly concentrated in Gujarat and Maharashtra. In the 19th century, however, their trading activities spread also to other parts of India particularly the south. The Parsis for example, controlled the major part of the maritime trade of the Karnatak and Kerala already in the early years of the last century and began to settle there in increasing

62 W. H. Coates, *The Old Country Trade*, 52.
63 *Ibid.*, 51-2, 59.
64 *Ibid.*, 137-145, 150-60.
65 *Ibid.*, 203.

numbers after the British seized these regions. Besides the Parsis, Banias from Gujarat and Marwaris also emigrated to the Karnatak and Kerala during this period.[66]

The activities of sub-contractors engaged in shipbuilding and in the arsenals of the East India Company are also of considerable interest. In the thirties of the 18th century the East India Company set up a shipyard in Bombay. As we already know, the first shipbuilding establishment of the East India Company on the west coast was in Surat where, from 1673 onwards, the Parsis—whom A. Hamilton called excellent shipwrights—[67] built vessels for the Company. In 1735 an officer taking over a ship constructed in the shipyards of Surat was struck by the skill and knowledge of the shipwright Lowjee Nushirvan and suggested to him that he should take charge of the work at the docks which were, at that time, under construction in Bombay.[68]

But we also have a more modest version of the beginning of Lowjee's career in Bombay. Maria Graham, who visited Jamshet Bakhman the great-grandson of Lowjee in 1809, wrote that the latter "came to Guzerat to work in the dock-yard as a day-labourer" and thanks to his great ability later became a shipwright.[69]

In 1742 the Council of Bombay examined Lowjee's application for a loan of Rs 1,000 to build a house. Taking into consideration the merits of the applicant, testimonies as to his capability, and his loyalty, the Council decided to comply with the request of the master carpenter Lowjee.[70] When Lowjee died, in 1774, he left a house and £3,000 to his heirs.[71] He was the ancestor of the Wadias, a family from which came many leading shipbuilders of Bombay and later on, at the close of the 19th century, a number of big industrialists. The surname Wadia does not appear in any of the old sources which refer to Lowjee Nushirvanjee.

Lowjee's grandsons Manikjee and Bakhmanjee, who died in 1790 and 1792 respectively, did not manage to leave large fortunes to their sons Framjee Manikjee and Jamshetjee Bakhmanjee who succeeded them.[72] In his work on the Anglo-Indian navy, published in three volumes, C. R. Low referred to the great services of J. Bakhmanjee who began to build ships of the line in the shipyards of Bombay.[73] In 1802 J. Bakhmanjee launched the frigate "Cornwallis", which was the signal

66 Sarada Raju, n. 4, 188.

67 A. Hamilton, *A New Account of the East Indies, Being Observations and Remarks*, (Edinburgh, 1727), I, 160.

68 *Handbook for India*, (Bombay, 1859), II, 279.

69 Graham, n. 45, 44.

70 *Materials towards a Statistical Account of the Town and Island of Bombay, Part I History (Bombay Gazetteer, XXVI)* (Bombay, 1893), 191.

71 n. 68, Pt. II, 279.

72 *Gazetteer of Bombay City...*, I, 391.

73 Ch. R. Low, *History of the India Navy* (London, 1877), II, 176.

for the East India Company to embark on a feverish building programme of big men-of-war that were launched in the dockyards of Bombay.[74]

Information as to the conditions in which Indian capitalists participated in the work of the shipyards is rather incomplete. It seems that the docks were, either entirely or to a considerable extent, the property of East India Company. In any case we have no indication of any Indian dock owners. One can, however, say with certainty that Indians who played a part in the shipbuilding industry were not merely workers and foremen.

Even the size of the inheritance bequeathed by Lowjee Nushirvan Wadia indicates that he probably was a contractor. Lowjee's great-grandsons owned a large tract of land in Bombay. Maria Graham wrote in 1809: "Pestengee (a brother of J. Bakhmanjee) told me that he received not less than £15,000 a year in rents, and that his brother received nearly as much".[75] Postans, an Englishwoman who visited the Wadia family thirty years after Maria Graham, relates that the splendour of Lowjee's castle astonished her. In the course of his conversation with her the master of the house mentioned his extensive trade with China and referred to the cost of the valuable cargo which had just been brought to Bombay in one of his own ships "Lowjee Family". He then observed that the Parsis were greatly indebted to the Europeans for the help they had received from them at the start of their commercial activities.[76]

The *Asiatic Journal* of 1838 reported that many Parsi craftsmen who began work in the shipyards of Bombay as ordinary workers, had, through their own skill and enterprise, become rich shipbuilders.[77] This is undoubtedly also a reference to the numerous members of the Wadia family.

If the dockyards belonged entirely to the East India Company, it may be asked, what Indian capitalists could do there. A considerable field remained open to private Indian initiative. W. Hamilton remarked that the shipyards were full of Parsis who had gained monopoly positions in all departments. The supplier of timber was a Parsi, as was the man who inspected the finished ships.[78] The supply of timber for the shipyards was indeed in the hands of Parsi merchants. A copy of an agreement for the supply of timber signed as early as 1741 by the representative of the Company and the Parsis Bhikha Ratan and Runjee Dhanjee, is still in existence.[79] As far as one can see, the shipyards of

74 N. 68, Pt. II, 279.

75 Graham, n. 45, 45.

76 Postans, n. 53, I, 106.

77 The extract is taken from the *Gazetteer of Bombay City...*, (Bombay, 1909), II, 149.

78 W. Hamilton, *East-India Gazetteer....* (London, 1828) I, 261.

79 N. 70, 190.

Bombay were a capitalist enterprise, the fixed capital of which belonged to the East India Company and the circulating capital to Indian capitalist contractors.

An official document gave the following information with regard to the building activities in the shipyard of Bombay (Table 4.2).[80]

TABLE 4.2
Shipbuilding in Bombay

Years	*No. of ships built*	*Years*	*No. of ships built*
1735-44	7	1805-14	38
1745-54	10	1815-24	26
1755-64	2	1825-34	33
1765-74	17	1835-44	35
1775-84	14	1845-54	36
1785-94	22	1855	1
1795-04	24	1856	2

The battleship "Ganges" designed to carry 84 guns was launched in 1821, and subsequently also a number of sister-ships of the "Ganges", costing £50,000 to 60,000 each. Vessels built in Bombay were notable for their great seaworthiness and strength. Low quotes a letter written by the chief officer of a frigate hailing from Bombay to her builder Jamsetjee Bomanjee. The letter relates that a fleet of seventeen British ships spent the winter of 1808-9, in extremely difficult ice conditions, in the Baltic Sea, and that only the frigate which was built in Bombay escaped serious damage.[81]

The battleship "Asia", which carried 84 guns and had a displacement of 2883 tons, was launched in the shipyards of Bombay in 1824; it was the biggest man-of-war ever to have been built there. After the ship had taken part in the battle of Navarino, Admiral P. Malcolm sent a message to her builder Naorodjee Jamshedjee informing him that the battleship "Asia" had played a major role in the naval engagement and that the admiral was proud of the success of her builder.[82] The high quality of the ships launched in Bombay was not only due to the skill of the Parsi shipwrights but to a considerable extent also to the excellent timber used in their construction.

In 1838 the first steamship—the "Snake" an iron river-steamer with a displacement of forty tons—was built in the docks of Bombay. It was followed in 1839 by the steamsloop "Victoria", a sloop of 705 tons displacement, and a river boat with a displacement of 204 tons. Between 1838 and 1857 a total of 21 steamships was built in Bombay. The biggest

80 N. 72, 1, 391.

81 Low, n. 73, I, 279, 298.

82 *Ibid.*, II, 4.

of these were the steam-frigates "Assaye" and "Punjaub", with a displacement of 1800 tons each, built in 1854.[83]

This brief summary shows that, had India been a free country, Bombay could have become an important shipbuilding centre of sea-going vessels. But the shipyards of Bombay were, from the outset, subordinated to the interests of the British colonialists. For the East India Company it was advantageous to build for its own requirements good and cheap vessels in India, especially as they brought in big profits.[84] After the abolition of the East India Company, the British industrial bourgeoisie, who had gained direct control over India, saw in the shipyards of Bombay only a dangerous competitor. Shipbuilding was, in fact, discontinued in Bombay after 1857. Steam vessels were no longer built at all, and as regards sailingships only a few small coasting vessels were launched.[85]

The closing down of Bombay's shipyards cannot be explained by purely economic considerations. Indian-built vessels were stronger than British ones and cost 25 per cent less. Taking into account savings on repairs while the ship was in service, say for a period of fifty years, the total expenditure would amount to only a quarter of that needed for a British vessel.[86] The decision of the colonial government was based on "higher" consideration, namely, to deprive India of her shipbuilding facilities and to establish a British monopoly of maritime transport. In this respect, British capital succeeded to a high degree. By the close of the 19th century India had lost her mercantile marine; this is evident even from the official data which give the nationality of the vessels calling at Indian ports[87] (see Table 4.3).

TABLE 4.3

Nationality of Ships Calling at Indian Ports

	Indian		*British*		*Others*	
Year	*Number*	*Tonnage*	*Number*	*Tonnage*	*Number*	*Tonnage*
1857	34,286	1,219,958	59,441	2,475,472	—	—
1899	1,676	109,813	6,219	7,685,009	1,165	1,297,604

Parsi capitalists organised the production of gunpowder for the' East India Company. Existing documents show that, as early as 1677, Manjee Dhanjee received a contract for building the first large powder mill in Bombay for the East India Company, and carried it into effect.[88]

83 *Ibid.*, I, App. 4.
84 N. 68. Pt. II, 279.
85 Low, n. 73, I, 540, 541
86 W. Dighy, *"Prosperous" British India,* (London, 1901), 870.
87 *Cf. Ibid.*, 88.
88 N. 70, 186.

From the thirties of the 18th century, the East India Company's powder supplier—or to be exact, its powder-maker—was a certain Manok Manuwakh. His sons inherited this position from him in the eighties. In 1797 Bomanjee Hirjee was the supplier of gunpowder and in 1840, Merwanjee Rustamjee.[89]

A gun factory belonging to the East India Company existed in Bombay during the first half of the 19th century. We know that the foreman of this establishment was the Parsi Sorabjee Shapurjee. His position in the factory was, apparently similar to that occupied by Wadia in the shipyards, for in 1852 he was able to build a steel foundry in Bombay. Shapurjee went to England in 1850 to buy the equipment and machinery for his foundry. That this capitalist was a very rich man is also confirmed by the fact that he was the first to build a cotton-cleaning plant and a flour-mill in Bombay. His grandson was a big manufacturer and supplier of textile machinery.[90]

For a long time Bombay possessed an industry producing luxury articles which conformed to the taste of both the English and the well-to-do strata of the Indian population who imitated English fashions. As early as 1808 the Parsi Pallonjee Bomanjee opened a workshop for the manufacture of carriages, in which he at first invested only Rs 500 and assumed the name of P. B. Pankhiwalla (manufacturer of palanquins). Soon P. B. Pankhiwalla grew rich. His workshop became a fairly large establishment, apparently run on capitalist lines. It is in any case known that he paid his workers Rs 15 to 20 per month and his carriages, made in the European style, were bought not only in India but also in Iran, Afghanistan, and Singapore. The firm flourished until the introduction of the motor car, in the 20th century, struck it a heavy blow.[91]

The merchants of Bombay also derived large profits from the real estate they owned in the town. According to Maria Graham: "The Parsis are the chief landholders in Bombay. Almost all the houses and gardens inhabited by the Europeans are their property."[92]

Extremely favourable conditions thus existed for the collaboration of the big Gujarati merchants with British industrial capital, during the first half of the 19th century. The sphere of collaboration which covered a great variety of activities, included broking in commercial transactions, export of opium, credit operations, shipbuilding and other industries in Bombay. Probably no other group of Indian merchants established such firm, and one can say cordial, relations with the colonialists. But just because they had such favourable conditions for

89 H.A. Joung, *East-India Company Arsenals* (Oxford, 1937), 73, 74.

90 *Bombay Industries : The Cotton Mills*, ed. S. M. Rutnagur (Bombay, 1927), 725.

91 N. 72, I, 478.

92 Graham, n. 45, 45.

collaboration with the British, the merchants of Bombay were able to build industrial enterprises earlier than those in other parts of the country,[93] and this led subsequently to an intensification of contradictions between them and the British.

Marwari Traders and Moneylenders in the first half of the 19th Century

New opportunities for the big trading and moneylending capital arose in the first half of the 19th century not only in the coastal regions, but also in the interior of the country. The further development of commodity-moneyrelations in the Indian village received a fresh impetus early in the 19th century when British industrial capital turned India into a market for its industrial commodities, the yoke of taxation became heavier and the export of agricultural commodities—i.e. cotton, jute and indigo—began.[94] The transformation of the Indian patriarchal peasant, who was a member of the village community, into a small commodity producer created additional opportunities for his enslavement by the moneylender.

While in feudal India the usurer could use as means to enslave the peasant, who conducted a natural economy, only the debts the latter incurred to pay taxes, a natural calamity or extraordinary expenses of the peasant household; the peasant's dependence on the market now gave the usurer wider scope to exploit him either during commercial transactions or by lending him money. Moreover it was at a time when the metropolitan country exchanged, not equivalents, but unequal values with its colonies and was carrying out an unprecedented tax robbery, that the peasant household began to produce a growing proportion of commodities relative to its total output.

The former system of feudal tax-farming had been replaced by a new system of exploiting the peasant by means of commerce and

---

93 "If the cause be sought" (of the active participation of the Indians in the industry of Bombay—*V.P.*), "some indication of it may be found in the fact that Indians have held a large and important share in the trade of Bombay since the city first came into English hands. The Mahomedans of the west coast, especially, traded by sea with the Persian Gulf, Arabia and East Africa from much earlier times. The Parsees and Hindus from the northern Bombay coast districts" (i. e. from Gujarat—*V.P.*) "are recorded, at the beginning of the British occupation, as taking with the Mahomedan sects of Khojas, Memons and Bohras, a most important share in the trade of the port as contractors, merchants, financiers and shipbuilders, and have throughout shown themselves little, if at all, inferior to the Europeans in enterprise, and usually in command of more capital", *Indian Industrial Commission*. (London, 1919) I, 65.

94 For a detailed description of the methods of colonial exploitation applied during this period, see Reisner, n. 3.

moneylending. The primary unit of this new form of exploitation was the village trader and moneylender. The very fact that this local network of trading and moneylending capital was so widespread created favourable conditions for a new mass emigration of members of the Marwari caste from Rajputana.

Ravaged by feudal strife, Rajputana was, during the first half of the 19th century, by no means an ideal place for large-scale trading and moneylending operations. No provisions for the safety of life and property existed there. Bishop Heber declared that in the twenties it was as dangerous to travel in Rajputana as in Central Africa.[95] The activities of big trading and moneylending firms of the beginning in the 19th century still included the carrying of goods and money from one place to another protected by armed detachments which they hired, granting of loans to princes at high interest rates, and active participation in the commerce with neighbouring regions.[96]

The great trade route of medieval India, which started in Gujarat and led through Rajputana to the centre of the Mogul Empire finally lost its former importance in the first half of the 19th century. But a lively local trade was still carried on in the towns of Rajputana. One has to remember that the towns in Rajputana were the nuclei of agricultural oases, that were surrounded by desert regions whose inhabitants were engaged in cattle breeding. For this reason, it seems, the towns of medieval Rajputana became centres where the agriculturists and cattle breeders exchanged their produce. In any case, a document dating from the middle of the 19th century—when the feudal features were still fully preserved in the economic structure of Rajputana—stressed that there was an abundance of animal produce in town bazaars.

The principal commodities sold in the bazaar of Jodhpur, for instance, were camels, horses, cattle, sheep, hides, and horns. Only after having enumerated these, the handbook proceeds to list the traditional wares of the Indian feudal bazaar such as silk, cotton fabrics, sandal-wood, camphor, dyes, sugar, spices, salt weapons, metals, and so on.[97] There was a shortage of agricultural produce and Jodhpur, like Jaisalmer, imported rice and wheat from Sindh.[98]

But although local trade was relatively brisk, its volume remained fairly constant and thus afforded only limited scope for merchant's capital. The trading and moneylending capital of Rajputana went, therefore, beyond its borders in search of the new opportunities already provided by the colonial exploitation. The mass emigration of traders

---

95 R. Heber travelled in India in 1824-1825

96 N. 8, II, 421.

97 Thornton, n. 9, II, 724.

98 *Ibid.*, 674, 724.

and moneylenders from Rajputana was connected with their attempt to make use of the new, colonial conditions.

The Indian economist T. R. Sharma wrote that the Marwaris originally inhabited a small district in the neighbourhood of the towns of Nawalgarh and Pilani on the river Shekhavati, in Rajputana, north of Jaipur. After the establishment of British rule, their hunt for profit took them to almost all parts of India, and especially to the industrial and trading centres such as Calcutta.[99] The Bihar Banking Committee—one of the members of it was a big local Marwari shroff—declared: "They (i.e. the Marwari and Gujarati shroffs) are essentially the product of British rule".[100]

In the first half of the 19th century the Marwaris were already the strongest group among the traders and moneylenders of India. Thornton's *Gazetteer* pointed out that the inhabitants of Jodhpur were trading not only in their own country, but had flooded the neighbouring provinces, where they had managed to seize control of the majority of commercial companies.[101] In Tod's opinion "nine-tenths of the bankers and commercial men of India are natives of Maroo-desh (one of the names of Marwar) and these chiefly of the Jain faith (the majority of the Marwaris were adherents of Jainism).[102]

Tod undoubtedly exaggerated the importance of the Marwaris among Indian merchants and moneylenders. One may assume, however, that he had in mind only that region which he knew best, namely the upper and middle course of the Ganges. His views regarding the position of the Marwaris as expressed in the following passages seem to have come closer to reality: "More than half of the mercantile wealth of India passes through the hands of the Jain laity (Tod refers here to the Oswalls). The officers of the state and revenue (in the native states) are chiefly of the Jain laity, as are the majority of the bankers, from Lahore to the ocean."[103]

The Agarwal Marwaris were the strongest caste of traders and moneylenders in Bihar in the twenties of the 19th century.[104]

Maharashtra, where the cultivation of cotton led during this period to a considerable development of commodity-money relations in the countryside, became the object of special attention of Marwari traders and moneylenders. The advance of the Marwaris into Maharashtra can be traced especially clearly on the basis of data on their immigration into the western part of the region, where almost no petty Marwari

99 T. R. Sharma, *Location of Industries in India* (Bombay, 1948), 277.
100 *Bihar and Orissa Provincial Banking Enquiry Committee* (Patna, 1930), I, 186.
101 Thornton, n. 9, II, 72.
102 J. Tod, *Antiquities . . . .* (London, 1832), II, 166.
103 *Ibid.*, I, 518, 519.
104 Montgomery Martin, *The History...*, II, 161.

moneylenders lived before the 19th century. In the Nasik district, for example, the Marwaris made their appearance in the first quarter of the 19th century.[105] As regards Poona the *Bombay Gazetteer* informs us that "the Marwar Vanis came later than the Gujaratis, but were settled in the district in large numbers before the beginning of British rule."[106] The majority of Marwaris who lived in the Ahmednagar district arrived there after the establishment of British power. The *Gazetteer* of Sholapur district mentioned in 1884 that the Marwaris immigrated there about fifty years earlier.

Why did members of the Marwari community of traders and moneylenders migrate to all parts of India as a result of the establishment of colonial rule? The principal reason was that British industrial capital required the cooperation of the indigenous trading and moneylending capital in order to exploit the conquered country. For this purpose the trading and moneylending capital had to have an organisation that was sufficiently widespread—so that every peasant household could be caught in its network—and at the same time sufficiently centralised to enable British capital, which had attained a high degree of concentration by means of commerce and moneylending to exploit the working people of India, and in the first place the peasants both as producers and sellers of raw materials and as consumers of British commodities. In the rural economy of colonial India such a system was based on the financial and commercial organisation of the trading and moneylending castes, whose members formed a complicated hierarchy starting from the petty village trader and moneylender up to the big city merchant and banker. The castes were firmly held together by credit arrangements and financial relations that had developed between caste members. The trading and moneylending groups constituting the Marwari community were best suited to meet the needs of British capital not only because they formed the largest organisation of Indian traders and moneylender—apart from the Gujarati Banias—but also because Marwari bankers were already established in almost every town of North India at the time the country was conquered.

What was the nature of the business transacted by the Marwaris at this period? One has to stress that broking, or acting as middleman, played a proportionally smaller part in the business activities of Marwari trading and moneylending capital than in those of the merchants of Bombay or the Gujarati merchants in general. The reason was that the Marwaris carried on their business chiefly in remote parts of the country, where the volume of the home trade was far greater than the amounts involved in the commercial deals in which they

105 *Nasik, (Bombay Gazetteer*, XVI), 44.

106 *Poona, (Bombay Gazetteer*, XVIII, Pt. 2) (Bombay, 1885) 99.

collaborated with the British. In addition, the bankers still continued to engage, although to a diminishing extent, in the monetary, commercial and financial operations that were customary in feudal India.

Jenkins, an Englishman who visited Nagpur in 1823, wrote in his memorandum to the Council of the East India Company: "Most of the sowkars (moneylenders) in this part of the country are Marwaris. There are only two banking houses in the city conducted by Brahmans (apparently Maratha Brahmins). It is difficult to enumerate and describe their various speculations."[107] Jenkins laid particular stress on such operations as money-changing, remittance of money, commerce in gold, silver and precious stones. But the activities of the Marwaris were not confined to monetary and commercial transactions. Relates Jenkins:

> Their country business is, besides the common affairs of money exchanging, to advance cash or grain to patels and ryots. For the latter purpose, some have large stores of grain, for the loan of which they take 25 per cent for eight months, the time of repayment being usually at the harvest. They may also lend money to artisans and merchants.[108]

In addition therefore to the older kinds of business transactions—money-changing and remittances—the Marwaris began to advance grain to the cotton-growing peasants of Maharashtra.

In the Maratha country, just as in Bengal, adjustment to the new, colonial conditions necessitated a radical reorganisation of the trading and moneylending capital. The *Poona Gazetteer* writes:

> Under the Peshwas much of the revenue from their widespread possessions centred in Poona. The money came either by bills drawn from the districts upon the Poona banks, or if it was paid in cash it passed through the hands of bankers who profited by the exchange of coins before the collection reached the public treasury. Poona bankers had their agents in the districts and the ramification of the money trade in loans to the people and to the renters of villages created a wide circulation of specie, which returned to the coffers of the Poona bankers with an abundant accumulation of interest. Loans of this nature were usually repaid in grain which was received at a price much below the market rate, and thus brought great returns to the lenders. Under the British revenue system all these advantages to the capitalists disappeared.[109]

The ruin of their principal clients, the military and administrative

107 *Central Provinces Provincial Banking Enquiry Committee* (Nagpur, 1930), I, 333.
108 *Ibid.*, 334.
109 *Poona Bombay Gazetteer*, XVIII, Pt. 2, 978.

top strata of the Maratha state, dealt a heavy blow at the big moneylenders. As a result, around 1821, the business life of Poona became paralysed. Many rich, bankers were reduced to poverty.[110] But in the middle of the 19th century, when British capital started to exploit Maharashtra as a market and a source of raw materials, the business of the Marwari moneylenders in Poona began to revive.

Maharashtra's trading and moneylending capital had to adjust itself to the new, colonial conditions. Big bankers and merchants suffered heavy losses since their best customers, the Peshwa state and the great feudal lords, were crushed.[111] But when the colonial government imposed the excessive land tax, which had to be paid in cash, and destroyed the village community, it condemned the Maratha peasant to an existence outside the pale of law and to grievous dependence on the moneylender. Since the tax was collected either before the harvest began or, directly after its completion, the peasant had not enough time to sell his products, and if he did manage to sell them he could only get the low prices prevailing at this time of the year. To pay the land tax in time the ryot was, therefore, inevitably forced to borrow from the moneylender.[112]

The ryotwari land-tax system, which the British introduced in Maharashtra,with the small and middle landholdings, overburdened with taxation, that were a characteristic feature of it, accelerated the enslavement of the peasants by the moneylender. To be able to pay their taxes the peasants had to sell their cotton and wheat, the principal marketable products of the rural economy, to the moneylender.[113] The tax oppression thus increased artificially the ratio of commodity output in the semi-natural peasant household and intensified the peasant's dependence on trading and moneylending capital.

But in the twenties, and partly also in the thirties, of the 19th century, the colonial regime hampered the activities of the moneylending capital to a certain extent, for it appropriated not only the surplus product but also part of the necessary product. It is significant that the first big influx of Marwaris into Thana district, on the sea coast opposite Bombay, occurred in connection with the sharp decrease of the tax in 1835-37, which made land valuable.[114]

---

110 *Ibid.*

111 *Ibid.*, 188.

112 Choksey, n. 16, 107. According to Chaplin who occupied an important position in the Indian Civil Service in Maharashtra, the exertions of the ryot to rid himself of his debts could be compared "to the hellish torments of Sisyphus who had no sooner rolled his burden to the summit of the hill than it fell back on him with redoubled violence" (*Ibid.*, 186).

113 *Ibid.*, 309.

114 *Thana, (Bombay Gazetteer*, VIII, Pt. I). (Bombay, 1882), 308.

Merchant's capital, deprived to a considerable extent of orders from its feudal customers, began to participate in the cotton export trade as early as 1820. The necessity to import grain into Maharashtra was moreover increased by the ruin of the peasant economy and harvest failures. The colonial authorities, who mercilesely fleeced the ryots, naturally granted tax privileges to the moneylenders.

No documentary evidence exists showing that Marwari moneylenders were ruined. It seems that the Marwaris were able to adjust themselves to the conditions obtaining in Maharashtra during the period of transition, when the old system of feudal exploitation was already wrecked and the system of colonial oppression, which made use of commercial and money capital and of the remnants of feudalism surviving in the countryside, only began to take shape. What is more, the increasing penetration of small traders and moneylenders into the villages during the first half of the 19th century prepared Marwari capital for the role it was to play as agent of British capital when India was exploited by imperialist methods.

Thus in the period of the colonial exploitation of India by British industrial capital, the representatives of Indian trading and moneylending capital who collaborated with the British considerably increased their monetary resources. These accumulated funds were made up of both that part of the colonial plunder which British capital was forced to forgo in favour of their Indian collaborators, and profits from independent commercial and moneylending operations, mainly in the countryside.

During the first half of the 19th century, the big Indian merchants and moneylenders continued, as a rule, to act as reliable political supporters of the British intruders. Lieutenant-Colonel W. H. Sleeman, who served in India for many years, declared: "There is no class of men more interested in the stability of our rule in India than that of the respectable merchants; nor is there any upon whom the welfare of our government, and of the people, more depends".[115]

Many big Indian traders, independent of their nationality and caste, continued during the national uprising to serve faithfully those who were inflicting punishment on the insurgents. The gazetteers of those districts of the United Provinces that were affected by the revolt were full of reports about the "loyalty" of the top strata of the native merchants and moneylenders. For the services they rendered during the uprising—making available money and provisions and organising detachments to fight against the insurgents—many traders and

115 W. H. Sleeman, *Rambles and Recollections of an Indian Official* (London, 1844), II, 143.

116 *Ghazipur*, 110; *Banda*, 109; *Allahabad*, 189; *Moradabad*, 168; (published in the series : *District Gazetteers of the United Provinces*, Allahabad, 1909-1911).

moneylenders were rewarded with estates and titles.[116] Among the recipients of these rewards was Abirchand Daga, a forefather of the contemporary monopolists of the same name.[117] Merchants of Panipat supplied grain to the British troops at Delhi.[118]

It is true that several merchants gave financial support to the government of Bahadur Khan in Delhi. In one day alone bankers contributed Rs 100,000 to the coffers of the insurgents.[119] But Bahadur Khan applied strong pressure to obtain these loans. The following incident is well-known. The emperor ordered that two bankers be brought to his palace and asked them for a loan; when the bankers declared that the war had ruined them, Bahadur Khan angrily reminded them of the fact that one of their partners had already given the British Rs 30,000. Thereupon the bankers loosened their purse-strings and handed over Rs 50,000.[120] To pay the sepoys, some commanders of the insurgents simply imposed levies on the bankers towards the end of the uprising.[121] The merchants of Delhi besieged Bahadur Khan with complaints about the losses they suffered as a result of requisitions made for the needs of the mutineers.

By no means all Indian merchants, however, supported the colonial regime. Anti-British sentiments were apparently still rather strong among a section of the merchants, particularly in the interior of the country where they were to a smaller extent able to offset the loss of their traditional business by acting as middleman of the British.[122] Some information exists, although it is rather scanty, showing that merchants participated in the national uprising. For instance, letters of Punjabi Banias have been discovered addressed to sepoys of the local forces, in which they tell them that soon the day will be fixed when the uprising is to begin, and that all Indian soldiers should come out against the British raj. After the insurrection had broken out in Delhi, the shops of the Punjabis became centres of political discussions during which the question was examined whether a repetition of the events which had

117 N. 107, II, 495, 496.

118 C. T. Metcalf, *Two Native Narratives of the Mutiny of Delhi* (Westminster, 1892) 155.

119 *Ibid.*, 113.

120 *Ibid.*, 174.

121 *Ibid.*, 200.

122 On the basis of documentary sources Gadgil stresses that commerce and the handicrafts declined in Lucknow the capital of Oudh, after the annexation of this principality by the English and the suppression of the uprising. The section of the population that had been attracted by the special conditions existing for commerce under the native government, left the town (Gadgil, n. 30, 9).

123 *The Crisis in Punjab, from the 10th of May until the fall of Delhi*, by a Punjab Employee, (Lahore, 1858), 17, 18.

taken place in Delhi was necessary.[123]

Little investigation has so far been undertaken to discover—why a section of Indian merchants from Hindustan and the Punjab supported the uprising. But whether their assistance to the insurgents was given voluntarily or involuntarily the reason for it can on no account have been that the economic contradictions between these merchants and the colonial regime had become more intensive and had developed further than the contradictions that existed between the colonial regime and the bourgeoisie that had come into being in the older colonial centres of British India, for example, Bombay or Calcutta. We consider, their attitude during the insurrection was determined by the fact that the century-old links between the merchants of Delhi, the Punjab and Oudh on the one hand and the local feudal chiefs and the feudal economy as a whole on the other, were still comparatively strong. The patriotism of these merchants was an offspring of feudal patriotism and perished with it in the fire of destruction.

Considered from an historical point of view the future belonged to those first shoots of bourgeois nationalism, that were still weak and sometimes twisted but which, from the middle of the 19th century onwards, began though still rather timidly to force their way through to the political life of India. To study this development seriously one must first of all examine the press of that period. But so far we did not have this opportunity. Therefore, we shall merely give a few examples.

In 1853, when the British Parliament considered a new bill dealing with the East India Company's rule in India, many Indian public organisations and private individuals sent petitions to the House of Commons in which they expressed their wishes regarding the political and economic course of the colonial regime.

The petition presented by the Bombay Association asked the House of Commons to grant India a constitution which was to retain the "best elements" of the existing system but make the administration less cumbersome, and at the same time more accessible (to the Indians, of course) and overt and also to a greater extent responsible, effective and acceptable (again to the Indians).[124] Seeking to limit the powers exercised by the oligarchy of the East India Company, the Bombay merchants suggested that the Council for Indian Affairs should be directly responsible to the House of Commons. The petitioners also made the request, though it was hedged in by various reservations, to reduce the salaries of English officials in India. Furthermore, they declared "that the time has arrived when the Natives of India are entitled to a much larger share than they have hitherto had in the administration of the

124 *Minutes of Evidence Taken before Select Committee on the Government on Indian Territories* (Parliamentary Papers, 33), London, 1853, 228.

affairs of their country".[125] Therefore, they proposed that Indians be admitted to the provincial councils of the government and to judicial and administrative bodies. The members of the Bombay Association also stressed that the industry of their presidency needed railways and highways and an extension of harbour facilities.[126] Finally they pointed out that it was wrong to spend a mere £12,500 on the education of ten million inhabitants of the presidency while the land-tax alone exceeded £1,000,000.[127]

The Madras Native Association underlined that the amount of land-tax levied by the colonial administration was without parallel in the history of India and asked that at least part of the tax be used for irrigation and the construction of roads. Thanks to the ryot's labour, wrote the petitioners, money was always available to wage wars of self-aggrandisement, to pay British Civil Servants excessive salaries and grant them pensions of £300 per annum, and to pay dividends of 10 per cent to the stockholders of the East India Company; but when the ryot needed a new road to improve his condition he was told that he must build it himself.[128]

The British Indian Association of Bengal—in the leadership of which predominated rich Bengali zamindars but Parsi and other non-Bengali traders were also represented—asked in its petition for a reduction of the land-tax, which was paid by the zamindars in Bengal; encouragement of commerce and industry; construction of public works; the abolition of the huge monopoly of the East India Company and a restriction of the Free Trade, which led to a decline of the local industry. The petition suggested that appointment to the higher administrative posts should be based on the candidate's personal experience, ability and his knowledge of the languages and—laws of the country.[129] This was obviously in the interest of the feudal strata of Bengal, for, if promotions were made on the basis of these conditions, their representatives would undoubtedly have advantages over the young Civil Servants sent from Britain. The petition expressed the desire to alter the administrative system of India, because the Board of Control and the Board of Directors of the Company had not sufficient responsibility.[130] The familiar requests to lower the salaries of the officials and to abolish the salt and opium monopolies were not forgotten either. But the fact that opium was 'freely' sold in Bengal

125 *Ibid.*, 229. (The quotation is taken from R. Dutt, *Economic History of India*, Delhi, 1960, II, 140).
126 *Ibid.*, 231.
127 *Ibid.*, 132.
128 *Ibid.*, 212.
129 *Ibid.*, 216.
130 *Ibid.*, 217

fully satisfied the Bengali merchants.[131]

The petitions submitted by the representatives of the wealthy strata of the three Indian presidencies contain no essential differences. They all expressed their loyalty to the colonial regime, both in form and in substance. None of them uttered any desire for self-government, even in a limited form which preserved the sovereign power of the British Empire. The petitioners merely asked that the absolute rule of the Board of Directors of the Company and the Board of Control be, somewhat, restricted. They undoubtedly took into account that, in this respect, their request coincided with the aspirations of the British industrial bourgeoisie who urged their representatives in the House of Commons to hand over to them the direct government of this colony, the richest of the British Empire. The desire to lower the salaries of the colonial officials did not affect the British manufacturers either, for the Indian Civil Service consisted chiefly of the sons of ruined noblemen.

Their economic wishes merely amounted to a request for reduction of the land-tax (the taxes levied on commerce were quite small) and a rather vague reminder that some encouragement ought to be given to the native industry. To what extent these most loyal petitions reflected the true interests of the merchants in such big ports as Bombay, Madras and Calcutta is difficult to say. But it is possible that, at this time, their aspirations did not go further than to throw off the restrictions imposed by the East India Company and to become free contractors in relation to the British industrial and commercial firms.

Bholanath Chunder's book, *The Travels of a Hindoo to various Parts of Bengal and Upper India,* helps, us to understand the views of the rising Indian bourgeoisie. At first the work appeared in an English newspaper published in Calcutta, and was then issued in two volumes in London. The travels—or to be more accurate, business trips—of the author, a Bania from Bengal, took place between 1845 and 1866. The whole book, written in good English, is pervaded by loyalty to the colonial order. It begins with a dedication to Sir John L. M. Lawrence, Viceroy and Governor-General of India. The author glorifies British "law and order", the administration and the railways.[132] Reading the table of contents of this book, which consists of an enumeration of the remarkable places through which Chunder passed in the course of his journeys, one gets the impression that he was trying to see his country through the eyes of a European.

The author wrote with bitterness about the neglected state in which he found the palace of the Jagat Seths and about the decline of the urban handicrafts. Although a European traveller might also have noticed this, only an Indian capitalist could deplore the fact that Indians

131 *Ibid.*, 258.
132 Chunder, n. 1, I, 64, 65, 140, 141.

were obliged to wear clothes made exclusively of British textiles and look forward to the day when their sons and grandsons would wear garments consisting entirely of Indian cotton cloth produced by Indian manufacturers.[133] Chunder reproached the colonial powers with extravagance, because they constructed magnificent administrative buildings and residencies in Calcutta.[134]

But feudal conceptions had still a very strong hold on this newly-fledged Indian bourgeois. He could only cherish a faint hope that perhaps in the 20th century or the 21st Indians would be able to sink mines and build factories, although at that time he could have seen factories in Bombay that belonged to Indian capitalists. According to Chunder, India's industrial future depended on the dissemination of knowledge and enterprise, and not on the national liberation of the country.[135] These considerations were not set out merely in deference to the colonial censorship, for the author declared in his conclusion that Indian reasoning had never known and never tried to understand any form of government except despotism.[136] Since, in his opinion, neither constitutional monarchy nor a republic was appropriate to Indian conditions, he suggested that the Indian princelings should be taught the elements of good government and good conduct.[137] Apparently, his political aspiration went no further than a sort of enlightened Indian monarchy under the aegis of the British.

The incipient bourgeoisie of India was for a long time unable to free itself of the illusion that it could become an equal member of bourgeoisie that embraced the whole empire. The Indians who drew up the petitions mentioned earlier stubbornly repeated that the protection of their rights as Her Majesty's most loyal subjects was all they desired. Indian merchants sent their children to the Elphinstone Institution of Bombay and other colleges where the young Indian bourgeois were educated in the English manner. Even at the close of the 19th century so clever and advocate of the interests of the Bombay bourgeoisie as Dadabhai Naoroji tried to use the rostrum of the House of Commons—to which he was elected on the ticket of the British Liberal Party—to convince the British bourgeoisie that the colonial government they practised in India was at variance with bourgeois common sense. These illusions of the precursors of the Indian bourgeoisie are reminiscent of the hopes cherished by the representatives of the third estate in Europe who strove for admission into the ranks of the aristocracy.

---

133 *Ibid.*, 169.
134 *Ibid.*, II, 273.
135 *Ibid.*, I, 169.
136 *Ibid.*, II, 408.
137 *Ibid.*, 408, 409.

The Indian bourgeoisie had to learn its lesson from its own lengthy economic and political experience before it recognised that it could not merge into the bourgeoisie of the ruling nation. In the capitalist era, the individual capitals of entrepreneurs from different nations began to show wide variations not only in their composition and the sphere of their activity (which meant that the specific weight and importance of trading and moneylending capital differed from those of the industrial capital) but also in the rates of profit they commanded. The boundary which divided British industrial capital and Indian merchant's capital was simultaneously the barrier separating the representatives of these different forms of capital, i.e. the British industrial bourgeoisie and the Indian merchants.[138] Similarly, in the imperialist period, the Indian bourgeoisie personifying trading, moneylending and industrial capital was separated by an insuperable barrier from the British monopolists who represented financial capital. The fact that British and Indian entrepreneurs participated in the same companies did not substantially alter the position, for it did not signify the merging or fusion of their capitals but simply meant that British capital subordinated and utilised Indian capital. But this problem will be considered in the next part of the book.

138 One of the manifestations of this division was the racial discrimination shown by British imperialists in relation to the Indian bourgeoisie. For instance, Dadabhoy Naorojee who, at the beginning of his public activities, made every effort to improve relations between the British and the Indian bourgeoisie was called by Lord Salisbury "a black man". By insulting in this manner the representative of the Indian bourgeoisie who had dared to stand for Parliament in Great Britain, the British imperialist wanted to put him in his proper place (*The Voice of India, January*, 1885, 52-58).

PART II

ORIGIN AND DEVELOPMENT OF INDIAN BOURGEOISIE

CHAPTER V

EARLY CAPITALIST DEVELOPMENT

As we have stated earlier, already in the second and third decades of the 19th century began the import, on a mass scale, of British machine-made commodities into India and the export of Indian raw materials. These were the first steps taken by British industrial capital towards the transformation of India into an agrarian and raw material appendage. The export of Indian raw materials and the importation of British machine-made goods had substantially increased by the middle of the 19th century, but had not yet reached an extent justifying us in describing the utilisation of India as an agrarian and raw material adjunct, as the principal method of exploitation employed by British capital in this country. Revenue from tax robbery still occupied the first place in the colonial loot

Although it is true that we do not possess records of the profits obtained from either the sale of British commodities in India or the export of indigenous raw material from there, the volume of the foreign trade proves that it was impossible for commercial profits to surpass tax receipts. For example, the gross revenue of the colonial treasury for the financial year 1856-57 was £31,691,000 and £17,722,000 of this total was derived from the land-tax alone. It is difficult to calculate the "net" revenue from the fiscal receipts. But it must, in any case, have been very large if one considers that the home charges alone amounted to £3,529,000 while the trade turnover of Britain and India in the fifties fluctuated between £20 and £30 million per annum. Even if trade brought in a very high rate of profit, the sum total could hardly have been higher than the "net" revenue obtained by the tax robbery which was perpetrated on the Indian population.[1]

The conversion of colonial India into an agricultural appendage which supplied raw materials for Britain was accelerated in the fifties

1. See Romesh Dutt, *The Economic History of India* (Delhi, 1960) II, 160-212. In 1852, the duties levied on the opium trade alone brought the colonial administration Rs 26,800,000 or 10 per cent of its fiscal receipts. J. W. Kaye, *The Administration of the East India Company*, 148.

and sixties, when the British capitalists sharply stepped up the export of raw materials, especially cotton, from India. But the export trade was hampered by lack of roads. That is why the British began to build railways in the 1850s. Marx wrote in 1853: "the English millocracy intend to endow India with railways with the exclusive view of extracting at diminished expenses the cotton and other raw materials for their manufactures."[2] The export of British capital to India, which started in the middle of the 19th century, was at first not an independent measure, for its immediate purpose was to speed up as much as possible the supply of raw materials.

Railways remained the main object of British capital investments in India throughout the latter half of the 19th century. By 1870, more than 7,700 km of railway track had been laid in India and Rs 900 million spent on this construction; the corresponding figures for 1900 were 39,000 km and Rs 3,295 million[3]—part of the money came from the British colonial authorities and Indian princes and capitalists. The investment of British capital in manufacturing enterprises, mining and the extractive industries in general began in the middle of the 19th century. British capitalists started to operate the first jute mills near Calcutta in the 1850s and the cotton mills of Kanpur in the sixties. Thousands of small mechanised enterprises sprang up in the cotton and jute growing regions to carry out the initial processing of these agricultural raw materials.

Another important sphere of British capital investment aiming at the exploitation of the country as an agrarian and raw material base was the construction of irrigation works. During the last quarter of the 19th century its chief objects were the Punjab and Sindh, two regions which rapidly became the main producers of cotton and wheat for the export trade. Construction of irrigation works in other parts of the country were also undertaken with the view of increasing the cultivation of export crops. By 1902, £24 million had been invested in irrigation works.[4] The building of an irrigation system proved a very profitable enterprise for the British. By utilising the taxation machinery, the colonialists had by 1900-01 obtained a net profit of Rs 20,700,000 from the state irrigation works.[5]

In 1890-91 the total capital invested in the state railways and other installations belonging to the colonial government amounted to Rs 957 million. The direct investments of British capital in India reached £365

---

2 Karl Marx and Frederick Engels, *The First Indian War of Independence 1857-1859*, (Moscow) 35-6.

3 *Indian Railways.One Hundred Years*, (Delhi, 1953), 187-88.

4 Dutt, n. 1, II, 550.

5 *Report of the Indian Irrigation Commission*, (London, 1903), I, 24.

million in 1909-10. In other words, at the beginning of the imperialist era, capital investment became the principal means of extracting colonial tribute from India.

The import of British capital—invested in the construction of railways and enterprises for the processing of raw materials—created the conditions which made it possible to expand rapidly the exportation of agricultural products.

Value of Agricultural Raw Materials Exported from India

(In £ thousand)

				Year		
Raw Materials		*1849*	*1865*	*1880*	*1914*	
Cotton		...	1,700	37,573	11,145	22,000
Jute	...	...	68	1,410	4,370	8,600
Grain		...	858	5,956	6,170	19,300

Source: Statistical Abstract Relating to British India, (London, 1870, 1882) R. Palme Dutt, *India To-day*, (London, 1940), p. 1[illegible]1-2.

The proportion of India's traditional export commodities, indigo and opium, decreased at the same time, within the total volume of her foreign trade. In 1862-63 opium in terms of value made up a quarter of the total exports, while in 1883-84 it only amounted to one eighth.[6] Indian economists stressed the fact that goods were exported under coercion. Romesh Dutt, for instance, wrote:

> India presents a busy scene to the winter globe-trotter when these transactions take place in every large town and market; but under the cheering appearance of a brisk grain trade lies concealed the fact that the homes and villages of a cultivating nation are denuded of their food to a fatal extent, in order to meet that annual tribute which England demands from India.[7]

During the last three decades of the 19th century imports of British commodities continued to grow rapidly. Their volume in the five-year period in 1885-89 had quadrupled as compared to the five-year period 1855-59.[8]

Between the sixties and nineties of the last century, the increasingly colonial character of Indian foreign trade was also reflected in its commodity structure, although in connection with the beginning

6 *Statistical Tables for British India*, (Calcutta, 1885), 156.

7 Dutt, n. 1, II, 261.

8 W.W. Hunter, *The Indian Empire: Its Peoples, History and Products*, (London, 1892), 665.

capitalist development of the country a few new articles also made their appearance. In 1890-91 the chief exports were grain (which amounted to 19 per cent of the total export trade), cotton (provided 16.5 per cent), opium (9 per cent), and jute (7.5 per cent); but cotton twist and yarn (6.5 per cent) and cotton cloth (2.4 per cent) already occupied a significant place. The main imports were textiles, which made up 40 per cent of the total, while machinery and railway equipment only amounted to 2 per cent each.[9]

The relation between import and export prices did not change substantially in the period under review. But the production costs of the commodities produced by the British machine industry fell owing to technical advances, while the conditions of production of the Indian export goods remained unaltered. The consequence was a growing disparity in the values that were actually exchanged between India and Britain.

The excess of exports over imports, substantial though it was, did not reflect the whole weight of the colonial exploitation. The crux of the matter was that the commodity exchange which took place between colonial and semi-feudal India on the one hand and capitalist Britain on the other, was by its very nature not an exchange of equivalents. The amount of socially necessary labour expended in the production of the commodities that were exchanged was considerably smaller in Britain than in India. The price of Indian commodities should, therefore, have been higher, but while in reality British commodities in India were sold more or less in accordance with their cost of production, the Indian peasants and craftsmen were forced to sell the products of their labour without taking into consideration their costs of production, for they urgently needed the money to pay the huge land tax, the rent due to the landlord, or the debt incurred with the moneylender. Brute force was also frequently used to fix the price, for example, in the cultivation of indigo and the opium poppy. Marx wrote about the export of agricultural commodities from India: "These products were sold without regard to price of production, they were sold at the price which the dealer offered, because the peasant perforce needed money without fail when taxes became due."[10] Sale without regard to the cost and price of production—achieved by the colossal pressure of colonial exploitation to which the Indian peasant was subjected—made it possible to sell the agricultural products of colonial and feudal India on the capitalist world market.

Although the weight of taxation was somewhat reduced, in the 1880s India still remained the country with the highest level of taxation.

9 *Ibid.*, 668, 671.

10 Karl Marx, *Capital*, (Moscow, 1959), III, 710.

Dadabhai Naoroji declared that during this period taxes absorbed 14.5 per cent of India's national income, while British taxes represented only 6.92 per cent of Britain's national income.[11] For a country as poor as India such a level of taxation was an excessive burden.

The land tax was still the principal revenue of the Indian budget. It amounted, in 1871-72, to 42 per cent of the total tax receipts.[12] Although the rate of taxation was reduced in the sixties and seventies as compared with the middle of the 19th century, the total volume it brought in did not decrease at all, but on the contrary rose from Rs 181 million in 1858-59 to Rs 240 million in 1889-90.[13]

The revenue of the Indian colonial government, whose main source was direct and indirect taxation, jumped from Rs 361 million in 1858-59 to Rs 851 million in 1889-90.[14] The growing tax burden was an indication of the increasing exploitation of India as an agricultural and raw material appendage of Britain. The taxes compelled the peasant to sell a considerable part of the production of his household. This helped the British to extract the raw materials from the country. Describing the development of the international grain trade, Marx pointed out that the peasants in Russia and India "had to sell a portion of their produce, and a constantly increasing one at that, for the purpose of obtaining money for taxes wrung from them—frequently by means of torture—by a ruthless and despotic state".[15] Old methods of colonial exploitation were, thus, at the beginning of the new historical epoch, made to serve new aims, namely, the extortion of raw materials for the requirements of the home country.

It has, so far, not been possible to establish the exact size of the tribute extracted, for some of its constituent elements have been completely omitted and others not fully revealed in the British statistics; this was partly due to methodological weakness but chiefly to understandable political considerations. W. Digby, perhaps the only British economist who tried to examine the question objectively, quoted the following data: at the beginning of the eighties the Indian public debt—imposed on India by the colonialists and chiefly in the hands of British shareholders—had reached £150 million and private British investments in production (mainly in plantations) came to a similar figure. Adding to this the capital invested in railways and the capitalised income of British officials, Digby concluded that British interests in

11 *The Voice of India*, (October, 1887), 476.

12 *Statement Exhibiting the Moral and Material Progress and Condition of India during the years 1871-1872*, 150.

13 *Statistical Abstracts Relating to British India, from 1880-1881, to 1889-1890.* (London, 1891), 300.

14 *Ibid.*

15 Marx, n. 10, III, 709-10.

India amounted to £500 million.[16] Even on the assumption that the rate of interest was 8 to 10 per cent (which is obviously an underestimate), the British bourgeoisie must have drawn £40 to 50 million a year from India.

The well-known British official, H.J.S. Cotton, reckoned that, according to the lowest estimates, Britain received annually from India £30 million, of which 17 million were compulsory transfers to the metropolitan country the so-called home charges.[17] W. W. Hunter asserted that between 1885 and 1891 two items of the colonial tribute alone—namely the sum total of dividends yielded by British investments and the money transmitted by the Indian treasury to that of Britain, the so-called home charges—added up to £30 million per annum.[18]

One has to remember that even these estimates only cover "net dividends" received by the British bourgeoisie. They do not take into account such important, visible and invisible, components of the colonial tribute as the profits arising from the existing disparity in the exchange of commodities and from shipping profits reinvested, the enormous sums spent on the maintenance of the military and administrative apparatus of colonial oppression and on predatory wars. The army and administration absorbed three-fifth of the fiscal revenue, half of which was sent abroad.[19] If these indispensable elements of the colonial tribute are included, the total must, undoubtedly, have exceeded £100 million per year.

The direct result of the imperialist and feudal exploitation was the impoverishment of the great mass of the population. According to the estimates of Dadabhai Naoroji, who played an outstanding part in the national movement at this time, the average income per head of the population at the end of the 1870s amounted to only 40 shillings per annum.[20]

In years of harvest failure huge regions suffered from disastrous famines. According to official data, in 1860-61 famine affected an area with a population of 20 million; in 1865-66 it affected 48 million people; in 1868-69, 44 million people in 1873-74, 21 million and in 1876-78, 58 million people.[21] The intensification of the colonial exploitation of the country led to more frequent famines and to an enormous rise in the mortality. While between 1825 and 1850 India suffered twice from famines, in which 400,000 persons died, famines occurred six times

16 W. Digby, *India for the Indian—and for England* (London, 1885), 201–02.
17 H. J. S. Cotton, *New India or India in Transition* (London, 1896), 61, 113-15.
18 Hunter, n. 8, 662.
19 Digby, n. 16, 85.
20 Dadabhai Naoroji, *Poverty and Un-British Rule in India* (London, 1901), 2.
21 *Report of the Indian Famine Commission*, Part I, (London, 1880), 24.

between 1850 and 1875 and eighteen times between 1875 and 1900 causing 5 million and 26 million deaths respectively.[22]

The beginning of the imperialist stage of India's colonial exploitation, which led to a deterioration in the material conditions of the great bulk of the population, caused radical changes in its social and economic structure.

As early as the sixties and seventies of the 19th century, British industrial capital introduced additional methods of exploitation in India characteristic of imperialism, namely, capital import and export of raw materials at an increased rate. It conforms to the laws determining historical development that Britain transformed India so early into an object of imperialist exploitation. Lenin pointed out that "two important distinguishing features of imperialism were already observed in Great Britain in the middle of the nineteenth century, viz., vast colonial possessions and a monopolist position in the world market".[23]

The presence of imperialist features in Britain as early as the middle of the 19th century was, to a large extent, due to the fact that by exploitating the nations inhabiting its immense colonial empire, British industrial capital considerably accelerated its own development and, even at that time, showed signs of decay. The influence which the tribute received from the colonies exerted on the capitalist development of Great Britain has been recognised and studied for a long time. It is of considerably greater interest that each new stage in the development of capitalism in Britain gave rise to new methods of colonial exploitation and had a strong influence on the economic structure of the colonies. The determining role in the economic interaction of Britain and India obviously belonged to the home country, that is, British capitalism created conditions in the colony that were most favourable for the extraction of tribute which helped to accelerate its own development.

Lenin stressed that the precapitalist methods of exploitation caused the colonies to participate only in the commodity exchange and not in the capitalist mode of production itself. "Imperialism changed this. Imperialism is, among other things, the export of capital. Capitalist production is being transplanted to the colonies at an ever increasing rate".[24] It is true that the methods employed by merchant's capital, and later on by industrial capital, merely involved India in the commodity exchange with the home country, but did not give rise to new relations of production. It was only when methods characteristic of the last stage of capitalism were used to exploit the country that a stimulus was given to the growth of capitalism in India, the basis for which had

22 M. B. Nanavati and J. J. Anjaria, *The Indian Rural Problem* (Bombay, 1947), 19.

23 V. I. Lenin, *Imperialism, the Highest Stage of Capitalism* (Moscow, 1961), 184.

24 V. I. Lenin, *Questions of National Policy and Proletarian Internationalism* (Moscow, 1960), 172.

undoubtedly been prepared by the country's preceding development.

It would be a mistake to underestimate the economic progress which had taken place in India between the middle of the 18th century and the middle of the 19th. The destructive work of the British cleared the ground, although by no means sufficiently for the emergence of capitalism. The old social division of labour, based on natural interrelations within the community, had been undermined, as was the former system of landownership and land tenure.

In addition to these negative prerequisites, a number of positive preconditions necessary for the advance of capitalism also came into being during the first century of colonial rule. In the course of their collaboration with British industrial capital, the Indian merchants set up a commercial organisation that was able, when the need arose, to serve local capitalist production as well. The first rudiments of industrial production made their appearance, for example, the shipyards in Bombay, enterprises for the processing of cotton and indigo, mines, and so on. And finally, the Indian merchants and handicraftsmen, especially in the big ports, formed a mental picture of modern capitalist techniques; they advanced, so to speak, in their thoughts from the Middle Ages to the era of industrial capitalism. As early as 1853 Marx wrote: "the Hindus are allowed by British authorities themselves to possess particular aptitude for accommodating themselves to entirely new labour, and acquiring the requisite knowledge of machinery."[25]

One must, however, emphasise that the "grafting" of capitalism by means of British capital export (including reinvestments of profits derived from India) led only to the formation of capitalist relations in a very narrow section of industry and transport, i.e., in the railways and some dozens of industrial establishments, in the main textile factories. In other words, a trifling proportion of large-scale industrial enterprises and the total absence of the production of modern means of production are characteristic features of the "industrialisation" of colonial India.

According to British estimates 177 cotton mills operated in India in 1898, employing 156 thousand workers, that is on the average 800 workers per factory. £14,900,000 were invested in this branch of production of which one-third belonged to British capitalists. Capital investments in the jute industry amounted to £4,985,000. We have no information with regard to the nationality of the owners, but all the 33 jute mills, employing 95 thousand workers—which represents a still higher level of concentration—were controlled by British managing agencies.[26]

---

25 Marx and Engels, n. 2, 36.

26 Managing agencies frequently acted as founders of companies and bought the necessary machinery after; the enterprise started working they provided it with the resources required to meet current expenditure, were responsible

In the other spheres of industrial and agricultural production—such as wool-weaving and paper mills, cotton-ginning enterprises, oil-mills, rice-husking factories, sugar refineries, tea, coffee and indigo plantations—three quarters of the capital belonged to the British. If one takes further into account that Indians owned no more than £10 million out of the joint-stock capital of £35.5 million[27] the dominating position which, at the end of the 19th century, British capital occupied in the large-scale enterprises of India, becomes obvious.

Notwithstanding the transplantation of the capitalist mode of production to the colonies, a factor which at first accelerated the rate of capitalist development, imperialist exploitation played an essentially antagonistic role and, in the final analysis acted as a drag on the development of capitalism in the colonies. The reactionary influence which imperialism exerted in the colonies was most forcefully revealed during the period of the general crisis of capitalism, that is, after the first World War. But already from the close of the 19th century onwards, British capitalism made use of the state apparatus to suppress all tendencies towards independent progress, which the young Indian capitalism was bound to exhibit. British colonial oppression could, of course, not cancel the effects of the objective laws governing the development of Indian capitalism, but could only distort them. The British and the Indian bourgeoisie were, therefore, unable to overcome the contradictions that arose between them, although each side tried hard to maintain their former "cordial" relationship in the new conditions.

In the course of imperialist exploitation an economic environment was created which was conducive to the formation of capitalist relations on a mass scale; this was of great importance for the development of Indian capitalism. Such an environment favourable to the growth of capitalism arose in the branches of agriculture and industry which rapidly lost the patriarchal features of the natural economy and evolved a structure appropriate to small commodity production. The cultivation of agricultural raw materials for export irrevocably destroyed the natural self-sufficiency of the Indian village community, accelerated the formation of a capitalist home market, including a market for labour power which consisted of expropriated handicraftsmen and peasants. As Marx wrote: "Modern industry, resulting from the railway system, will dissolve the hereditary division of labour".[28] But while imperialism destroyed the old relations, it retarded the growth of new capitalist

---

for the sale of its products and in fact, controlled the whole of its work. Subsequently many British, and later also Indian, managing agencies became monopoly organisations.

27 W. Digby, *Prosperous British India*, 108–09.

28 Marx and Engels, n. 2, 36.

relations and this was the objective reason chiefly responsible for the antagonistic conflict which existed between imperialism on the one hand and the peasants and craftsmen of India on the other.

The new, imperialist methods of exploitation gave a certain impetus to the development of capitalism in India. But the restriction of capitalist development within the narrow framework of colonialism and feudalism was the necessary condition for this form of exploitation and of the colonial rule in general. British imperialism, therefore, substantially strengthened its hold on the political and economic life of its colony.

The colonialists made use of the slogans of the Free Traders to hold back the development of the Indian national industry. They asserted that a vigorous enterprise required no assistance from the state. But in the latter half of the 19th century when the uneven development of capitalism became particularly apparent in individual countries, the economic progress of the countries that were lagging behind depended to an increasing extent on state support. Even if under these conditions the colonial apparatus had merely refrained from interfering in the economic life of India, it would already have been a strong impediment. But British imperialism did not simply ignore India's development but hampered it on purpose. With the aid of the powerful military and political apparatus which it had built up in the colonies, imperialism, for many decades, mercilessly suppressed any protest of the masses of the population against the oppression to which they were subjected by the landlords, moneylenders, and the colonialists. That was why the colonial regime had to be overthrown before the progressive forces of the Indian society were, in the course of the class struggle, able to abolish the medieval relations of production that were holding back the capitalist development of the country. Right up to the time they "went", the British put down the smallest manifestation of the peasant movement and maintained the feudal property rights of the landlords, which were the greatest obstacle blocking the path of India's social progress.

From the very beginning of the colonial conquest, it was the aim of the British agrarian policy to adapt the feudal relations prevailing in the country for the exploitation of the peoples of India by British capitalism. Changes in the methods of colonial exploitation, in their turn, introduced new elements into the agrarian policy pursued by the British authorities. The increasing exploitation of India as an agricultural and raw material appendage of capitalist Britain, employing methods of industrial capitalism in the latter half of the 19th century, obliged the colonial powers to introduce land-tax reforms in the ryotwari and temporary zamindari systems, which were accomplished in the sixties and seventies.

The legal sanctification and consolidation of private landownership and the reductions in the rate of the land tax carried through at the same time, meant that feudal land property held by individuals had been definitely established in India. But this process took place when India's exploitation as an agricultural and raw material appendage of the home country exerted an increasing influence on its economy, when India gradually became part of the world system of capitalist economy, and when a capitalist structure of society developed in India. The strengthening of the private property rights of the Indian landlords—although it indicated that the feudal relations were preserved as an important feature of the whole system of the country's colonial exploitation—under these circumstances, became the direct prerequisite for the decline of feudal property and the rise of capitalist property. The appearance of mature forms of feudal relations in colonial India was quickly followed by their decay.

The pre-capitalist exploitation of the peasants was to an increasing extent accomplished by means of capitalist market relations and therefore assumed a semi-feudal character. Feudal landownership became essentially a feudal relic preserved by the British colonialists.

The fact that the colonial state remained the supreme landowner gave rise to a certain antagonism between the colonialists and the Indian landlords. In the economic sphere, this became evident when the rent levied on the peasants was divided between the landlords and the colonial state. It is worth noting that where the land tax, which was paid by the landlords, was not permanently fixed, the colonialists raised it in the course of their tax revisions.

In the political sphere this antagonism manifested itself in the growing opposition among landowners and the landed intelligentsia. The dissatisfaction within some particular sections of the landowning class was also connected with the confiscation of part of the feudal estates by the British, and the reduction in the income of certain feudal strata.

But the contradictions which we just mentioned did not determine the relations between the feudal landowning class of India and the colonial powers. During the second half of the 19th century, the Indian landlords finally became the intermediaries with whose aid the British bourgeoisie exploited the peasantry. This became especially evident in the areas where the zamindari system operated but the Permanent Settlement had not been introduced and the land tax was calculated as a part of the rent, the amount of which was determined by officials of the colony's fiscal administrative apparatus in the course of the assessment of the land tax. In preserving the property rights of the feudal landlords the aim of the British was to exploit India by means of feudal and semi-feudal relations. The rent legislation of the sixties to eighties served a similar purpose.

Private feudal property and small peasant property were consolidated in the last third of the 19th century, when commodity-money relations rapidly penetrated the countryside. This prepared the ground for the chief element of primitive accumulation—the expropriation of the peasants, which deprived them of the means of production, first and foremost of their land. The small commodity producers who were ruined provided labour power for the market, one of the main preconditions for the development of capitalism.

But while the imperialist exploitation at first accelerates the development of both capitalism and the bourgeoisie in India, later on it strengthens the feudal relics in the countryside whose existence depended on the prevalent property rights of the landlords. It was, therefore, a characteristic feature of colonial India that the process of primitive accumulation remained incomplete: the peasant deprived of his land was reunited with it on a semi-feudal basis (the existence of the metayage system and of enslaving conditions for the wage labourer are evidence of this); the craftsman who lost his economic independence to an increasing degree became inevitably more and more dependent on the capital of the buyer-up, the early forms of which appeared in the small industries as trading capital.

The expropriation of the agricultural producer from the soil forms the basis of primitive accumulation—a process which in different countries, as Marx noted, assumes different aspects, and runs through its various phases in different orders of succession, and at different periods.[29] The huge gap that existed between the expropriation of the small producer and the time when capitalism made use of them, i.e., turned them into proletarians—a gap resulting from the fact that, due to the colonial and imperialist oppression, capitalism was not sufficiently developed in India—condemned India's labouring masses to pauperisation and under-employment. It caused extreme destitution, because the value of the labour power, which was already very low, was not fully replaced, and thus led to constant malnutrition and a high mortality from starvatios.[30]

According to the calculations which the British economist, W. Digby, made on the basis of official data, 26 million people died of starvation

---

29 Marx, n. 10, I, 716.

30 In June 1863, Sir Charles Wood declared in the House of Commons: "In Cuddapah, in Guzerat, and other parts of India, the native weavers and spinners have been thrown out of employment. Happily for many of these poor people, other employment has been found for them on the railways and other public works carried on by the Indian Government, and thus they have been saved from severe suffering". *Hansard's Parliamentary Debates*, Vol. 172. (Third Series, London, 1864) 219. But for how long? And how many millions have not been saved from suffering even for a short time?

in India between 1876 and 1900, or five times more than in the preceding 25 years.[31]

The inevitable clash of these contradictory aspects, which were part of the single process of the capitalist development in the colonial country, gave rise to fundamental conflicts during the latter half of the 19th century—conflicts that became decisive for India in the imperialist era. The principal one of these was the fight of the national democratic forces for the independent political and economic development along capitalist lines against the imperialist policy which endeavoured to slow down the economic development of the country and to subordinate it to the interests of the bourgeoisie of the metropolitan state.

The preservation of feudal relics created conditions in which the trading and moneylending capital operating in the countryside and in the handicrafts was able to develop a greater independence in India than, for example, in the European countries at the time when capitalism was evolving there. Here we are, of course, concerned with its independence in regard to the domestic capitalist industry and not in relation to the British factory. It was precisely the dependence of Indian trading and moneylending capital on the British industry, and later on British finance capital, which impeded the development of capitalist enterprise in India, especially in agriculture. During the differentiation process of the peasantry a top stratum was created in the countryside, which was conspicuous not so much for the amount of agricultural produce it supplied but rather for the size of their landed property and, especially, their pecuniary resources. The trader and moneylender were the main products of the evolution of the bourgeoisie in the countryside whose activities reflected the whole ugliness of capitalist development. Capitalist landlords and rich peasant entrepreneurs only arose in exceptional circumstances.

When the colonialists abolished the feudal system of tax-farming they provided new opportunities for expansion of trading and moneylending operations. The increasing tax burden, the fact that British capital proceeded to exploit India as a market and the beginning export of agricultural raw materials led to the further development of commodity-money relations in the countryside and to their penetration even into the remote parts of the country as early as the first half of the 19th century. Because of the survival of the feudal vestiges, the growth of commodity-money relations in colonial India was accompanied by an intensification of the enslavement of the peasantry by the moneylenders. The comparatively strong and permanent dependence of the peasant on the market which arose during the latter half of the 19th century, and especially in the early 20th century, created new opportunities for his exploitation by means of commercial and

31 Digby, n. 27, 131.

moneylending operations. A factor which contributed to the enslavement of the small peasant commodity producer by the moneylender was that the further development of commodity production in India took place under conditions of unequal, or non-equivalent, commodity exchange with the metropolitan country and an unprecedented tax burden.

The sphere of activities of the village trader and moneylender, who formed the primary link in the trading and moneylending system of exploitation of the peasant, was greatly expanded. With his help the colonialists foisted British machine-made products on the country and extracted raw materials. The extension of the trading and moneylending network in the countryside also caused members of the trading and moneylending castes, primarily from Rajputana (including the Marwaris) and from Gujarat, to emigrate in large numbers. This migration of Marwari and Gujarati traders and moneylenders already began at a time when India was exploited by methods typical of industrial capital, that is, in the first half of the 19th century. It continued at an increasing rate during the imperialist exploitation of the country, which is evident from the numerous reports about the influx of moneylenders from Rajputana and Gujarat into other Indian provinces printed in reference works at the close of the 19th and early 20th centuries. This migration was necessarily brought about by the system of market relations and the oppression of the peasant by the trader and moneylender which helped British capital to exploit the peasant as a tax payer, as a consumer of machine-made commodities and a supplier of raw materials for the home country.

The small shopkeeper and moneylender usually did not have sufficient means to be able independently to conduct trading and moneylending operations covering, let us say, a whole village. An interesting system, which was widely practised within the trading and moneylending castes, namely grant of credit to fellow members on preferential terms, therefore, played an important role in the exploitation of the peasants. A reference work on the Gujarati Banias related that a member of the caste who possessed a small capital borrowed money on easy terms from the richer members of his own caste and used it in moneylending operations or in marketing textiles, grain or other commodities.[32] Similar relations existed also among the members of the Marwari trading and money lending castes.

We have here encountered a phenomenon peculiar to the economy of India. The provision of credit within the caste was undoubtedly already practised in feudal India, and was one of the circumstances enabling certain castes to occupy, what amounted, in fact, to a monopoly position in commerce and finance. One may also assume that this

32 *Bombay Gazetteer,* (Vol. IX, Part I), 78.

practice was a direct economic condition of the very existence of the trading and moneylending castes. We have called it a "direct" condition, for in the final analysis the preservation of the trading and moneylending castes, just as the granting of credits that was practised within the framework of the caste, were manifestations of feudal relics surviving in the social and economic structure of colonial India; these survivals persisted both in India's economy as a whole and in the field of finance in particular. The colonial exploitation, which was conducive to the preservation of feudal relics, was responsible for the protracted existence of the trading and moneylending castes and for the system of granting loans which was practised within the castes.

The growth of the trade in which the Indian merchants collaborated with the colonialists and of internal trade, and the intensification of the exploitation of the peasants by moneylenders required a financial mechanism that was, on the one hand, sufficiently centralised and, on the other hand, sufficiently widespread. The colonial banks and British managing agencies formed the top of this mechanism and the various categories of Indian merchants and moneylenders represented its intermediate and lower links. Only big merchants who collaborated with the British and indigenous bankers could obtain loans direct from the British banks; the latter moreover, only granted them short-term credit. Thus even big Indian capitalists were unable to get long-term loans except through the native credit system. The small moneylender, who could not furnish sufficient security from the point of view of the British bank, usually received loans from the rich shroff who was a member of the same caste as he. The bills of exchange circulated within a small group of dealers and moneylenders. Regular quotations existed for bills of exchange, wrote the *Gazetteer of the Central Provinces*, which were well known to the brotherhood of Saukars, who used them in their transactions with one another but they made no scruples to get as much as possible out of strangers.[33]

Loans to other members of the caste were often given without any security or the drawing up of any formal documents.[34] The creditor could do this because through the existing traditional links he was very well acquainted with the business circumstances of the debtor, whose "honesty" was moreover vouched for by the customs prevailing in the caste; infringements of these customs were punished by expulsion from the caste and even from the family.[35] It is obvious that a hereditary

33 *The Gazetteer of the Central Provinces*, (Nagpur, 1870) 333.

34 "Few cases occur in which a Marwary, however unscrupulous in his dealings with other men, is false to his employer or partner", *Bombay Gazetteer*, Vol. XIX, (Bombay, 1885), 181.

35 Such rules existed, for example, among the Chettiars, the members of a trading and moneylending caste from Tamilnad. See *Burma Provincial Banking Enquiry Committee*, (Rangoon, 1930), I, 207, 20[illegible].

moneylender who was ostracised in this way was deprived of any chance to become rich. The credit system obtaining within the caste permitted the big shroff to build up a network of agents consisting of village shopkeepers and moneylenders who depended on him, and who robbed the peasants directly. In case he needed it the shroff could get a loan from another big shroff who was a member of the same caste. Since the members of the trading and moneylending castes had at their disposal a widespread network of correspondents and the possibility of obtaining large credits, they naturally possessed considerable advantages over those merchants and moneylenders who were not members of such castes.

As a result of the economic advantages which their caste organisation and their mutual relations gave the members of the trading and moneylending castes, the Indian bourgeoisie arose mainly from them. Jawaharlal Nehru writes that in the latter half of the 19th century "Commerce and industry grew slowly, and it is interesting to note that the classes who took to them were predominantly those whose hereditary occupation for hundreds of years had been trade and commerce."[36] Nehru mentions in particular trading and moneylending groups consisting of Gujaratis, Marwaris, Sindhis and Chettiars.

Both the general weakness of industrial capital due to the colonial conditions and its dependence on trading, moneylending and comprador capital prevented the disappearance of the feudal credit system and the formation of a capitalist credit system. It is well known that the main source of loan capital is money capital which is temporarily not required in the circulation process of industrial capital. The fact that its volume was exceedingly small in India set narrow limits to the formation of loan capital. But even the small amount which was set free in the turnover process of industrial capital was, with rare exceptions, not used in the sphere of capitalist credit. In the small-scale and cottage industry it fell into the hands of the buyer-up, that is, it was used as trading and moneylending capital; the part arising in large-scale industry was sucked into the sphere of the commercial operations conducted in collaboration with the British, that is, in fact it was sucked into the sphere of circulation of British industrial capital.

One can form an approximate idea both of the size of the profits which the merchants and moneylenders received and of the proportion which these profits represented in the total income of the exploiter classes in India, from the figures supplied by W. Digby. The aggregate national income of the country was £392,400,000 at the beginning of the 20th century. The share of the ten thousand ruling princes, titled rajas, zamindars, and other feudal landlords amounted to £50 million per annum, the income of the 75 thousand bankers, moneylenders,

36 Jawaharlal Nehru, *The Discovery of India*, 309.

wealthy merchants, and so on, came to £75 million a year; a similar amount fell to approximately 750 thousand smaller traders and shopkeepers.[37]

The existence of a capitalist credit system "on correct European lines", as Lenin put it, would have reduced to zero the advantages of the caste organisation and destroyed the trading and moneylending castes as economic institutions. But British capital utilised the caste organisation of the merchants and moneylenders for their own purposes as an indispensable element of the colonial exploitation system, taking advantage of it in the same way as of the other feudal relics.

How important the caste organisation of the Indian merchants and moneylenders was for British capital is demonstrated, for example, by the method applied in the cotton export from Maharashtra as far back as the fifties of the 19th century, which Chapman described in the following way:

> The great moneylender makes advances to the little moneylender, and he in turn to the cultivator. The cultivator, bound by inextricable indebtedness to his immediate creditor, cares little for his crop beyond its satisfying the immediate claim on him. The little moneylender takes the crops of, perhaps, 100 cultivators, and the great moneylender the collected crops of, perhaps, 100 little ones.[38]

In this way, the big moneylenders exploited many thousands of peasants who cultivated cotton. The cotton went from the big moneylenders, either through the hands of Gujarati merchants who collaborated with the foreigners or direct through British export firms, to the ports and was sent from there to Great Britain.

British capital, therefore, extracted the raw material for export purposes by means of the most cruel, semi-feudal exploitation and the enslavement of the peasantry through the moneylenders. The Indian merchants and moneylenders charged the enslaved cultivator not only high rates of interest, but took his crop at an "agreed", i.e. very low, price.[39] In 1850, an employee of a British firm drew the following picture of the cotton-grower in Maharashtra. Although the cotton crop was, as a rule, good the ryots were usually in debt to the shroffs to such an extent that they took little interest in the harvest. The shroffs, on the

37 Digby, n. 27, 615-16.

38 J. Chapman, *Cotton and Commerce of India*, 90-91.

39 Even in the sixties of the 19th century during the comparatively favourable period of the cotton boom, the price the Maratha peasant received for his cotton depended entirely on the advances made by the moneylender. See R. D. Choksey, *Economic History of the Bombay Deccan*, 222. The Marwari moneylenders gave the tenant farmers advances before the harvest and received the grain at a low price. *Narsingpur, Central Provinces District Gazetteer*, (Bombay, 1906), 146.

other hand, extracted such high profits that the quality of the produce did not matter to them.[40] The cotton trade brought huge profits to the British and native Indian merchant's capital. In the 1860s, a pound of cotton, for which the ryot received two pence, was sold for six pencehalf penny in London. Despite the relatively smaller share of overhead expenses in the price of American cotton, it was, during the same period, sold for nine pence to one shilling two pence per pound.[41] The low monopoly prices of Indian raw materials and high monopoly profits made by the British bourgeoisie rested on the same basis: the many-sided exploitation of the Indian peasant—as a tax payer, tenant and debtor. An admission, which is interesting in this connexion, was made by a member in the House of Commons during the debates of measures designed to increase cotton exports from India. After expressing his concern about the diminished cotton yields in the West Indies and Brazil after the abolition of slavery in those countries, he cynically declared: "And it is worthy of remark, that in India alone free labour has been able to sustain a competition with that of slaves."[42]

The trading activities of the Indian merchants were, however, not merely confined to collaborating with thę British capital, which exploited India as a market and a source of raw materials. Side by side with the expansion of foreign trade, the home trade was growing in India during the second half of the 19th century. Unfortunately, we have only incomplete data regarding the commodity exchange carried on over a number of years in some towns in the interior of India. But it is possible to draw certain conclusions from the information we possess about trade in a number of towns in the Central Provinces.

In 1867-68 the proportion of British commodities (mainly textiles) imported into such a large centre as Nagpur amounted to 6.4 per cent of the total volume of imports, or Rs 605,000 out of Rs 9,464,000 while for example the value of the grain imported into Nagpur during the same years reached Rs 2,600,000. The import of locally made cloth was twice as big in quantity as that of British cloth.[43] The proportion of British commodities was roughly the same in the export trade of other towns in the Central Provinces.[44]

---

40 M.Z. Dantwalla, *Hundred Years of Indian Cotton* (Bombay, 1948), 71.

41 *Hansard's Parliamentary Debates, Vol.* 163, (London, 1861) 364, 496.

42 *Ibid.*, Vol. 172, (1863), 178.

43 *The Gazetteer of the Central Provinces*, 344.

44 In 1868 British imports into Jabalpur came to Rs 802,000 (including Rs 486,000 worth of textiles) out of a total of Rs 4,641,000; in Raipur the value of British textiles amounted to Rs 278,000 that of locally manufactured to Rs 171,000, while the total import was Rs 1,799,000; in Arvi, a town in the Wardha district, the value of imported British textiles came to Rs 32,600 that of locally manufactured cloth to Rs 54,000 and cotton to Rs. 389,000 while total imports added up to Rs 986,000; in Bilaspur British textiles made up 10-

Up to the beginning of the 20th century, the turnover of foreign commerce grew simultaneously with the expansion of home trade; it is therefore not likely that any significant changes occurred in the ratio of the commercial transactions which the merchants in the interior districts of India undertook on their own account and those operations in which they acted as middlemen. One should, however, keep in mind that, in the wider economic sense, the commerce in which they served foreigners as intermediaries cannot be limited to export and import operations. The import of commodities and, especially, the export of raw materials caused a sort of chain reaction as a result of which some new trends appeared in the home trade. For example, the introduction of the single-crop system for export, e.g. cotton or jute, created in the regions specialising in the cultivation of an industrial crop of this kind the need to import foodstuffs, above all, grain. The corn trade became an indispensable condition for the production of agricultural raw materials for industrial purposes. Therefore, on the one hand it served British capital, on the other it formed part of the domestic inland trade and was a result of the increasing division of social labour within the country.

The deep-seated contradictions in the structure of the Indian market and commodity exchange were, in the final analysis, brought about by colonialism, which disrupted and distorted the course of the social division of labour. The division of labour between industry and agriculture was not so much a division of labour between the Indian town and countryside as a division of labour between the British town and the Indian countryside, and when this process developed further it became a division of labour between individual branches of British industry and of Indian agriculture.

The colonial regime destroyed those obstacles which prevented the moneylender from taking over the lands the peasant held in feudal India. As R.D. Choksey says:

> In pre-British days there were two restraints on the moneylenders; firstly, the existence of vigorous village communities, and secondly, the apathy of the State toward the recovery of loans; a function that was entrusted to the village punchayets (i.e. to the organs of village self-government). It was the disintegration of the village communities that gave the sawkars and land grabbers their opportunity to exploit the ryot.[45]

In the latter half of the 19th century peasant lands began to pass

15 per cent of the import total, in Deol one per cent, in Garkhakot 8 per cent, Hinganhat 1.5 per cent, while locally produced textiles amounted to 9 per cent of the aggregate imports. See *Ibid.*, 6, 120, 183, 193, 204, 227, 420.

45 Choksey, n. 39, 187.

rapidly into the hands of traders and moneylenders. Even in the United Provinces, where most of the land belonged to the landlords, the moneylenders began quickly to acquire landed property. The expropriation of the peasant from the soil took on truly catastrophic dimensions in Maharashtra in the 1870s, when it was turned by the British into the principal cotton-growing region of India.

Many members of the Gujarati bourgeoisie became landowners, although their landed property did not reach the dimensions of that held by Marwari shroffs.

The rise of the big Indian bourgeoisie was thus accompanied by the acquisition of land by the Indian merchants and moneylenders constituting the capitalist class.

As far back as the latter half of the 19th century, two contradictory currents became apparent in the flow of accumulations emanating from the sphere of commerce and moneylending; productive capital investments which went into industry, on the one hand, and unproductive investments moving into landed property, on the other. The stream directed towards the acquisition of landed property was, moreover, incomparably broader than the flow of capital investments into industry. The favourable conditions for investments in landed property, created by the agrarian policy of the colonial government, seriously retarded the industrial development of India, and consequently the emergence of the bourgeois entrepreneur. The firm bonds linking the big Indian bourgeoisie to the real estates of the landlord strengthened its reactionary features, in particular its hostile attitude towards the peasant movement.

The fact that the development of capitalism in India took place under conditions of imperialist exploitation decisively affected the process of its formation. The rising big Indian bourgeoisie accumulated money capital both by, more or less independently, exploiting the working masses, first and foremost the peasant, and by appropriating a certain portion of the colonial tribute which the imperialists extorted. The absolute size of their share grew during the imperialist period, for the increasing export of agricultural raw materials made British capital more dependent on the collaboration of the Indian propertied classes. The operations in which the Indian acted as middleman also increased as a result of the development of the home market which created the conditions necessary for a steep rise in the import of British machine-made commodities in the second half of the 19th century.

Side by side with the introduction of new, imperialist methods of exploitation, the exploitation of India as a market for British commodities continued to grow up to the beginning of the general crisis of capitalism. It should, in general, be emphasised that although at each stage of its development British capitalism put forward and principally used a new method of exploiting colonial India the methods applied during one stage were nevertheless retained and sometimes even reached the summit of their development during the next stage. For instance, the export of raw materials had begun already during the epoch of industrial capitalism in Great Britain, but it reached its widest scope during the imperialist period. Imperialism combined all the methods of colonial exploitation—taxation, import of industrial commodities, export of raw materials—besides export of capital into the colony. For this reason the Indian bourgeoisie that collaborated with the foreigners during the imperialist era had various sources of accumulation at its disposal while, on the other hand, the sphere in which it could invest these accumulations was limited.

CHAPTER VI

GROWTH OF THE INDUSTRIAL PROLETARIAT

The most important result of the early capitalist development in India was the growth of an industrial proletariat. The colonial exploitation of the working people of India by British capital exerted a decisive influence on the conditions of the working class of India and its principal features—such as its numerical strength and its structure the wages and the length of the working day, unemployment and the fluctuation of manpower.

The first detachments of the industrial proletariat arose in Bombay and Calcutta in the 1860s. Its total strength reached 400 thousand workers at the beginning of the nineties. In line with the uneven development of large-scale industry in the different areas of India, the industrial proletariat was concentrated in two centres: Bombay, which had 118 thousand workers, and Bengal with 120 thousand. There were considerably fewer workers in the other parts of the country, the Madras Presidency, for example, had only 24 thousand.[1] The total number of workers employed in the factories, railways and mines did not exceed 700-800 thousand.

A characteristic feature of the Indian industrial proletariat was the absolute predominance of the textile workers employed in the cotton and jute mills. Workers employed in the engineering industry—in arsenals, railway workshops and repair shops—numbered a few tens of thousands. The rest worked in enterprises of the food, cement and other branches of large-scale industry which had but a secondary importance for India.

The Marathas and Gujaratis (in the Bombay Presidency) and the Hindustanis (in Calcutta) predominated within the working class, as a result of the uneven distribution of industry in the country, and the fact that the decay of the feudal relations took on diverse forms and reached

1 *East India (Factory Inspection). Copies of Recent Correspondence with the Government of India on the Subject of Inspection of Factories and of the Factory Inspectors' Report,* (London, 1894), 51, 56, 108.

varying degrees among the different nationalities. Many Santals worked in the mining industry of Bihar. Among the Telugus, Oriyas and Punjabis the custom was rather widespread to seek seasonal work in town.

The caste and age composition of the working class was determined by the extremely difficult colonial living conditions. On the face of it, it may seem surprising that at the close of the 19th century members of the peasant castes predominated among the workers; for one might have expected the working class to obtain its recruits, chiefly from the ranks of craftsmen ruined by the colonial oppression. But the point is that the price of labour-power in colonial India did not include the cost of maintaining a family. Therefore the family of a worker could live in town only if, in addition to the worker himself, the other members of the family were also employed. But the low level of wages and the enormous supply of labour-power enabled the capitalists to use in the main only the most valuable section of workers, namely young men.[2] From 5 to 25 per cent of the workers were women and children (5 per cent in Madras and 25 per cent in Calcutta); they were usually employed on work of secondary importance which was badly paid.

Under these circumstances the worker himself was usually forced to find the means to support his family. After the craftsman went to work in the factory, his family could as a rule not subsist in town. The family was more likely to find an opportunity to maintain itself in the village. The tilling of either their own or a leased plot of land, day labour or seasonal work enabled the women and children to earn a meagre living.

The hold which the moneylender, the landlord and the tax departments had over the debt-ridden craftsmen and poor peasants was another factor determining the extent to which certain sections of the peasants and artisans merged in the working class. Debt slavery retarded the migration of the poorest strata to the town. This explains why members of the higher peasant castes who were relatively well off, predominated among the workers of Bombay and Ahmedabad. For example, the report of the factory inspection notes that, although some of the immigrants in Bombay were members of craft castes, the majority derived from the agricultural population that provided almost all unskilled and semiskilled workers in Bombay.[3]

The value of labour-power as is generally known, is first of all determined by the historical conditions in which the working class has arisen and in which it is reproducing itself in a given country. In this respect the proletariat of colonial India was placed in an extremely unfavourable condition. The retarded development of capitalism in agriculture and the extremely narrow sphere of capitalist production in industry, brought about by colonialism, gave rise to a vast relative

2 N. 1, 55.
3 N. 1, 67.

surplus population. The surplus population existed not only in the countryside but also in the towns (consisting of unemployed craftsmen, coolies, small traders and intellectuals), which is a characteristic feature of colonial countries. The pressure of this army on the labour market was already considerable during the first stages of the development of the proletariat and henceforth was inevitably growing. The supply of labour-power, which greatly exceeded the number of workers that could possible be employed by the capitalists, was one of the main reasons for the exceptionally low value of labour-power in India. This itself ensured supersrofits for the capitalists.

However low the value of labour-power, its natural limit is the cost of the reproduction of labour-power, including the necessary expenditure for the maintenance of a family. Even if one takes as the point of departure the minimum expenditure—as established by bourgeois economists—needed to provide the "normal" quantity of food, clothing and housing without any comforts, even then, the actual price of labour-power in Bombay fluctuated between one-fifth and one-half of its value at the beginning of the 20th century.[4] This meant that labour-power was being exhausted, while the exploiters received additional profits.

Up to the early 20th century the working day in the factories of Bombay was limited to the daylight hours, since artificial light was not used in the shops. The working day, therefore, began 15 minutes before sunrise and ended 15 minutes after sunset, i.e. it lasted from dawn to dusk, totalling from eleven to thirteen and a half hours, depending on the season.[5] Similar working hours existed in the factories of Ahmedabad.[6] But after the introduction of electric light the manufacturers forced the workers to labour 13-14 hours, and more, per day.[7]

The colonial statistics do not provide sufficient material for an analysis of the position of the Indian working class in the last third of the 19th century. Separate data, however, enable us to form some idea of the standard of life of the workers during this period. In Bombay, where their living standard was higher than in the rest of the country, the spinners—the category of textile workers with the highest skill—earned from Rs 7 to Rs 20 per month in the early nineties, women earned Rs 7-8 and children Rs 6-7. The average earnings of a worker's family in Bombay totalled Rs 25-26. The wages earned in the jute mills of Calcutta were rather similar, but wages in the industrial centres of the

4 *Natsional'no—osvoboditel'noe dvizhenie Indii i deyatel'nost B.G. Tilaka*, 446.

5 *Ibid.*, 451.

6 *Bambay Gazetteer*, IV, 75-76.

7 *Hansard's Parliamentary Debates, Third Series*, Vol. 245, (London, 1879), 351. James Cair, *India;Land and the People* (London, 1883) 15-16, 154, *Bombay Gazetteer* IV, 75-76.

provinces were 10-30 per cent lower.[8] One has to keep in mind that the earnings of the workers in the two principal industrial centres were higher than in remote towns. That was why, for example, the manufacturers of Bombay were interested in a constant influx of labour power especially from the remote districts of India. The rates of pay in Bombay, as an official investigation noted (in 1894), had already been established for a long time and had acquired the force of law in the eyes of the regular workers. According to the investigators, attempts to reduce the rates might have led to a general strike. It was precisely this circumstance which caused the manufacturers to draw up a plan for the export of cheap labour from the northern provinces of India.[9]

As we have stated earlier, the colonialists extracted a heavy tribute from the national industry. Hence, British capital exploited the proletarians of India, engaged not only in British-owned enterprises, but in enterprises belonging to the national bourgeoisie as well. The working class of India, thus, had to carry a twofold capitalist yoke.

In fact, the capitalists did not conceal that the super-exploitation of the Indian workers was the source which provided them the means to acquire machinery, pay the engineers and technicians, and buy materials at high monopoly prices. Sir Charles Wood observed in a speech, which he made in the House of Commons in 1860, that vast sums were saved on wages in India; while a small enterprise in Lancashire paid £400 a week in wages, the price for the same manpower in India would only come to £100.[10] A similar ratio between the prices of labour-power in Great Britain and India was maintained also in the following decades of the 19th century. This ratio was even more favourable to the British textile worker than it appears at first sight, for the calculations do not take into account that the Indian worker, worn out by the back breaking toil without any rest days, had to stay away from work considerably more often than his British opposite number.

One of the reasons why surplus value in the Indian industry was produced under worse, and more difficult conditions for the working class was that modern means of production were a monopoly of foreign finance capital. It will be recalled that to reproduce relative surplus value it is necessary to increase the productivity of labour and continuously to revolutionise the capitalist industry itself by means of changes in the method of production.[11] Colonialism, which prevented India from creating its own engineering industry and its own qualified technical personnel forced the Indian factory to use techniques already discarded in Europe. We do not even speak of agriculture where

8 N. 1, 56-57.

9 N. 1, 67-68.

10 Hansard's n. 7, Vol. 160, 46.

11 See Karl Marx, *Capital*, I, 315, 510-11.

technical methods were kept altogether at a medieval level.

Capitalist exploitation was supplemented and aggravated by various kinds of bondage. The worker usually was in debt to the moneylender, who took an interest of 70 per cent per annum.

The worker who lived in town was compelled to turn to the moneylender not only because his earnings were so scanty but also because his wages were paid at extremely irregular intervals, sometimes involving a delay of two months.[12] The jobber (labour recruiter and overseer) extorted bribes from him. Ultimately, the worker, who did not sever his connections with the village had to bear the burden of tax and rent payments, that is, he was subjected to the colonial and semi-feudal exploitation.

The worker had to toil under conditions of military discipline and was subjected to outrageously brutal treatment on the part of the numerous overseers. "Each mill in India is a garrison, and the domineering sepoy exacts discipline with his bamboo cane",[13] wrote a British eyewitness.

But for the workers the worst sections of the colonial and capitalist hell were the coal mines and tea plantations belonging to the British. An official investigation admits that "the working hours" in the pits "are from 6 a.m. to 6 p.m., and, perhaps, later when extra work is required". The miner worked at the coal-face without ventilation, in a fetid atmosphere saturated with vapour, without any safety arrangements. To quote again the official report:

> The ignorant native has not yet realised that his health and longevity are in question, and he has, besides, helped much to prevent ventilation becoming a necessity, by the wonderful power of endurance he has shown . . . in an atmosphere which is fetid and laden with steam.

Women and children were employed in the carrying of coal and rock. The investigators were able to observe a truly "idyllic" scene, which they have described in the following terms: "The women often take their babies, two and three months old, down the mine, taking with them also a small cot on which the child sleeps or plays while its parents are at work".[14]

In the eighties the tea plantations of Assam became places of penal servitude for tens of thousands of peasants from Bihar and other regions of the country who went there in search of additional earnings. The plantation coolies were exposed without any defence to the arbitrary treatment of the owners. The Indian press strongly protested against

---

12 N. 1, 67.

13 *Hansard's*, n. 7, Vol. 245, 353.

14 *Imperial Institute (Indian Section)*, (London, 1899), 83, 85-86.

the revival of slavery in the plantations, and pointed out that out of a thousand coolies 46 died every year.[15]

The capitalists made use of the downtrodden and dispossessed workers from the lowest castes as an additional means of oppression. They gave them the heaviest and the worst paid work. For example, the miners were members either of the lower castes or of tribes considered to be untouchable.[16]

Owing to colonialism the capitalist development in agriculture was inadequate and capitalist production in the towns covered an extremely narrow sphere. This led to the development of a vast relative surplus population: a surplus population that existed not only in the countryside but also in towns (there were many unemployed coolies, craftsmen, small traders and intellectuals), which is a specific feature of the colonial countries.

Since the majority of workers maintained their connections with the village and could return there if they lost their jobs, the relative surplus population exceeded open unemployment. Incidentally, although there were no statistics on this subject, one can say that many thousands of unemployed were concentrated in the big centres of colonial India. An indication of this is, for example, the great number of partially employed workers. In the early nineties, for instance, the number of part-time workers in the cotton mills of Bombay amounted to 25 thousand, that is, approximately one half of the textile workers of the town.[17]

The living conditions of the proletariat, especially housing, were appalling. The workers of Bombay lived in low huts, covered with leaves and without any windows. A grown-up person could enter them only by crawling on all fours. The huts of the miners consisted of one or two tiny rooms with a floorspace of 4-9 square metres; often they contained not only men but also cattle. Such "dwellings" had of course no conveniences at all.

The 400 thousand workers of Bombay lived in 50 thousand rooms.[18] The overcrowding of the living quarters was not due to the fact that Bombay was overpopulated, for there were approximately 63 thousand empty rooms[19] in the town. But the meagre earnings of the workers forced them to spend as little as possible on housing. Each dwelling consisted of a small room with a floorspace of 10-12 square metres. It was usually inhabited by a worker with his family and two or three single workers who rented a cot or a corner of the room. Two to three families, sometimes

15 *The Voice of India* (July 1888) 375-81; n. 1-, 84.
16 Caird, 7, 15-16; n. 14, 84.
17 N. 1, 67.
18 *Times of India*, April 4, 1908, 16-17.
19 *Ibid.*, August 17, 1907, 19.

as many as 12-20 persons, lived in the larger rooms.[20] The congestion and lack of sanitary arrangements gave rise to dirt and epidemics. Fresh air could apparently not penetrate into the rooms, since the gutters, which were full of dirty water and sewage, were running alongside the houses. The terrible stench of these gutters poisoned the atmosphere of the whole neighbourhood,[21] reported the Factory Labour Commission. Another dispassionate English source relates that when an outbreak of plague or any other infectious disease occurred, the epidemic immediately spread among the inhabitants, who were crowded together in a small space in complete defiance of all sanitary standards.[22]

Undernourishment, excessive toil and the terrible conditions of life rapidly exhausted the organism of the worker and led to premature death. The average weight of an adult male worker of Bombay was 100 pounds; at the age of 30-40 the worker was already unable to continue his labour in the factory. The mortality of Indians in Bombay was three to four times higher than that of Europeans.[23]

The production of relative surplus-value was under these conditions extremely difficult. The principal method used to increase the surplus-value was the lengthening of the working day, i.e., a method producing absolute surplus-value. In the last third of the 19th century, the working week in the Indian factory was 80 hours, while it had only 56 hours in the English factory.[24]

In their efforts to weaken the ability of the Indian industry to compete with them, the Lancashire manufacturers demanded—through their representatives in the British Parliament—the introduction of labour legislation in India. But this demand was in contradiction not only to the interests of the Indian entrepreneurs but also to those of the British owners of industrial enterprises in India. The efforts of the colonial philanthropists with regard to labour legislation, therefore, produced only trifling results. In 1881 the employment of children under seven years of age in factories was prohibited; minors over that age who worked 12-13 hours per day were permitted to take four rest days per month. In 1891 the minimum age of the worker was raised to nine years and the working day of children under 14 years was limited to seven hours. It is understandable that this legislation, which was, moreover, not strictly observed, did not have any significant influence on the rate of exploitation of the Indian proletariat.

The physical exhaustion, low cultural level, and insufficient training of the worker, and the technical backwardness of the colonial factory

20 *Natsionalno—osvoboditel'noe dvizhenie Indii i deyatel'nost' B. G. Tilaka*, 476.

21 *East India, Factory Labour Commission: Report*, I, (London, 1909), I, 7.

22 *Times of India*, October 26, 1905, 14.

23 N. 21, I, 91; *Times of India*, February 25, 1905; September 16, 1905.

24 *Hansard's*, n. 7, Vol. 245, 386.

tended to reduce the productivity of labour. But considering the conditions, the labour of the Indian worker was relatively effective. Even the millowners of Bombay, who were inclined to underestimate their workers' productivity of labour, admitted that, at the close of the seventies, 1,200 local workers were able to produce in a given time as much as 500 British textile workers—that is, the workers whose productivity, at that period was the highest in the world.[25] The productivity of labour of the Indian workers was, moreover, growing. For instance in the Empress mill in Nagpur, which belonged to the Tata Company, the productivity of labour increased two and a half times between 1882 and 1891.[26]

The extremely high costs of machinery spare parts, chemicals and other imported materials were more than balanced by the low costs of labour power, which ensured super-profits for the manufacturers. A spinning mill of the same size might, for instance, cost £50 thousand in Lancashire and £150 thousand in Bombay; but the dividends of the former totalled £2,500, that is 5 per cent per annum, while the dividends of the latter amounted to £13,500, or 9 per cent.[27] The greater part of the difference in the cost of the Indian industrial enterprises was pocketed by the British bourgeoisie.

These were the conditions under which the surplus-value was extracted which, after the deduction of the tribute paid to British capital, provided the income of the Indian industrialists.

The proletariat of India though weighed down with unprecedented poverty and back-breaking toil had, as a class possessed immense vigour, tenacity and heroism to wage the economic and subsequently also the political struggle in defence of its vital rights.

The spontaneous strike action undertaken by the Indian proletariat to assert its economic rights began in the 1870s. In 1884 the Bombay Association of Textile Workers, the first trade union organisation, was set up on the initiative of N. M. Lokhande, who was an employee in a mill. Lokhande also published the newspaper Deenabandhu which had a philanthropical character. The close of the eighties and the nineties were marked by several large strikes in Calcutta and Bombay.

The first mass strike flared up in Bombay in 1892. Three thousand workers employed in the mills of Heeramanek's company participated in it in protest against a wage-cut. During the following year eight thousand workers took part in strikes. The strikes affected the enterprises of both Indian and British millowners.[28] In 1901, 20,000 workers went on strike in Bombay. In its economic fight the proletariat

25 Caird, n. 7, 15
26 W. W. Hunter, *The Indian Empire*, 714-15.
27 *Ibid.*, 715.
28 S.D. Mehta, *The Cotton Mills of India*, (Bombay, 1954), 82.

was justified in making no distinction between British and Indian manufacturers, since there were no essential differences in the methods they used to exploit their workers.

The proletariat of Bombay directed its first political mass action against British imperialism, the chief enemy of the Indian people as a whole. We refer to the famous strike which took place in Bombay in 1908. It was the culmination of the national liberation movement in the early 20th century. It is not necessary to touch upon the events of this strike, for it is analysed in sufficient detail in Soviet literature.[29] We will merely mention that Lenin gave a high evaluation of the action of the Bombay workers.

"In India the native slaves of the "civilised" British capitalists have recently been causing their "masters" a lot of unpleasantness and disquietude. There is no end to the violence and plunder which is called British Rule in India. Nowhere in the world, with the exception of Russia, of course, is there such poverty among the masses and such chronic starvation among the population. The most liberal and radical statesmen in free Britain, like John Morley, who is an authority in the eyes of Russian and non-Russian Cadets (right-wing party in pre-revolutionary Russia) the star of the "progressive" (in fact, lackeys of capital), publicists, are, as rulers of India, becoming transformed into real Genghis Khans, capable of sanctioning all measures for "pacifying" the population in their charge, even the flogging of political protestants. The little British Social-Democratic Weekly *Justice* is prohibited in India by liberal and "radical" scoundrels like Morley. And when Keir Hardie, the leader of the Independent Labour Party and member of Parliament, had the presumption to go to India and talk to the natives about the elementary demands of democracy, the whole of the English bourgeois press raised a howl against the "rebel". And now the most influential English newspapers, gnashing their teeth, are talking about the "agitators" who are disturbing the peace of India, and welcoming the purely Russian Plehve[30] sentences pronounced by the courts and the summary punishment meted out to Indian democratic publicists. But the Indian masses are beginning to come out into the streets in defence of their native writers and political leaders. The despicable sentence that the English jackals passed on the Indian Democrat, Tilak (he was sentenced to a long term of exile, and in reply to a question in the House of Commons it was revealed that the Indian jurymen voted for acquittal, whereas the conviction was passed by the *votes of the English Jurymen!*),

29 See I. M. Reisner, *Ocherki klassovoi borby v Indii;* A. I. Chicherov, *Protess's B. G. Tilaka v iyule 1908 goda i bombeiskaya zabastovka* (B. G. Tilak's trial in July 1908 and the Bombay Strike). Jn; sb. *Natsionalno—osvoboditelnoe dvizhenie Indii i deyatel'nost B. G. Tilaka.*

30 Plehve, Minister of the Interior in 1902-04, an outstanding reactionary and brutal suppressor of the revolutionary movement. Assassinated in 1904.

this act of vengeance against a democrat on the part of the lackeys of the moneybags, gave rise to street demonstrations and a strike in Bombay. And the Indian proletariat too has already matured sufficiently to wage a class-conscious and political mass struggle—and that being the case, Anglo-Russian (i.e., colonial and semi-feudal) methods in India are played out. By their colonial plunder of Asiatic countries, the *Europeans have managed* to harden one of them, Japan, for great military victories which ensured her independent national development. There is not the slightest doubt that the age-long plunder of India by the English, that the present struggle of these "advanced" Europeans against Persian and Indian democracy, will harden millions and tens of million of proletarians of Asia, will harden them for the same kind of victorious (like the Japanese) struggle against the oppressors. The class conscious workers of Europe now have Asiatic comrades and their number will grow by leaps and bounds."[31] The first political movement of the Indian proletariat was directed against the system of colonial and feudal oppression. Objectively seen, the fight was waged to secure the greatest possible freedom and independence for the capitalist development of India, which was bound to create the most favourable conditions for the rise of the working class and the development of its classconsciousness and class-discipline.

31 V. I. Lenin, *Selected Works, IV. The Years of Reaction and of the New Revival (1908-1914)*, (Moscow-Leningrad, 1935).

CHAPTER VII

RISE OF THE BIG GUJARATI BOURGEOISIE

During the second half of the 19th century, Bombay, along with Calcutta, became the principal stronghold of British capital. In general there were many similarities between Bombay and Calcutta during this period. The transformation of India into a source of raw materials for the industry of Great Britain during the 1860s was accompanied by a steep rise in the volume of raw material exported via these two ports. Jute was the main commodity exported from Calcutta, while the first place among the goods exported via Bombay belonged to cotton. A big ute industry was built up in Calcutta during those years, and a big cotton industry in Bombay.

The outward resemblance in the economy of the two most important cities concealed serious differences. Calcutta grew up as a centre of colonial exploitation which was, in the main, carried on direct by British firms concentrated in the city. Bombay, on the other hand, remained a centre of colonial exploitation which was accomplished by means of comparatively independent native capital. As a result of the colonial policy, which excluded the native commercial strata of Bengal as much as possible from business ventures, tendencies towards independent capitalist development began to take shape relatively late in Calcutta. In Bombay, where the resistance of the freedom-loving Marathas, which lasted for half a century, forced the colonialists to grant the native propertied classes greater independence and more favourable terms for their collaboration, capitalist trends appeared earlier, with greater force and—from the capitalist point of view—at a higher level of development. The development of the sector of national capitalist economy in Bombay took place under the most favourable conditions possible in colonial India.

It was precisely in Bombay that the first big group of the national bourgeoisie took shape and its ideologists—Dadabhai Naoroji, Ferozeshah Mehta, and M. G. Ranade originated. The first detachment of the Indian working class also arose there. The heroic struggle waged by the Marathas against the colonialists was, therefore, historically important not only because it enriched the patriotic traditions of the people but also because it helped to bring about the conditions for the emergence of the new classes of the Indian society.

The favourable conditions existing for the collaboration with British capital were chiefly responsible for the fact that in the middle of the 19th century the big merchants of Bombay who collaborated with the British and Gujarati shroffs were the first Indians to build cotton mills.

In 1919 the Indian Industrial Commission—among whose members were F. E. Currimbhoy and D. J. Tata, the descendants of the biggest capitalists of Bombay in the middle of the 19th century—wrote in its report that most of the capital invested in the cotton mills of Bombay consisted of profits derived from the opium export to China and, of course, of the gains which the cotton boom brought to Bombay in the 1860s.[1] The accumulated capital required for the building of textile mills was, however, as we have seen, not only derived from the trade in opium, cotton, and British textiles, but was also built up during the course of the many-sided collaboration with the colonialists. One must admire the enterprise and scope of these Bombay merchants who boldly embarked upon the building of factories—a new venture that had not yet been tried. The emerging bourgeoisie of Bombay laid the foundations for the factory industry of India. British capitalists began to construct the jute mills at Calcutta two years later and their enterprise was much less ambitious. This fact alone is sufficient to refute the hypocritical complaints raised by some western economists about the alleged timidity and conservatism of the Indian capital. It is quite a different matter, that under the conditions of the colonial economy the Indian bourgeoisie, in the race for profits, sometimes refrained from investing its accumulated capital into the large-scale industry but confined itself to the traditional spheres of activity—commerce, moneylending, and so on. The Bombay merchants who collaborated with the British were, moreover, from the subjective point of view also better prepared to undertake industrial ventures than other groups of Indian traders. The merchants of Bombay learned much from their business connections with British capitalists and especially from their relation with the representatives of the Manchester industry, which lasted for many years and dispelled their prejudices against the risk which the investment of capital in the modern industry involved.

The commercial relations which these merchants of Bombay maintained with the cotton-growing areas of India and with overseas markets—in the Middle East and, above all, in China—contributed to the fact that the first Indian mill-owners arose from their ranks. As far back as the 18th century, Bombay merchants acting as middlemen

1 Indian Industrial Commission Report (London, 1919) I, 65.

helped to sell British commodities in these markets, especially in the Chinese ones. The marketing of British yarn in China acquired great importance in the middle of the 19th century. It was precisely this trade in yarn which suggested the idea of building spinning mills to the Bombay merchants. T. R. Sharma, an Indian economist, writes:

> Some of these Parsi merchants realised that Bombay itself could provide a very good venue for the manufacture of yarn from the Indian cotton for export to the China market. The import of coal from England solved the problem of power and the first cotton mill in Bombay was started by Cowasji Nanabhoy Davar in 1851, and by 1860 two more mills were added. Thus the early cotton mill industry of Bombay was not started to serve the home market but was rather intended to supply yarn to the overseas foreign market in China and the Far East.[2]

That was the reason why up to the early 19th century the output of yarn in the mills of Bombay far surpassed the production of cloth, although part of the latter was also exported. The orientation of the cotton mills of Bombay towards the overseas markets was obviously forced upon them by the circumstance that the weak native industry was as yet unable to compete with the British textiles which were already firmly established in the Indian market. The industrial activity of the rich citizens of Bombay appeared therefore, during its first stage to be simply the continuation of their collaboration with the foreigners, for this had included assistance in the sale of British yarn in China.

Although these factors helped, in the beginning, to tone down the contradictions between the emerging Indian-owned factory and British capital, the fact itself that the Bombay dealers who had collaborated with the British started to build factories signified a new stage in their relationship with the colonial regime, which differed essentially from the preceding one. It was not without reason that as early as 1860 anxious voices were raised in the British Parliament by the representatives of Manchester, who demanded the imposition of an excise duty on Indian cloth equal to the customs duties that were levied on British textiles imported into India, alleging that these customs duties created privileged conditions for the building of cotton mills in Bombay.[3] The colonialists moreover, claimed that the workers would be torn away from their work in agriculture.[4] In other words, they were afraid that the creation of an industry would hamper the exploitation of India as an agricultural appendage of the home country.

The first company for the building of a cotton spinning mill in

2 T. R. Sharma, *Location of Industries in India*, 15.

3 *Hansard's Parliamentry Debates*, (Third Series, Vol. 160, 1860), 1256.

4 *Ibid*.

Bombay was set up in 1851. The mill was put into operation on February 5,1854.[5] Its equipment was supplied by a British firm, Platt Brothers and Co. of Oldham,[6] which became the principal supplier of machinery for the factories built later in Bombay.

There is no information available regarding the composition of the board of directors in charge of the first factory built in Bombay. We only know that a Parsi merchant Cowasjee Nanabhoy Daver (sometimes called Davar) was the promoter of the company. Apparently he was not a very rich merchant; in any case, his name did not appear in the list of Bombay merchants who owned mills.[7] But the same Cowasjee Nanabhoy Daver was able to open another spinning mill in 1857, thanks to the success of the first enterprise. Three years later the price quoted for the shares of this enterprise was 5 per cent higher than their nominal value.[8] After 1857 Daver's name is no longer mentioned.

The first weaving mill of Bombay, the Oriental began to operate in 1860. A few months later, its shares were already quoted at 38 per cent above par value. The productive capacity of the Oriental comprised fifty thousand spindles and one thousand looms. A joint-stock company was set up to run this enterprise which, for those times, was very large. Its managing board consisted of the biggest commercial magnates of Bombay and two British capitalists.

The chairman of the board of directors, Cursetjee N. Cama (1831-1905), came from an old family of merchants. R. P. Masani, the biographer of Dadabhai Naoroji relates that C. N. Cama was for a time the closest comrade-in-arms of Naoroji in his work of enlightenment. In 1855 when Cama's firm opened a branch in London, it became the first Indian commercial company with an office of its own in Great Britain. Naoroji was appointed to represent Cama in London.[9] But a rupture in the relations of the two friends occurred in 1858. Masani explains that this was due to the fact that Naoroji could not reconcile himself to the opium and liquor trade carried on by the firm of Camas.[10] The opium was sold in China, while the liquor was imported from Europe into India. This explains why Cama maintained commercial relations with British and Chinese ports.[11] Already in 1859, a year after his break with Cama, Naoroji was able to start a firm of his own in London. The commercial activities of this firm included trading in

5 Some authors give other dates; M. P. Gandhi, for instance, February 1856.

6 *Bombay Industries* . . . 9.

7 See *Guide to Bombay* (Bombay, 1877).

8 *Journal of the Royal Asiatic Society*, (1860), 374.

9 R. P. Masani, *Dadabhai Naoroji, the Grand Old Man of India*, (London, 1939), 78.

10 *Ibid.*, 72.

11 N. 6, 702.

cotton and acting as broker.[12] After having established the Oriental, C. N. Cama played no important role in the building of textile enterprises.

A member of the board of directors was Byramjee Jeejeebhoy, a son of the big merchant Jamshetjee Jeejeebhoy whom we already encountered earlier (see p. 108 of this voulume). Subsequently, Byramjee Jeejeebhoy became director of a number of other cotton mills. Another director of the Oriental mill Maneckjee Petit, was one of the richest Parsi merchants in Bombay. From the age of eighteen onwards he was engaged in commerce and sailed to the shores of Arabia. Maneckjee Petit later secured a more stable, though no less profitable position when he served British firms in Bombay as a broker.[13] At the same time, Petit continued to conduct commercial transactions on his own account, which assumed large proportions. This is indicated by the fact that Petit became the owner of the large merchant vessel Charles Grant, with a displacement of 2,000 tons, which was rather large for those days. The Charles Grant made regular trips between India and China. Petit was one of the organisers of the drainage works in Colaba, a suburb of Bombay. For his services to the British empire, this merchant was made a baronet by Queen Victoria.[14]

The general manager and largest shareholder of the Oriental mill, the Parsi Merwanjee Framjee Panday, was the broker of three British firms in Bombay which were engaged in the import of textiles.[15] Panday the manufacturer should have, therefore, become the rival of Panday, the collaborator, with the British. This is only one of many examples showing the contradictory position in which the Bombay merchants who worked together with the British found themselves when they began to build industrial enterprises of their own.

Another director, the Hindu Vurjivandas Madhowdas, was a member of the Kopal Bania community. Madhowdas was closely linked to the financial interests of the colonialists and occupied the post of a director of the Bank of Bombay, a great honour for a Bombay dealer.[16]

The director Elias David Sassoon (1819-80) hailed from an ancient family of merchants. According to tradition, as early as the 12th century a rich Jewish family called Ibn-Shashun lived in Toledo. At the end of the 15th century the Shashuns escaping from the stake and fire of the Holy Inquisition moved to distant Baghdad. They reached a high standing in Mesopotamia. The grandfather of Elias was treasurer of the Turkish vice-regent in Baghdad. David Sassoon, the father of Elias,

12 Masani, n. 9, p. 78.

13 D. H. Buchanan, *The Development of Capitalist Enterprise in India*, (New York, 1934), 201,

14 N. 6, 720.

15 *Ibid.*, 718.

16 *Ibid.*, 729.

was a banker in Baghdad; in 1822 he migrated to Basra.[17] But Basra, apparently did not offer enough opportunities to the rich merchant and he moved to Bombay. In 1832 David Sassoon started a business firm in Bombay where he carried on commercial and financial transactions. Four years later he was already a member of the board of administration of the Bombay Chamber of Commerce, which had just been set up. As a rule only representatives of British firms were admitted to the board. Apart from David Sassoon, the only other 'native' member of the board of administration in 1836 was Dadabhoy Pestonjee.[18]

The business operations of Sassoon fully explain the trust placed in him. His transactions extended to the Chinese ports where he was selling opium. Elias Sassoon was sent to China in 1844 to establish an office there. From that time up to the Second World War the orientation towards China remained a tradition of the firm of Sassoons. David Sassoon and his sons did not content themselves with the Chinese market but subsequently began to send ships with cargoes of opium to Nagasaki, Yokohama and other Japanese ports.

During the lifetime of David, the Sassoons already started to become Anglicised. David Sassoon himself, to judge by his portraits, wore the turban and oriental robes, which were the traditional dress of the merchant in the orient. It is characteristic of him that though the languages he knew included Hindustani, Arabic and Turkish, he did not speak English. His eldest son had been given a curious combination of names—Albert Abdullah David. Albert Sassoon (1817-96) received a European education, but the 'universities' from which he really graduated were the offices of his father. He became the head of the firm after his father's death in 1864. Even before that, in 1856, the head office of the Sassoons was transferred to London. In addition to opium, the Sassoons began to trade in cotton. In 1877 they established an office in Liverpool and in the same year Albert Sassoon received the Order of the Bath. He attained a high position in society circles in London. The Prince of Wales was a frequent visitor in the fashionable drawing-room of Sir Albert Abdullah David, who was made a baronet in 1890.

Neither the transfer of the firm's business centre to Great Britain, indicating that the Sassoons had become British capitalists, nor the operations they conducted in the Far East, diminished their activities in India. In the 1860s David Sassoon built docks for the repair of ships in Colaba, a suburb of Bombay.[19] The Sassoons owned factories for the

17 See *The Jewish Encyclopedia,* (London, 1925), and *The Dictionary of National Biography* (London).

18 R. Sulivan, *One Hundred Years of Bombay, 1836-1936,* (Bombay, 1936).

19 N. 7, 164. The British branch of the Sassoons has, in recent times, consolidated its position in the upper strata of the British bourgeoisie. They intermarried with the Rothschilds and one of the Sassoons became a member of the Baldwin cabinet.

processing of cotton and raw silk in Bombay. Finally, they also participated in the building of industrial enterprises, but we will refer to this later.

This brief sketch could merely give a few facts regarding the first owners of the large-scale modern industry in Bombay.

Besides the Oriental, six other factories were put into operation in 1860. Dinshaw M. Petit, the son of Manekjee N. Petit, started to operate the spinning mill Victoria and the weaving mill Manekjee Petit. Baronet Dinshaw Petit (1823-1901) was the biggest manufacturer in Bombay, but he did not abandon the commercial dealings of his father. The *Indian Textile Journal* wrote in the obituary about him that to give an account of the commercial activity of D. M. Petit, it would be necessary to write a history of commerce in Bombay during the last fifty years.[20] D. M. Petit was the only Indian director of the Bank of the Presidency of Bombay. A characteristic feature of the business-men of Bombay was the combination of industrial activity with commerce carried on in collaboration with the British.

The weaving mill Royal was started by Kesowjee Naik, a member of the Bhattia community. This newly-fledged manufacturer had been a broker of a British firm and later a cotton merchant.[21] Another weaving mill, the Great Eastern was set up by a company which was headed by B. Jeejeebhoy, Khatau Makanjee, a Bhattia merchant, and Morarjee Gokuldas. Like the majority of the Indian manufacturers, Morarjee Gokuldas (1833-80) was a member of the Bhattia community. He began his business career as associate in the firm of his uncles, who were selling British textiles.[22] We will later meet the descendants of the third partner, Khatau Makan.

The Parsi Bomanjee H. Wadia opened the cotton mill Coorla in the same year. He was a member of the family of shipbuilders which we already know. Finally, the sixth of the enterprises that began to operate in 1860 was built by Nathubhoy Mangaldas, a member of the Kopals, a sub-caste of the Banias,[23] who was the head of the Hindu community of Bombay. We will merely point out that a descendant of a caste of merchants was only elevated to the ranks of the British aristocracy if he had rendered services to the colonial regime.

By the end of 1860, nine factories were operating in Bombay, six of which had been built in 1860. The time seemed near when Bombay would become the Manchester of India. But within a few months civil war broke out in the U.S.A. The fleet of the Northern States blockaded the cotton ports of the slave-owners, and the prices of Indian cotton trebled and quadrupled, rising from Rs 139 per

20 N. 6, p. 95.
21 *Ibid.*, 13.
22 *Ibid*, 715.
23 *Gazetteer of Bombay City and Island* (Bombay, 1909), I, 168.

kandi (approximately 7 cwt.) in 1861 to Rs 585 in 1864.[24] The first timid steps towards modern industry were followed by an orgy of speculation. The capital of the Bombay merchants which should have gone into industry got tied up in the so-called big cotton boom. None of the schemes proposed for the setting up of joint-stock companies seemed absurd to the investors. Banks, finance corporations and land companies, each with a nominal capital of crores of rupees, were launched every month.[25] The delay in the building of new factories was not only due to the possibility of making a fortune in the boom, but also to the fact that the high cotton prices deprived the local industry of one of its advantages, cheap cotton.

But cotton prices fell when the defeat of the slave-holder confederation removed the obstacles which had blocked the way to the British ports for American cotton. Sad days followed for the speculators of Bombay. Merchants and other business-men were ruined in their thousands.[26] The Bank of Bombay, which got involved with the speculators, crashed at the same time.

The business-men of Bombay managed, nevertheless, to make a profit of Rs 50 crores out of the cotton boom.[27] The big business-men who collaborated with the British grew rich through the cotton trade. Many traders of average means also made fortunes during this period. Some of these merchants became the promoters and managers of new companies, but more often they were just ordinary shareholders. A certain amount of pressure was also exerted by millowners; when signing contracts for future deliveries cotton suppliers had to promise that they would acquire a number of shares.[28] The cotton fever forced the colonial authorities to introduce a tariff scale for railway transport with the aim of encouraging the export of cotton. The new tariff also lowered the charges made for the delivery of cotton to the mills situated in Bombay, which became the most important railway junction in Western India in the 1870s. The transport of finished cloth from Bombay to the inland markets became considerably cheaper, because, for the benefit of the British importers, the railways reduced freight charges for the carriage of textiles from the ports to the interior of the country. The policy, which the colonial authorities pursued with regard to railway freight charges led to the concentration of the cotton industry in Bombay which is comparatively distant from both the cotton-growing regions and the main markets.

---

24 Department of Statistics: *Index Numbers of Indian Prices 1861-1918*, (Calcutta, 1919), 7.

25 *Imperial Gazetteer of India*, II, 211.

26 N. 6, 18.

27 E. D. Wacha, *The Life and Works of J. N. Tata*, (Madras, 1912), 10.

28 N. 6, 47.

The cotton boom and the subsequent growth of the cotton trade were conducive to the appearance of the second group (chronologically speaking) of Bombay manufacturers risen from the ranks of cotton dealers. To big capitalists who played a particularly active role in the industrial building programme of the sixties were the Parsi P. R. Kolah and the first Muslim millowner, Kassumbhoy Dharamsey, a member of the Khoja, a Gujarati Muslim caste of traders. They were both well-known cotton merchants. P. R. Kolah was a business partner of Dadabhai Naoroji.[29] After becoming a millowner, K. D. Dharamsey continued to conduct large-scale commercial operations in collaboration with the British, and was considered one of the richest men in India.[30]

The Parsi Jamshedji Nusserwanji Tata, the most prominent figure among the Indian capitalists of the latter half of the 19th century, began his industrial career in 1869. Nusserwanji Tata, the father of Jamshedji, broke away from the traditional occupation of his ancestors who were Zoroastrian priests. N. Saklatvala, a relative of the Tatas and one of the managers of the Tata concern, wrote that J. N. Tata was the first in the family to give up prayers for a business career, and that his pockets were empty when he arrived in Bombay.[31] J. N. Tata managed for the first time to earn good money on war supplies in 1857 when the British attacked Iran. Having acquired a fortune Tata became independent and turned towards the well-tried commerce with China. In December 1859, the firm Nusserwanjee and Kaliandas was established in Hong Kong (Kaliandas, a Hindu merchant, was Tata's partner at the time when he sold supplies for the military expedition in Iran). During the same year Jamshedji Tata joined the firm of Nusserwan jee and Kaliandas, which imported opium and cotton into China and exported tea, silk, camphor, copper, and gold from there.

In 1861, during the cotton boom, the firm began to speculate in cotton. Jamshedji was sent to Manchester to conclude agreements for the supply of cotton. The young trader from Bombay saw there the most up-to-date machine industry of that time. As a result of the cotton speculations, carried on without due regard for the financial limitations of the firm, and the sudden end of the war in America, the Tatas and their partners went bankrupt. The biographers emphasised the extraordinary honesty shown by J. N. Tata in the way he settled with his creditors, but the rapid re-establishment of the firms makes these assertions appear to be rather too bold.

It is true that another profitable business turned up just then; the British started a colonial expedition as they had done ten years earlier. This time they marched against Ethiopia. J. N. Tata, together with a

29 Masani, n. 9, 78.

30 *Indian Textile Journal*, (July, 1934).

31 *Ibid*.

few other Bombay traders, set up a company for the purpose of supplying this expedition. Although the campaign was notable for the intrigues which the British carried on with the Ethiopian feudal traitors rather than military actions, the money spent during the expedition amounted to £11 million instead of the one million allocated for it. This greatly perplexed even the worldly-wise members of the House of Commons.[32] Inquiries were made, but it was not without reason that N. Saklatvala called the supplies for the Ethiopian expedition, "the first real opportunity which Jamshedji found."[33]

This "real opportunity" which he seized provided him with enough money to build the cotton mill Alexandra in Bombay in 1869. The cotton mill brought in high profits, but if Tata, the business-man collaborating with the British and military supplier, had been satisfied with such ordinary returns, he would have hardly become the founder of an enterprise which comprises one of the largest iron and steel works in the British Empire. He realised that the place to build cotton mills, if one wanted to extract super-profits, was in the interior regions where labour power was especially cheap, cotton close at hand and the markets within easy reach. Already in 1871, Tata, therefore, sold the Alexandra mills to Kesowjee Naik and chose Nagpur as a convenient place for building a new mill. The mill was put into operation in January 1877 and was called the Empress, in honour of Victoria, Queen of Great Britain, who had assumed the title "Empress of India". In addition to a practically unlimited working day, Tata used a sort of allround method of exploitation at the Empress mill. He had barracks there and introduced a premium system for uninterrupted attendance at work and for length of service, to induce the exhausted workers to continue the back-breaking toil in the mill for as long as possible; there was also a workers' joint-stock company with a capital of Rs 50,000 which issued shares of ten rupees carrying a dividend of 4 per cent, to utilise even the pitiful savings of the workers.[34] It was precisely at this mill, that in 1877 the first strike of Indian workers took place.

J. N. Tata began to draw huge profits as a result of combining such methods of exploitation with up-to-date techniques and the favourable position of the mill. The dividends paid by the Empress mill reached 16 per cent as early as 1881; the average dividends for the first twenty years were 20 per cent, while the average annual profit yielded, including deductions made for the reserve fund of the enterprise, was 43 per cent. By 1920 the total returns of the Empress mill for the 43 years it had been in operation amounted to Rs 75,000,000 that is 50 times the capital initially invested. Between 1877 and 1907 the capital

32 Wacha, n. 27, 21.

33 N. 30.

34 F. H. Harris, *The Life of J. N. Tata*, (London, 1925), 37.

of the company grew from Rs 1,500,000 to 4,700,000.[35] The exploitation of the textile workers yielded an enormous surplus value and led to a vast capital accumulation, which Tata subsequently invested in the building of iron and steel works and a hydro-electric power station.

Besides Tata, the Bombay manufacturer M. Gokuldas, whom we mentioned earlier, and Sunderdas Jeitha—a Bhattia business-man who collaborated with the British—began to build factories in the interior of the country. Jeitha was the biggest cotton merchant and the owner of ships and numerous enterprises for cleaning and pressing cotton in Maharashtra.[36] He built three mills one after the other; the first one was opened in Bombay, in 1872; the next in Madras, in 1874; and the last in Jalgaon, (in Maharashtra) in 1872.[37] The cotton merchant Thakersey Mooljee, also a member of the Bhattias, became a manufacturer in 1873.

Among the new millowners who emerged after the cotton boom of the sixties, cotton merchants, who had made their fortune by collaborating with the British capital that exploited India as a source of raw material predominated. But it would be wrong to assume that in this period the big bourgeoisie arose only from the ranks of merchants trading in cotton. Merchants acting as middlemen in other spheres of commerce also became manufacturers. Moreover, cotton merchants frequently combined the export of cotton with trade in other commodities that were exported and imported.

In 1874, eleven new mills were put into operation in Bombay—a record number which was surpassed only in 1883. The Petits started two mills in this year and became the biggest manufacturers in India. The Sassoons—who, during the time of the cotton boom became big cotton merchants and opened an office in Liverpool, the principal British port for the import of cotton—also put a cotton mill into operation. Among the other capitalists who opened mills in 1874 were A. Habibbhoy, B. R. Mody and A. H. Wadia. The Gujarati Muslim Ahmed Habibbhoy was one of the two Indian directors of the Bank of Bombay,[38] which shows that he was closely associated with British capital. Burjorjee R. Mody, a Parsi began to build his mill as soon as he returned from China where he had represented the Tata enterprise.[39] The Parsi Ardeshir H. Wadia was a descendant of the family whose members were shipbuilders and contractors of the East India Company.

35 *Ibid.*, 35, 42.

36 The cotton trade, incidentally, called forth numerous small enterprises, ran on capitalist lines, for the initial processing of cotton. A considerable part of these enterprises, including those situated in Maharashtra, belonged to Gujarati merchants from Bombay. See n. 25, IV, 1910.

37 N. 6, 725.

38 See, n. 7.

39 N. 6, 715.

If one does not take into consideration the enterprises of the Sassoons, British capital began to operate its first cotton mill in Bombay in 1874. There are good grounds for believing that even earlier, British capitalists had interests in the cotton industry of Bombay. For example, two British dealers were members of the board of administration of the Oriental, one of the first cotton mills built in Bombay. But only in 1874 did an Englishman for the first time become managing director, that is, in fact chief, of a cotton mill in Bombay. This was James Dunckerly, an agent of a British firm which supplied machinery for mills built in Bombay. Many British millowners in Bombay went there originally as representatives of British machine-building firms and then became rich.[40]

The fact that the agents of machine-building enterprises became millowners showed that the developing large-scale industry in India was completely dependent on Britain for the supply of machinery for the factories. The colonial regime, which delayed the industrial development of India, first and foremost obstructed the creation of machine-building industry; this strengthened and deepened the dependence of the Indian industrialists on British capital, forcing them to 'collaborate' with the latter on unfavourable terms.

The dependence of the Indian industry on the supply of machinery from Great Britain determined to a great extent the methods used by British capital to penetrate it. The British suppliers of machinery granted Indian capitalists who were building factories deferred payment terms for the machinery they bought. Only a third of the price was usually paid in cash. A high rate of interest—approximately 6 per cent—was charged for the remaining amount, until it was completely paid off. It is obvious that if delays occurred in the payment of the debt, the British suppliers of the machinery, in fact, became joint owners of the enterprise.[41] Using their monopoly position in respect of the supply of machinery, they not only forced the manufacturers in Bombay to give them a share of the profit, but seized direct control of the large-scale industry through their agents, who became managers and directors.

---

40 The *Indian Textile Journal* wrote later in February 1928, that the founders of the mills in Bombay were local cotton traders and bankers who were helped by the owners of engineering works in Lancashire, and by mechanics and craftsmen sent to India by the factory owners. A few years later, they were joined by several building firms and successful factory managers. Some of those who set up factories of their own were interested in the sale of machinery, for they were agents of the British engineering works which manufactured them. All these founders worked jointly on the boards of directors, which had a rather cosmopolitan membership. The actual leadership, however, was in the hands of managing agencies. Certain firms or families by right of succession almost always held these managing agencies.

41 N. 6, 47

Outwardly this often took on the form of cooperation of British and Indian capitalists in one and the same company and the apparent fusion of their capitals. But in reality the Indian partners did by no means enjoy equal rights.

The British machine-building companies were represented by their commercial agents in the industry of Bombay. The building of mills enabled these agents to make a pretty penny. The agents usually charged a commission of 5 per cent on the value of the machinery they sold. Since the machinery of one mill cost from Rs 700,000 to Rs 800,000, the agent could, at that time, earn up to Rs 50,000 during the building of one enterprise, if the inevitable additional receipts such as bribes and premiums are taken into account.[42] Frequently the agents invested the money they accumulated in the building of new enterprises. By this means, moreover, they eliminated the competition of other British suppliers of machinery; for the agent, who became a shareholder, could influence the business of the company. After the mill was put into operation the agents usually sold their shares. They invested the money they realised in another mill about to be built, thereby making sure of receiving the new orders for the supply of machinery.

However, these earnings could not, of course, provide sufficient funds for the rate of building undertaken by agents in their capacity as independent manufacturers. In 1883, for instance, the firm of the former agents George Cotton and John Greaves started five cotton mills in Bombay. Greaves and Cotton, obviously, could not have managed to do this without help from Great Britain. This aid was not confined to purely financial assistance. The fact that these manufacturers were members of the British bourgeoisie, which ruled India, gave them a real advantage over the Indian managing agents. By relying upon their dominating position in the economy and the state apparatus, the British managing agents could mobilise and place under their control the investments of numerous Indian shareholders. The greater part of the ordinary share capital of British industrial companies usually belonged to Indian shareholders. The British managing agents received not only their portion of the super-profits but, in the shape of founder's shares, premiums, commissions and other deductions, appropriated that part of the super-profits which should have accrued to the capital of their Indian partners. The rate of profit obtained by the British managing agents was usually considerably higher than the rate of dividends of the Indian shareholders.

The Indian stockholders who owned ordinary shares, therefore, had to be satisfied with dividends corresponding approximately to the average rate of profit obtained on Indian industrial capital, which was

42 *Ibid.*

however considerably lower than the actual colonial rate of surplus value extracted at the given enterprise. Indian capitalists, thus, helped the British companies which were acting as managing agencies to extract huge profits by exploiting the proletariat and peasantry of India. At the same time, such a partition of profit gave rise to serious contradictions between British capital and the Indian bourgeoisie which was dependent on it.

After a certain revival of the industrial activity in 1874, a slack period followed which lasted up to 1882. During these eight years only two industrial enterprises were built in Bombay. The new factory owners were the Hindu Premchand Roychand, a partner of Tata and the biggest speculator in landed property in Bombay, and the Hindu Munmohandas Ramjee, who traded in British textiles and was the representative of Ralli Brothers, the leading cotton export company.[43]

In 1883, a record year in the history of the cotton industry of Bombay, thirteen mills were built. Five of these belonged to the British firm Greaves, Cotton and Co. Three other British companies, including the Sassoons, built one mill each. Thus British capital made in 1883 a particularly serious encroachment upon the cotton industry of Bombay.

The big businessmen of Bombay, such as Dinshaw M. Petit, N. B. Jeejeebhoy and a few other merchants, also put new mills into operation. The Parsi Kaikhusro Heeramanek was particularly enterprising. After having set up a company of small Parsi shareholders, he started a weaving mill, the Queen, in 1883 and two spinning mills in 1888. Heeramanek began his career as a cashier of the Bombay-Baroda railway line; in 1868 he became a broker on the stock exchange, and in 1880 he began to trade in cotton and built several cotton pressing establishments. The favourable economic situation of the eighties gave Heeramanek the opportunity to become quickly rich. But after his death in 1893, the company he had established could not withstand the difficulties which arose at the turn of the century and was ruined. In general one can say that the attempts of the small capitalists of Bombay to establish independent industrial enterprises inevitably ended in failure.

In 1884, Nusserwanji Ardaseer Wadia, another member of the family of former shipbuilders, opened his first industrial enterprise. N. A. Wadia increased his fortune by the sale of machinery. His firm N. Wadia and Sons acted as agent for four British engineering works which specialised in textile machinery.[44] This firm fitted out fourteen mills in Bombay alone. Two more Indian brokers dealing in machinery built cotton mills in 1896; they were Naoroji Wadia, the son of Nusserwanji Wadia, and Shapur Sorab, the grandson of the gunsmith and contractor

43 C. H. Rao, *Indian Biographical Dictionary*, 34.
44 N. 6, 647.

of the East India Company whom we have already mentioned. Naoroji Wadia (1849-99) received his education in Liverpool and was, perhaps the first Indian to become a trained engineer. After his return to Bombay in 1866, he worked as manager in the factories of Petit. In 1878 he opened a firm for the supply of machinery, which was connected with four British companies manufacturing textile machinary.[45] Shapur Sorab (1863-1932) received higher technical education in Great Britain and gained practical experience in British factories. Before his return to India, in 1887 Sorab was presented to Queen Victoria by the Secretary of State for India. At that time, Indians trained as engineers were very rare and did not endanger the monopoly of the British specialists.

Incidentally only very few Indian engineers graduated during the following decades. The Victoria Jubilee Technical Institute, which was opened in Bombay in April 1889, trained only skilled mechanics; although the bourgeoisie of Bombay had spent much money on this institution, it did not obtain Indian engineers for its factories.[46]

We have seen that not only did British firms supplying machinery exist in Bombay but also Indian firms, which were dependent on British suppliers. One can say with certainty that the British firms maintained a considerably higher rate of profit than the Indian firms. That all these Greaves, Cottons and later Bradys and Bradburys could build industrial enterprises so quickly and on such a large scale, was to a considerable extent due to the fact that the bourgeoisie of Bombay had to hand over a large portion of its profits to the representatives of British capital. The only Indian agents for the supply of machinery who gradually became big manufacturers were the Wadias, but it took them several decades.

The pace of industrial building in Bombay was, for Indian conditions, fairly rapid up to the end of the 19th century. Sixty-seven cotton mills operated already in the town by 1891.[47] At the close of the 19th century British capital continued to strengthen its positions in the industry of Bombay. In 1895 and 1896 the Sassoons built two more mills and became the biggest millowners in the cotton industry of India. The biggest British firm in India for the import of textiles, Killick, Nixon and Co. opened its first enterprise in 1896.[48] It is rather characteristic that this British firm combined the manufacture of cloth in India with the export of cloth from Great Britain.

Of the 57 new enterprises started in Bombay during the twenty

45 *Ibid.*

46 W.W. Hunter, *Bombay 1885 to 1890, A Study in Indian Administration* (London, 1892), 171.

47 *Indian Cotton Textile Industry 1851-1950, Century Volume,* (Bombay, 1959), 20.

48 A. S. Pearse, *Cotton Industries of India* (Manchester, 1930), 189.

years from 1881 to 1900, British capitalists, including the Sassoons, built 18 mills. The participation of British capital in the building of industrial enterprises in Bombay reached its peak during this period, for before 1880 the British built three mills and after 1900 one mill. By 1895, fourteen of the seventy mills operating in Bombay were directly controlled by British capitalists.[49]

At the close of the 19th century the merchants who collaborated with the British and formed the top strata of Bombay continued to strengthen their position in the industry of the town. In 1888 Ebrahim Currimbhoy, the founder of the richest dynasty of Muslim manufacturers, put his first spinning mill into operation. Currimbhoy was a member of the Khojas, a Gujarati trading caste. He began his business career by setting up a firm in Hong Kong; afterwards he opened offices in Calcutta, Singapore, Shanghai and Kobe in Japan. The commodities which this big merchant handled included opium, cotton and yarn which he exported to the Far East, and tea which he imported from China. Currimbhoy built a number of enterprises in Maharashtra and Indore for the initial processing of the cotton he exported.[50]

Let us examine some of the results of the economic development of Bombay and the emergence there of the big bourgeoisie during the latter half of the 19th century. Data regarding the building of cotton mills are presented in Table 7.1.

Despite the closure of several mills in the early nineties, the cotton industry occupied the leading place in the economy of Bombay; 102 thousand workers were employed in the cotton mills and 33 thousand in the other branches of large-scale industry in 1908.

TABLE 7.1

Development of Modern Cotton Industry in Bombay

Year	*Mills*	*Spindles in 1000s*	*Looms*
1866	13	303	3,400
1876	32	992	9,100
1881	47	1,100	10,900
1885	49	1,347	12,000
1891	67	1,909	14,300
1905	69	2,124	20,200

Source : See Indian Cotton Textile Industry 1851 1905, 20.

Side by side with the machine industry, several tens of thousands

49 N. 6, 54.
50 Rao n. 43, 137.

of handicraftsmen were still engaged in certain branches of small-scale industry. In addition to the mills, whose products were sold not only in India but also in the countries of the Near and Far East, there were small weaving shops which manufactured local varieties of cloths to satisfy the needs of the different sections of the population in Bombay. In 1901 there were 7,500 weavers. In other branches of manual production craftsmen—such as shoemakers, potters, jewellers, tobacco workers, butter and oil manufacturers, confectioners, and bakers—catered to the requirements of the half million inhabitants of the town.

In the second half of the 19th century, as we have already noted, Bombay continued to develop as the major gateway through which the commerce between Great Britain and India was conducted. By the 1890s the total turnover of Bombay's foreign trade had increased elevenfold as compared with the forties. Among the imported commodities cloth and yarn occupied the first place, making up 40-45 per cent of the total value of the imports. It was followed by liquor which made up approximately 20 per cent, and sugar, approximately 10 per cent of the total. Therefore the by far greater part of the import trade consisted either of consumer goods which by the end of the 19th century India could have already produced by modern industrial methods or of alcoholic drinks which were mainly consumed by British officials, officers and soldiers. But the beginning of the import of British capital and the building of industrial enterprises by Indian capital led to the appearance of a new import item, machinery, which was still small but steadily growing. At the end of the 19th century it amounted only to 5 per cent of the total value of the commodities imported into Bombay. Each machine that was imported into India increased the extent of the contradictions that would arise in the future between imperialist Britain and colonial India.

From the 1850s onwards cotton supplanted opium as the principal commodity exported from Bombay; it made up one-third of the total value of exports by the close of the 19th century. Next came oil seeds and wheat. The volume of the opium export increased up to the seventies and only then began its gradual decline. Even at the close of the 19th century Rs 30 million worth of opium was annually exported from Bombay to Asian countries. Thus the export consisted chiefly of the type of commodities that are characteristic of a colony, i.e. a source of agricultural raw materials. But the composition of the export trade too was altered by the growth of industrial production and in the last decade of the 19th century yarn and cloth amounted to over a quarter of the total value of the commodities exported from Bombay.[51] The growing large-scale industry of India, thus, led to changes in the structure of Bombay's foreign trade.

51 *Gazetteer of Bombay City...,* Vol. I, 401.

The merchants of Bombay continued to participate actively in the foreign commerce of their town, although seafaring by Indians was greatly restricted by the almost complete British monopoly of sea transport. The Parsis transported goods even to Europe, let alone China and Japan. Indian and Muslim merchants carried on a lively trade with the countries of the Near East and the British colonies in Eastern Africa.[52]

The semi-government Bank of Bombay and the British exchange banks occupied a dominant position in the financial sphere both in Bombay and in the other towns. The Indian financial organisation was still in the early stages of development. There were no indigenous joint-stock banks and the merchants and manufacturers used their individual connections and relied on the trading and credit relations that existed within the caste organisation to obtain loans, especially long-term ones. The leading figure in this financial system was the indigenous banker, or shroff, who represented big moneylending and loan capital. Between the indigenous financial system and the British banks existed complicated relations based on competition and subordination. While in the interior of the country these relations were facilitated by many intermediate links, in such a centre as Bombay direct contracts between the native bankers and the British banks took place in which the former had to accept a subordinate position.[53]

The Marwari moneylenders played an important part in the credit system of Bombay. The first reference to them can be found in the *Gazetteer of Bombay City* published in 1909. Their penetration into Bombay must have taken place in connection with the powerful expansion of the moneylending capital of Rajputana in Maharashtra, which began in the second quarter of the 19th century after the final defeat of the Peshwa state. In the early 20th century Marwari

52 *Ibid.*, 168.

53 The American consul in Bombay, Henry D. Baker, describes the business activities of the shroff and his connections with the banks in the following way: "An important factor in Indian banking is the 'shroff', who acts as an intermediary between the trading community and the banks. This may be illustrated in the following manner: A shopkeeper in the bazaar, with limited means, finds that, after using all his own money, he requires, say, Rs 25,000 to stock his shop suitably. He approaches the 'shroff', who, after careful inquiries as to the shopkeeper's position, grants the 'accomodation', if satisfied that the business is sound. The demand on the 'shroffs' are often greater than they are able to meet out of their own money, and it is at this point that the assistance of the banks is called into requisition. The 'shroffs' do this by taking bills which they already hold to the banks for discount under their indorsement, such bills being accepted to an extent determined by the standing of the 'shroff' and the strength of the drawers. Past experience has shown that this class of business is one of the safest the banks engage in." H. D. Baker, *British India with Notes on Ceylon, Afganistan and Tibet*, (Washington, 1915), 22-23.

moneylending capital was already rather firmly established in Bombay, where the Marwari dialect was spoken by seven thousand of its inhabitants.[54] In the beginning of the 20th century moneylending remained the chief occupation of the Marwaris in Bombay. The *Gazetteer of Bombay City* relates that the Marwaris headed the group of professional moneylenders, adding that the latter comprised also a number of Parsis and Hindus from the Deccan who, having fallen a prey to the Marwaris, started their own independent business.[55]

By the beginning of the 20th century the Marwari moneylenders had spread their net among all sections of the population of Bombay; they found their clients in all walks of life, from the heir apparent to the mill hand.[56] The colonial legislation provided dependable legal securities for moneylending transactions. An official record admitted that legal proceedings were the principal weapon of the Marwaris.[57]

Data regarding the joint-stock companies operating in Bombay in 1908 give an idea of the branches towards which the enterprise of the Bombay bourgeoisie was mainly directed. Cotton mills absorbed almost half the share capital of all existing companies, that is Rs 91.5 million out of a total of Rs 186.5 million. The aggregate capital of all industrial companies of Bombay (including cotton presses, mining, mills for grinding corn, etc.) amounted to approximately Rs 117 million. Among the other objects in which share capital was invested were banks (Rs 12.7 million), railways and tramways (Rs. 18.8 million), shipbuilding (Rs 7.9 million), landed property and building (Rs 10.2 million).[58]

But these figures need to be amended to a considerable extent. For the greater part of the commercial and credit operations of Indian businessmen in Bombay were undertaken by private firms, that is not joint-stock companies. The hundreds of millions of rupees used in commerce and banking in Bombay considerably surpassed the capital of the industrial enterprises. However, it is characteristic that it was precisely in the national industry that the higher organisational forms of the local capital were evolved and where they predominated.

As to British capital, since the overwhelming majority of British commercial firms and banks operating in Bombay were registered in Great Britain, they were not included in the figures quoted earlier. Thus we can assert that the relation between industrial capital on the one hand and commercial and banking capital on the other were even more favourable for the latter. Although the national capital

54 N. 23, I, 205, 293, 296. The Marwaris were moneylenders and speculated in opium, cotton, silver and gold. Immigrants from Rajasthan were mostly traders.

55 *Ibid.*, 303.

56 *Ibid.*, 304.

57 *Ibid.*, 303.

58 *Ibid*, 309.

strengthened its position in Bombay, the city in the early 20th century continued to be chiefly a centre of British commercial and banking capital which exploited India as a source of raw materials and a commodity market.

The national composition of the population of Bombay changed in the course of the centuries. But, as the records testified Bombay was never a cosmopolitan town. Some tens of thousands of people representing the most diverse nationalities, religions, and citizenship, were, of course, always living in Bombay as in any international port. Incidentally, among the foreigners living in this important colonial centre of the British Empire, Englishmen predominated. According to the information provided by British censuses which were taken during the 19th century, the number of inhabitants of Bombay who were born beyond the borders of India did not exceed 23 per cent of the city's population. It follows, that changes affecting the national structure of Bombay's population could take place only among the Indian inhabitants of the city.

Before Bombay was taken over by the British, the island as well as the seaboard were inhabited by Marathas. When Bombay became the principal factory of the East India Company on the west coast of India, many Gujaratis settled there, and during the 18th century they, perhaps, constituted the largest section of the inhabitants of Bombay. But after the conquest of Maharashtra, in the 19th century, the Maratha population of Bombay grew rapidly. The ruined Maratha peasants and craftsmen, and people who simply left the village in the hope that the additional earnings they made in town would enable them to improve their economic position, flocked in great numbers into Bombay. By 1901 the absolute majority of the population of Bombay, i.e. 51 per cent, consisted of Marathas.

The percentage of Marathas among the working population of Bombay was even larger.

Approximately 75 per cent of the factory workers of Bombay were Hindus, the rest Muslims. Within the Hindu section the *Gazetteer* distinguishes the immigrants who had come from the Konkan, the Ghats (literally "the people from the mountains", a name given to the inhabitants of the mountainous coastal regions of Maharashtra), and the members of the Pardesi community. The Julahs, members of a caste of weavers, formed the majority of the Muslim workers.[59] More than half of the Marathas living in Bombay were members of the Maratha caste,[60] the principal caste in Maharashtra, whose members enjoyed full rights in the village community. These peasants, who had either been ruined or came to town in the hope of additional earnings, worked

59 *Ibid.*, 322.
60 *Ibid.*, 272.

in almost all branches of industry and urban economy of Bombay; their diligence won the admiration even of the officials of the colonial administration.[61] Many Marathas were members of the castes of craftsmen, the Shimpi, Sonar and Teli.

The next national group—according to numerical strength—were the Gujaratis, who made up 26 cent of the population of Bombay. Within the Gujarati section, the Banias formed the largest community, more than 20 per cent of the total. It would be wrong to think, however, that all Gujaratis in Bombay were businessmen. Naturally, a smaller number of peasants who had lost their share of the land were ejected from the relatively well-to-do Gujarati villages than from Maratha villages. Gujarat, moreover, had its own big commercial and industrial centre—Ahmedabad. But among the working population of Bombay were many thousands of Gujaratis, who came in particular from the Surat district which was closest to Bombay. There were especially the members of the caste of village servants—the Dheds or Mahars—who worked in the factories and cleaned the streets.[62]

At the beginning of the 20th century, the big Indian bourgeoisie of Bombay still consisted in the main of Gujaratis; although strong groups of Marwari and Hindustani bourgeoisie began to emerge. Commerce in Bombay remained to a considerable extent in the hands of people who spoke Gujarati; and the local traders usually rendered their accounts in Gujarati, remarked the *Gazetteer of Bombay City*.[63]

The Gujarati merchants of Bombay did not, however, monopolise the trade of this city. Bombay was considered a rich town and, as W. Digby wrote, a sufficiently large amount of capital circulated there to satisfy all the requirements of this great port. Where did this capital come from? The greater part belonged to foreigners, to European mercantile banks and European merchants (most of these were from countries other than Great Britain); the bulk of the indigenous capital did not come from local sources either but belonged to Indian bankers and merchants from the native principalities, who owned approximately Rs 60 million of the capital that circulated in Bombay. An important group of rich merchants who had more or less settled down in Bombay were, moreover, emigrants from the native states.[64]

The majority of these capitalists, apparently, were local bankers and merchants from the Gujarati principalities of Kathiawar and Baroda. But among them were undoubtedly Marwari, Hindustani and other

61 *Ibid.*, 224.

62 *Ibid.*, 226.

63 *Ibid.*, 3. H. R Baker, the American consul in Bombay observed that Gujarati was the great commercial language of Western India and was used by the Parsees as well. Marwari, another commercial language, was equally important. Baker, n. 53, 35.

64 W. Digby, *Prosperous British India*, 185.

non-Gujarati merchants. Generally speaking, non-Gujarati capitalists played a more important part in the commerce of Bombay than in its industry, where the families of hereditary Bombay merchants predominated. One can assume that the indigenous merchants of Bombay were induced to invest their accumulations in industry as a result of a certain amount of competition by merchants hailing from the interior.

According to the *Gazetteer of Bombay City* the leading group of capitalists included members of the following Gujarati castes and communities: Bhattias, Banias, Bohras, Khojas and Parsis in addition to Marwaris, and Memons (a Hindustani community of Muslim merchants).[65] The only Maratha caste mentioned is the Brahmins from the Deccan, listed among the castes that have produced some of the wealthy inhabitants of Bombay. Since there were no businessmen among the Brahmins at that time, one can assume that the wealthy Marathas were either landowners who lived in Bombay or prosperous members of the free professions, in the main, lawyers.

Data concerning the nationality and religious or communal group to which the millowners of Bombay belonged are interesting. (see Table 7.2).

TABLE 7.2

Ownership of Cotton Mills Cotton Millowners : Communitywise

Years	*Number of Mills Built*	*Number of Mills Built by :* *Parsis*	*Hindus*	*Muslims*	*Total Indians*	*British including Sassoons*
1854-70	13	9	3	1	13	—
1871-80	17	4	8	2	14	3
1881-90	39	17	6	3	26	13
1891-1900	18	6	4	3	13	5
1901-15	9	5	2	1	8	1
Total	96	41	23	10	74	22

Sources : Data in *Bombay Industries: The Cotton Mills.*

65. "The capitalists of Bombay belong to various classes: Bhattia, Jain, Marwari, Bania, Khoja, Memon, Bohra, Parsi, and Jew; while there will be found a certain number of rich individuals; among the Gujarat and Deccan Brahmans, the Sonars (a caste of jewellers), the Arabs and the Hindus from Multan.

"The Bhattias are chiefly cloth merchants, landlords and millowners; the Jains of Gujarat are bankers, jewellers, shroffs, and commission agents, while those of Cutch are grain merchants and cotton-brokers; the Marwadis are moneylenders and speculate in opium, cotton, silver and gold; the Banias do the same and are traders of every denomination; the Khojas are landlords millowners, general merchants, contractors and do a large trade in imports and exports; the Bohras and Memons are landlords, contractors, stationery merchants and general traders. The Parsis are ubiquitous in every branch of trade; the European capitalist is usually a large importer and exporter." N. 23, I, 293.

Three quarters of the cotton industry were therefore, built by the Indian bourgeoisie. It is obvious that Parsi capitalists played a leading role in setting up new cotton mills in Bombay. They were followed by the Hindu capitalists, who founded approximately a quarter of the cotton mills, and by the British. During which years did the capitalists of the various communities display a particularly intensive building activity? The Parsis built nine mills during the first 16 years, 1854-70, representatives of other communities four. The dominance of the Parsis during these years is understandable if one takes into account that they dominated the commerce of that time. During the following years too—except during the decade 1871 to 1880—a relatively larger number of mills were set up by the Parsis. The Hindus managed to take the lead only in one decade (1871-80), although they continued to build a considerable number of enterprises. The majority of Hindu millowners, as we have already seen, were engaged in the cotton trade. Their appearance in the industry of Bombay must, therefore, be connected with the fact that in the sixties Bombay became the principal port for the export of cotton. The Muslim merchants who collaborated with the British were slow to invest their accumulations in industry.

Since Table 7.2 is concerned with the founders of mills and not with their owners, it does not reflect the transfer of mills from one owner to the other. The table reproduced by Rutnagar (see Table 7.3) shows the actual number of mills which were controlled by Indian capitalists, communitywise, and by the British.

TABLE 7.3

Control of Cotton Mills in Bombay

Religion or Nationality	*Firms*	*Mills*	*Firms*	*Mills*
	1895		*1915*	
Hindu	27	30	11	18
Parsi	15	22	14	25
Muslim	4	4	7	11
Total controlled by Indians	46	56	32	54
British Including Sassoons	4	14	8	29
Grand Total	50	70	40	83

Source : *See Bombay Industries. . .*, p. 54.

Indian capital investments have, therefore, always exceeded British investments. But at the same time one must emphasise that the number of mills controlled by the British has been steadily growing, both in absolute figures and in relation to the total number of mills. The rather frequent assertions, made by bourgeois economists, that British capital played an insignificant part in the industry of Bombay, do not correspond to the facts.

The reason why the number of mills built exceeded the number in operation (see Table 7.2) was that some mills were closed down, some were burnt down and some were amalgamated with other mills.

In the beginning of the 20th century, during the depression and the subsequent technical reorganisation, the Hindu capitalists who had up to then controlled a larger number of mills than any other section of capitalists, had to relinquish their leading position to the Parsi manufacturers.

One can form an idea of the wealth of the Bombay bourgeoisie on the basis of the data for 1905 which have been published by the revenue authorities (see Table 7.4).[66]

TABLE 7.4
Biggest Taxpayers of Bombay

Annual Income,	*Taxpayers*			
Rs 1000s	*Parsis*	*Hindus*	*Muslims*	*Total*
20-30	23	72	29	124
30-40	11	36	15	62
40-50	9	8	2	19
50-100	13	15	9	37
Over 100	6	7	4	17
Total	62	138	59	259

Naturally these figures do not provide a picture of the actual size of the capital owned by the bourgeoisie of Bombay, the more so, as the revenue departments of colonial India, just as those of any other capitalist country, always quote excessively low figures regarding the income of the big bourgeoisie.

The industrial capitalists of Bombay were still carrying on commercial operations on a large scale, especially transactions in which they acted as intermediaries of foreigners. Even Tata, one of the biggest industrialists of Bombay, extended his activities in this sphere. For instance, simultaneously with the building of the iron and steel works, the Tatas were the first Indian merchants who began to export cotton for the Japanese industry which was ousting Indian yarn from the Chinese market. For the services he rendered the Japanese textile monopolies, R. D. Tata was awarded "The Order of the Rising Sun"[67] The combination of industrial activity and commerce was not infrequent

66 N. 23, I, 294-95.

67 C. N. Vakil and D. N. Maluste, *Commercial Relations Between India and Japan*, (Bombay, 1937), 89.

in European and American countries, but it became the rule in colonial Bombay. It is, in fact, impossible to name any big manufacturer in Bombay who was not a merchant at the same time; many were, moreover, chiefly merchants. The Bhattia and Khoja capitalists were big landowners. As we have noted earlier, the Parsis were the richest owners of landed property in Bombay. The estates referred to in the present case were apparently situated in the countryside. Since this is not mentioned in earlier sources, it can be assumed that the capitalists of Bombay began to lay hold of the land in the second half of the 19th century. The process in which the bourgeoisie of Bombay became landed proprietors in the countryside was directly connected with the transformation of the country into a source supplying agricultural raw material for the industry of imperialist Britain, and was engendered by the general economic conditions in colonial India. On the whole, however, landed property was not a principal object of the business activities of the Bombay bourgeoisie.

Important changes took place in the cotton industry of Bombay at the beginning of the imperialist period, at the close of the 19th century and in the early 20th century. First of all it should be noted that it had to change its orientation. While it previously worked for the foreign markets, mainly those of China, it turned now towards the home market. The cotton industry of Bombay, as we have already mentioned, was designed for the export of yarn to China. The output of fabrics for the home market continued to be comparatively small. In the latter half of the 19th century, the export of yarn from Bombay to China grew rapidly, rising from 19,817 bales in 1876 to 77 thousand bales in 1881 and 403 thousand in 1891. It reached its highest level in 1905, when it totalled 651 thousand bales.[68] How important a proportion of the yarn produced in Bombay was exported to China can be seen even from the fact that between 1901 and 1904 the average annual output of the Bombay mills was approximately 800 thousand bales.[69] But from 1905 onwards the export of yarn from Bombay decreased continuously, falling from 405 thousand bales in 1913, to 108 thousand in 1908 and a few tens of thousands of bales in the twenties.[70] The changes caused in the marketing of the manufactures were to a large extent due to the fact that the Far Eastern countries, first of all Japan and to a certain extent China as well, set up their own machine industry. Imperialist Japan began to supplant colonial India in the Chinese market.

The sale of its products in the gradually expanding home market provided a certain compensation for the industry of Bombay. But the

68 *Minutes of Evidence Taken Before the Committee Appointed to Inquire into the Indian Curency,* (London, 1893), 244.

69 N. 47, 21.

70 N. 6, 433.

manufacturers of Bombay encountered two serious difficulties in the home market. First, the ultimate capacity of the internal market was limited by the colonial conditions under which capitalism developed in India. The semi-feudal system of landownership, which was preserved by imperialism, hampered the differentiation process of the peasantry and thereby held back the development of the home market. Secondly even, in this restricted market the Gujarati bourgeoisie had to face two competitors, in the first instance British capitalism, and also the emerging bourgeoisie of the other Indian nationalities, whose sphere of activity was in the main, handlooms.

The following figures, taken from official statistics, show that the consumption of both machine-made and handloom fabrics was growing.

TABLE 7.5
Consumption of Textile in India

Variety	1896-1990 Million Yards	1896-1990 Per cent	1918-1922 Million Yards	1918-1922 Per cent
Machine-Made	301	9.8	1,432	38.8
Handmade	846	27.5	1,058	29.6
Imported	1,932	62.7	1,166	31.6
Total	3,079	100	3,656	100

Source : Indian Textile Journal, January 1931.

Although the data indicate that the import of British cloth dropped in the first two decades of the 20th century, they do not fully reflect the real position. Firstly, since British textiles were more expensive than the Indian textiles, their share in terms of value was greater than these figures show; secondly, the output of cloth in British enterprises in India went up, i.e., the export of commodities was superseded by the export of capital. We will later deal at greater length with the question of handloom production. Here we will merely note that the overall increase in both production and consumption of handloom fabrics, as indicated by the figures quoted earlier, seems rather unlikely. The colonial statistics apparently, recorded, in the main, cloth that was sold in the market. The output of these fabrics increased undoubtedly, because the small industries extended their connections with the market as a result of the development of capitalism within these industries. But the production of cloth in the auxiliary rural industries simultaneously decreased at least to the same extent.

The change in the orientation of the modern machine industry of Bombay meant not only that the sale of cloth on the home market led to an increased competition with the handloom weaver, but also that the connections between the big and small cotton producers were widened. This was because the Indian machine-made yarn that had been ousted from the Chinese market was partly sold to local weavers. That was the reason why such an influential representative of the Bombay manufacturers as Thackersey considered it necessary to announce that the immediate revival of handloom weaving on a commercial basis was a question requiring the most serious attention of all those who were favourably disposed towards India.[71]

The beginning of the imperialist epoch was marked both by the intensification of the contradictions existing between the Indian bourgeoisie and imperialism in the foreign and home markets in the early 20th century, and by the emergence of conflicts within the Indian bourgeoisie itself based on the division of the Indian market. The "cordial relations" that existed between the propertied strata of Bombay and the colonialists were broken off at the end of the 19th century. The interests of the Bombay bourgeoisie, who had gained strength, clashed with the growing expansion of British imperialism. The Indian National Congress—which its founders, the capitalists of Bombay, and its sponsors, the colonial administrators, had intended to be a most loyal organisation—was, to the great surprise of both these groups, turned into a tribune against colonialism by the emerging bourgeois opposition.

The rise of this opposition was precipitated by the discriminating policy of the British authorities. The import duties on British textiles, which had been abolished in 1882, were re-introduced in 1894. At the same time an excise duty was inposed on cotton goods produced in India. In this way the British authorities created equal conditions of competition for the comparatively weak Indian industry and that of Great Britain, the most powerful cotton industry in the world. Discriminative measures were carried through with particular force during the administration of Curzon (1899-1905). The financial reform, in particular, struck a heavy blow at the national industry during this period.[72]

The new orientation of the industry of Bombay towards the home market demanded a sharp increase in the production of cloth and a reduced output of yarn for sale. This necessitated an expensive technical reorganisation of the machine industry; during the decade 1906-15 the number of weaving looms operating in Bombay was increased by 85 per cent. The famine and plague which raged at the close of the 19th century and the financial measures of Curzon caused additional difficulties. The changed situation in the foreign market combined with

---

71 *Times of India*, February 3, 1906.

72 Regarding Curzon's financial reform see N. D. Grodko, *Kreditno-denezhnaya sistema Indii v period kolonialnoi zavisimosti*, (The Credit and Financial System during the Period of India's Colonial Dependence), Moscow, 1956.

the above-mentioned conditions at home, which had arisen because India was a colony, led to a sudden drop in industrial construction.[73] Only eight mills, all of them weaving mills, were built in Bombay between 1905 and 1915.

The weaker companies could not withstand the difficulties of reorganisation, and, between 1895 and 1915, 44 companies, owning 58 enterprises—that is more than two-thirds of the cotton industry of Bombay—went bankrupt. Even some firms belonging to big merchants who collaborated with the British failed as a result of the reorientation towards the home market. The oldest enterprise of Bombay, the Oriental mill was one of the first to go bankrupt. It was taken over by Peerbhoy Adamjee, a member of the Bohra community. In 1861, at the age of seventeen, Adamjee came to Bombay where he engaged in small-scale trade to start with; later he was connected with the commissariats of the Anglo-Indian army. He worked his way up from sutler to big military supplier. Adamjee set up several leather works and furnished not only the army of Bombay but also that of Madras with footwear. For his loyal services Adamjee was knighted by the colonialists.[74]

The ruin of a number of companies led to a greater centralisation of production. The majority of enterprises which became insolvent were taken over either by the British firms Brady and Bradbury, Sassoons or by the stronger Indian companies such as those owned by the Petits, Currimbhoys, Gokuldas, and Habibbhoys.

Among the new Indian manufacturers the Parsis Shapur B. Broacha and Hormuz M. Mehta deserve to be mentioned. S. B. Broacha made a fortune serving the biggest princes of India as attorney. Being closely connected with the business life of the principalities, Broacha took an active part in financing big industrial enterprises. One has to take into account that it was precisely the period preceding the First World War, when many princes started to invest the money they had obtained from their subjects by tax robbery, in industry, banking and commerce. S. B. Broacha was the biggest agent of the princes investing their accumulations in industry. In 1915 alone, Broacha bought four spinning mills from Greaves, Cotton and Co. and managed to install weaving looms in the enterprises he had acquired, even under the difficult war

73 "The cloth trade with Africa and Arabia and the yarn trade with China had become important by 1882. The closing of Indian mints in 1893 to the free coinage of silver, together with the industrial development in recent years of Japan, which now not only supplies its own needs, but is a keen competitor with India in the China yarn market, have to some extent retarded the rapidity with which the Bombay yarn industry was previously expanding and have turned the attention of those interested in the production of cloth on a larger scale." See n. 1, I, 65.

74 Rao, n. 43, 50.

conditions when the import of machinery into India almost ceased. By 1920 Brocha was managing agent of seven mills.[75]

The Parsi Hormusjee M. Mehta was the last big manufacturer to rise from the ranks of commission agents supplying machinery. Having set up his firm in 1897, H. M. Mehta had already by 1917 become the managing agent of three mills. It is significant that even Mehta, who was a supplier of machinery, refrained from building new mills and preferred with the assistance of Parekh, the biggest manufacturer of Ahmedabad, to get hold of enterprises that belonged to ruined companies. In 1915 H. M. Mehta founded a firm which specialised in the import of cars, and in 1918 he established the commercial company Uganda and a large insurance company.

The stagnation which affected the building of new mills in Bombay since the early 20th century showed itself in the fact that older companies preferred to acquire managing agencies rather than start new enterprises; this saved them from worries, helped to increase the capital and reduced the risk, as Vera Anstey wrote.[76] Of the nine industrial enterprises built in Bombay in the pre-war years, two belonged to N. Wadia, a commission agent for the supply of machinery, and one each to Tata, Currimbhoy and James Finlay and Co., a British firm specialising in the export of cotton. The early 20th century was, on the whole a period during which both British capital and the strongest individual representatives of Indian merchant capital who collaborated with the British were consolidating their positions in the textile industry of Bombay.

The growing number of looms in operation led to a considerable increase in the output of cloth, which jumped from an annual average of 293 million yards in 1901-04 to 618 million yards in 1911-14. However, in spite of this, it was precisely in the beginning of the 20th century that Bombay started to lose its dominating position in the cotton industry of India. Its share in the total output of yarn in India fell during these years from 57 per cent to 52, and in the production of cloth from 54 to 53 per cent.[77] The remoteness of Bombay from the cotton-growing districts and the comparatively obsolete machinery used in its mills already began to have an effect.

At the beginning of the 20th century the bourgeoisie of Bombay put forward plans for the construction of iron and steel works and hydro-electric power stations. It was impelled to do this by the stagnation which affected the building of cotton mills and by the desire to reduce its dependence on British capital by creating its own technical and power base. Jamshedji Tata stood at the head of this undertaking.

75 N. 6, 252, 701.

76 V. Anstey, *The Economic Development of India*, (London, 1931), 114.

77 N. 47, 21.

At first Tata tried to obtain a loan from the bankers in London, but he did not succeed. There upon in 1902, Tata went to the U.S.A.[78]

As a result of negotiations with the largest iron and steel company of the U.S.A., Carnegie Steel Company, and with J. Kennedy, who was in charge of the biggest construction projects in the American steel industry, Jamshedji Tata received from the American monopolies technical aid but they refused to grant him financial assistance.[79] One of the first American experts sent by the Carnegie Steel Company was R. Watson, who became later vice-president of the United States Steel Corporation.[80] According, to Keenan, one of the American directors of the Tata combine, Jamshedji Tata wrote to his son from America that the management of his works must be American.[81] The Tata enterprise was, indeed, predominantly directed by American engineers.

After having failed to obtain financial support from the British and American monopolies, Tata turned towards native capital. The nominal share capital of the Tata combine originally amounted to £1,630 thousand. One quarter of this sum came from the Scindia, the remaining shares were bought by Indian capitalists, in the main from Bombay, within the next few days. The rapid sale of the shares exposes the conjectures of the British economists who alleged that the timidity and passivity of the Indian capitalists induced Tata to appeal to the British and American monopolists. The real reason for Tata's appeal to the British monopolists was his desire to secure the support, or at least a favourable reception from the state apparatus of the colonial dictatorship, and his wish to obtain technical assistance from British firms. When he failed in this he had to apply to the American monopolies for financial and technical assistance. But both the American and British monopolists declined to make any investments in the steel industry of the colony, preferring to gain control of it by other, rather effective, means. The British hoped to achieve this by taking advantage of the dependence of the Indian steel industry on government orders, while the Americans counted on the supply of machinery on credit and on the technical aid which they were to furnish.

The colonial powers, moreover, endeavoured altogether to prevent the creation of a modern Indian steel industry. They tried, in particular, to make prospecting in southern Bihar impossible by placing all kinds of obstacles in its way, and Tata's geological prospecting parties were not permitted to work in the native states of Central India. After the first section of the factory was built the colonial administration hampered its work by discriminating against it when orders had to be

---

78 See J.L. Keenan, *Steel Man in India*, (New York, 1944), 29.
79 *Ibid.*, 29, 30.
80 *Ibid.*, 43.
81 *Ibid.*, 38.

placed, and by introducing a number of changes in its customs policy. During the First World War, however, when the Tata combine was the only big iron and steel enterprise in any of the British possessions situated in the area of the Indian Ocean, the British were forced to give it some very profitable military orders. During the five-year period, 1912-16, the net profit of the company added up to Rs 23,509 thousand, that is, it exceeded the total share capital which amounted to Rs 23,175 thousand. In 1917 alone the company extracted a profit of Rs 10,569 thousand.[82] Deliveries of ferro-manganese to American steel furnaces, which were implementing military orders, also brought Tata huge profits.[83] The money capital which a section of the Gujarati bourgeoisie, headed by Tata, had accumulated during the First World War, led in the twenties to an aggravation of the antagonism between the bourgeoisie of Bombay and the colonial regime which hindered the transformation of this capital into productive capital.

In addition to the Gujarati bourgeoisie of Bombay, another group of big Gujarati bourgeoisie emerged in the latter half of the 19th century. It arose in Gujarat proper and consisted exclusively of members of Hindu and Jain castes of traders and moneylenders, in the main, Banias.

The *Bombay Gazetteer* described in the following way the activities of the Gujarati Banias in the beginning the 20th century:

> Of Gujarat Vanias a few are landholders and some are in government or private service, but the bulk are traders and shopkeepers. Most Vania landholders have invested in land money made in trade or as pleaders. The rest are mortgagees or holders of lands granted for services rendered as district revenue superinten-dents *(desais)* and as district accountants *(majumdars)*. Of those in service the greater number are in native firms, some in posts of trust well paid and with chances of private trade and profit; others are simpler clerks poorly paid and badly off. Of the rest some are in government employ, most as clerks and a few in high positions. Some, especially among the Modhs (a subcaste), are clerks and administrators in the native states of Kathiawar and in Cutch; some are in European merchants' offices and in railways and in spinning companies in Bombay.[84]

One can, therefore, outline three fields of activity of the Gujarati Banias during the second half of the 19th century: government and private service, landownership, and trading and moneylending operations. Service in the colonial revenue departments and in those of the native states was, in a way, a continuation and modification of

82 G. Pilcher, *Steel as a Factor in India's Progress*, (Calculta, 1923), 28.

83 Keenan, n. 78, 63.

84 *Bombay Gazetteer*, IX, Part I, 77.

tax-farming which the Gujarati moneylenders had practised for a long time. The acquisition of landed property by the Banias was also a result of their moneylending operations. Trade and moneylending remained, therefore, the economic basis of the business activities of the Banias.

Gujarat was one of the regions which, during the second half of the 19th century, British capital converted with special energy into a source of raw material and a market for British commodities. In the 1850s Gujarat supplied three quarters of the cotton exported from Bombay.[85] Although Maharashtra's total output and export of cotton afterwards outdistanced that of Gujarat, the latter still remained the second largest cotton producing area in India. The ratio of commodity output to the total output was comparatively high in the peasant households of Gujarat, which created favourable conditions for the activities of trading and moneylending capital in the countryside.

In addition to cotton export the Gujarati merchants traded in corn on a large scale; corn was needed by not only the urban population but also by the peasants who were growing cotton. In periods of famine the merchants sold their grain at inflated prices.[86]

The trader and moneylender was the basic unit of the Gujarati trading and moneylending capital in the countryside. The *Bombay Gazetteer*, writes: "Of moneylenders who live in the country, the village shopkeepers and cotton dealers are Vanias by caste."[87] here follows a description of how he, like a spider, spreads his web.

> A moneylender starting in life borrows a few rupees in the town, buys small supplies of clarified butter, oil, molasses (jaggery) and stocks his shop. The villagers, having no money, barter small quantities of their grain or cotton for as much oil as will keep their evening lamp burning for an hour, or for little supplies of groceries. They are unaware of the market value of their raw produce, and are satisfid that they have made a bargain if the shopkeeper, with a polite show of liberality, throws in a little more of the article he is selling, under the name of a bonus. When he has gathered enough raw produce, the trader carries it to the town, sells it, and returning to the village resumes work on a larger scale.

This picture, which relates to 1855, still describes a comparatively patriarchal mode of rural commerce when agriculture in Gujarat was on the threshold of commodity production.

But even this example illustrates the evil role played by the harmless rural commerce. For the merchant in the countryside, wrote the *Gazetteer*, the shop was mainly useful as a means which forced the village poor to open an account with him

85 J. Chapman, *Cotton and Commerce of India*, 193.
86 Postans, *Western India in* 1838, II, 222-3.
87 N. 84, II, 449.

> If a villager has lost a bullock the trader offers him money to buy a new one. If another has a child to marry or has to give a funeral feast, the trader supplies clarified butter, molasses and cloth, charging for them twice their value. (One need not wait long for the denouement). After a time the moneylender tells his customers that they must draw up a bond showing how the account stands. The paper is prepared, the cultivator scrawling beneath it his mark, a rude plough. When the crop is reaped and the government share is paid, the debtor with much entreaty, gets enough to live for a short time, and on account of the remainder is credited with whatever the shopkeeper is pleased to allow him.[88]

From whom does the village Bania borrow a few rupees when he is in town, or to be more precise, from whom does he receive the financial support necessary to set up his moneylending business? The answer is provided by the *Bombay Gazetteer.* "Those who have a small capital borrow money on easy terms from some wealthy member of their caste and employ it in usury or in dealings in cloth, grain, and other articles."[89] Thus once again we find evidence indicating that members of the trading and moneylending castes were in the habit of granting loans to one other.

One of the principal conditions for the flourishing of the moneylenders in Gujarat was the direct assistance they received from the British administration especially the judiciary. How effective this support was can be seen from the fact that, in 1874 alone, 6,623 debtors appeared before the district court of Surat, representing 4.36 per cent of the total number of families living in the district. Only 136 cases, or 2.5 per cent, were decided in favour of the debtors.[90]

While the business activities of the village moneylenders and shopkeepers were going well during the latter half of the 19th century, the situation was rather different for the big bankers in the towns of Gujarat. The collection of taxes and the payments to the troops were taken out of the hands of the Gujarati shroffs after the establishment of British rule. In consequence their branches in Delhi, Poona and other feudal headquarters had to curtail their operations.

R. Heber, who stayed in India from 1824 to 1826, gained the impression that commerce was quite insignificant in Surat. It consisted mainly of the export of cotton which was sent to Bombay. All industrial commodities, except shawls, which were not in great demand, passed through the hands of the British. The business of the local merchants was in a bad state. For instance, an ancient Muslim family, which had

88 N. 84, IX, Pt. I, 78, fn 3.

89 *Ibid.*

90 N. 84, II, 201.

formerly been famous for its wealth, supported itself by selling the beautiful family library. Armenian merchants too were in a deplorable condition. Only the Bohra merchants, who were engaged in banking throughout the whole of Gujarat, were flourishing; and the Parsis, who owned half the houses in Surat. They had learnt to accumulate vast fortunes, wrote Heber.[91]

In their search for new spheres in which to invest their capital the shroffs of Gujarat turned towards the opium trade, the annual turnover of which was estimated to have reached Rs 5 million in 1849. With the expansion of the cotton export many merchants of Gujarat either became agents of Bombay firms or set up their own business. Many big shroffs became rich by financing the cotton trade.[92] The shroffs of Ahmedabad in general preserved their money capital. In the 1870s there were many rich men among them, whose wealth, even according to the figures of the tax departments, reached Rs 1 million to Rs 1.2 million.[93] The family history of the Nagar Seths,[94] the most influential banking dynasty of Ahmedabad, gives an idea of the commercial and financial transactions undertaken by the bankers of Ahmedabad in the 19th century. Seth Hukumbhai (died in 1858), whose business activities extended to Bengal and Delhi, traded in fabrics and spices, and was a moneylender. His son Premabhai was well known for his extremely cordial relations with the East India Company, which received considerable assistance from him during the Sepoy uprising in 1857. Hathising (1796-1845), another member of the Nagar Seth family, was mainly engaged in the export of opium to China. His cargoes were reported to have amounted to two thousand chests of opium at a time.[95]

The indigenous bankers of Kathiawar granted loans only to the big landowners and made regular advances to merchants for commercial purposes. Big merchants used their own capital mainly in the cotton trade, making advances to the small traders. Some of the capitalists of Bhavnagar had a capital of Rs 1 million to Rs 1.2 million.[96]

In the eighties the business of the biggest bankers of Baroda experienced a certain decline, for the times when "they lent money on interest to the state and to the military class"[97] had passed, and

---

91 R. Heber, *Voyage dans les provinces superieures de l'Inde*, (Paris, 1835), 399.

92 N. 84, IV, 64.

93 *Ibid.*, 63.

94 Seth (from Sanskrit *shreshthin*, the head of a guild, a moneylender) is an honorary prefix placed before the name of a rich member of the trading and moneylending caste. It makes it possible to establish that a given person is a member of this caste.

95 N. 30 (February, 1931).

96 N. 84, VIII, 208.

97 The bankers of Baroda granted loans to the small states of Kathiawar as late

important new spheres were not available for their business activities, since Baroda was not an important commercial centre and the bankers of Baroda did not engage in commerce. Their top layer however, which consisted of the princely bankers, retained their accumulated wealth. For example, the fortune of only two of the princely bankers was valued at Rs 7.5 million.[98]

The information we have indicates that the Gujarati shroffs encountered a certain amount of difficulty in the wholesale trade. Taking advantage of the proximity of Gujarat and the fact that it had been opened up, the British firms and the Gujarati merchants of Bombay, who collaborated with the British managed in a number of cases without the help of the local bankers in the ports, thereby limiting their participation in the wholesale trade.[99] The competition of the Bank of Bombay in the financial sphere increased in the 1870s, when this British-controlled bank began to issue bills of exchange in respect of the cotton exported from Bombay.[100] In consequence several local bankers either became agents of Bombay firms[101] or migrated into the interior of the country.

The traders and moneylenders of Gujarat, thus, had ample opportunity to take part in the exploitation of the population of Gujarat, especially the peasantry, when this province was turned into a source of raw material (cotton) for export purposes. But the British banks and commercial firms and the Bombay merchants collaborating with the British were in some instances able to establish direct contacts with the village dealer, and to restrict the opportunity of the local bankers and merchants to act as intermediaries. This was one of the circumstances inducing the merchants and bankers to invest their accumulations in the cotton industry.[102]

During the latter half of the 19th century, the Gujarati castes of traders and moneylenders extended their activities beyond the borders of Gujarat, and especially in west Maharashtra. The purely commercial operation—excluding moneylending—of the Gujarati businessmen who collaborated

---

as the middle of the nineteenth century. See G. Le Grand Jacob, *Western India Before and During the Mutinies,* (London, 1871), 37.

98 *Ibid.*, VIII, 123.

99 "But as the native bankers" (in Broach-V. P.) cannot compete with the low rates of discount charged by the Bombay Bank, the greater part of the cotton trade is now [1875] carried on by Europeans and Eurasians, only about one-eighth remaining in the hands of local capitalists... Cotton is now bought in one of two ways, either by the local agents of Bombay firms, or by the owners of ginning-factories in Broach." *Ibid.*, II, 446, 429.

100 *Ibid.*, IV, 65.

101 *Ibid.*, 444.

102 Some of the bankers of Broach invested their capital in enterprises for the cleaning and pressing of cotton. *Ibid.*, 446.

with the British covered to a smaller or larger extent the whole of India.

Apart from the Marwaris, the Gujarati Banias were the strongest group of merchants and moneylenders in the western part of Maharashtra. The Gujarati moneylenders settled in Maharashtra as far back as the 17th and 18th centuries. "Gujarat Vanias . . . are said to have come to the Deccan about 250 years ago when Surat was the chief centre of trade in western India." But the Gujarati moneylenders were "still considered foreigners",[103] wrote the *Gazetteer.*

Since we will later examine the activities of the merchants and moneylenders of Maharashtra in greater detail—using the Marwaris as an example—we will here only describe the principal features denoting the size and character of the business operations of the Gujarati merchant and moneylenders. As in Gujarat, the basic unit of their trading and moneylending activity was the village shopkeeper and moneylender, who was, just as much as the Marwari, an indispensable figure in the Maratha village.[104]

With the support of the village trader and moneylender, the big Gujarati moneylenders and commercial firms collaborating with the British seized the leading positions in the wholesale commerce of Maharashtra. *The Gazetteer* relates, "The importers are chiefly Gujarat and Marwar Vanias" in the Poona district, and "nearly three-fourth of the cotton grown is sent by rail from the eastern subdivisions to Bombay by Bhattias and Marwar and Gujarat Vanis".[105]

The methods which the Gujarati moneylenders used to exploit the Maratha peasants and craftsmen differed in no way from the devices employed by the Marwaris, although the compilers of the gazetteers tried to depict the Gujarati moneylenders as kinder and more loyal than their Marwari colleagues. How little the kind and loyal Gujarati moneylenders differed from the Marwaris can be seen even from the burning hatred with which they were regarded by the Maratha peasants. Driven to despair, the peasants often resorted to savage reprisals against them. Peasants from the village of Chinch in Satara killed a Gujarati moneylender with axes in 1873, for this the colonial court sentenced four of their fellow villagers to be hanged, and one to penal servitude for life.

In how far the robbed peasants were justified in falling back upon such acts of violence against the local moneylenders can be judged from the tragic story, which we are quoting in the impassive words of a colonial official.

> At Visapur in Tasagaon (a district in Satara) one Appa Ravji owed money on a bond to Hirachand Gujar. Hirachand threatened to sell Appa Ravji's land, but promised he would not sell it if Appa

103 *Ibid.*, XVIII, Pt 2, 98-99.

104 *Ibid.*, 106, 166; XIX, 181.

105 *Ibid.*, XVIII, Pt 2, 167, 170.

Ravji got one Appa Mali to go bail for him. Appa Mali accordingly passed a bond for £20 (Rs 200) to the Gujar, giving his house and land as security. The agreement was that Appa Ravji should at the same time in consideration of this and other debts pass Appa Mali a bond for £40 (Rs 400) giving his land as security. This bond was never forthcoming. Appa Mali was put off time after time. Meanwhile the Gujar enforced Appa Mali's bond for £20 (Rs 200). After all due proceedings in the civil court Appa Mali's lands and house were seized, and his land given to Appa Ravji to cultivate. Appa Mali despairing of redress waylaid Hirachand Gujar and murdered him in open daylight in the presence of several witnesses. He confessed everything and courted the fullest inquiry into his money transactions. Appa Mali was hanged.[106]

Thus, the Gujarati moneylender doomed to starvation a naive and noble peasant, who in fact did not owe him a farthing. With Jesuitical calculation the moneylender leased the land he had taken away to precisely that peasant who had unwittingly been the cause of his neighbour's ruin. A truly virtuous follower of the doctrine of non-resistance could argue about the hypocrisy of the colonial judges sending a person who was robbed to the gallows.

The revolts of the Maratha peasants, which broke out in the spring of 1875, were in equal measures directed against the Gujarati moneylenders and the Marwaris.[107] The uprising in the Poona district was started by peasants who burned the houses and warehouses of Gujarati moneylenders. The police which arrived immediately restored order and arrested fifty peasants. Recovering from their shock the moneylenders filed a claim for the recompense of the losses they had suffered, which they valued at Rs 150 thousand. Even the *Gazetteer* reckoned that in reality their losses amounted to no more than Rs 25 thousand.[108] The Banias, therefore, attempted to appropriate another Rs 25 thousand. During May and June 1875, many Gujarati moneylenders were attacked by peasants in Poona, Satara, Ahmednagar and other districts of Maharashtra.

Several big firms of Gujarati bankers operated in Hindustan during the period under consideration. The firm "Beni Ram Madho Ram" of Banaras was founded by bankers serving at the courts of the princes of Oudh and Nagpur. One of them, a diwan of the Bhonsle, saved the life of Warren Hastings when the latter escaped from Banaras in 1780. As a reward for this feat the Gujarati banker was granted a big piece of land

106 *Ibid.*, XIX, 187.

107 The causes and nature of these revolts and the conduct of the colonial authorities will be examined in the chapter dealing with the Marwari bourgeoisie.

108 *Ibid.*, XVIII, Pt. I, 120-21.

and a pension. The founders of another banking-house in Banaras, "M. Dvarkanath", which was established in the beginning of the 18th century, hailed from Ahmedabad. In 1903 more than 15 thousand acres of land in the Banaras district alone was in the possession of Gujaratis.[109]

The biggest landowner in the Hamirpur district was the Gujarati Seth Sham Karan, who owned the lands of twelve villages in the beginning of the 18th century. His forefathers, who moved from Gujarat to Hamirpur, became the financial agents of the local nawab. In the period under review, the business of Sham Karan did not go well; he was greatly encumbered with debts and sold some of his villages.[110] In general, the *Gazetteer of the United Provinces* contains many references to the impoverishment, indebtedness or even the ruin of Gujarati bankinghouses. It seems that in the United Provinces the Gujarati bankers were unable to adjust themselves to the new colonial conditions, because they did not have at their disposal a sufficiently widespread network of moneylenders in the countryside.

The accumulations which the Gujarati shroffs retained since the times of the independent feudal states, and which they augmented during the colonial period, formed the principal source from which the building of cotton mills in Gujarat was financed. The Gujarati shroffs, who invested merchant's capital in large-scale industry, had been in a certain degree, prepared for this by the development of the commercial relations which they established in the course of their activities as intermediaries for the sale of British fabrics and the purchase of cotton.

Ahmedabad became the centre of the modern cotton industry of Gujarat. This city, which had formerly been the magnificent capital of the Mogul viceroys of Gujarat, numbered only 97 thousand inhabitants in 1851. Its commerce had a purely provincial character. The handicrafts of Ahmedabad, as of the other towns in Gujarat, experienced a serious decline in the middle of the 19th century. The British conquest deprived it of its foreign markets and undermined its principal home market which was closely linked with the existence of the Indian feudal states, i.e. the court, army, administration and feudal class. The Gujarati towns were ruined by the colonial wars. After Gujarat was conquered by the British, the handicraft production which still existed encountered a powerful competitor in the shape of the British factory. A British source, dating from 1854, which in general provides only extremely scanty information about the economy of the towns that were ruined by the colonialists, had to admit that the decline of the handicrafts of Ahmedabad and Broach, which had formerly flourished, was caused

109 *District Gazetteer of the United Provinces, Benares,* (Allahabad, 1909), 54-55, 114.
110 *Ibid., Hamirpur,* 84–85.

by the wars which the British waged against the Marathas and by the British competition.[111]

While the British conquest destroyed the handicrafts, it simultaneously created the conditions necessary for the establishment of an industry based on the new, capitalist principles. The agriculture of Gujarat, as we have already mentioned, became the supplier of cotton for the mills of Lancashire. The cultivation of cotton for the market brought commodity production to the countryside and led to the formation of a capitalist home market in Gujarat. Gujarat was, moreover, connected by railway with markets all over India since the second half of the 19th century.

Industrial production on capitalist lines developed simultaneously in the form of the manufactory and of the modern factory in Gujarat, as in other parts of India, although the pace of development varied. But in Gujarat, and this distinguishes it from the other regions of India, the predominating role played by the factory in the capitalist development of the national industry became apparent as early as the close of the 19th century. The reason for this has to be sought in the fact that from the outset the cotton mills of Gujarat worked for the all-Indian market or the foreign market, while the development of the manufactory was restricted to the local market of Gujarat.

Figures relating to the 1870s indicate that trading and moneylending capital penetrated deeply into the urban handicrafts of Gujarat. The craftsmen obtained advances from the moneylenders to buy raw materials. As in other parts of India, the influence of the buyer-up increased when the artisans started to use imported semi-finished products. For example, if the weaver manufactured his cloth from yarn which was locally produced, he bought the yarn himself with money borrowed from the moneylender; but if the yarn was imported from Great Britain, the weaver obtained it on loan from the buyer-up. The financial dependence of the artisan was used by the buyer-up to set up a system of scattered manufacture. The dyers, for instance, received from him fabrics, which they undertook to dye by a specified date. If there was a delay the dyer had to pay a fine to the buyer-up.[112] The buyer-up paid piece rates for the goods manufactured by the craftsmen from the raw materials and semi-finished products which he advanced to them. Similar relations existed in weaving, butter and oil manufacture, soap-making, wood-working, and other small-scale industries in Ahmedabad. Payment on the basis of a piece-rate system was so firmly established that standard rates applied to the basic production processes; for example, the weaver received one rupee if

111 E. Thornton, *Gazetteer of the Territories. . .*, (1854), I, 42, 528.

112 N. 84, IV, 68-69, 129-30.

he manufactured a piece of cloth thirteen feet long and two feet wide from the yarn the dealer supplied.[113]

The description of Ahmedabad in Hunter's *Imperial Gazetteer of India* contains valuable information on the activities of the buyers-up who owned scattered manufactories. They were united in a special corporation, which Hunter calls a guild stating that "the objects of the trade guild are to regulate competition among the members, and to uphold the interest of the body in any dispute arising with their craftsmen".[114] Thus, the guild of buyers-up on the one hand functioned like a medieval corporation, which regulated production, and was on the other hand a class organisation of manufacturers directed against the home-workers. Nowhere but in a colonial country, where pre-capitalist relations survived not only in agriculture but also in industry, could capitalist buyers-up join a medieval guild which regulated production.

A fierce struggle was carried on between the buyers-up and the craftsmen, who were in essence workers employed in scattered manufactories. During the cotton boom of the 1860s, for example, when the prices for foodstuffs rose, the potter's community in Dhandhuk, a town in the Ahmedabad region, decided on a corresponding increase in the prices of their wares. The guild of merchants and bankers replied by banning the sale of earthenware crockery, and even obtained the permission to use metal vessels during religious ceremonies, which had previously been prohibited. The funds of the merchant guild were later used to buy earthenware crockery from potters in remote rural areas and to bring it to the bazaar in Dhandhuk. But the urban potters continued to hold their ground, and apparently sold their wares themselves. In a few months' time the right to work the pit from which the potters obtained their clay was due to be auctioned. The guild of merchants decided to acquire this right irrespective of the expenses. Having deprived the potters of their raw material, the buyers-up forced them to capitulate. The barbers and carpenters of the same town were more successful in defending their price increases. Attempts which were made to import barbers from other districts failed, and pouring rain, which destroyed the roofing forced the merchants to make concessions to the carpenters.[115]

Another episode throws light not only on the existing class relations, but enables us to form an idea of the degree of division of labour prevailing in the scattered weaving manufactories of Ahmedabad. The buyers-up of fabrics were members of a special caste organisation, the purpose of which was to restrict competition between its members and

113 *Ibid.*, 76.
114 N. 25, I, 87.
115 N. 84, IV, 109.

to defend their common interests in any conflict with the artisans.[116] In 1872 the buyers-up of fabrics decided to lower the pay of the sorters; the sorters, on the other hand, refused to prepare the cloth at the reduced rate. The conflict lasted for six months, during which time the sorters remained without work.[117] The class struggle waged by the proletarian home-workers against the pro-bourgeois buyers-up, therefore, still took on the form of conflicts between the corresponding caste groups of the craftsmen and merchants.

The organisation of craftsmen protected its members not only against the arbitrary practices of the buyers-up but also safeguarded the monopoly of the caste to follow its traditional trade. A case is known when the community of bricklayers of Ahmedabad frustrated the attempt of newly arrived bricklayers to obtain orders by offering to do the work at a lower rate. The bricklayers of Ahmedabad reached an agreement with the community of potters to deprive the newcomers of the building materials they needed, thus forcing them to abandon their plans.[118]

Not only the wealth accumulated by the local merchants, but also the extremely cheap labour power which was available in great abundance, and the proximity of raw material sources and markets helped to turn Ahmedabad during the latter half of the 19th century into one of the biggest centres of the modern cotton industry in India. The building of cotton mills in Gujarat began in the early 1860s. At the end of the seventies four mills were already operating in Ahmedabad employing more than two thousand workers.[119]

Seth Ranchhodlal Chotalal opened a small spinning mill in Ahmedabad in 1861. This was the first modern industrial enterprise of the city. Chotalal was one of the Banias closely connected with the colonial apparatus and the princes. Among the forefathers of Chotalal, who was a member of the Nagar Seth family, were three ministers of princely states, and he himself had been employed as a customs official by the British for several years.

The idea to build a mill struck Chotalal as far back as 1846. He came to an understanding with a British firm which worked out the plans for the building of a mill. But it became immediately clear that the collaboration of Gujarati capitalists with British capital was beset by a number of difficulties. The shroffs of Ahmedabad considered that the building costs were too high and rejected the project. Chotalal's attempts to make the American J. London, a manager of a cotton-cleaning mill, his

---

116 N. 25, I, 87
117 *Ibid.*
118 *Ibid.*, IV, 109-10.
119 *Ibid.*, 132. *Indian Textile Journal*, 1931, January.

partner also ended in failure.[120] The personal endeavours of the future Indian millowner to establish contacts with foreign capital in an industrial joint-stock company encountered many obstacles.

R. Chotalal's business relations with the princes developed on completely different lines, since the latter saw in industry a sound opportunity for investing their vast accumulations of money. It was precisely the financial support of the princes which provided Chotalal with the necessary means for building his first mill. The prince of Rajpipla and the diwan of the Bhavnagar state were his biggest shareholders.[121] Close links between the millowners and the local feudal lords were a characteristic feature of the industrial development of Ahmedabad from the outset. The very existence of the principalities helped to preserve vestiges of feudal relations and hampered the development of the capitalist industry. But some of the princes began to act as sponsors of the national industry as early as the second half of the 19th century. They became the biggest shareholders of a number of industrial companies. Enterprises that were set up in the native principalities were granted a number of privileges, such as credits, subscriptions for shares, land, temporary exemption from taxes and the transfer of factories built at the expense of the public purse for next to nothing.

Chotalal's first mill had a capital of Rs 100,000. Dadabhai Naoroji handled the buying of the machinery for it from British firms. The machines had to be transported on carts, drawn by buffaloes, from Cambay to Ahmedabad.[122] At first the company paid a dividend of 6 per cent, later it went up to 9 per cent. But a considerable part of the profit was apparently reinvested, for by 1879 the share capital of the enterprise had reached Rs 654,000. The mill itself already consisted of 22 thousand spindles and 300 looms employing more than 900 workers.[123]

In 1872 Chotalal built a new and considerably bigger mill which had 14,500 spindles and 800 looms. The enterprise, which was not insured, burned down in 1875 but Chotalal quickly rebuilt it. In addition to his own mills, Chotalal controlled several other mills in Gujarat whose owners he patronised. Having become a big millowner, this former colonial official joined the British regime's loyal opposition. In 1893 he took part in the session of the National Congress, and in 1896 he protested against the excise duty which had been imposed on Indian machine-made fabrics.

Several other big manufacturers of Gujarat, besides Chotalal, were

120 N. 30 (January, 1931).
121 *Ibid.*
122 N. 47, 129.
123 N. 84, IV, 132.

members of trading and moneylending castes who had worked as officials in the colonial administration or that of a native state. It is significant that many of them continued to serve in the administrative apparatus of the native states after they became millowners. For example, in 1908 H. K. Kantawala, an official of the native ruler of Baroda, set up the mill Maharajah in this state. A short time after the mill started to work, the newly-fledged manufacturer was promoted and became minister in the state of Lunawada.[124]

At the close of the 19th century K. M. Mehta, who came of a family of hereditary ministers in the principality of Palanpur, took part in the building of the mill Fine in Bombay. His father, uncle and other relatives became shareholders. Industrial dividends were apparently to their taste and in 1905 at the urgent request of his relatives and with their support K. M. Mehta built a mill in Ahmedabad.

One could name quite a number of Bania officials who later became manufacturers, but we will merely mention Samaldas Lalubhai (1863-1936), who became one of the biggest capitalists during the first three decades of the 20th century. His father was a diwan in the state of Bhavnagar. Samaldas himself was in his youth private secretary of the Maharajah of Gwalior and subsequently became a tax inspector. In 1899 he resigned and worked as a broker in Bombay. Samaldas was afterwards one of the founders, and, later on, one of the directors, of the Tata Iron and Steel Company and of several other important industrial and shipping companies. During the period when Samaldas turned into one of India's biggest capitalists, his connections with the princes became even closer. In the nineties Samaldas was no longer a simple official in one of the states; he had been made chairman of the Board of Directors of the Bank of Baroda, established by the Maharajah of Baroda, and had become the owner of a mill in Mysore and of a number of companies which were connected with various Indian princes.[125] Towards the end of his life he played an active part in setting up monopolistic amalgamations in the steel and cement industries. This is in brief the outline story of one of the biggest capitalists of Gujarat; which illustrates very well how a section of the trading and moneylending capital serving in the tax administration of the British and the princes developed into the capital of monopolistic corporations.

A section of the big bourgeoisie of Gujarat, therefore, consisted of Banias employed in the British civil services or in that of the states. Mohandas Karamchand Gandhi, the outstanding ideologist and leader of the liberation movement that was headed by the national bourgeoisie, came from this background.

A numerically larger group of millowners in Gujarat was composed

124 N. 30 (April 1929).
125 *Ibid.*, (January 1936).

of descendants of big merchants and bankers who were members of the Bania caste. We have already indicated earlier that with the establishment of British rule the shroffs of Gujarat got the opportunity of greatly expanding their commercial and moneylending operations. Their connections with the colonial regime and the princes were no less close than those of the group of Bania officials which we have examined. The relations of the latter with the colonial and feudal oppressors were merely more overt and formal because they served in the state administration.

As in Bombay, the cotton trade occupied a particularly important place in the business activities of the big bourgeoisie of Gujarat who collaborated with the foreigners. Balabhai Damodardas Parekh, Seth J. Udhamshi, the owner of three mills,[126] and other manufacturers and shroffs were cotton merchants. Many of them, including Parekh and Udhamshi, also imported machinery for cotton mills. The shroffs of Gujarat proper participated in the sale of British fabrics only to a comparatively small extent, for the British capitalists and Gujarati merchants of Bombay kept a firm grasp on this commerce. The trade in cotton, machinery, and also in cloth, enabled the shroffs not only to accumulate money, but also created the commercial links necessary for the development of the cotton industry. This facilitated the investment of these accumulations in the building of industrial enterprises.

The first shroff to become a millowner was Seth Bechardas Ambadas Lashkari. His father, a military supplier, maintained close relations with the British military authorities and the Maharajah of Baroda. Bechardas himself, who was born in 1818, served in the colonial military administration from 1835 to 1845, and later rendered important services to the punitive expeditions during the National Uprising of 1857-59. Afterwards, B. Lashkari set up a firm in Bombay and established good relations with British firms in that town. He was in the main, a moneylender and shroff.[127] In 1865, supported by numerous merchants of Ahmedabad and Bombay and by his fellow officials, Lashkari founded a company, the purpose of which was the building of a second cotton mill in Gujarat. The mill started to operate in 1867 and by 1878 it employed more than 500 workers and had 15 thousand spindles and 170 looms.[128]

At the close of the 19th century Seth Balabhai Damodardas (born in 1858) joined the ranks of the mill owners of Gujarat. His father, a shroff of Ahmedabad, became rich by means of speculations during the cotton boom of the sixties. In his youth Balabhai became apprentice

126 *Ibid.*, (August 1931).
127 *Ibid.*, (February 1931). *Ahmedabad (Bombay Gazetteer,* Vol. IV) p 132.
128 N. 84, IV, 132.

in R. Chotalal's mill and worked as a storekeeper and commercial agent. His biographer refers to the symbolic monthly salary consisting of a few rupees which this heir of a cotton magnate received. Hypocritical sentiments about the allegedly modest beginnings of rich sons can be often found in the writings of their apologists. After finishing his training in the mill of Chotalal, Balabhai Damodardas started to build cotton enterprises of his own. Between 1884 and the end of the 19th century he built no less than six mills and several enterprises for the processing of cotton.

In 1877 the shroff Mansukhbhai Bhagubhai (1856-1913) opened the fourth mill of Ahmedabad. The new mill, which contained 27 thousand spindles and 620 looms, brought big returns, and as early as 1881 Mansukhbhai set up a second huge enterprise comprising 72 thousand spindles and 1800 looms. In addition Mansukhbhai gained control of four more mills, one of which was situated in Bombay. Having become a big millowner, he still continued to work as a banker and to be engaged in commerce. The author of a series of articles on the manufacturers of Ahmedabad considered that Mansukhbhai's role in the further development of the city's textile industry was similar to the part which Ranchhodlal Chotalal played in launching it.[129]

Seth Mangaldas Girdhardas Parekh (1862-1930), the son of a big shroff of Ahmedabad, was the most outstanding figure among the Gujarati millowners at the close of the 19th century. Just as many other future manufacturers of Ahmedabad M.G. Parekh began his training in the mill of Chotalal, where he worked as storekeeper in 1883. Half a year later, having gained a certain amount of experience, Parekh set up his own commission house for the supply of British machinery for textile mills. Having become rich through this type of trade, he built his first mill in 1892, and his second, three years later. The enormous profits he made—the result of such intensive an exploitation of the workers that it was unprecedented even in India—enabled Parekh to seize control of one enterprise after another. Between 1902 and 1922 eight cotton mills in Gujarat and one in Bombay fell into his hands, apart from the fact that he helped to finance another six mills. The Industrial Bank of Eastern India, with a capital of Rs 4 million, and two insurance companies which he had established helped him to get hold of the enterprises of other capitalists. Parekh was not only the biggest textile manufacturer of Gujarat, but also owned coal mines in Western Bengal and was a director of the first Indian cinematographic company "Oriental Film". Towards the end of his life he was a director of 24 different companies.[130]

---

129 N. 84 (February 1931).

130 *Ibid.*, (January, September 1931; August 1946).

Many other millowners of Gujarat, besides B. Lashkari, Balabhai Damodardas, Mansukhbhai Bhagubhai and M. G. Parekh, rose from the ranks of the shroffs.

The representatives of big trading and moneylending capital of Gujarat who became big entrepreneurs, especially millowners, did not only continue to act as moneylenders and shroffs, but in a number of cases even extended these operations on the new basis created by the imperialist exploitation.

The millowners of Gujarat, on the one hand, produced fabrics and, on the other, assisted in the manufacture of British cloth—by supplying cotton—and helped to sell it in India, thereby restricting the market for their own industrial output. This was an unusual but very real contradiction facing the bourgeoisie of Gujarat who were acting both as manufacturers and as agents for the British; the industry of Gujarat moreover, as distinct from that of Bombay, consisted from the outset mainly of weaving mills and not of spinning mills, and worked not for export but for home market. The fact that the Gujarati capitalists were acting as moneylenders as well as industrialists was another real contradiction, since moneylending retarded the development of the capitalist market and in the final account impeded the growth of the modern factory industry. Because capitalism developed under colonial conditions these contradictions existed within the economic life of the big bourgeoisie of Gujarat and exerted a definite influence on their political attitude.

The third and smallest group of Gujarati millowners rose from the ranks of the owners of capitalist manufactories. Only two such manufacturers who managed to become millowners are known. But even they had to pass through a number of intermediary stages, such as, working in the offices of a mill and becoming small shareholders. To judge by their titles these two millowners, Seth J. Girdharlal and Seth M. Gagaldas, were not members of a community of craftsmen but of a caste of merchants and moneylenders. It is most likely that they were buyers-up who had invested their capital in manufactories run on capitalist lines.

Towards the end of the period under review Ahmedabad was one of the principal centres of the Indian cotton industry, next only to Bombay. Approximately 700 thousand spindles and 20 thousand looms operated in its mills in 1914. The mills of Ahmedabad produced 10 per cent of the yarn and 21 per cent of the cloth manufactured in the whole of India in 1911-14, their average annual output was 260 million yards.[131]

At the outbreak of the First World War, the Gujarati industrialists of Bombay and Gujarat owned more than a hundred mills—i.e.,

131 N. 47, 21, 131.

approximately 70 per cent of the productive capacity of India's cotton industry—the only large iron and steel works in the country, and numerous small enterprises for the processing of agricultural raw materials.

The big bourgeoisie of Bombay and Gujarat thus consisted of representatives of trading and moneylending capital who worked as agents (in the wide sense of the word) of the British, were employed in the fiscal apparatus of the princes and were in some cases, landowners. When the big bourgeoisie of Gujarat began to build modern industrial enterprises, it maintained its connections with the British capital and the princes, and this determined the contradictoriness of its economic and political interests.

The old tradition of political and economic collaboration with the colonialists was a major subjective factor, which introduced a certain moderation into the mutual relations of the Gujarati bourgeoisie and the colonial regime. W. W. Hunter, an important British official who was a well-known expert in Indian affairs, wrote with satisfaction that in Bombay

> the competition of races, European and Indian, although as keen as in any other province, is tempered by common interests, mutual forbearance, and a certain reciprocal respect, which impart a moderation to Bombay public opinion and to the Bombay press in political crises.[132]

But the objective economic processes inevitably caused an increasing antagonism between the Gujarati bourgeoisie and the colonialists. Before the former became industrial entrepreneurs the conflicts amounted to no more than haggling about better terms for the transactions in which they acted as intermediaries, that is, the contradictions remained within the bounds of collaboration. But when the bourgeoisie acquired independent industrial interests the nature of their relations with the foreign capitals and its colonial administration changed radically. The principal elements of the deepening contradictions between the Gujarati bourgeoisie and imperialism caused by the industrial development were: the struggle for cheaper machinery and technical advice; opposition to the taxation, excise, customs and financial policy of the colonial administration; and, finally, the growing competition between Indian and British capital in the Indian market. These contradictions were no longer developing within the framework of their collaboration with British capital, as previously, but were brought about by the development of independent economic interests of the Gujarati bourgeoisie and their opposition to the expansion of British capital.

The intensified competition in the markets led to a drop in the

132 Hunter, n. 46, 14.

income of the Bombay manufacturers. While the net profits of the mills of Bombay amounted to Rs 23.5 million in 1905, they fell to Rs 16 million in 1909, and the financial year 1910-11 showed even a loss. But the First World War created extremely favourable market conditions, and the manufacturers of Bombay rapidly grew rich.[133] The duality inherent in the national bourgeoisie of the colonial and semi-colonial countries manifested itself in the position of the big Gujarati bourgeoisie earlier, and in more developed forms, than in the other groups of Indian capitalists; while the Gujarati bourgeoisie was subject to the discriminating practices of the foreign imperialism, it exploited and oppressed the workers in its own factories. It was precisely in the factories of Bombay and Ahmedabad that the most numerous and politically conscious section of the industrial proletariat of India developed, which consistently defended both the national interests and its own independent class interests. The objective class antagonism which existed between the national bourgeoisie and the proletariat developed within the colonial and semi-feudal society of India, long before the beginning of the general crisis of capitalism, although it found its ideological expression only during this crisis.

At the outbreak of the First World War the antagonism of the Gujarati bourgeoisie to both imperialism and the proletariat had reached such an advanced stage that one can regard the capitalists of Bombay and Gujarat as the first section of the national bourgeoisie to have evolved by that time. The formation process of this bourgeoisie was, however, not yet completed; this applies to both the economic aspect and, to an even greater extent, the political aspect. This process was basically concluded only in the post-war period which brought a sharpening of the contradictions of the Gujarati bourgeoisie to imperialism and led to class struggles with the proletariat in the 1920s.

---

133 N.H. Thakkar, *The Indian Cotton Textile Industry during the Tweentieth Century*, (Bombay 1949), 38.

CHAPTER VIII

THE MARWARI BOURGEOISIE

When we divided the Indian bourgeoisie into various sections, we did so on the basis of their national origin. But the specific features of the development of capitalism under colonial conditions caused some groups of the Indian bourgeoisie to take shape within the framework of certain trading and moneylending communities or castes (for instance the Multanis in North India or Chettiars in Burma). The most powerful of these groups was the Marwari bourgeoisie consisting of descendants of trading and moneylending castes from Rajputana, whose members had, by the middle of the 19th century, spread throughout the country with the exception of the southern part of the Deccan Its economic interests show that the Marwari bourgeoisie has never been the national bourgeoisie of Rajputana. The Marwari bourgeoisie did not merge, in the course of its development, with the bourgeoisie of the nationalities among whom it worked. The Marwari bourgeoisie appears as a separate community of capitalists, firmly held together by the ties of their caste.

While wholesale trade in which they acted as middlemen formed the bulk of the commercial transactions of the Gujarati bourgeoisie—whose business activities centred in Bombay, one of the most important trans-shipping points, the Marwari bourgeoisie—who operated chiefly in the internal regions—combined direct participation on a wide scale (far wider than that of the Gujarati bourgeoisie) in the growing home trade with business activities in which they collaborated with the British. This does not mean, however, that the Marwari bourgeoisie were more interested in the advance of capitalism than were the Gujaratis. The trading and moneylending capital of the Marwaris, who lived parasitically on the semi-natural or small-scale commodity economy of the peasants and craftsmen, began to flow into large-scale industrial production much later than the capital of the Gujarati merchants who collaborated with the colonialists. The role played by Marwari capital in the development of capitalism was, on the whole, very contradictory. It accelerated the natural economy, but at the same time, under the conditions of the colonial economy, it delayed the maturing of capitalist relations in agriculture and the handicrafts and retarded production during the lower stages of capitalism.

The Marwaris in Rajputana

In the period under review Rajputana became a backwater of colonial India. The handicrafts declined, while modern large-scale industry did not develop. Before the First World War, Rajputana had only one small cotton mill—employing 500 workers, which was opened in Kishangarh in 1897.[1] The urban population fell from 1,533 thousand at the end of the 19th century to 1,352 thousand in 1921.[2]

As earlier in Bengal, the consolidation of the colonial regime in Rajputana restricted the opportunities of the local bankers to make direct use of the treasury of the feudal state to enrich themselves (tax-farming, loans, remittance of taxes, and so on).[3] In the seventies the local bankers were only remitting the tribute paid by the states of Raiputana to the colonial administration.[4] Under these circumstances Rajputana was by no means a sphere of action favourable to the trading and moneylending capital of the Marwaris. The *Gazetteer* relates:

> The employment of capital in Rajputana is becoming less productive, and is diminishing since the peculiar source of profit formerly open have been disappearing. At the beginning of the present century, great firms often remitted goods or spices under the guard of armed companies in their own pay, and loans were made (to the princes) at heavy interest for the payment of armies or the maintenance of a government. Now, railways and telegraphs are gradually levelling profits on exchange and transport of goods, while the greater prosperity and stability of the States, under the wing of the Empire, render them more and more independent of the financing bankers. (This was due to the reduction in the military expenditure and the increased exploitation of the "subjects" and not to "the greater prosperity"). Of course, there is an immense amount of moneylending to the peasantry.[5]

Marwari trading and moneylending capital could indeed live parasitically on the feudal landed property and the peasant economy. But the business opportunities were diminishing, for the feudal landholders *(istimrardars)* applied to the courts for extensions of the term of payment of their debts to the moneylenders. The authorities,

1 *Rajputana, Imperial Gazetteer of India* (Calcutta, 1908), 56.
2 *Census of India 1941*, Vol. 24 (New Delhi, 1941). 14.
3 N. 1, 57.
4 *The Rajputana Gazetteer* (Calcutta, 1879), 11, p. 60.
5 *Imperial Gazetteer of India*, XI, 421.

moreover, fixed a low rate of interests for debts incurred by *istimrardars*.[6]

The position of the peasants differed widely from that of the *istimrardars*.[7] The rate of interest, which the moneylenders charged them, was not limited by law and fluctuated between 12 and 48 per cent. According to the estimate of the *Gazetteer* the amount which the moneylenders took in interest was higher than either the tax receipts or the income of the landowners.[8] At the close of the seventies, for example, the moneylenders of Ajmer received approximately Rs 280 thousand from peasant members of village communities as interest payments on loans, a sum exceeding the taxes collected by the state.[9] But the exploitation of the semi-natural peasant economy of sparsely populated Rajputana could not satisfy the powerful moneylending capital. The existing legislation, moreover, made the transfer of land into the hands of the moneylenders difficult.[10]

The numerous reports about flourishing banking houses in Rajputana seem to contradict these facts. For instance, the *Imperial Gazetteer* of India writes, "Whilst the mass of the people is occupied in agriculture, in the large towns (of Rajputana) banking and commerce flourish to a degree beyond what might have been expected in so backward a country".[11]

The reason for the prosperity of the local bankers in backward Rajputana was that it remained the Marwari financial centre for the whole of India, in spite of the consolidation of such new financial centres as Calcutta, Kanpur, Lahore and Nagpur. For instance the heads of several important firms of Seths—which had branches throughout Rajputana and other parts of India where they traded in grain, cotton and opium—resided in Ajmer. Their principal, and almost exclusive, business in Ajmer consisted of banking operations.[12] According to official data, which are undoubtedly incomplete, there were, in the eighties, seven big banking houses, owning a capital of Rs 60 million, and several smaller firms with a total capital of Rs 5 million, in Jodhpur alone.[13] An important role in the sphere of finance was also played by

---

6 N. 4, II, 115. The business activities of the bankers of Ajmer shrank considerably, according to the *Gazetteer*, because their principal clients, the *istimrardars*, nor tended to avoid borrowing money and also because of the many court decisions which permitted the *istimrardars* to defer the repayment of their debts. *Ibid.*, 60.

7 *The Rajputana Gazetteer* observes that similar relief could not be granted to the small landowners in the village communities. *Ibid.*, II, 115.

8 *Ibid.*

9 *Ibid.*

10 *Ibid.*, 114.

11 N. 5, XI, 420.

12 N. 4, II, 60.

13 N. 5, VII, 60.

small moneylenders, who frequently granted loans direct to moneylenders and traders working far beyond the borders of Rajputana.

These vast accumulations of money could not be used in commerce, which was comparatively insignificant during the latter half of the 19th century. For example, in 1877-78 goods worth Rs 2,780,900 were imported into Ajmer; the import, moreover, of British cloth amounted to Rs 562,000 while that of locally produced cloth came to Rs 124,700.[14]

Rajputana, just as Central India, had a favourable balance of trade mainly because of the opium exports,[15] which also contributed to the capital accumulations of the local merchants and bankers.

The heads of the biggest moneylending clans continued to occupy leading positions in the administrative apparatus of the local states during the nineteenth century.[16] The most important Marwari capitalists of contemporary India have the same surnames as many high officials in the native states. But service in the administration of the states did not hold out such good prospects as in earlier times. The campaigns of the military leaders were a thing of the past, and in consequence the influx of war loot ceased. The feudal lords of Rajputana could no longer count on receiving high posts in rich viceregencies. The Rajputana states themselves became powerless vassals of the colonial administration. The income a person was likely to receive as a result of service in the administration of these states was much more moderate than the profits of the merchants and bankers in British India.

Thus, the economic situation which had arisen in Rajputana during the second half of the 19th century was conducive to ousting trading and moneylending capital from this region, and to the spreading of the Marwari castes throughout India, especially in those parts of British India which had already begun to produce agricultural crops for the market.

---

14 N. 4, II, 58.

15 W. Digby, *Prosperous British India*, 185.

16 The Bhandaris, who belonged to the Oswal community of Jains, filled the principal posts in the state of Jodhpur or Marwar, namely those of *diwan*, *bukhshi* and *musabat*. For many years—while the Maharajah Ajit Singh, who lived at the close of the 17th century, remained in Delhi—Bhandari Rudhnath governed Marwar in the name of his prince. The Oswal Mokhnots occupied just as prominent positions as the Bhandaris. Mokhnot Nains was a famous minister in the government of Maharajah Jesvant Singh, who died in 1681. The most important posts in the state at the beginning of the 19th century were occupied by the Muhtas—apparently the same as Mohta—and Singhs, both Oswal families. Finally, in the 1870s the positions of *diwan* and *vakeel* of the durbar were firmly held by the Lodhis, who were Oswal moneylenders. See N. 4, II, 248-49; see also *Ibid.*, III, 27, 32, which contain similar information in regard to the Mewar state.

The Marwaris in Maharashtra

To show how the capital of the Marwaris operated we will examine its progress in Maharashtra in greater detail. It is true that Maharashtra was not the only part of western India where the Marwaris were active. A community of Marwari merchants and moneylenders existed also in Gujarat, but it was comparatively less numerous, although rather firmly established. According to the census of 1872, 6,800 Marwaris lived in the Gujarat districts of the Bombay Presidency, amounting to approximately 5 per cent of the total membership of the trading and moneylending castes. The majority of Marwaris, about 6,000 in number, lived in the Surat district.[17] Most of them settled in Gujarat after the establishment of British rule there.[18] The Marwaris usually began their business career in Gujarat as village shopkeepers and moneylenders But in contradistinction to Maharashtra, there were considerably fewer Marwaris in Gujarat than those of the local castes of merchants and moneylenders.

Two considerations have caused us to give so much attention to the business activities of the Marwaris in Maharashtra. Firstly, the Marwaris were exceptionally active in this region, particularly in its eastern districts; secondly, Maharashtra offered the Marwaris an extremely wide field in which to conduct their commercial and moneylending transactions, because of the specific features of Maharashtra's economic development, which had been strongly influenced by British capital during the second half of the 19th century.

On the basis of very convincing data quoted in documentary sources one can conclude that, during the last quarter of the 19th century, the Marwaris were the strongest, although certainly not the only, group of merchants and moneylenders in Maharashtra, and especially in its eastern region. The *Imperial Gazetteer of India* relates in the eighties that "in the interior of the Bombay Presidency (comprising Gujarat and Maharashtra) business is mainly divided between two classes, the Baniyas of Gujarat and the Marwaris from Rajputana".[19] In 1881 the Jains alone numbered approximately five thousand in the Central Provinces; they were, for the main part, merchants and commercial agents from Rajputana.[20]

The district *Gazetteers* of eastern Maharashtra published at the

17 "When these Marwaris first began to settle in the villages of the Surat district has not been ascertained." It is said that a few families have lived there since the end of the seventeenth century. " Newcomers constantly appear, and generally for the first generation keep a close connection with Marwar." *Bombay Gazetteer*, IX, Part I, 103.

18 *Ibid.*

19 N. 5, VI, 591.

20 *Ibid.*, III, 317; *The Gazetteer of the Central Provinces*, 204, 214, 333.

beginning of the 20th century also indicate that the Marwaris predominated among the local merchants and moneylenders. The Marwaris made up 62 per cent of all moneylenders in the Buldana district.[21] The biggest merchants and moneylenders in the Amraoti district were Marwaris.[22] The most important of the moneylenders in the Yeotmal district were Marwaris.[23] At the close of the 19th century the Marwaris began to be predominant also among the traders and moneylenders in western Maharashtra, which formed part of the Bombay Presidency.[24]

The basis of the Marwari capital in the countryside was the village shopkeeper and moneylender. The classic description of the Marwari Bania's business activity in the Maratha village has been given in the *Imperial Gazetteer of India*. It relates that the Bania from Marwar who wished to become a moneylender usually brought his capital with him consisting of bills of exchange and gold and silver ornaments. After his arrival he met many members of his caste and other acquaintances who were prepared to give him a helping hand in the form of credits. It is characteristic that the capital of the Marwari did not consist of money but either of valuables, which were to serve as security for loans, or of bills of exchange—hundis—which circulated among the moneylenders and local bankers who were working in close contact with each other.

Then the Marwari travelled about in the district for a month or two studying the local conditions of trade. In the end he settled down in the village which seemed to offer the best opportunities for profitable business operations. The Marwari rented a small house, opened a shop and began to trade in fabrics, grain and groceries. He never miscalculated and never sold anything without making a profit. He showed great restraint in his personal expenditure. Within a short time he was lending small sums of money taking as security household

---

21 *Buldana, The Central Provinces District Gazetteers*, 230. See also N. 5, I, 401; V, 421; VI, 104; XI, 66, 348.

22 *Amraoti District*, 130, 228.

23 *Yeotmal District*, n. 21, 123.

24 "The professional village moneylender" in the Sholapur district "is... usually a Gujar or Marwari, but sometimes a Lingayat Vani. (i. e. a Bania belonging to the Shaiwaite denomination in the Kanara districts.) The small urban moneylender too "is usually a Marwari". *Sholapur Bombay Gazetteer*, Vol. XX, Bombay, 1884, p. 244. "Of all moneylenders (in the Satara district) the Marwar Vani has the worst name and is harshest and most unscrupulous in his dealings with his debtor... Next to Marwari moneylenders come Gujarat Vanis and local (i.e. Maratha) Brahmans... Though they generally charge the same rate of interest as Marwaris, the Gujars are less unscrupulous and harsh than the Marwaris in enforcing payment of debts." N. 17, XIX, 181. "The importers are chiefly Gujarat and Marwar Vanis" in the Poona District. *Ibid.*, XVIII, Part 2, 167. "Moneylenders, traders, and shopkeepers" in the Nasik District are "chiefly Marwar, Gujarat and Ladsakka Vanis". *Ibid.*, XVI, 114.

goods and ornaments. As soon as his connections expanded the Marwari began to grant loans on the security of land or the future harvest. His stock of grain was growing every year. He sent some of the grain to Poona or Bombay and kept the rest as a reserve to be used in case of a bad harvest or a rise in prices.[25] Lending grain to the peasants —especially those who were growing cotton—became not only one of the principal forms of the moneylending activity of the Marwaris but it was often the starting point which led to the enslavement of the peasants.[26]

The close connection between the commercial and moneylending operations of the Marwaris is obvious: the grain bought on the cheap from peasants who were beforehand entangled in usurious loans was then advanced at high rates of interest to the same peasants. By applying pressure the moneylender squeezed grain out of the peasant for his wholesale operations too. The grain was sent from the countryside to a town—for instance to Nagpur, the commercial centre of eastern Maharashtra—where the grain trade was, with few exceptions, controlled by Marwari merchants. From the commercial centres the grain was taken to the cotton-growing regions, and also to Bombay and other big cities.

Subsequently the life of the moneylender took approximately the following course. Having lived in the Deccan for eight to ten years, he returned to Marwar to take his family to his new place of residence. His profits grew year by year and he became rich; he built himself a big house, married off his children to the children of other local Marwaris and did not leave the Deccan any more.

Apart from grain, cotton and locally produced fabrics were the principal commodities in which the Marwaris conducted a wholesale trade. The Marwari wholesale dealers participated to a large extent in the cotton trade with Bombay. As early as 1865 the government commissioner for cotton in Bombay noted that cotton was delivered from the countryside to Nagpur, the biggest cotton market, in the main by Marwari traders. The cotton was resold to the big export merchants in Nagpur.[27]

The buyers-up of cotton—Gujarati and Marwari Banias—advanced money to the peasants and often bought the crop before it was fully

25 N. S, I, 165,

26 "... the new Marwari usually establishes himself in some small village, and, with the headman's leave, begins to make grain advances, to be repaid at harvest time, at from twenty-five, *sawai,* to a hundred per cent, dumi, and occasionally on bad security and during times of scarcity, at the rate of three to one, *tipat*... From grain he gradually passes on to selling cloth and lending money." N. 17, XVI, 44-45.

27 M. L. Dantwalla, *Hundred Years* . . . , 50.

grown. The cotton was sent by the buyers-up to their agents in Ahmednagar, who were Marwari Banias. The latter made advances to the buyers-up. The firms in Ahmednagar and other big towns in Maharashtra sold the cotton to British and Indian companies in Bombay.[28]

In addition to the export of agricultural products, mainly cotton, in which he acted as intermediary, Marwari merchant played an active part in the sale of imported industrial commodities—above all textiles—in the markets of Maharashtra.[29] A part of these commodities was at that time, imported from Great Britain. How close the links were between Marwari and British merchant's capitals is shown even by the fact that local bankers frequently granted loans to British commercial firms.[30]

We will examine closer the activities of two of the biggest Marwari banking houses in eastern Maharashtra, Bansilal Abirchand and Mohta.

Indrabhan, the founder of the firm of Bansilal Abirchand came to western Maharashtra about 1820, that is soon after it had been conquered by the British. Together with his brother Bansilal he opened a shop in Amraoti where they traded in grain and later on began to lend money as well. Their moneylending operations enabled the brothers to build up a stock of grain, and Bansilal was selling grain to the British army before the Indian national uprising of 1857-59. Bansilal's son was granted the title "Rai Bahadur" for the assistance he rendered to British punitive detachments during the uprising. The same title was conferred on the younger son of Bansilal, who supplied the British army with provisions during the second Anglo-Afghan war of 1878-80. The members of Bansilal Abirchand's family grew rich as a result of making deliveries to the British army and subsequently became the biggest bankers in Maharashtra.[31]

The founder of the firm of Mohta, who apparently was a member of the clan of Muhta from Jaipur, began his business activity in the cotton-growing regions of the Central Provinces in the thirties of the 19th century. His son Raikchand expanded the cotton and grain business and seized the lands of many villages. He was the first Marwari to build a cotton mill, and later on a second. In addition, Mohta owned ten cotton processing enterprises.[32]

Nagpur was the centre of both the banking and commercial

28 N. 17, XVII, 343.

29 The Marwari was not only a moneylender and general broker, but also a retail and wholesale dealer in groceries, grain and textile fabrics, wrote the *Gazetteer.* N. 17, XVIII, part 2, 99.

30 *Central Provinces Provincial Banking Enquiry Committee*, II, 495-96.

31 *Ibid.*, 497.

32 *Ibid.*

activities of the Marwaris in eastern Maharashtra. Almost all banking operations in this town were carried out by Marwaris, although a few banking houses also belonged to Maratha Brahmins.[33] The bankers of Nagpur themselves did not usually grant small loans but preferred to act through their agents who were established in every small town of the district and gave loans to the poor at high rates of interest.[34] The bankers made advances to the small moneylenders at a rate of 12 per cent and more.[35] Firm relations regarding bills of exchange existed between the bankers of Nagpur and the businessmen in Bombay, Banares, Indore, Amraoti and Hyderabad, and, of course, the bankers of Jaipur, originally the main base of the Marwaris. The Nagpur bankers had their own representatives or permanent agents in these towns. It is interesting that the bills of exchange of the Nagpur bankers were discounted in Bombay after 13 days, and in Calcutta after 61 days. Only the general gravitation of the economic relations of the Nagpur district—just as of Maharashtra as a whole—towards Bombay can be the explanation of this considerable time difference.[36] The system of discounting bills in existence among bankers indicates that the practice of granting loans to other members of one's own caste was firmly established. "There are regular quotations of bills of exchange" records the *Gazetteer* "well known and kept to by the Sahukar brotherhood in their dealings with one another, but they are not the least ashamed to make as much as they possibly can out of chance customers".[37]

The Marwaris were in the habit of granting usurious loans on the security of land, which led inevitably to the transfer of peasant holdings into the hands of the moneylenders. The acquisition of peasant holdings by members of the castes of traders and moneylenders did not lead to the consolidation of capitalist relations, but merely converted the peasant into a tenant without any rights, that is, it reunited him with the land under semi-feudal conditions.[38] The *Gazetteer* writes that the Marwaris "are bad landlords, spending no money in improving their property and grinding their tenants to the uttermost farthing... During harvest they spend most of their time in the fields securing their share of the crop".[39]

33 *The Gazetteer of the Central Provinces*, 333.
34 *Ibid.*
35 *Ibid.*
36 *Ibid.*, 334.
37 *Ibid.*, 334.
38 According to the *Gazetteer*, the Gujarati or Marwari Bania, as a rule, permitted the debtor who had pledged his land to cultivate it as a tenant under the condition that be handed over from one half to three quarters of its product to the landlord. N. 17, XIX, 189.
39 *Ibid.*, XVII, 78.

Colonial statistics conceal the extent of the expropriation of the peasantry, but occasionally some information appears which gives an idea of the magnitude of this national calamity. Even the *Gazetteer of the Satara District* admits that by the 1880s "about one third of the arable land has virtually passed into moneylenders' hands".[40]

During the second half of the 19th century, the Maratha peasants fought against the attempts of the Marwari moneylenders to seize their lands. The peasants in the Jalgaon region of Berar organized a boycott against the Marwari moneylenders. Anybody working for the Marwaris was expelled from the caste, and in those cases where this was considered insufficient the peasants resorted to threats. In consequence the moneylenders suffered heavy losses. The crops on their land were not harvested and in one instance even a big garden belonging to a Marwari moneylender was destroyed by lack of water.[41]

The peasant movements sometimes used more violent methods. For example in 1845, the banker Janraj Sahu, the founder of a big commercial firm in Amraoti, who speculated in grain after a bad harvest, was killed by the enraged inhabitants.[42] During the great national uprising of 1857-59, the partisan detachments of Bhils operating in Maharashtra often made short work of the village moneylenders.[43]

Moneylending had particularly disastrous consequences for the Maratha peasants after Maharashtra became the cotton supplier of Lancashire. The cotton boom of 1862-65 induced large numbers of peasant households to turn to the cultivation of cotton, which required considerable expenditure on the part of the peasants. Moreover, the rise in the price of cotton was accompanied by nearly as big an increase in the price of grain, which the peasants who grew cotton were forced to buy. Hence, the peasants rapidly ran into debt. The moneylenders, who grew rich in the boom, readily granted loans to the peasants in view of the rise in the price of land. The boom brought the peasants "the fatal gift of unlimited credit".[44] When the price of cotton suddenly dropped after the end of the war in the United States of America, the debt-ridden peasants found themselves in a very difficult position; their debts grew, and they were forced to pledge their land even more frequently than before. The bad harvest of 1871 and another fall in the prices of cotton which occurred in 1871-74 led to a further intensification of the enslavement of the peasants by the moneylenders.[45]

Moreover, the tax burden carried by the peasantry became even

40 *Ibid.*, XIX, 180.
41 N. 21, 236.
42 *Ibid.*, 176.
43 N. 17, XVI, 201
44 N. 17, XVII, 317.
45 *Ibid.*

heavier during the seventies. Taking advantage of the temporary, and in fact only nominal, rise in the income of the peasant households during the cotton boom, the British imposed unusually high tax rates.[46] It was difficult for the peasants to pay these taxes even though the prices for cotton were high. When the depression set in, the peasants were in arrears of tax payments. The moneylenders refused to give credit to the indebted peasants, because their land was not sufficient security. All this created a very tense atmosphere. According to official data, moneylenders were attacked eighteen times in one mountainous region alone on the border of the Poona and Ahmednagar districts between April 1871 and October 1874.

In May 1875 the movement against the moneylenders grew into peasant disturbances in the Poona, Ahmednagar and Satara districts. Although these disturbances were also directed against the Maratha Brahmins who were moneylenders, the peasants considered that their main enemies were the Marwari and Gujarati moneylenders;[47] the reason for this was that the peasants regarded the latter groups of moneylenders as aliens because of their different language and religion, while the Brahmins were able to take advantage of the privileges of their caste and also of the fact that they shared the same religion with the population.[48] The actions of the peasants were to a certain extent caused by the agitation of the Maratha propertied strata especially in the countryside, who endeavoured, with their talk about the predominance of the Gujaratis and Marwaris, to divert the anger of the peasants from themselves. It was not without reason that "in many cases the movement was led or shared by the heads of the villages".[49] Maratha landlords and moneylenders later resorted, more than once, to similar stratagems.

During the disturbances the peasants destroyed the records of their debts kept by the moneylenders, and distributed their stocks of grain among the peasants.[50] Although no moneylenders were killed in 1875, the colonial authorities mobilised not only the police but also regular military units, for instance, the cavalry regiment in Poona as well as infantry—and savagely dealt with those who had taken part in the peasant movements. More than 500 peasants were flung into prison in two districts alone, Poona and Ahmednagar. Whole regions were, moreover, occupied by regular troops and the police, and the population had to bear the cost of the punitive expedition.[51]

* * * *

46 R. D. Choksey, *Economic History of the Bombay Deccan...*, 165, *Part 2*, 122.
47 N. 17, XVIII, Part 2, 122.
48 *Ibid.*, 124.
49 *Ibid.*, 123.
50 *Ibid.*, n. 17, XVII, p. 319.
51 N. 17, XVII, 319.

The economy of colonial Maharashtra provided only very limited opportunities for the creation of large-scale capitalist industry. But Marwari trading and moneylending capital did not make use even of these slender opportunities, since collaboration with the colonialists provided it with a sufficiently high rate of profit. The cotton mills existing in Maharashtra, therefore, belonged either to Gujarati or British capitalists.

The following episode is rather significant. In 1876, when J. N. Tata, who was building a cotton mill in Nagpur, required money for the construction of a dam; he turned to a local Marwari moneylender and suggested that he should become a shareholder of the company; but the Marwari refused saying that it did not befit him, who was used to get money from under the earth, to bury it again. The investment of Marwari capital in industrial enterprises for the initial processing of agricultural raw materials which occasionally occurred before the First World War, was in effect, a supplement or continuation of their commercial and moneylending activities and did not involve considerable expenditure, since these enterprises required little fixed capital.

During the latter half of the 19th century, the Marwari merchants and buyers-up took advantage of the growing dependence of the producers in Maharashtra on loans and the supply of machine-made semi-finished products which were mostly imported—such as yarn, metals and dyes—to strengthen their control over the principal branches of manufacture. In this respect the Maratha and Gujarati merchants and moneylenders did not lag behind the Marwari buyers-up. At the close of the 19th century the Marwari buyers-up, who had established close relations with British import firms and had wide opportunities to obtain loans, gained a firm hold on the handicrafts in Maharashtra. The dominance of the buyers-up and moneylenders over the handicraft industries retarded the development of the higher forms of capitalist enterprise and condemned the small producer to an exceedingly painful expropriation.

So far, very little is known about the scale and nature of the business activities of the Marwari capitalists in Bombay at the close of the 19th and the early 20th century. As we have stated already, the Marwaris were engaged in widespread financial and moneylending transactions. We have however, reason to believe that Marwari merchants occupied prominent positions as brokers in the wholesale trade of the town. Among indigenous bankers, hailing from the native states, who had settled in Bombay—whose aggregate capital according to Digby amounted to Rs 60 million—were certainly Marwari bankers too. This is, in particular confirmed by the fact that the commercial operations of the local bankers and merchants were directed towards Rajputana and central India. The Marwaris, however, did not play any significant part in the mill industry of Bombay. Their names in any case do not appear either among the managing agents or the directors of Bombay factories.

* * * *

A few words about the language of the Marwaris who lived in Maharashtra. All gazetteers of Maharashtra relate that among themselves the Marwari moneylenders spoke Marwari, while in public they spoke a rather poor Marathi.[52] The Marwari language spoken by the Marwari merchants and moneylenders was just as distinct from the Marwari dialect, as the community using it was distinct from the Marwari people. The Marwari spoken by the caste of traders and moneylenders was one of those class dialects which it would be more correct to call jargons, for they do not serve the mass of the people but a narrow social group, and they possess neither a grammatical structure nor a basic vocabulary of their own. The *Bombay Gazetteer* related that their language in the way they wrote it permitted so many variations in respect of both spelling and grammar that one rarely met a Marwari able to read a letter written in Marwari unless it happened to be in his own handwriting.[53]

The Marwaris in Hindustan

The Marwaris remained the most important local community of merchants and moneylenders after the consolidation of the colonial regime in Hindustan. The *Gazetteer of the Central Provinces* declared in 1908 that the most influential group of the commercial community was the Marwaris from Rajputana, who maintained such close relations with their homeland that they could not be considered a local group, even if they had lived in these parts for a long time. The biggest native bankers and merchants in Hindustan, and in Kanpur, its economic centre, were Marwaris.[54] Just as in Maharashtra, the Marwaris in Hindustan were merchants and moneylenders, and managed also to acquire a considerable amount of land. The Marwaris acted as brokers for export and import commodities such as textiles, indigo, sugar, hides, and mineral oil. The trade of the Marwaris in agricultural products was, as in Maharashtra, based on till exploitation of the peasants by a combination of usurious and feudal methods. "The Marwari Banias... make advances to the tenants before harvest and get grain at cheap; rates",[55] to quote again the *Gazetteer.*

52 N. 17, XI, 48, XX, 85, XIX, 60.

53 *Ibid.*, XVI, 44.

54 *Cawnpore, District Gazetteers of the United Provinces*, (Allahabad, 1909), 47.

55 *Narsingpur*, n. 21, 148. .

The appropriation of peasant lands by representatives of Marwari merchant's and moneylender's capital was rather widespread in Hindustan.

> Every moneylender of importance is a landlord, and many landlords are moneylenders. The capitalists have invested largely in land, partly for its profits as a property, and partly for its advantages as a field for money and grain lending business. Such speculators are usually Palliwal Brahmins, Marwaris, and Mahasri or Agarwal Banias.[56]

Members of the trading and moneylending castes in the Aligarh district owned 21 thousand acres in 1840, 119 thousand acres in 1870, while by 1908 they had already acquired 158 thousand acres, or 13 per cent of the cultivated land of the district.[57] In the Saharanpur district 22.3 per cent of the land belonged to moneylenders.[58] In the Budaun district, 12 per cent of the acreage was in the possession of Banias in 1870 and since then they have doubled their holdings.[59] Members of the Agarwal community owned approximately 9 per cent of the land in the Benares district.[60] The portion of the land which the Banias owned in Allahabad increased from 6.7 per cent in 1840 to 12 per cent in 1907.[61]

At the beginning of the 20th century, many members of the Marwari castes became big landowners in the United Provinces. For example, Jambu Prasad, an Agarwal Jain, acquired 21 thousand acres in the Saharanpur district alone. Several other members of the Agarwals owned from 7 to 9 thousand acres each in Saharanpur.[62] An Agarwal banker, Bhagvati Prasad, had appropriated the land of 115 villages in Horahpur.[63]

The Marwari Gokul Das was the biggest landowner in central India. He appropriated the land of 131 villages in the Mandla and Narsingpur districts alone.[64] A forefather of Gokul Das immigrated from Jaisalmer shortly before the establishment of British rule. Members of this family faithfully served those who organised punitive expeditions during the Indian national uprising, and Gokul Das donated Rs 1,000 to the British army during the Böer War.[65] The wealthiest Bania in the Chhindwara district was Seth Narsinh Das, who made himself master of 16 villages.

---

56 *Hoshangabad District*, n. 21, 155.
57 *Aligarh*, n. 54, 91.
58 *Saharanpur, ibid.*, 116.
59 *Budaun, ibid.*, 76.
60 *Benares, ibid.*, 144.
61 *Allahabad, ibid.*, 104.
62 *Saharanpur, ibid.*, 116.
63 *Gorakhpur, ibid.*, 112.
64 *Mandla District*, n. 21, 105: *Narsingpur*, n. 21, 117.
65 *Mandla District, ibid.*, 105.

His ancestors immigrated from Jaisalmer in the beginning of the 19th century.[66] Several Oswals, members of one of the Marwari castes, living in the Betul district, had already managed to acquire several villages in the district, although they had only recently settled there. Two of the principal moneylenders in Badpur were members of the same subcaste.[67]

Land seizures by members of the merchants' and moneylenders' castes were accompanied by a reduction in the landholdings of the Rajputs, members of a military feudal caste. But, as we have already pointed out, the acquisition of land by the trading and moneylending castes did by no means lead to the consolidation of capitalism in agriculture but, on the contrary, gave rise to enslaving forms of semi-feudal tenancy.

During the period under review, objective conditions favouring the investment of Marwari trading and moneylending capital in industry were absent in Hindustan, just as in Maharashtra. The industrial interests of the Marwaris were limited to the small industries engaged in the initial processing of agricultural raw materials. These industries were, in fact, ancillary to the commerce in agricultural products. For example, the Kanpur banker and cotton merchant Lala Mulchand owned 84 cotton-cleaning enterprises; Nihalchand Baldeo Sahai, a banker and cotton merchant owned 65 such enterprises; and Baijnath Juggi Lal, another banker and cotton merchant had 50 cotton-cleaning enterprises and one cotton pressing mill.[68] Three out of four cotton-cleaning mills in the Chhindwara district belonged to Marwaris or Maratha Brahmins.[69] The first three cotton-cleaning mills in Narsingpur were opened between 1901 and 1906. Two of these worth Rs 30-35 thousand belonged to the biggest landowner and banker Gokul Das.[70] At the beginning of the First World War, the majority of cotton processing enterprises in Hindustan were in the hands of Marwari merchants or Indian firms from Bombay and Ahmedabad, that is, Gujaratis.[71] But the biggest company engaged in the initial processing of cotton in Hindustan was a British enterprise set up in London in 1874 with a capital of Rs 150 thousand.

Since the exploitation of the peasantry provided an extensive field of activity, the Marwari merchant's and moneylender's capital did not even make use of those slender opportunities to build industrial enterprises which in fact existed in Hindustan. British capital was, therefore, in complete control of large-scale industry.

66 *Chhindwara District, ibid.*, 85.
67 *Betul District, ibid.*, 66.
68 *Cawnpore*, n. 54, 80.
69 *Chhindwara*, n. 21, 136.
70 *Narsingpur, ibid.*, 136.
71 *Indian Industrial Commission*, (London, 1919) I, 24.

The Marwaris in Bengal and Assam

After the suppression of the Indian uprising of 1857-59, the British continued to exercise undivided rule over the economic life of Bengal. This led to various specific features in the development of trading and moneylending capital, and in particular that of the Marwaris, in Bengal. British capital made it difficult for the businessmen collaborating with the British in Bengal to act as independent brokers, a difficulty not encountered by the Gujarati merchants who collaborated with the British. An outward sign of this was, incidentally, the fact that, in contradistinction to Bombay, there were no big firms of Indian brokers engaged in overseas trade in Calcutta. The jute industry—the only important large-scale industry in Bengal—was entirely controlled by the British. The network of British banks in Bengal was considerably stronger than in Bombay. Finally, since the latter half of the 19th century, the Bengali landlords, the zamindars, who were the most privileged section of the Indian landowners, firmly kept almost all the cultivated land of the province in their hands. The Marwaris in Bengal, therefore, exploited the peasants mainly by means of commerce. This was facilitated by the fact that the colonialists encouraged the cultivation of jute, a monoculture, which made the peasants dependent on the market.

The *Imperial Gazetteer of India* relates that during the last quarter of the 19th century, "many of the upper classes of Shudras (a general name for the castes whose members were craftsmen and traders in Bengal) have devoted themselves to wholesale trade; although here also the Jain Marwaris from Rajputana and the North-west occupy the front rank. Their headquarters are in Murshidabad district, and Jain Marwaris are found throughout the valley of the Brahmaputra, as far up as the unexplored frontier of China". They even penetrated among the primitive tribes.[72] Many other sources also stress that the Marwaris played a leading role in the commerce of Bengal. In another volume of the *Gazetteer* we read:

> Though the great banking house of Jaget Seth has long fallen into decay, the Jain merchants of Murshidabad still rank as the wealthiest of their class in Bengal. Their dealings in gold and silver bullion are especially large; and some of their number almost monopolize the local traffic on the Brahmaputra, as far up as the northeast frontier of Assam.[73]

72 N. S., VI, 592.

73 *Ibid.*, X, 39. "A large part of the local trade of Bengal is in the hands of natives from other Provinces of India, and the enterprising Marwaris in particular have established firms in all the important commercial centres." *Ibid.*, II, 311.

During the First World War the Industrial Commission noted that the greater part of the trade in Calcutta was in the hands of Indian merchants, mostly Marwaris. The Indian merchants did not, however, directly control foreign trade—apart from the import of textiles, cheap iron and tin-plate—but conducted their export and import operations through European firms.[74] The principal buyers of jute in the provinces and in Calcutta were either agents of European merchants and manufacturers or rich Marwaris.[75]

The Marwaris in Bengal were not only traders but also moneylenders. Since the land in Bengal was not the legal property of the peasants, the moneylenders acquired from the indebted peasants the right of the so-called privileged land-tenure, i.e. the right to use the land on condition of a rent payment consisting of a fixed sum of money.[76] Having acquired this right, the moneylenders sub-leased the plot on terms which reduced the peasants to servitude. The moneylender, who appropriated that part of the rent which exceeded the legally established payment, in fact shared (with the zamindar) the ownership of the land. The position of the Marwaris in Bengal with regard to landed property was nevertheless considerably weaker than in the Hindi region or Maharashtra.

There is hardly any information about capital investments made by the Marwaris in the industry of Bengal. Some of the Indian shareholders of the jute companies, which were controlled by British capital, were undoubtedly Marwaris. According to the data of a government investigation carried out during the First World War, 55 per cent of the shares of the Jute companies in Bengal were owned by Indians.[77] R. Mukerji, the well-known Indian economist, states that, of a total of 55 small mechanised enterprises which existed in Calcutta at the beginning of the First World War, 19 belonged to the cunning and enterprising Marwari merchants.[78]

The custom to grant each other loans, which persisted in their caste, held the Marwaris together in Bengal, as in the other provinces. The isolation of the Marwari community of traders and moneylenders led in 1898 to the foundation of the Marwari Association in Calcutta. According to the statute of this association its aims included not only the furtherance of the commercial interests of the Marwaris but also the promotion of the social, moral and cultural well-being of the

74 N. 71, I, 16-17.

75 *Ibid.*, I, 24.

76 *Murshidabad, Eastern Bengal District Gazetteers*, 75.

77 G. S. Slater, *Southern India, Its Political and Economical Problems*, (London, 1936), 229.

78 R. Mukerji, *The Foundations of Indian Economics*, 366.

merchants and moneylenders who were members of the Marwari community in Calcutta.

* * * *

The development of the tea plantations in Assam, which began at the close of the 19th century, provided the Marwaris with many opportunities to carry on their commercial and moneylending operations. The "active and enterprising Marwari merchants from Rajputana", writes the *Imperial Gazetteer of India* as far back as the eighties, "carry on most of the import and export trade of the Brahmaputra Valley".[79] Information from the various districts shows that the Marwari middlemen predominated in the trade of Assam.[80]

The commerce of the Marwaris was closely connected with the deliveries of goods to the tea plantations of the British. "Jorhat on the Disai river in the centre of the (Sibsagar) District is the home of several Marwari and Muhammadan traders, who supply the wants of the labourers on the tea-gardens.[81] The Marwaris had their shops in most of the big plantations.[82]

The trading and moneylending capital began, at the end of the 19th century, to subjugate the craftsmen of Assam. For instance, the gazetteer records that in the Sibsagar district, "the braziers are almost entirely supported by a system of advances made by Marwari capitalist."[83] The weavers of the mountain tribes in the Lakhimpur district in eastern Assam began to dye their yarn with aniline dyes with which the Marwari buyers-up supplied them.[84] Thus moneylending and collaboration with the British (aniline dyes and metals were imported commodities) became the means that helped to bring the craftsmen of Assam to submission.

Marwaris in the Southern Deccan

Marwari traders and moneylenders began, in the second half of the 19th century, to penetrate through Hyderabad into Andhradesha.[85] As early as the 1880s, the *Gazetteer* writes about the Kistna district in northern Andhradesha: "the traders are chiefly Marwari settlers".[86]

79 N. 5, I, 359.

80 "The trade of the District (Kamrup) is mainly in the hands of Kaya, or Marwari merchants from Rajputana (chiefly from Bikaner), and of Muhammadan shopkeepers". *Ibid.*, VII, 363-64. "The trade of the District (Sibsagar) also, is mainly confined to the Marwaris. *Ibid.*, XII, 469.

81 *Ibid.*, XII, 465.

82 *Ibid.*, 472.

83 *Ibid.*, 469.

84 *Ibid.*, 435.

85 By the early twentieth century, the Marwaris had already established a wide spread network of traders and money-lenders covering the country-side of Hyderabad. See n. 5, XIII, 265.

86. *Ibid.*, VII, 42.

Marwari trading and moneylending capital began to gain control of the still existing considerable weaving industry of Andhradesha supplanting the local buyers-up.

> The weavers of both cotton and silk are largely in the hands of the capitalists who advance them the thread, take the finished cloths and pay them piece-work wages for their labour. These capitalists are often Marwaris and the purchases of yarn and dyes and the sale of the manufactured article are managed by them.[87]

The Marwari buyers-up, who reduced the weavers to utter dependence thus became, in fact, proprietors of scattered manufac-tories.

The documentary sources of the period under review hardly ever mention the business activities of the Marwaris in Karnatak. The only exception is the *Gazetteer of Bijapur*. In the early eighties, there were only 235 Marwaris—the figure includes all the members of their families—in the Bijapur district. They only began to settle there in the middle of the 19th century, for as late as the eighties the *Gazetteer* still stressed that they were all immigrants from Marwar.[88]

The Marwaris in the Dravidian Deccan encountered strong competition on the part of the merchant's capital of the Gujaratis and Chettiars, a Tamil caste of traders and moneylenders. For this reason the activities of the Marwaris in the southern Deccan were chiefly concentrated in Andhradesha and, to a certain extent, in Karnatak. It was only in the beginning of the 20th century that Marwari capitalists became important moneylenders in the extreme north of Tamilnad.[89]

The exploitation of India by imperialist methods and the development of capitalism in the country led to substantial changes in the business activities of the Marwaris. Marwari dealers began to an increasing extent to participate in the export of cotton and other raw materials to England, and in the sale of British cloth and other industrial commodities. This type of trade did not, however, form a sufficiently large proportion of the total trade turnover in the interior regions to allow us to assume that the majority of local Marwari dealers acted chiefly as intermediaries of the British. Apart from the colonial centres, the commerce of the Marwaris catered mainly to the internal commodity exchange. But the role played by Marwari capital within the system of colonial exploitation should not be underestimated. The more so that in a number of cases the internal commodity exchange served the requirements of foreign capital, for instance, the supply of foodstuffs to the cotton and jute-growing areas and to the tea plantations.

Because the Marwari merchants, especially those in the colonial

87 *Anantapur, Madras District Gazetteers*, (Madras, 1909), 64.

88 N. 17, XXIII, 127.

89 In 1908 moneylending in the Chingleput District was, in the main, in the hands of Marwaris. N. 5. X, 263.

centres, were involved in commercial transactions that served the British and since their investments in the national industry were quite insignificant—for the capital of the buyers-up cannot really be regarded as industrial capital—separate groups of the Marwari bourgeoisie, at times, projected their own narrow interests against the rest of the Indian bourgeoisie. This happened, for instance, during the Swadeshi movement in Calcutta where the local Marwari merchants refused to take part in the boycott of British goods and suffered heavy losses.[90]

Jawaharlal Nehru described in the following way the wide range of business activities in which the Marwaris engaged during the second half of the 19th century:

> The Marwaris from Rajputana used to control internal trade and finance, and were to be found at all the nerve centres of India. They were the big financiers as well as the small village bankers; a note from a well-known Marwari financial house would be honoured anywhere in India, and even abroad. The Marwaris still represent big finance in India but have added industry to it now.[91]

Nehru regards investment of Marwari capital in industry as a recent development. Up to the time when India was turned into an agrarian and raw-material appendage of Great Britain, and agricultural products were, in consequence, transformed into commodities, the peasant was occasionally forced to ask the moneylender for a loan to pay his taxes in a year of famine or to meet exceptional family expenses. But, the natural or semi-natural economy of the peasant did not constantly require money. It was not till the latter half of the 19th century, when India was exploited by imperialist methods, that the Indian peasant became completely dependent on the market both as a producer of raw materials and as a consumer of the necessaries of life, especially foodstuffs. Under these conditions the peasant household was constantly in need of loans, a need which was increased by bad harvests and the inevitable price fluctuations on the world market. The debt-ridden peasant was obliged to hand over his harvest to the moneylender for next to nothing. By adapting the system of usury and feudal exploitation to its own use, British capital was able to extract super-profits from India by extorting raw materials at monopoly prices. Thus we see that during the period of imperialist exploitation, which saw the completion of India's transformation into an agrarian and raw material appendage of Great Britain, economic factors emerged whose

90 Interesting data are quoted in the article of A. I. Levkovsky. *Dvizhenie svadeshi* In: sb. *Natzional 'no-osvoboditel'noe dvizhenie Indii i deyatel 'nost' B. G. Tilaka,* p.p. 329-30.

91 Jawaharlal Nehru, *The Discovery of India*, 310.

continuous pressure was conducive to the enslavement of the peasants by moneylending capital; while on the other hand the operation of moneylending capital became the principal condition which facilitated the extraction of colonial superprofits by the British monopolies.

During the second half of the 19th century, land passed into the hands of Marwari traders and moneylenders at an increasing rate. In the feudal era as well as during the period of primitive accumulation of capital by the British the landed property of the Marwaris had grown mainly on account of grants received from the feudal lords and the colonialists. The seizure of land by economic means was of minor importance, its chief form being the transfer of the land of indebted feudals to Marwari moneylenders. During the epoch of industrial capitalism, and especially imperialism, the acquisition of land through the exploitation of the peasant ryots became prevalent; but the transfer of landlords' estates to Marwaris played a subordinate role, and occurred mainly in regions where the non-permanent zamindari system prevailed, for instance, in the United Provinces. The combination of moneylender and landlord came about as the result of the exploitation of the Indian peasant by a fusion of semi-feudal methods with commercial and usurious methods, which was a specific feature of the colonial economy.

The penetration of Marwari capital into industry began during the imperialist exploitation of India. In this connection it should be noted that Marwari capital operated in four spheres.

A. In the *small industries where capitalist relations began to reappear during the second half of the 19th century.* The peculiar strength of the merchant's and moneylender's capital in the Indian manufactures, as well as the stability and scope of the moneylender's capital that exploited the direct producer were due to the colonial conditions. Marwari capital usually assumed the higher form of merchant's capital in the small industries, the form under which the buyer-up directly hands out materials to the handicraftsmen to be worked up for a definite payment. The handicraftsman becomes in fact a wage worker, working at home for the capitalist; the merchant's capital of the buyer-up is here transformed into industrial capital.[92] Under colonial conditions, however, the merchant's capital which was turning into industrial capital continued to exploit the producer by usurious methods. It is well-known that this type of exploitation is typical for the lower form of merchant's capital in small industries which, as Lenin pointed out, consists in a combination of merchant's capital with usury: the craftsman who is constantly in need of money, borrows it from the buyer-up and repays the debt with his goods. The sale of his goods in this case always takes place at artificially reduced prices, which often

92 See V. I. Lenin, *Collected Works*, III, 369.

do not leave the handicraftsman as much as a wage worker could get. Moreover, the handicraftsman who has run into debt becomes personally dependent on the buyer-up.[93] The exploitation of the producer by a combination of capitalist and usurious methods is characteristic of the activity of Marwari capital in the small industries during the imperialist epoch.

B. The *industry engaged in the initial processing of agricultural raw material* began to develop on a capitalist basis during the second half of the 19th century, when the export of agricultural raw materials increased. The participation of Marwari capital in this industry was linked with its business collaboration with the British, i.e., the dispatch of raw materials to the ports.

C. In the *large-scale industry owned by British capital* the Marwari capitalists took part as junior partners of the British (as shareholders and commercial agents.)

D. The participation of the Marwaris in the *large scale national industry* was limited to a few cotton mills. These enterprises were situated in the internal regions of the country where the competition of British imports was weaker.

In spite of their growing industrial interests the Marwari merchants and moneylenders cannot as yet be considered as an industrial bourgeoisie during the second half of the 19th century and early 20th century. The Marwari bourgeoisie took shape as a commercial and moneylending bourgeoisie whose business activities were concentrated in the spheres of both the internal commodity exchange and commerce in which it collaborated with the British.

93 *Ibid.*, 368.

CHAPTER IX

THE MARATHA BOURGEOISIE

The economic processes which began in India during the latter half of the 19th century, perhaps, reached their greatest maturity in Maharashtra. The towns in the interior of Maharashtra increasingly became centres of a widespread intermediary trade and of small-scale capitalist industries. The cotton boom of the sixties, which was connected with the reduction of cotton exports from the southern States during the Civil War in the U.S.A, led to important changes in Maharashtra's economy. It was precisely Maharashtra, and in particular Berar, which became the principal supplier of cotton both for export to Great Britain and for the use of the first mills of Bombay.

The construction of railways was of great importance for the economy of Maharashtra, and above all for the production of cotton. In 1867 the Great Indian Peninsula Railway line, traversing the whole length of Maharashtra, connected Bombay with Nagpur, the centre of the cotton trade. The railway replaced tens of thousands of carts drawn by buffaloes which were previously used to transport cotton from the remote districts to the ports. This reduced the cost and speeded up the transport not only of cotton but also of British industrial commodities. In consequence the volume of foreign trade doubled in the Central Provinces during the sixties.[1]

The railways disorganised the old commercial relations which had grown up between Maharashtra and the neighbouring provinces and led to a one-sided development. For example, the cotton from East Maharashtra was previously sent to the United Provinces and Orissa, while after the construction of the Bombay-Nagpur railway line almost all of it was transported to the west coast. Individual regions began at the same time to specialise in a particular commodity; the cultivation of cotton in one region stimulated the growing of food crops in another.[2]

---

1 *The Gazetteer of the Central Provinces*, CL.

2 *Ibid.*, 332. By the end of 1867 the export of grain from the Central Provinces had reached one million maunds (in this, case, the maund equals 35.15 kg), that is, it had doubled in the preceding six years.

Thus at the end of the sixties the land under cotton in the Central Provinces amounted to approximately 5 per cent of the sown area. In the Nagpur, Wardha and Rajpur districts the corresponding figure was 50 per cent.[3] The growth of foreign trade, therefore, led to the weakening of Maharashtra's commercial relations with India as a whole and to the intensification of certain trends in its internal commodity exchange, primarily the sale of foodstuffs to cotton-growing regions.

Cotton prices went up as a result of increasing British purchases of cotton. But the Maratha peasants, especially the middle and lower strata, gained little by the cotton boom. The reason being that under the conditions of extensive agriculture the growing demand for marketable foodstuffs was not accompanied by a corresponding increase in supplies to the market and inevitably led to a rise in the prices of the peasants' means of subsistence, first and foremost, grain.[4] The switchover from the growing of cereal crops to the cultivation of cotton caused a famine in 1861, since lack of transport made it impossible to bring a sufficient supply of provisions from other regions.[5] This made the increased nominal income of the peasants largely fictitious. If one also takes into account that the colonial authorities, taking advantage of the cotton boom, considerably increased the rate of taxation, it becomes clear why the position of the peasants in Maharashtra deteriorated sharply during the 1870s.

The cotton boom and the general expansion of commodity-money relations had a completely different effect on the strata of merchants and moneylenders in the town and countryside of Maharashtra. It was precisely in this period that the local commercial and financial system finally took shape which, till recently fulfilled the principal functions of an agent to the foreign capital that exploited Maharashtra as a market and as a source of agricultural raw materials.

During the second half of the 19th century British commercial firms set up their own branches in Nagpur and other Maratha towns and began persistently to push back the Indian merchants in an attempt to reduce as far as possible their activities as brokers and to intercept the greater part of the profits derived from trade in cotton, British fabrics and other business operations connected with foreign trade. To a certain

3 *Ibid.*, 535.

4 It has been pointed out in the *Gazetteer of the Central Provinces* that the grain prices reached so high a level in the sixties that it became impossible to expand further the area under cotton. To facilitate the supply of grain to Wardha, a cotton-growing region, it was intended to improve the communications between the latter and the granary of Central India, Chattisgarh. The authors, moreover, considered it possible that Chattisgarh might specialize exclusively in the production of grain. *Ibid.*, CLI.

5 Karl Marx, *Capital*, I, 353.

extent they succeeded in eliminating Indian capital from big wholesale trade, but the commercial and credit transactions which were concluded direct with the peasants and handicraftsmen remained, as previously, in the hands of Indian merchants, and moneylenders.

Gujaratis and Marwaris predominated, as before, among Indian merchants and bankers in Maharashtra. But local landlords and the village rich, especially Brahmins, played an important role in trading and moneylending operations in the countryside. The Maratha merchants and bankers in the towns were far weaker than the Gujarati and Marwari shroffs. Nevertheless, a few large Maratha firms came into being during the 19th century.[6]

Rukam Randiv, the founder of the banking house of Chitnavis in Nagpur, was in the middle of the 18th century, a *chitnavis* (i.e. clerk) of the local prince.[7] In 1844, after the death of Raja Raghoji, the head of the banking house took service with the British who had seized Nagpur. At that time he owned 15 or 16 villages. After the death of the Raja he began to lend money and grain on interest, thereby increasing his property. The Raja had kept a stock of grain in his storehouses, which the British sold after his death for one rupee per khandi. Chitnavis bought the grain and expanded his business by making further advances of grain. Thus after the establishment of the colonial regime and the development of commodity-money relations this Maratha landowner, utilised the accumulations made by the feudal lord to conduct usurious operations on a large scale.

The founder of another Maratha firm, Gopalroa Ghatate, had been employed in the firm of a Marwari businessman in Pardi, a town which at that time—that is, before the railway connecting Nagpur with Bombay and Calcutta was built—was the principal market in the Nagpur district. Ghatate scraped together a little money and began to

6 "Maharashtra provides an interesting example of a commercially retarded region. There was no important community, Hindu or other, which was indigenous to this region, specialising in commerce and trade. To some extent, particularly in the east, the Yajurvedi Brahmins took considerable part in moneylending and indigenous banking. It is also recorded that in the early part of the 18th century, with the increasing migration of Chitpavan Brahmins to the Desh tract, a number of these were also engaged in moneylending and indigenous banking. Trading activities in South Konkan, were associated with Saraswat Brahmins. The fact itself (that Brahmin subcastes should appear prominently in some activities in the trading and banking field) is indicative of the lack of the Bania element in the indigenous caste structure." D. R. Gadgil, *Origins of the Modern Indian Business* Class, 19.

7 In the reports of the British Resident at the court of the Maratha Princes of Sindhia (Gwalior), written in the 1790s, Appa Chitnavis is mentioned several times as the real head of the financial administration in this state. It is quite possible that he was member of the banking house. *Mahadji Sindhia and North India Affairs* 1785-1794, (Bombay, 1936) 105, 376-77, 385, 386.

lend it out on a small scale and, later on, he also started to trade in grain. He soon became rich and, at the end of his life, had already amassed about Rs 100 thousand. Gopalrao's grandson owned not only a big banking firm but vast tracts of land, as well.[8]

The local Maratha bankers, thus, fell back upon the lending of grain, one of the principal methods used by moneylenders to enslave the peasants. It is obvious that opportunities for this type of lending arose on a large scale only when the Maratha peasant households switched over from the cultivation of millet and wheat to that of technical crops, i.e., cotton. It is not without reason that Nagpur—the centre of the cotton-growing region of East Maharashtra—became the stronghold of the local Maratha bankers.

During the second half of the 19th century essential changes took place in the position of the handicraftsmen in Maharashtra. The development of commodity-money relations in the Maratha countryside, especially in the sixties as a result of the cotton boom, created a home market for the handicrafts. The growth of commodity-money relations accelerated the decline of the peasant industries, above all weaving. The economic self-sufficiency of the village community was finally destroyed. In particular, the craftsmen of the village community, who were formerly linked to the peasants by natural relations, became small commodity producers doomed to a hopeless struggle against the encroachment of imported machine-made commodities. The manufacturers of Manchester sold their fabrics cheaper than then local weavers in their own villages.[9] It will be recalled that the British cloth competing against the products of the local weavers was manufactured from cotton grown in Maharashtra. This was the result of the division of labour between the British town and the Indian countryside.

While the rural industries were slowly, but inevitably, disappearing, the urban handicrafts continued to exist in Maharashtra, although the craftsmen had to pay a high price. The fact that the British abolished the state apparatus of the Maratha rulers—the Peshwa in Poona and the Bhonsle dynasty in Nagpur—had disastrous results for the handicrafts which worked for the court, the army and the administration of the principality. For example, in the sixties the manufacture of expensive fabrics ceased almost completely in Pauni, a small town near Nagpur.[10]

Artisans working in handicrafts which catered to the feudal class were especially deeply enslaved by the capital of the buyers-up. The buyers-up took advantage of the poverty of the craftsmen, who were unable to buy the expensive material they needed for their work—

8 *Central Provinces Provincial Banking Enquiry Committee*, II, 490, 503.

9 N. 1, ICL.

10 *Ibid.*, 66.

gold and silver thread, ivory, etc.—and to sell their wares profitably to customers occupying high positions. The buyers-up reduced the craftsman to bondage by giving him loans and were able to dictate their terms to him.

The switch-over of the urban handicrafts from the production of expensive goods for the feudals to manufactures satisfying the requirements of the peasantry led to a crisis in the relations of production which had grown up in the handicrafts. For example, in Burhanpur, an old handicraft centre, the weaving industry had been flourishing thanks to orders received from the Bhonsle and Sindhia, and to the export of cloth to countries beyond the sea, even as distant as Turkey and Poland. In the sixties, however, as the *Gazetteer* relates, the position of the weavers manufacturing coarse cloth was better than that of the weavers working with gold and silver threads, who had never enough capital to work on their own account.

> Till lately the whole command of both the wire-drawing and weaving trades was in the hands of the merchants of the city (of Burhanpur). They found all the materials, and merely paid the stated ṛates for piece-work executed by the operatives; the latter were always kept under heavy advances, and under Sindhia's rule they could not leave their employers while these were unpaid, unless their new masters chose to clear them; in short they were regularly bought and sold like slaves. The employers now complain of their inability to keep them to their work, and seldom now make advances, as the operatives frequently abscond, and being without chattels, debts cannot be recovered from them under our (that is British) legal procedure. Of course this is altogether advantageous to the operative class; they are thus gradually emancipating themselves from the thraldom of the capitalist merchants; and a good deal of the outcry made by the latter about the decay of the trade may mean only the transfer of a part of their old profits on fine goods to the independent manufacturers of coarser stuffs.[11]

It is worth noting that the position described here, even if it did correspond to the facts, soon changed—the colonial legislation assisted the buyers-up in reducing the craftsmen who ran into debt slavery.

The weavers of Maharashtra experienced serious difficulties during the cotton boom of the sixties.[12]

---

11 *Ibid.*, p. 131.

12 "The native cloth manufacture has been severely tried by the development of cotton trade. In the first years of the scarcity cotton became almost too precious to be worked up into the coarser native fabrics, and the weavers were under-sold by the Manchester manufacturers even in their own villages". *Ibid.*, CLII.

The sharp rise in the prices of cotton, which was exported to Great Britain, increased several fold the circulating capital needed by the weaver to buy the raw material. The weavers, who had no ready money, depended on the credits granted by merchant's capital, which grew rich by speculating in cotton. It was precisely at this time that the buyers-up seized hold of the supply of raw material to the weavers and made the producers of cheap cloth no less dependent than the weavers manufacturing expensive fabrics, whom they had earlier enslaved.

The increased demand by the peasants for marketable industrial commodities during the seventies and eighties created favourable conditions for the renewed development of the lower forms of capitalism—primarily scattered manufactories controlled by the capital of the buyers-up—in the urban handicrafts of Maharashtra. The development of manufacture in some handicraft centres was accompanied by a general increase in the production of handmade goods. Thus, according to the estimates of the *Ahmednagar Gazetteer*, the number of weaving-looms in the district rose from 2,300 in 1850 to 3,135 in 1884.[13] The number of workers engaged in the working up of copper doubled between 1868 and 1883.[14] But, on the whole, the development of large centres of manufacture did by no means indicate a growth in the total productive capacity of the handicraft industries, for, at the same time, the rural handicraftsman, who was unable to compete with foreign industry and with manufacture, was ruined. Moreover, in the course of the development of capitalism in the small industries a decline began in the small urban centres of artisan production.[15]

A more or less comprehensive pattern of handicraft industries had grown up in every town of feudal Maharashtra. But the increasing social division of labour caused some towns in Maharashtra to specialise in one or two key industries as early as the second half of the 19th century. The other branches of industry either disappeared entirely or dragged out a miserable existence. For example in the eighties cotton weaving, the largest of the handicrafts in Poona—where earlier a very complex structure of handicraft industries existed—not only failed to recover from the decline it had experienced in the middle of the 19th century, but even continued to deteriorate. In 1883 cotton fabrics were manufactured on only 400-600 looms out of a total of 1100-1300 weaving-looms in operation.

As far as the output of silk cloth, metal-wares and the processing of tobacoo were concerned Poona occupied a leading position in Maharashtra, but in regard to the manufacture of cotton fabrics and other handicraft products it had to surrender pride of place to other

13 *Bombay Gazetteer*, XVII, 348.

14 M. P. Joshi, *Urban Handicrafts of the Bombay Deccan* (Madras (1936), 57.

15 *Ibid.*, 49.

handicraft centres.[16] 2,300 persons were engaged by 1883, in the processing of copper in Poona. Small workshops ran along the lines of manufactories—their equipment was worth Rs 300-400—and controlled by buyers-up predominated in this handicraft.[17]

The establishments in which tobacco was worked up by hand were owned by Maratha Brahmins and had an annual output of 700 tons consisting of bidi cigarettes and snuff; the greater part of it was sent abroad.[18]

But in spite of the growth of some branches, the handicraft industry taken as a whole did not reach the level it had attained when Poona was the capital of the Peshwa state.[19] Footwear production, in which 600 leather workers were employed in Poona, suffered greatly as a result of foreign competition. By working on orders from the army the craftsmen managed to make both ends meet. The position of the craftsmen engaged in the production of illuminating vegetable oils was not better, they were unable to stand up to the competition of imported oil.[20] Only seven or eight establishments manufacturing paper were left in Poona by 1883. Each of these employed five to six workers. The rest of the industry had been stifled by foreign competition.[21]

Sholapur became the largest centre in Maharashtra for the manual production of cottons. According to official estimates, five thousand craftsmen—weavers, spinners and dyers worked there in the eighties.[22] In 1883, according to other sources there were 6,405 handlooms in Sholapur,[23] 2,240 in Malegaon[24] and 1,200 handlooms in Ahmednagar.[25]

The fact that certain towns specialised in particular handicrafts and that thousands of artisans working in one trade were assembled there was inevitably accompanied by an expansion of merchant's capital in the handicrafts; it organised the sale of the finished products and the supply of raw materials and semi-finished goods. The strengthening of the position of the buyer-up and the gradual submission of the small commodity producer to him became characteristic features of the development of capitalism in the handicraft industries of Maharashtra.

---

16 D. R. Gadgil, Assisted by some others *Poona : A Socio-Economic Survey*, Part I, (Poona, 1945) 104-06.
17 Joshi, n. 14, 56-57.
18 Gadgil, n. 16, 175.
19 Poona was no longer so big a centre of commerce and industry as it had been under the Peshwas, wrote the *Imperial Gazetteer of India*, XI, 213.
20 Gadgil, n. 16, 56-57, 171.
21 *Ibid.*, 63.
22 N. 19, XIII, 421.
23 Joshi, n. 14, 49.
24 N. 13, XVI, 116.
25 Joshi, n. 14, 49.

Data provided by the *Gazetteers* and the research work of M.P. Joshi make it possible to form a fairly complete picture of the development of capitalist relations in the handicrafts of Maharashtra. For example, in the eighties the weaving industry of Sholapur consisted mainly of weavers who acquired their raw material from the local trader on credit, and on market days sold the finished articles to the same trader.[26] This is the primary form of scattered manufacture with the buyer-up distributing raw material to home-workers.

In 1883, 925 looms were in operation in Yeola, the biggest silk-weaving centre in the Bombay region of Maharashtra. But the town had only 95 independent weavers the other weavers were controlled by 48 buyers-up.[27] A detailed division of labour existed in the section of the handicraft which was under the control of the buyers-up. For instance, the production of gold-brocade was subdivided into four or five separate operations, and that of cotton into three or four.[28]

In Ahmednagar, the big cotton weaving centre, small craftsmen predominated who received raw material on credit from the trader and were paid by the piece for the finished cloth which they returned to him. In the eighties *karkhanas* consisting of 5 to 10 looms, began also to appear in Ahmednagar.[29] The traders managed to gain control over the weaving industry in Poona as well. Only in Malegaon did the majority of weavers consist of small independent commodity producers, who were not yet enslaved by buyers-up and sold their wares to the merchant offering the highest price.[30]

Scattered manufacture, which came into being when the craftsman became subordinate to trading and moneylending capital, was dominated to a large extent by Gujarati capitalists and partly by Marwari capitalists, who had obtained a number of privileges while the Maratha state was still in existence. During the latter half of the 19th century the Gujarati and Marwari dealers who collaborated with the British captured the supply of the principal raw materials and semi-finished products to the small industries. Yarn produced in Britain and Bombay was brought by Bohra and Gujarati Banias to Poona and distributed to the small weavers scattered throughout the district.[31]

The craftsmen who manufactured silk cloth in Poona either borrowed money from the buyers-up—the latter were either Marwari Banias or Shimpis that is members of a Maratha caste of tailors—and

26 *Ibid.*, 44.
27 *Ibid.*, 51.
28 *Ibid.*, 59-60, 65.
29 N. 13, XVII, 688.
30 Joshi, n. 14, 45.
31 N. 13, XVIII, Part 2, 168.

bought themselves yarn and gold thread, or they were home-workers who were supplied with semi-finished products by Shimpi and Marwari Banias and received piece wages for their work.[32] In the beginning of the 20th century, when Poona had, to a considerable extent, been pushed into the background other centres where copper and bronze manufacture existed, its own metal-working industry was controlled by Marwari and Gujarati Banias who had captured the supply of raw material (metals from Great Britain and Australia) and the marketing of the finished articles.

Gujarati merchants had reduced the weavers of Ahmednagar—apart from Sholapur, the most important centre of cotton manufacture—to a state of utter dependence, turning them into home-workers forced to hand over their products to the traders at piece rates.[33] Silk-weaving manufactories in Ahmednagar, employing 600-700 workers, belonged to Gujarati Banias who were also the suppliers of the raw silk, which was imported from China.[34] A few weavers in the Satara district had some capital and hired workers, but the majority had to borrow money from Gujaratis and Marwaris to buy yarn and paid their debts with cloth.[35] Regarding the position in Khandesh the *Gazetteer* writes:

> Though many of them (i.e. of the weavers) are small capitalists, handloom weavers are generally employed by men of capital, most of them Vanis and some Bohras and Khatris (members of a Maratha caste of weavers) who supply them with yarn chiefly spun in local and Bombay steam mills.[36]

Their wages were usually two to six annas per day. How big the capital of the buyers-up was can be seen even from the fact that the buyers-up of silk in Yeotmal owned from Rs 5 to 300 thousand each.[37]

In addition to scattered manufacture—the lowest form of capitalist enterprise in industry—centralised manufacture was also coming into being. As early as the seventies a Telugu capitalist set up the first weaving workshop organised on capitalist lines in Sholapur. By 1880 the workshop had 20 looms, among them were the first looms with a flying shuttle to be used in Sholapur.[38]

Hiring of weavers was a widespread practice in East Maharashtra. For example, at the end of the sixties there were 1,150 looms in Umrer, a town in the Central Provinces, which were operated by 2,300 weavers.

---

32 *Ibid.*, 186.
33 Joshi, n. 14, 47.
34 N. 13, XVII, 688-89.
35 *Ibid.*, XVIII, Part 2, 222.
36 *Ibid.*, XII, 229.
37 *Ibid.*, XVI, 156.
38 Joshi, n. 14, 44.

The weaving industry was in the hands of a few rich weavers. It is rather interesting that—to judge by official data quoted in the *Gazetteer*—the earnings of an apprentice weaver were fairly high—Rs 10 to 25 per month, depending on his qualification.[39] This is considerably higher than the income of the home-worker who had become dependent on the moneylender. We have not sufficient information to compare in detail the earnings of the enslaved home-workers with those of the wage workers employed in capitalist workshops. But it seems that in India, as in other countries, the wage worker lived better than the petty master who clung to his illusory independence.

In the middle of the 19th century an industry for the initial processing of cotton began to grow up in Maharashtra. By 1875, already 2,575 steam-driven plants for the pressing and cleaning of cotton were operating in the Bombay Presidency alone.[40] The leading positions in this sphere were from the very beginning occupied by big British firms which exported cotton and also by Gujaratis who were collaborating with the British and by Marwari capitalists. But among the owners of cotton-processing enterprises were also Maratha capitalists who were descendants of landowners. For example, one of the four cotton-cleaning enterprises in the Chhindwara district belonged to a local landlord, the other three to Martha Brahmins and Marwaris.[41]

Ruthless and savage exploitation of the producer was the specific feature distinguishing manufacture in colonial India. In this respect the cotton processing establishments were, perhaps, the worst. On the basis of a primitive mechanisation they introduced an unprecedented intensification of labour and increased the working hours considerably. A report from India published in the London *Times* asserts that during the season, lasting four months, the women employed in cotton-cleaning enterprises worked more than twenty hours a day. During this working day the women rested for only two or three hours, while they were replaced by friends or relatives.[42] The readiness of these friends or relatives to take on the work, even if it lasted only two or three hours, indicates, apart from anything else, how strong a pressure the enormous hidden army of unemployed exerted on the labour market—this was one of the principal conditions which made the inhuman exploitation of the Indian worker and craftsman possible.

The intensification of labour reached an unheard-of degree. When

39 N. 1, 40.
40 N. 19, IV, 191.
41 *Chhindwara*, n. 13, 136.
42 *The Times*, 12, 18, September 1891. The author of the report K. H. Bahadurji, an Indian physician who was representing the interests of the Bombay manufacturers at a London congress dealing with problems of hygiene, was by no means inclined to exaggerate the difficulties of the Indian workers.

the women workers were eating or suckling their babies they continued to throw cotton into the machine (the movement which the mother made with her hand was repeated by the hand of the child). In these enterprises, wrote *The Times* in its leading article, child labour was not used, for the rates of pay of adult workers were so low that the employment of children would not have brought any advantage.[43] The atrociously long working day, the inhuman intensification of labour and the beggarly wages not only undermined the health of the women workers, but literally killed them. R.F. Wadia, the manager of an establishment for the cleaning and pressing of cotton in Khandesh, admitted that when the management noticed that the female workers were quite exhausted they brought new workers from Bombay to replace them, and that the death of operatives working long hours was a frequent occurrence.[44]

The tragic position of the craftsman and manufactory worker was made worse by the fact that in addition to the capitalist exploitation they were dependent on the moneylender. Not only the buyers-up but also the owners of weaving workshops used usurious methods to enslave the home-workers and the workers who were concentrated under one roof in manufactories. The enslavement of workers by usurious methods brought the owners of manufactories additional profits, and enabled them to reduce wages far below the value of labour power prevailing in colonial India. The *karkhandars*, owners of workshops, for instance, gave the weavers advances of Rs 20 to 100. In return for this favour the weavers who had run into debt were obliged to work in the workshop during the five months when trade was brisk—i.e. December to April, the so-called wedding season—they were then dismissed and told to return in December.[45] Usurious methods to enslave weavers who were members of their own caste were, in particular, applied by Telugu manufactory owners. They were members of either of two castes: *Padmasali* and *Kamathi*, the former specialised in the weaving of cotton, the latter in silk weaving.[46]

As early as the seventies owners of weaving manufactories arose from among Telugu craftsmen who had grown rich. We have noted already that the first weaving manufactory in Sholapur was set up by a Telugu weaver in the seventies. In addition to centralised

43 *The Times*, 15 September, 1891.

44 *Ibid*.

45 Joshi, n. 14, 92.

46 N. 13, XVIII, Part 2, 174. These Telugu castes of weavers immigrated into Maharashtra during the sixties to eighties of the 19th century. The migration of castes of craftsmen provides, incidentally, additional evidence showing that the productive capacity of the manufactories was at the time expanding in connection with the growth of the internal market.

manufactories, in which the workers were concentrated in one building, Telugu capitalists also controlled home-workers, whom they reduced to bondage with the help of loans.[47] By using relations which had grown up within the caste and debt bondage, the Telugu capitalists to a large extent monopolised the exploitation of weavers who were members of their caste. This monopoly position enabled the Telugu capitalists to pay their fellow countrymen Rs 10 for 8-10 saris, while Maratha weavers received Rs 13 for the same amount of cloth. The weavers worked 14 hours a day. The whole family of the craftsman, including women and children, took part in the work.[48] The Telugu owners of manufactories were in fact, however, only agents of big merchant's capital. In Sholapur and Ahmednagar, for example, they were obliged by contracts to supply certain quantities of cloth at agreed prices to the merchants who gave them credits.

The terrible exploitation of the craftsman was the inevitable result of the colonial economy. The import of British cloth and other machine-made commodities exerted a decisive influence on the price level in the Indian market, which had no protective customs. The market value in India was determined by imported commodities produced in Great Britain which had long since changed over to factory production. British manufacturers, even if they extracted super profits, were therefore able to sell their goods in India at prices which were considerably lower than the cost of production of similar commodities manufactured by Indian handicrafts—provided labour power was paid in accordance with its value. The reduction of the price of labour power paid to the worker in manufacture—of course, including the home-worker—below the physical minimum, was the principal reserve fund of Indian manual production in the merciless competition against the British factory.[49]

Debt bondage was an additional, pre-capitalist means of reducing the price of labour power and was to a certain extent an inevitable feature of manufacture under colonial conditions.

Another reserve fund on which manual production fell back was the use of semi-finished products, both imported and local (yarn, metals, dyes and so on); they were comparatively cheap and could be obtained from the buyers-up. Indian manufacture, thereby, became in effect an external department of British—and partly also of Indian—large-scale industry. The control of the prices of semi-finished products became

47 Joshi, n. 14, 71,112.

48 *Ibid.*, 71, 112.

49 For example, a weaver in Burhanpur (Central Provinces) earned Rs 5-10 per month in the sixties. All members of the weaver's family had to work to make both ends meet. In addition to spinning and dyeing the weaver's wife and children took on various kinds of occasional work. A weaver in Bilaspur earned two to three annas for day. N. 1, 131.

an effective method which enabled the British and Indian factory owners to exploit the workers of the manufactories.

The debt bondage of the immediate producer, the dependence of manufacture on the supply of machine-made semi-finished products and, finally, the fact that a capitalist credit system had not yet developed increased the dependence of the small Indian industry on the trading and moneylending capital of the buyer-up. But the trading and moneylending capital, which controlled the small industries, was itself only an intermediary subordinate to British capital and big Indian capital.

The countryside, in which commodity-money relations were developing, was the principal market for the products of manufacture. The orientation of the weaving industry towards the home market of Maharashtra already began at the close of the 19th century. Sholapur, for instance, produced coarse saris and pasodis which were sold to poor peasants in almost all parts of the Bombay Deccan, the Konkan and, especially, Ratnagiri; the manufactories, moreover, which supplied the market of Maharashtra as a whole, were mainly concentrated in the big weaving centres. Their products were in demand both in Eastern and in Western Maharashtra (Central Provinces, Berar and Hyderabad). The cotton fabrics manufactured in the small centres of handloom weaving were intended for the consumer who lived in the neighbourhood, that is, also for the home market. The product of the silk-weaving manufactories, too were sold within the borders of Maharashtra.[50] Thus, the fight of the Maratha manufactories for markets was, from the outset, a fight for the home market of Maharashtra.

A specific feature of the Indian market was the great variety in the tastes and demands of the consumers. A unified market for consumer goods did not exist, and could not exist, in feudal India. Because the markets were for centuries isolated from each other numerous and diverse traditional designs of articles of general consumption had been evolved; the use of consumer goods of particular pattern had become firmly established and sanctified by religion or ritual. The members of each caste and subcaste—and there are several thousands of them in India—wore distinct garments, headgear and ornaments, used distinct utensils, etc.

The import of British machine-made commodities gradually unified the tastes of the consumers. But up to now, the peasant who is a little better off prefers the sari woven on the handloom with the traditional design of his caste to the standardised cloth manufactured in the factory. It is true that the mills, especially the Indian mills, endeavoured to

50 Joshi, n. 14, 44, 49, 77.

bring their products into line with the requirements of the Indian consumer;[51] often however, they did not succeed.[52] Manufacture could easier adjust itself to the varying requirements for it arose on the technical basis of the handicrafts and made use of the habits of work and the skill of the craftsmen, who had for many generations succeeded in satisfying the tastes of their customers. An extremely wide range of products, intended for the manifold local requirements, became a characteristic feature of manufacture in India. Hence close ties—based on the technique of production—existed between most branches of Indian manufacture and the local market. Lenin wrote with regard to this feature of handicraft production: "The insignificant scale of production easily adapts itself to the slightly fluctuating local demand".[53]

It has been stated already that the exploitation of the working people of Maharashtra through commerce and moneylending was carried on by British and also Gujarati and Marwar capital which to a considerable degree ousted the Maratha propertied classes from this sphere. This fact exerted a strong influence on the development of the big, as well as the petty Maratha bourgeoisie. Machine industry in Bombay, Sholapur, Nagpur, Poona and other towns of Maharashtra belonged to British or Gujarati capital. Non-Maratha capitalists—Gujaratis, Marwaris and Telugus—occupied strong positions in the small industries, too, as we have already said.

A considerable number of weavers in East Maharashtra were Momins and Julahs—members of Muslim castes of weavers. The majority of them came to Maharashtra from other provinces of India. In the eighties 1,700 looms, out of the 2,240 looms which operated in Malegaon, belonged to Momins, who hailed from the United Provinces.[54]

Simultaneously with the development of capitalist manufactories, small Maratha capitalists—mainly members of craft castes who had grown rich—began to appear. For example, the capitalist merchants who predominated in the cotton-weaving industry of

51 *The Gazetteer of the Central Provinces* records that some common kinds of cloth typical of Nagpur and Umrer were imported from Britain and sold well since their prices were much below those of the local fabrics which they imitated. See 332.

52 Describing the position of the weavers in Burhanpur, the same gazetteer stresses, that the population still preferred the cheap cloth which the local weavers produced to the textiles imported from Manchester. The common people did not consider that the cloth from Manchester was suitable for everyday use, because of both its quality and price. *Ibid.*, 129, 132.

53 V. 1. Lenin, *Collected Works*, III, 543.

54 N. 13, XVI, 116.

Poona were Shimpis,[55] members of a Maratha caste of tailors.[56] Tikekar who became owner of a small weaving mill and of several manufactories during the nineties, was a Maratha by birth. Existing evidence shows that he was closely connected with the textile industry of Bombay.[57] Apparently, he grew rich by supplying weavers with machine-made yarn. The owners of workshops in the metal-working industry were members of Maratha castes of craftsmen, in the main Kansars (braziers).

Among the Maratha merchants and small industrialists were also Brahmins and members of the highest peasant caste—the Maratha. Both these castes occupied a high social position in feudal Maharashtra. Brahmins and Marathas served not only in the state apparatus but were also merchants and sometimes industrialists.

Brahmin and Maratha industrialists, as we have stated before, owned tobacco and cotton processing enterprises. It can be added that during the eighties a considerable number of grain-dealers in Poona belonged to members of the Maratha caste. Most of the owners of furniture workshops were Brahmins and Marathas.[58] Medicines were usually made by Brahmins. In general, the Brahmin and Maratha small entrepreneurs carried on their business in those handicrafts where production was not the monopoly of a particular craft caste. According to data at our disposal, Brahmins and Marathas extended their activities in the small industry of Poona during the 1830s. Certain urban groups of these castes, the highest castes in the Maratha social structure, were, therefore, strongly interested in the fate of handicraft production. Because of their recent prosperity, which was still fresh in their memory, and their relatively high educational level the petty Brahmin and Maratha proprietors were particularly sensitive to coercion exerted by the colonial regime, whether it was direct—political—or indirect, but no less painful—economic—coercion.[59]

Although as a result of the development of manufacture a fairly numerous group of capitalist manufactory owners emerged from among the Maratha castes of craftsmen as well as from the Brahmins

---

55 Joshi, n. 14, 47.

56 R. V. Russels, *Tribes and Castes in India* (London, 1916), I, 409.

57 *Indian Textile Journal*, September 1926.

58 Gadgil, n. 16, 162, 167, 194.

59 Since the Brahmins predominated in the government apparatus of the Peshwa State, which was hostile to the East India Company, the colonialists continued after the conquest for some time to treat them with unconcealed animosity. Although this attitude was subsequently modified the Brahmins did not regain their former privileged position. The numerical strength of the Brahmins within the Maratha population was considerable; in the Bombay districts of Maharashtra they made up 4.5 to 11 per cent of the population. R. D. Choksey, *Economic History of the Bombay Deccan*, 181.

and Marathas, it should not be forgotten that Gujarati and Marwari merchant's capital seized the commanding positions in the manufacture of Maharashtra; for it acted as the commercial agent of British and Indian big industrial capital which monopolised the supply of semi-finished products to the principal branches of local manufacture. In the final analysis, the domination of merchant's capital over the manufactory owners was, essentially, a manifestation of the domination of large-scale industry over manufacture. The fact that a considerable part of the surplus-value created in the small industry of Maharashtra was appropriated by the capital of the buyers-up and with its aid by British, and partly by big Indian industrial capital hampered the accumulation of the means necessary for reproduction on a progressively increasing scale. Under these circumstances, the small masters who directly extracted super-profits from the workers employed in their manufactories were really only middlemen between the merchant and their workers; the merchant, moreover, pocketed the lion's share of the surplus-value.[60]

It should be noted that during the epoch of primitive accumulation—to which the preceding passage of Marx refers—in contradistinction to Europe, the merchant (buyer-up) in colonial India did not play an independent role and, since he was only a middleman, he was forced to pay too high a price for the semi-finished products like yarn, dyes and metals and to hand over the greater part of the surplus-value which passed through his hands to the foreign monopolists, and in some measure also to Indian industrialists. Accumulation was, therefore, retarded not only in the sphere of small industrial capital but also in that of the merchant's capital operating in the handicrafts of India.

The lack of financial resources experienced by the small manufacturers greatly impeded the technical reconstruction of the small industry. The few innovations that were introduced remained within the bounds of manual production—for instance, the flying shuttle in the weaving industry. The transformation of manufactories into factories was a very rare occurrence in India. Up to the First World War it happened only twice, as far as we know, that weaving manufactories in Maharashtra were turned into establishments resembling modern factories. The combination of machine and manual production was a characteristic feature of these establishments. For instance, Tikekar's factory in Sholapur had more handlooms than power looms.[61] In addition to this factory the same company owned several other weaving enterprises.[62]

At the end of the eighties the Maratha Anandrao Bhau Godambe

60 See Karl Marx, *Capital*, III, 329-30.

61 N. 57, September 1926.

62 Joshi, n. 14, 104.

set up a large workshop for the production of copper and bronze utensils in Poona. But after 20 years, in 1908, the workshop was closed, and the Gujarati merchant Hukamchand Ishwardas, who had been previously selling the wares produced in this workshop, acquired it. There is no evidence that machines were used in this establishment. But since it was specially mentioned in the research work we used, it seems to have been considerably bigger than other *karkhanas* manufacturing copper utensils in Poona.[63]

Certain circumstances—in addition to those affecting the Indian bourgeoisie in general—held back the development of the Maratha bourgeoisie in particular. One of the principal reasons for the slow emergence of the Maratha bourgeoisie was that the local merchants and moneylenders were comparatively weak when the colonial regime was established in their country. This allowed the Gujarati and Marwari capitalists, who had been for a long time connected with British merchant's capital, in a large degree to monopolise the exploitation of the Maratha working people through moneylending and commerce, in which they acted as middlemen of the British.

The development of the Maratha bourgeoisie was also retarded by the fact that the money accumulated by the wealthy strata in the Maratha town was used to acquire landed property. When the colonialists introduced their land tax legislation they expected—according to G. Keating, who ought to know, for he was director of the Department of Agriculture in the Bombay Presidency—that, if landed property was freely transferable, traders and persons receiving a pension would be induced to invest their money in the purchase and improvement of land.[64]

The agrarian policy of the British turned the pecuniary resources accumulated by the urban propertied strata in Maharashtra, as in the whole of India, towards landed property. Keating relates that these expectations proved to be correct; it was, however, not foreseen that many landowners, who were deeply attached to the soil and did not wish to part with it, were inadvertently deprived of all property rights in their land, which passed into the hands of moneylenders thanks to the incompetent civil courts, according to Keating.[65] At the beginning of the twentieth century one-sixth of the land in the Bombay Deccan (i.e. in West Maharashtra) belonged, as Keating admits, to non-agricultural classes, who did not wish to spend any money on its improvement but preferred to lease it on enslaving conditions.[66]

All this caused the big merchant's capital of Maharashtra to be slow

63 Gadgil, n. 16, 126.

64 G. Keating, *Rural Economy in the Bombay Deccan* (London, 1912), 21.

65 *Ibid.*, 22.

66 *Ibid.*, 37.

in investing its accumulations in the factory industry. The capitalist development of industry in the interior of Maharashtra proceeded chiefly along the lines of scattered and centralised manufacture, in which capitalist exploitation was aggravated by the fact that the direct producer was enslaved by moneylenders. The emerging Maratha bourgeoisie consisted mainly of small traders and manufacturers. Its transition to the higher stages of capitalist enterprise was retarded by colonialism.

The petty Maratha bourgeoisie, thus, suffered directly from the insufficient development of capitalism in India, which was impeded by colonialism. Its industrial activities were restricted by the narrow limits set by consumer demand in the semi-feudal countryside, the competition of British machine-made products in the home market the capacity of which was in any case very limited, the absence of a proper capitalist credit system and the dependence on the supply of imported semi-finished products. The petty Maratha bourgeoisie was, therefore, driven to an uncompromising struggle against imperialism in spite of the religious, communal and caste limitations of its conceptions and the archaic character of its ideology. The weakness of the big Maratha bourgeoisie caused the prevalence of petty bourgeois slogans in the programme of the national movement of the Maratha people. This circumstance was, in effect, conducive to the emergence in Maharashtra of the political group headed by B. G. Tilak which expressed the anti-imperialist trend that demanded the free development of capitalism in India, with the greatest consistency and force.

The participation of Maratha princes in the building of industrial enterprises occupies a special place in the business activities of the Maratha propertied classes. While Maharashtra itself was, after its conquest, divided up between several provinces of British India and Hyderabad, and the native rulers were deprived of all political power, the Maratha princes beyond the borders of Maharashtra—in regions inhabited by Gujaratis, Rajasthanis, Hindustanis, and other Indian nationalities—were able to retain what was left of their states.

At the close of the 19th century the Maratha princes of Baroda, Indore and Gwalior began, prompted by fiscal considerations, to encourage the building of industrial enterprises in their states. They assisted capitalists by granting them credits, taking up shares, allocating land, adjusting their customs policy, and so on. The merciless exploitation of the working class, which had no right in these states secured high profits. The princes often leased or sold for a song enterprises which they had built at the expense of the exchequer and which were not sufficiently lucrative They held shares in many big enterprises outside their states. The Maharajah of Gwalior, for instance, was one of the principal shareholders of the Tata Iron and Steel Co. We have already given some information regarding the industrial policy of the Prince of Baroda.

The Maharajah of Indore, Tukoji Rao II, built a cotton mill, which cost Rs 770 thousand in 1877. It manufactured cloth which was used as lining for opium chests. When the export of opium declined at the close of the 19th century, the mill had difficulties in selling its products—usually the weak point of enterprises run by native princes—and in 1912 it was leased to "Veper Uttejak", a private firm and subsequently in 1917 to a Marwari firm "Bhandari" and Sons. E. Currimbhoy, a native of Bombay, built two mills in Indore in 1900 and 1909. The Marwari Hukumchand set up the third and fourth mill of Indore in 1911 and 1917 respectively.[67] In 1913 the Prince of Sangli granted a loan free of interest and a rent-free piece of land to V. P. Velankar, a Maratha who owned a small textile mill in Poona. Attracted by these advantages Velankar transferred his enterprise to Sangli and expanded it considerably.[68]

Thus, since the end of the 19th century the policy of the Maratha princes was to encourage industry. The big Gujarati and Marwari capitalists profited most by this policy, not only because they were so powerful but also because through their activities in the spheres of taxation, commerce and finance, they had long established connections with the princes.

The Maratha princes granted large credits to the railway companies, at terms, which incidentally brought them nice profits. In 1876, for instance, the Prince of Indore lent the railways Rs 15 million for 101 years, which carried interest at 4.5 per cent per annum, and the Maharajah of Gwalior granted them a permanent loan of Rs 10 million at an annual interest of 4 per cent, increasing the loan later by another Rs 29 million.[69] It is obvious that these enormous sums considerably surpassed the investments made by the princes in the national industry.

The relations maintained by the Maratha princes with industry and commerce did not signify at all that their feudal nature had changed and that they had turned into bourgeois. On the contrary, under colonial conditions the income from industry, commerce and banking helped the princes to consolidate their economic position in their feudal domains, and strengthened the feudal reaction, whereas the building of industrial enterprises in the states made the big Indian bourgeoisie stronger.

---

67 N. 57, December 1931.

68 *Ibid.*, March 1935.

69 W. Digby, *Prosperous British India*, 230.

CHAPTER X

THE BENGALI BOURGEOISIE

The colonial oppression distorted the economic life of Bengal more profoundly than that of any other province of India. The specific features of the development of the Bengali bourgeoisie were determined by the fact that the whole economy of Bengal was subordinated to the aim of extracting colonial tribute. During the first half of the 19th century the peasant economy—which was strangled by the zamindars' monopoly of the land—and the small-scale commodity production of the handicrafts in the towns of Bengal were far too weak to give rise to capitalist relations. The handicrafts were bled white, first, by British merchant's capital, which led a parasitic existence, and then by the competition of British industrial capital. The Indian merchants and buyers-up, on the other hand, who depended on British capital and were independent in relation to the industry of Bengal, represented at that time pre-capitalist debt-bondage .

During the latter half of the 19th century certain opportunities of developing national capitalist enterprise arose in Bengal, as in India as a whole. One must, however, point out immediately that there were fewer opportunities in Bengal than in the other regions of India where the economy was relatively highly developed. This was not only due to British capital occupying a stronger position in Bengal, and especially in Calcutta, than anywhere else in India; but also to the agrarian policy of the colonial administration which evidently was no less an impediment to the development of local capitalist enterprise in the province.

The system of privileged landownership established in Bengal continued for a long time to attract the funds accumulated by the local propertied classes, thus preventing their investment in the national industry which involved a certain risk. These accumulations were used to acquire landed property, which provided a high and steady income. Land became to an even greater extent the object of business transactions in the eighties, when the colonial administration introduced for some categories of peasants a system of privileged lease whose rents could not be raised beyond a fixed amount. Moneylenders and landlords started to appropriate the plots of these tenants and then to lease them under inequitable conditions. In addition to the legal proprietors of the land in Bengal, the zamindars, a section of middlemen—sublease-holder came into being, who pocketed part of the rent. Thus as a result of the agrarian policy of the colonial government a class of semi-feudal landlords was brought into existence in Bengal, which was exceptionally numerous even in colonial India. As regards the big bourgeoisie, it should be said that it developed extremely slowly and arose for the main part from among the landlords who invested their accumulations in commerce, finance and industry under favourable conditions.

It was a sign of the weakness of capitalist enterprise in Bengal that the representatives of the local propertied classes were forced to become junior partners of British capitalists—they were agents or middlemen of British commercial firms, owners of small enterprises where agricultural raw material intended for export was processed, and shareholders in British companies without any rights.

Rich Bengalis lent money to British commission merchant houses, and were happy if they managed to get a job in one of these. While they were employed in one of the big British firms, they conducted trade, on a limited scale, for their own account. Regarding the *banyans*—that is the agents—of these firms Kabiraj Narahari tells us that the *banyan* was the translator or interpreter, the chief accountant and clerk, the cashier and, in general, the trusted servant of the firm. After the establishment of the British rule members of the best Hindu families were eager to secure such posts and were prepared to grant big loans to the firm in question. The desire of the Hindus to obtain employment with a British firm was due to the fact that such a position gave the employee great influence and a number of advantages which helped him in his own commercial transactions.[1]

Having destroyed the principal urban handicraft of Bengal, the weaving of cotton, and also jute fabrics,[2] the British capitalists proceeded—up to the close of the 19th century—to exploit the silk winding and indigo industries whose products were exported. Some enterprises in these branches of production reached quite a considerable size. For instance, a silk winding establishment in Jangipur (near Murshidabad), which belonged to the East India Company, employed approximately three thousand workers at the beginning of the 19th century.[3] But as soon as Indian silk and indigo encountered strong

1 Kabiraj Narahari, *Natsional 'no-osvobodites' noe dvizhenie v Bengali* (Moscow, 1956), 39.

2 The manufacture of cloth from jute was an important handicraft in Bengal. The export of jute cloth from Bengal began in 1795, while the first mills which worked up raw jute in Dundee (Scotland) only started to operate in 1835. Up to 1835 the export of hand-made jute cloth exceeded the export of raw jute. *Indian Industrial Commission*, (London, 1919), I, 19.

3 B. Chunder, *The Travels of a Hindoo . . .*, I, 85.

competition on the European market, the British capitalists abandoned these industries which ceased to be lucrative.

The *Imperial Gazetteer of India* relates in eighties that formerly the manufacture of indigo and silk in the Rajshahi district was mainly in the hands of European capitalists, but now both these branches had fallen into decay. In 1870 the output of only three enterprises was bigger than the total output of the district in 1881. The silk weaving industry had, during this period, cut its production by three quarters—from 400 thousand pounds of raw silk to 111 thousand pounds.[4] And in 1911 only 22 thousand pounds of raw silk were processed. Many of the European companies discontinued their business activities.[5]

Local Bengali capital played only a small part in the processing of raw silk. According to official data 45 silk reeling establishments with 3,500 vats belonged to the British in the Murshidabad district in 1876, while 67 establishments with 1,600 vats were owned by local inhabitants. Since two persons worked at every vat, there were more than 10 thousand silk-winders employed in the district. But the decline of the industry had already begun in the seventies.[6] Thornton writes that the production of silk in Murshidabad reached its greatest extent when the East India Company was a commercial enterprise.[7]

The enterprises for the processing of indigo belonged, as a rule, to the British. But as early as the middle of the 19th century the British entrepreneurs attracted funds accumulated by the propertied strata of the Bengali population to this industry. The participation of the Bengali capitalists in British enterprises had, at that time, not yet reached the stage when they acquired shares in British companies, but found its expression in loans which rich Indians advanced to the British owners of enterprises.[8] But the immature form of the participation not not change the nature of the process—the fact that the money of the wealthy Indians was utilised in the interests of British capital.

It is obvious that the job of a clerk in a British enterprise could not satisfy the rich Bengalis. In their endeavour to escape from a position which made them the direct subordinates of British capitalists, they set up independent companies. Several wealthy Bengalis, and first of

---

4 *Imperial Gazetteer of India*, XI, 435.

5 *Rajshahi, Bengal District Gazetteers*, (Calcutta, 1916), 108-11.

6 *Murshidabad, Eastern Bengal District Gazetteers*, 127-28.

7 E. Thornton, *Gazetteer of the Territories*. . . III, (London, 1854) 508.

8 A Member of the House of Commons declared that although a certain amount of British capital was indeed invested in the processing of indigo, he had been informed that a considerable part of the industry was run on borrowed capital, which was advanced by the natives at 16 to 20 per cent. *Hansard's Parliamentary Debates*, (Third Series Vol. 162, 1861) 811.

all Dwarkanath Tagore, established a number of firms, among them a coal mine and several banks.[9]

The efforts of the Bengali entrepreneurs to take part in the ship-repair industry which the British created in Calcutta in the middle of the 19th century are well known. The Albion dock was built by Mukerjee, a Bengali together with two Englishmen in 1874; three Indians built the East India dock two years later, and finally, in 1850, the Caledonia dock was bought by an Indian entrepreneur. The-Bengali ship-repair industry did not, however, make any significant impact on the development of the Bengali industrial bourgeoisie, for the Albion belonged to a considerable degree to Englishmen, the company which owned the East India dock went bankrupt in 1865, and only 105 workers were employed on the Caledonia dock in 1872 as against 500-600 in the British shipyards.[10] Indigenous capitalists, therefore, occupied only minor positions in industrial branches facilitating the colonial exploitation of Bengal.

With regard to independent business activities of the local rich, Kabiraj Narahari, a Bengali historian, writes that during the 19th century the wealthy Bengalis did not venture either to establish their own commercial enterprises or to conduct overseas commerce independently. For in the conditions prevailing under the British rule, new enterprises belonging to Bengalis were not able to develop successfully. They had to enter into competition with the British merchant houses on unequal terms; their fate, moreover, depended entirely on the goodwill of the British authorities. To preserve their fortunes the descendants of Bengali merchants were at that time forced to give up commerce and to invest their capital in land and to buy the estates of zamindars. Some of them, who spoke English, became employees in administrative bodies or in British commercial enterprises.[11]

Since the middle of the 19th century British capital held the world monopoly of jute production. The transformation of Bengal into a producer of jute based on single-crop farming was a further step in the colonial enslavement of this province. In contrast to indigo export, however, the export of jute developed at a time when India was no longer exploited by merchant's capital but by British industrial capital. The methods used to exploit the jute producer differed, therefore, considerably from those employed in the exploitation of the indigo producer. While the manufacture of indigo was forced upon the peasant by the government apparatus resorting to brute force, the cultivation of jute was stimulated by means of market relations and by taking advantage of the peasant's dependence on the landlord and

9 Narahari, n. 1, 40.
10 *Hourah*, n. 5, 104-05.
11 Narahari, n. 1, 40.

moneylender, who hoped that the introduction of a marketable crop would increase their income.[12] The cultivation of jute therefore on the one hand furthered the development of commodity-money relations in the countryside and the growth of the market, and on the other hand helped the landlords and moneylenders to grow rich, and was conducive to the retention of their accumulations in the spheres of agriculture, moneylending and commerce.

The growth of the home market in Bengal at the beginning of the 20th century gave an impetus to the capitalist development of the handicraft industries, especially in the countryside where they were still in a better state of preservation.[13] Buyers-up from other districts began to visit rural weavers. Prof. Mukerji, who himself investigated the economic position in the countryside of Bengal before the First World War, recorded that a great number of weavers had abandoned, their trade, adding however, that recently symptoms were appearing which indicated that an improvement was taking place in this important industry. The recovery of this industry in Bengal was particularly marked in 1906-07 thanks to the increased demand for commodities produced locally. The output of handloom weaving grew considerably, and many weavers who had given up the traditional trade of their caste took it up again.[14] Mukerji stressed that the recovery was greatest in the regions where weaving catered to the specific requirements of the local consumer.[15]

Other source material and investigations also indicate that at the beginning of the twentieth century a partial revival took place in the handloom weaving industry of Bengal.[16] Indian and English writers on economics usually explain that the expansion in the production of the handicrafts, which was not noticeable, was due to the Swadeshi

---

12 To make sure of their raw material, British firms also reduced the peasant to bondage. R. Mukerji relates that in regions where the peasant was hopelessly poor, deep in debt and unable to turn for help to the moneylender, he had to obtain advances from European firms and was forced to switch from the cultivation of crops for his own country to the growing of raw materials for the markets of Europe. R. Mukerji, *The Foundations of Indian Economics*, 41.

13 Cotton-weaving, after the cessation of the East India Company's commercial operation, languished in consequence of the competition of imported piece-goods. By the end of the 19th century, the latter had almost driven the products of the local looms out of the market... The number of persons engaged in cotton-weaving decreased by about 33 per cent in 20 years, and those who clung to their old handicraft had for the most part to supplement their earnings from other sources, such as agriculture, service, etc... Recently, however, in consequence of the Swadeshi movement and the preference for country-made cloth which it inspired, the fortunes of the weavers have improved and they are now able to make a fair living. *Hoogly*, n. 5, XXIX, 182.

14 Mukerji, n. 12, 162.

15 *Ibid*.

16 *Hoogly*, n. 5, 181; J.C. Mitter, *Recovery Plan for Bengal* (Calcutta, 1934), 283.

movement and the growing local demand which it called forth. In these explanations cause and effect are confused, for the Swadeshi movement itself was brought into existence by the desire of the rising national bourgeoisie to gain control of the home market, which developed in consequence of the growing commodity-money relations in the countryside and the decline of the home industry.

The revival of the handicrafts, as we have already said, was only partial, for although the market was expanding an ever-increasing proportion of the commodities sold consisted of British and Indian factory products. The workshops and small enterprises run along industrial lines which worked for the home market, belonged as a rule to Bengali and Marwari capitalists. In any case we have found hardly any references to proprietors of other nationalities. According to Mukerji, 367 enterprises in Calcutta belonged to Indians and 179 to Europeans, that is to the British before the First World War. But in spite of their numerical superiority (twice as many Indian establishments as British) the Indian enterprises were no match for the British, which included the biggest jute mills. The following figures are also rather interesting: out of 360 private Indian enterprises—that is, not joint-stock companies—65 were owned by members of the Kayastha caste (i.e. scribes), 61 by Brahmins, 18 by Sikhs and 19 by Marwaris.[17]

The relatively larger groups of small industrial capitalists, therefore, consisted not of descendants of the craft castes, but were composed of members of the higher Bengali castes, the Brahmins and Kayasthas. Representatives of the top layers of these castes were already for a long time employed in the colonial administration or acted as middlemen in commerce. The majority of the landowners in Bengal were also members of these top strata. It is natural, that in Calcutta, which had been up to fairly recent times the administrative centre of colonial India, these castes possessed great advantages over the castes of craftsmen, who were ruined by the British. The industrial activity of the Brahmins and Kayasthas, apparently, only began at the close of the 19th century and was connected with the development of capitalist manufacture in the small industries of Calcutta.[18]

The partial recovery of the handicrafts in Bengal, therefore, took place on the basis of the development of capitalist relations within them. But the inherent features of the colonial economy—such as the absence of a proper capitalist credit system, the limited market and the serious

17 Mukerji, n. 12, 365-66.

18 A noteworthy feature of Calcutta industrial life, which has become much more prominent in recent years, is the number of small organised industries (that is industries run on capitalist lines) recently taken up by Indians, such as tanning, pottery and pencil-making; also the many small power factories for oil milling and rice-husking owned by them. N. 2, I, 16.

competition of the British imports, the use of imported semi-finished products (yarn, metals, dyes, and so on), and, finally, the pressure of the vast surplus population on the labour market—confined the advance of capitalism in the handicraft industry almost completely to the development of the lower form of merchant's capital in the small industries, which consists of a combination of merchant's capital and moneylending.

On the eve of the First World War the cotton weavers of Bengal usually obtained yarn and other materials on credit from the village mahajans (moneylenders) and sold them the finished cloth at rates fixed by the mahajans who generally took advantage of the weaver's poverty to extract exorbitant profits.[19] A similar dependence of the producer on merchant's and moneylender's capital existed also in the other industries of Bengal. The mahajans advanced money to the silk weavers at high rates of interest and moreover, stipulated for the exclusive right to obtain the finished fabrics.[20] The shoemaker, too, received an advance from the mahajan, which consisted either of money or dressed leather. In return for the advance of, for instance, Rs 50 the shoemaker would in the course of a month hand over 20 pairs of shoes to the mahajan, who sold them at Rs 3 and 8 annas per pair. On each pair of shoes the mahajan made a profit of one rupee.[21] Thus in the course of a few weeks the Rs 50 brought the mahajan a profit of Rs 20 that is, an interest of 40 per cent on the capital lent.

R. Mukerji asserts that friendly relations existed between the mahajan and the craftsmen in the copper industry.[22] But, as the facts we are citing prove, the secret of this friendship was that, at this time, the copper industry of Bengal had difficulties in satisfying the current demands for its products. There was therefore, a shortage of skilled braziers. Craftsmen told him, writes Mukerji, that the demand for their wares had grown in the course of time, and that they were forced to hire workers who were members of other castes.[23] This shows that debt bondage was weakened as soon as the stagnant surplus population disappeared. But the situation in the copper industry of Bengal before the outbreak of the First World War was quite exceptional for India.

The information provided by the *Gazetteers* makes it clear that the relations described by Mukerji were merely an episode. One of the *Bengal District Gazetteers*, for instance referring to a number of villages in the Rajshahi district, in each of which 60 to 100 families were engaged in the manufacture of brass utensils writes:

19 Mukerji, n. 12, 168.
20 *Ibid.*, 189.
21 *Ibid.*, 213-14.
22 *Ibid.*, 236.
23 *Ibid.*, 235.

the industry is in the hands of mahajans who supply the workers with the raw material, i.e. brass sheets and old bell-metal utensils, and take back the finished articles from them after paying them wages at fixed rates per seer of the manufactured article . . . The earnings of the average worker average Rs 8 to Rs 12 per month[24] (a truly beggarly wage).

The examples we have given indicate that the principal figure in the small industries which developed in Bengal was the buyer-up or mahajan, who represented the merchant's and moneylender's capital. The mahajan controlled not only the home-workers but also the small capitalists.

But the merchant's and moneylender's capital did not, as a rule, commit itself by investing in the big national industry. In consequence of the growing home market and the increasing exploitation of Bengal as a market and a source of raw material, both the independent operations of merchant's capital and those in which it acted as an intermediary were up to the 1920s expanding; the funds it accumulated continued therefore to be employed in commerce and moneylending and also in landed property.[25] British and Marwari firms which were organising the buying-up of jute had to create a widespread network of agents, because more intermediaries were required in the jute trade than in the cotton trade, since the plots in Bengal were rather small.[26]

The dependence of Bengali merchant's capital on the British monopolies, which was especially marked in the wholesale trade where it acted as intermediary, hampered the concentration of accumulations and was one of the reason of its cautious attitude with regard to the creation of a large-scale national industry.[27] The *Indian Industrial Commission* remarked upon the striking contrast existing between

---

24 See *Rajshahi*, I, 5, XXIII, 107.

25 When communications were improved and India was brought into effective touch with the outside world (reports the *Indian Industrial Commission*), traders took advantage of the changed position merely to extend the scale of their previous operations. Like the landlord, they lent money to the cultivators and found a profitable investment in landed property. In trade and moneylending and, to a less extent, in financing village artisans, the trading classes found that large and certain gains were to be made; while modern (that is, large-scale) industries required technical knowledge, and offered only doubtful and, in most cases, apparently smaller profits. N. 2, I, 64.

26 *Ibid.*, 15.

27 Until recently, writes the *Indian Industrial Commission*, jute production was mainly financed by Bengalis. But the Bengali merchant in Calcutta, who had got used to trade in various kinds of goods, was apparently unable to switch from commerce to industry. Even in the commercial operations conducted within the country, he could not keep up with the greater enterprise of the Marwari merchant from Rajputana. *Ibid.*, 61.

Bombay and Calcutta with respect to the position which the Indians occupied in commerce and industry.[28]

At the beginning of the 20th century the objective conditions conducive to the investment of the funds accumulated by the Bengali landlords in industry, were still lacking. A passage in one of the *Bengal Gazetteers* reads:

> I am informed that zamindari in this district yields 9 per cent . . . on the capital invested, and there is therefore no inducement for a man who has money to spare to sink it in exploiting industries which will yield a smaller rate of interest than he can obtain from landed property.[29]

It is true that a few cases are known of Bengali landlords turning industrialists, especially during the time of the Swadeshi movement. In 1909 the Maharaja Mahindra Chandra Nandi and Babu Baikunth Nath Sen opened a pottery in the 24-Parganas district, which was equipped with German and British machinery.[30] Kishor Lal Goswami, who inherited a large zamindari estate and was a member of the executive council of Bengal, became a director of the British owned Bengal Provincial Railway and a cotton mill.[31] There are also other examples of landlords turning towards industrial enterprise. But, as the *Indian Industrial Commission* points out in its report, the ineffectiveness of the attempts made by the educated classes (i.e. civil servants and landlords) to take advantage of the new opportunities was particularly noticeable in Bengal, and contrasted strongly with the success of European enterprise.[32]

On the whole, the participation of Bengal landlords in industry was insignificant during this period. Sometimes patriotically minded landlords took a hand in industry not so much because of economic interests but spurred by a desire to keep abreast of the times and to join the anti-imperialist movement which gripped Bengal during the partition of the province in 1905-11.[33] This partition, incidentally, threatened the privileged position of the zamindars in regard to the land tax. To show how strong the subjective factor was, we recall an incident which really took place and which has been described with sad humour by Rabindranath Tagore.

---

28 *Ibid.*, 65.

29 *Rajshahi*, n. 5, 106.

30 *24-Parganas*, n. 5, 151.

31 C. H. Rao, *Indian Biographical Dictionary*, 165.

32 *Indian Industrial Commission*, Vol. 1, p. 64.

33 "It still remains to some extent effective", writes in 1916 the *Indian Industrial Commission* about the movement and it goes on to say that a few professional men and landowners are still found, in Bengal and elsewhere, who support "Swadeshi enterprises with such capital as they can afford". *Ibid.*, 66-67.

(Rabindranath's brother Jyotirindra, a big zamindar) had tried to light matches for his country, but no amount of rubbing, availed to make them strike. He had also wanted powerlooms to work, but after all his travail only one little country towel was born, and then the loom stopped. And then he wanted Indian steamers to ply, he bought an empty old hulk, which in due course was filled, not only with engines and cabins, but with loss and ruin as well...

On one side was the European Flotilla Company, on the other my brother Jyotirindra alone; and how tremendous waged that battle of the mercantile fleets, the people of Khulna and Barisal may still remember. Under the stress of competition steamer was added to steamer, loss piled on loss, while the income dwindled till it ceased to be worthwhile to print tickets. The golden age dawned on the steamer service between Khulna and Barisal. Not only were the passengers carried free of charge, but they were offered light refreshments *gratis* as well! Then was formed a band of volunteers who, with flags and patriotic songs, marched the passengers in procession to the Indian line of steamers. So while there was no want of passengers to carry, every other kind of want began to multiply apace.

Arithmetic remained uninfluenced by patriotic fervour; and while enthusiasm flamed higher and higher to the tune of patriotic songs, three times three went on steadily making nine on the wrong side of the balance sheet. . .

Then one day came the news that the steamer *Swadeshi* had fouled the Howrah bridge and sunk. With this last loss my brother completely overstepped the limits of his resources, and there was nothing for it but to wind up the business.[34]

Even when the Bengali propertied classes made investments in large-scale industry, before the First World War, they did so mainly by acquiring shares in British enterprises, above all jute mills. The first jute mill was built near Serampore in 1855. By 1901 the jute industry of Bengal comprised 16 thousand looms. In 1916 there were 71 mills in operation, which had 36,400 looms and employed 260 thousand workers.[35] The *Indian Industrial Commission* stressed that the Bengali and other Indian capitalists simply invested their savings in industry, but they played a very small part in the setting up of new enterprises and had nothing to do with their management.[36] As we have already said, 55 per cent of the shares of jute mills belonged to Indians as early as the First World War.[37] It is true that some of these shares were held by

34 Rabindranath Tagore, *Reminiscences,* (London, 1921), pp. 252-55.

35 *Indian Industrial Commission,* Vol. I, p. 14,

36 *Ibid.,* 15.

Marwaris and other non-Bengalis. The Indian investors, as a rule, owned preference shares which commanded the smallest dividends. This shows that the British monopolists made use of the dependent position of Bengali capital to retain the exclusive right of drawing super-profits.

At the beginning of the twentieth century Bengali capitalists outside Calcutta owned only a few small mechanised establishments for the pressing of jute and some local industrial enterprises run on factory lines. For instance, the only powerful jute pressing mill in the Dinajpur district belonged to Ralli Brothers while only a small establishment, which used semi-handicraft methods, was owned by Bengalis.[38] The same firm owned a jute pressing mill in the Rajshahi district, which was the only mechanised enterprise employing more than 50 workers in that district.[39]

In 1898 P. C. Roy opened an establishment for the preparation of medicines and perfumes in the 24-Parganas district. The share capital of this enterprise amounted to Rs 200 thousand in 1902, and the number of workers employed grew from 72 in 1908 to 190 in 1911. The owner had the degree of Doctor of Science which was quite common among the wealthy Bengalis of the upper castes.[40] Three small tobacco factories were set up in the same district before the war. The largest of them employed 487 workers which used imported machinery. All three enterprises belonged to Indians.[41]

In the middle of the 19th century the Bengali Babu Kishorilal Mukerji opened a metal working establishment in the Howrah district. Only 110 workers were employed there in 1908. The owners of the larger metal working enterprises were British. The British even owned corn mills and jute presses in Howrah.

It should be observed that at the beginning of the 20th century the tendency to develop independent industrial enterprises in Bengal became quite pronounced. The *Hoogly District Gazetteer* asserts that the growing desire of some Indians to invest their capital in industrial companies whose management was either entirely or predominantly in the hands of Indians was a new feature.[42] But the Bengali capitalists were merely taking the first steps towards becoming independent entrepreneurs in the sphere of modern large-scale industry. On the eve of the First World War the only really big enterprises owned by Bengalis were two cotton mills. In one of these 1,026 workers were employed in 1908. But even this offspring of Bengali capital changed its owners four times in the course of twelve years.[43]

---

37 G. S. Slater, *Southern India. . .*, 229.

38 *Dinajpur*, n. 6, 70.

39 *Rajshahi*, n. 5, 106.

40 *24-Parganas, Ibid.*, 51.

41 *Ibid.*, 150-51.

42 *Hoogly*, n. 5, 181.

43 The mill was built in 1894 by Sir Homer Petheram, the former chief judge of Bengal, but as early as 1897 the enterprise passed into the hands of British

The activities of Bengali capitalists in the coal mining industry of Bengal illustrate their inability at that time to manage independently large-scale enterprises. Coal output in the Raniganj Basin began to grow rapidly from 1854 onwards, after the railway connecting this district with Calcutta had been built. By 1917 the output of coal in Bengal reached 16,560 thousand tons per annum, while the output in the whole of India amounted to 18,120 thousand tons. The big mines belonged to powerful British managing agencies. The Indians owned only small mines, which had to close down as soon as the price of coal dropped. The British coal owners possessed the great advantage that coal was in the main consumed by the railways (28-33 per cent), the fleet (16.7 per cent), the jute mills (5.6 per cent), and metallurgical works (5.1 per cent).[44] This meant that the placing of coal orders depended on the colonial administration and the British capitalists themselves. The local zamindars, who were the proprietors of the mineral wealth concealed in the bowels of the earth, confined themselves to collecting a rent from the mine owners.[45]

Bengali capitalists participated in the British Bengal Iron and Steel Company which owned the only modern, though small, metallurgical works in Bengal. This company, which was set up in 1875, was, in contrast to the Tata enterprise, for a long time not very successful.[46]

Summing up the formation process of the Bengali bourgeoisie during modern times, one must stress that the principal factor affecting this process was the high concentration of all economic resources of Bengal in the hands of the British. So high a concentration was without parallel even in colonial India. The exceptionally heavy colonial oppression to which Bengal was subjected explains many of the special features in the development of the Bengali bourgeoisie; for example, the fact that the accumulations of the landlords surpassed those of the merchants, who were pushed aside both by British and Marwari capital; that manufacture came into being primarily in the disseminated form and mostly in the countryside; that comparatively independent industrial capitalists arose almost exclusively in the local industry run on the lines of manufactories; that many capitalists were descendants of the privileged castes connected with landownership and the colonial state apparatus; that Bengali capital played hardly any independent part in large-scale industry and that it was compelled to collaborate with the British monopolies.

---

merchants, who sold it within a short time to Mulraj Gordhandas, of Bombay. It was not till 1906 that the mill again became the property of Bengalis. See *Indian Textile Journal*, 1930, May; *Hoogly*, n. 5, 180.

44 N. 2, 20.

45 *Ibid.*, 21.

46 *Ibid.*, 22.

CHAPTER XI

RISE OF THE INDIAN ENTREPRENEUR AND IMPERIALISM

Although the specific feature of the rise of the bourgeoisie, and the whole process of capitalist development in India, were primarily determined by the colonial position of the country, this could not annul the general laws of capitalism, but could merely modify, change and distort their manifestations. The colonial rule was the decisive, but not the only important, factor determining the character of India's economic development. The colonialists themselves were forced in one way or another to take into account both the economic conditions which they found in the country when they conquered it and the economic processes which were taking place despite themselves in the national economy. Some British administrators tried to ignore these processes entirely, and to take into consideration only the needs of colonial plunder. But this adventurous policy led to economic dislocation and called forth the resistance of the masses of the people, i.e. it undermined the economic and political basis of the colonial regime.

While colonial rule, therefore, distorted the development of capitalism it could not deprive these processes of all their specific Indian features. Indian capitalism which in many important ways resembled the capitalism, for instance, of Egypt or the Philippines, did indeed differ essentially from them. But the fact that India's capitalist development differed from that of other colonial and semi-colonial countries was by no means the only result of the action of the objective economic laws. It was of considerably greater importance that the elements for a national capitalist development in India arose in rudimentary form within the colonial economy. The existence of these elements makes it possible to say that, owing to the action of the general economic laws, India if it had been politically independent could have produced a national version of capitalist development, just as Japan, another Asian country, has done.

Since, however, India was deprived of sovereignty the development of capitalism and the rise of the bourgeoisie followed a distorted, abnormal path, which although Indian was not national but colonial, containing nevertheless certain specifically national traits as a result of the action of the internal economic processes.

Before we pass on to describing the distinct features of the development of capitalism in Indian industry, let us consider for a moment the problems of dating and periodisation of this process. Historical works, unfortunately, do not always make a clear distinction between such different and independent concepts as "the appearance of the first nuclei of capitalist production", "the genesis or origin of capitalism" and "the development of capitalism".

The first nuclei of capitalist production already arose in the bowels of feudal society and became rather widespread at the stage of developed feudalism. As we have seen they were a common phenomenon in feudal India during the 17th and 18th centuries. But since the social division of labour was not sufficiently developed these nuclei could not yet form a distinct capitalist structure. The conquest of India by the British retarded the formation of this social structure.

It should be observed that the author's evaluation of the social and economic processes which took place in India during the first half of the 19th century is still under discussion and has been subject to criticism.[1] For example L. B. Alaev and L. I. Reisner, who on the whole agree with the author's thesis about the decline of the Indian handicrafts during the first half of the 19th century, declare at the same time that "the profound economic processes which were going on during that period should not be overlooked". That "the weavers turnout to the production of coarse cloth" in such centres as Dacca, "signified the reorientation of the petty commodity producer towards the home market—that is in the main the peasant consumer—and the growth of this market" are ranked by L. B. Alaev and L.I. Reisner among such processes, as is "the widespread practice of advancing yarn to the weavers".[2]

Such an interpretation of these developments cannot be accepted. The fact that a small section of weavers continued to work in Dacca by switching over to the manufacture of coarse cloth can hardly be considered a progressive phenomenon. The advancing of yarn to weavers does by itself indeed represent a new stage in the development of the handicrafts. But when under colonial conditions the weavers began to use imported British yarn it meant, in the final analysis, that the likelihood of Indian handicraft developing along capitalist lines had diminished.

1 See L. B. Alaev's and L. I. Reisner's review of V. I. Pavlov's book *Formirovanie indiiskoi burzhuazii*, (Moscow, 1958), published in *Problemy vostokovedeniya* (No. 2, 1959), 186–89.

2 *Ibid.*, 188.

As regards "the growth of the peasant market" during the first half of the 19th century, one must say that in view of the savage tax robbery and the extraction of not only the surplus-product, i.e. the potentially marketable output, from the peasant but also part of the necessary product—the proposition is, at least, doubtful and requires supporting data, which the reviewers fail to adduce. Moreover, the processes that took place in the sphere of agricultural production were precisely those which determined the general level of social and economic development of India. The reviewers commit the same error which is noticeable in Alaev's definition of the level of development in India during the 17th and 18th centuries, namely a reluctance to analyse the social and economic phenomena in their entirety.

In our view both the genesis of capitalism (that is the rise of the capitalist system) and its development (that is its transformation into the dominant system) took place in India during the latter half of the 19th century. These two processes, which usually follow each other, took place simultaneously. The reason for this unusual development was the dominant position of the British capital and its political overlordship. State finances, railways, banks, the foreign trade monopoly, overseas shipping, etc. were under the foreign grip from the very beginning.

At the same time in the field of agriculture developments characteristic of feudalism were taking place, such as the strengthening of feudal land property held by individuals, the beginning of expropriation of peasant households and the widespread development of commodity-money relations, etc. Petty commodity production which came into being in the Indian countryside was fettered by the domination of the feudal or landlord system and the supreme ownership of land being vested in the hands of the British.

Such a contradictory and unusual combination of processes belonging as a rule to different historical epochs tends to confuse research workers whose approach to the evaluation of the social and economic development of India at the close of the 19th century is one-sided. Indeed, if one confined one's observations to the village, one might arrive at the conclusion that during this period India was passing through the stage of late feudalism, since either feudal relations or feudal vestiges predominated in agriculture, which was in terms of volume the principal sphere of production. But the point is, that this late feudal foundation was surmounted and dominated by a colonial and capitalist structure, whose political and economic hold was extraordinarily strong although its own material and organizational base was relatively small. Finally, it is of great importance that, while the Indian economy was forcibly included in the system of world capitalist economy that was taking shape, the colonial capitalist system developed in close association with British capitalism and was powerfully supported by it.

Thus, India, as it were, in fact skipped the stage of late feudalism. The import of British capital, which began in the middle of the 19th century, played a decisive role in this leap. Under the conditions of social advance caused by the uprising of 1857-59, and the formation of a capitalist world economy, the capital import led to the comparatively rapid development of a colonial capitalist structure which dominated the economy of the country.

At the same time—i.e. during the latter half of the 19th century—a national capitalist structure also came into being in India. It was separated from the colonial capitalist structure by material and organisational barriers and by various important conditions and laws governing its own development—although this did not of course annul the action of the general laws of capitalism. The protracted co-existence of large-scale modern industry and petty production was a distinctive feature of the pattern of industrial branches which this structure comprised. As we have already seen, the development of Indian capitalism began with the building of modern cotton mills. This is quite natural, since the capitalist development of India began at a time when European, and above all British, capitalism—which forcibly included India first in the capitalist world market and then in the world system of capitalist economy—had already reached a high technical and organisational level. India could compete only on the basis of a correspondingly high initial technical and organisational level, and consequently a corresponding degree of concentration and centralisation of production and capital.

At the same time Indian capital developed also extensively, placing under its command manual production. Certain circumstances have already been pointed out which made possible the prolonged co-existence of large-scale and petty production in colonial India, such as the particular character of consumer demand, and the changeover to machine-made raw material and semi-finished products. But a still larger reserve fund of the handicrafts was the wretchedly low standard of life of the worker and the weakness of the large-scale industry.

One of the specific features of the Indian home market was that the price of the British commodities was a factor determining the prices of industrial goods. Whereas the market price of British commodities—even if it was an excessively high, monopoly price—was, as a rule below the production costs of Indian handicraft products, since they were manufactured under completely different conditions of production. The market prices of Indian handicraft wares, formed in competition with British imports, were therefore as a rule considerably below production costs. Not only did the market price fail to include the value of the surplus-product but also part of the necessary product. Taking into account the large profit of the buyer-up, which he realised by means of market price, we have to conclude that apart from rare exceptions, the craftsman recovered only a part of his necessary product when he sold his wares. Thus the extraordinary low standard of life of the craftsman was under colonial conditions, in a way, a pre-requisite of the very existence of the petty mode of production.

British industry had however two weak points: considerable overhead expenses incurred while its products were transported to and sold in India, and the comparatively high wages of the British workers. Had it been possible to produce the commodities in India under similar technical and economic conditions as those prevailing in Great Britain, their prices would, obviously have been so low that they would have definitely throttled the Indian handicrafts. But the colonial policy of retarding Indian industrial progress led to excessively high changes for machinery, for many industrial raw materials and for technical services which entered into the production costs of machine-made commodities produced in India.

The decisive factor was the absence of a national heavy industry. Modern industry had . . . itself to take in hand the machine, its characteristic instrument of production, and to construct machines by machines. It was not till it did this, that it built up for itself a fitting technical foundation, and stood on its own feet.[3] But large-scale production in India did not have its own technical foundation, which, on the one hand, made it dependent on British capital and, on the other, condemned it willy-nilly to co-existence with the petty mode of production. The absence of its own heavy industry was an important economic reason for the slowness, the semi-feudal nature and the very incompleteness of the process of primitive accumulation in colonial India.

On the basis of the general laws governing the development of capitalist enterprise, which the founders of Marxism-Leninism have investigated and clearly defined on the concrete example of European capitalism, we will endeavour—taking these preliminary remarks as a starting point—to reveal the specific forms in which the action of the general laws has manifested itself under the historical conditions obtaining in colonial India.

Let us first of all recall Marx's well-known passage describing the two ways in which the bourgeois manufacturer can arise:

> The transition from the feudal mode of production is two-fold. The producer becomes merchant and capitalist, in contrast to the natural agricultural economy and the guild-bound handicrafts of the me-

3 Karl Marx, *Capital*, (Moscow, 1956), , 384.

dieval urban industries. This is the really revolutionizing path. Or else, the merchant establishes direct sway over production. However much this serves historically as a stepping-stone—witness the English 17th century clothier, who brings the weavers, independent as they are, under his control by selling their wool to them and buying their cloth—it does not by itself lead to the overthrow of the old mode of production, but tends rather to preserve and retain it as its precondition.[4]

The data at our disposal show that a colonial variant of the second path leading to the emergence of capitalists definitely predominated in India's manufacture. The genesis of industrial capitalism along the first, the revolutionary, path was made difficult in colonial India, in the first place, by the ruin on a mass scale of the urban producer, the craftsman, at the close of the 18th century and the first half of the 19th century, which was brought about by colonial plunder, the general disorganisation of the country's economy, the destruction of the feudal home and foreign markets existing up to then, and by the competition of the British factory; an additional difficulty from the middle of the nineteenth century onwards, was the growing dependence of Indian handicrafts on the trading and moneylending capital of the buyers-up, who functioned as agents of British large-scale industry and also of the Indian factory. Widespread accumulation of capital in the hands of individual commodity producers—which, as Marx wrote, forms "the necessary preliminary of the specifically capitalist mode of production"[5]—could not take place in the Indian handicrafts under prevailing conditions. Such accumulation is the pre-condition of the direct transition from handicraft production to the capitalist mode of production. Those artisans who were, nevertheless, able to set up manufactories became dependent on the buyers-up. This, as Marx pointed out, is merely a modification of the second, the conservative path leading to the capitalist mode of production: the owners of the workshops "are really only middlemen between the merchant and their own labourers. The merchant is the actual capitalist who pockets the lion's share of the surplus-value".[6]

In describing the concrete situation that had taken shape in the small industries, one has to keep in mind that the capitalist workshop in the principal branches of the handicrafts arose and developed as an external department of the factory, and moreover not so much of the Indian factory as of the foreign factory. The merchant and buyer-up had therefore, to share the surplus-value extracted from the small

4 Karl Marx, *Kapital*, (Berlin, 1959), III, 336-37.
5 Marx, n. 3, 624.
6 Marx, n. 4, 330.

manufacturer with the British and Indian factory owners.

Because of the distorting influence of colonialism Indian manufacture was according to both its origin and its economic position essentially colonial. Foreign and native merchant's and moneylender's capital existing parasitically on Indian manufacture upset the process of reproduction on an expanded scale and, in the majority of cases, prevented it altogether, in particular impeding technical reconstruction. This process is, however necessary for the transition of small-scale industry to the higher, large-scale stage of capitalist production.

> The transition to large-scale industry depends on the technical development of these small owner-operated establishments—wherever they employ machinery that admits of a handicraft-like operation. The machine is driven by steam, instead of by hand. This is of late the case, for instance, in the English hosiery industry.[7]

This technical development of manufacture towards large-scale industry did hardly ever occur in colonial India.

To understand the specific conditions under which the big industrial capitalist arose in India, we shall compare this process with the genesis of the big industrial capitalist in Great Britain and Russia. Marx notes in *Capital* that the manufacturers of Manchester rose from among the petty masters of weaving manufactories, who in turn had been small artisans that made their way in the world. Marx wrote in *Capital*:

> Dr. Aikin says in a work published in 1795: "The trade of Manchester may be divided into four periods. First, when manufacturers were obliged to work hard for their livelihood... The second period, when they had begun to acquire little fortunes, but worked as hard as before... The third, when luxury began, and the trade was pushed by sending out riders for orders into every market town in the kingdom. . ." "The fourth period", the last 30 years of the 18th century, "is that in which expense and luxury have made great progress and was supported by a trade extended by means of riders and factors through every part of Europe".[8]

Lenin, who analysed the emergence of the big industrial bourgeoisie in Russia, wrote:

> Perhaps one of the most striking manifestations of the intimate and direct connection between the consecutive forms of industry is the fact that many of the big and even the biggest factory owners were at one time the smallest of small industrialists and passed through

7 *Ibid.*

8 Dr. Aikin, *Description of the Country from 30 to 40 miles round Manchester*, London, 1795, p. 182, sq, See Marx, *Capital*, I (1961), pp. 594-95.

all the stages from popular production to capitalism.[9]

Savva Morozov and many other big mill-owners (the Kuvayevs, Fokins, Zubkovs, Kokushkins, Bobrovs and so on) were formerly small craftsmen or even manufactory workers. An intermediate stage on the way from small commodity producer to factory owner was the possession of a work-distributing office (scattered manufacture) or a centralised workshop.[10]

Thus the genesis of the big industrial capitalist in Russia and Great Britain proceeded along the classical (but by no means the only) path which consisted of three stages: the small commodity producer; the owner of a manufactory (or of small establishment run on capitalist lines); and the millowner. This was "perhaps one of the most striking manifestations of the intimate and direct connection between the consecutive forms of industry" in the independent European countries.

The conditions in which Indian large-scale industry came into being were essentially different from those prevailing in Russia and Great Britain. The decisive difference was India's colonial position, which led first to the decline of the urban handicrafts and then to the complete dependence of the craftsmen and owners of the manufactories that sprang up on big merchant's and moneylender's capital. Economically and, especially, technically Indian large-scale industry was set up on the basis of machinery imported from the metropolitan country. As a result, the leading branches of large-scale industry developed not in the course of "a normal evolutionary process" leading from capitalist manufacture to the factory, but were, with few exceptions, built in "a vacuum".[11] It should be noted, moreover, that two radically different methods of building industrial enterprises were applied in India; on the one hand imported British capital was used or profits from already existing capital investments were reinvested, on the other hand capital accumulated by the local propertied classes was invested in industry.

The assertion that industrial enterprises were built in a 'vacuum' by no means denies the importance of the economic processes which took place within India and without which the factory could not have possibly come into existence. It is obvious that the machinery imported would not have become productive capital, unless the import of means of production was accompanied by the formation of a labour market, an internal consumer market, the concentration of money-capital in

9 V. I. Lenin, *The Development of Capitalism in Russia, Collected Works*, Vol. 3, p. 541.

10 *Ibid*.

11 The fact that the system of colonial oppression upset the "normal evolutionary process" of the domestic industry by way of manufacture to the factory has been noted by I. M. Reisner in his book *Ocherki klassovoi barby v Indii*, 55, as early as 1932.

the hands of the propertied classes, and other processes necessary for the rise of the capitalist mode of production. This proposition only means that the factory in India did not arise as a result of reproduction on an expanding scale in manufacture. In addition, the Indian factory, and even earlier the British factory, which competed with the manufactory upset the process of reproduction within the latter.

Owing to the combination of these circumstances in colonial India the direct connection between the consecutive forms of industry was interrupted, and occurred only by way of exception. Because of the break in the normal evolution of capitalism in the Indian industry, the development of the big industrial capitalist from the ranks of the small industrialists did not take place in accordance with the three stages of the classical process. In consequence of the interruption of "the normal evolutionary process" the majority of the big Indian industrial capitalists emerged almost entirely direct from among the representatives of big trading and moneylending capital, which had certain opportunities of expanding its operations in the conditions of the colonial dominion. The genesis of the big industrial capitalist in India consisted mostly of the stages: merchant—or moneylender—and factory owner.

That the genesis of the big industrial capitalists, in the main, followed along different paths in India and in Europe by no means signified that the general laws governing the rise of the industrial bourgeoisie—the direct connection of the stages of development of the industrial capitalists with the consecutively evolving forms of capitalist industry—did not operate. It was precisely the action of these general laws in the specific conditions of colonial India which led to a development that differed from the classical path taken by the rising capitalists in Europe.

Incidentally the emergence of the industrial bourgeoisie from among the representatives of merchant's capital did also rather frequently occur in Europe. We have already quoted Marx's proposition on the second path of development of the manufacturer in Western Europe where "the merchant establishes direct sway over production". This path was widespread in Russia, where "the combination of merchant's capital with industrial capital"[12] often took place already at the stage of manufacture, for "*the closest and most inseparable tie between merchant's and industrial capital* is one of the most characteristic features of manufacture. The buyer-up nearly always merges here with the manufactory owner".[13] Thus, the second way of development of the big industrial capitalist in Europe consisted of three stages: merchant, manufactory owner (buyer-up), and factory owner. A similar evolution

12 Lenin, n. 9, 441.
13 *Ibid.*, 440.

also took place in colonial India, although not so frequently. Two such cases are known among the bourgeoisie of Ahmedabad.

The enormous, almost insurmountable, difficulties encountered by the process of reproduction on an enlarged scale in Indian manufacture tended to keep the capital of the buyer-up at the lower stages of development through which merchant's capital passes in the small industries. The capital of the buyer-up remained for a long time parasitic on handicraft small-commodity production and manufacture without tying itself down by making industrial investments thereby in its turn exerting a retarding influence on expanded reproduction in manufacture and the transition from the manufactory to the factory. The accumulations made in the small industries could, of course, have been directly invested in the building of modern industrial enterprises. But the small industries were apparently, during the period under review, so lucrative that both the capital sunk in them and the resulting new accumulations were retained in this sphere. There is in any case no evidence indicating that the buyers-up transferred their capital, to any large extent, to modern large-scale industry.

However, as we have shown earlier, the merchant can, under certain condition, directly turn into a big industrial capitalist. The process of development of the big industrial capitalist, in this case, consists of only two stages: the merchant or moneylender, and the factory owner. This is the principal way of development in colonial India; a similar genesis of big industrial capitalists can also be observed in Western Europe and in Russia, for instance, the Guchkovs. Marx writes:

> Doubtless many small guild-masters and yet more independent small artisans, or even wage-labourers, transformed themselves into small capitalists, and (by gradually extending exploitation of wage-labour and corresponding accumulation) into full-blown capitalists . . . The snail's pace of this method corresponded in no wise with the commercial requirements of the new world-market that the great discoveries of the end of the 15th century created.[14]

The transformation of money-capital—formed by means of commerce and usury, and greatly increased by the blood and dirt of the colonial plunder—into industrial capital speeded up the industrial revolution first in Great Britain, and then in the other advanced countries of Europe.

It is difficult to say to what extent the transfer of capital from commerce and moneylending to industry in Europe was personified in the process of the merchant turning into a mill-owner. In all probability such a transformation took place fairly frequently. Marx mentions that the small cloth makers of Leeds petitioned for a law to

14 Marx, n. 3, 750.

forbid any merchant from becoming a manufacturer.[15] The history of the Artamonovs, a dynasty of manufacturers who arose from among the merchants, has been told by Maxim Gorky in his well-known novel *The Artamonovs*.

But it is clear, that just as trading and moneylending capital in colonial India differed from European merchant's capital so the circumstances and conditions of its transfer to industry were also different from those prevailing in Europe.

Finally, some landowners in Europe who invested their accumulations in industry became big industrial capitalists (for instance, the Putilovs in Russia). In recent times, many industrial capitalists arose in this way in India, especially in Bengal and the Deccan.

* * * *

The mutual relations between the big Indian bourgeoisie and imperialism differed from the attitude of the petty industrial bourgeoisie towards imperialism. The small industrialists had great difficulty in standing up to the competition of British imports, British capital made them pay a heavy tribute for the semi-finished products they required, and finally, the full weight of colonial arbitrary rule was directly experienced by them. The small industrialists were, therefore, opposed to British imperialism.

Far more complicated and contradictory were the mutual relations of the big bourgeoisie and imperialism. Up to the First World War the big capitalists who had become factory owners not only continued to act as agents of the British and as moneylenders, but frequently even expanded their operations in these fields. Since the foreign trade turnover of colonial India increased up to the beginning of the general crisis of capitalism, i.e. up to the First World War, objective conditions existed for the expansion of the operations in which they collaborated with the British, which tended to soften the antagonism between the big bourgeoisie and imperialism.

One should, however, keep in mind that it was precisely by means of the transactions in which the big bourgeoisie acted as agents of the British (especially in Bombay) that they accumulated the capital necessary for building the national industry; a fact that was fraught with serious contradictions. In its most general form the essence of these contradictions was that the capital accumulated by collaborating with foreign capital was invested in a section of national economy, the development of which brought it inevitably into collision with the imperialist tendencies of the foreign capitalists. It is true that during the latter half of the 19th century and the early 20th century the

15 *Ibid.*, 751.

contradiction between the source of these accumulations and the sphere towards which capital investments were directed was merely beginning to arise. Its most acute forms developed only during and following the world crisis of 1929-33, when the absolute volume of the transactions in which Indian capitalists collaborated with foreign capital declined and big industry became the principal sphere of expanded reproduction of the national capital. But one must take into account that during the period under review profits derived from large-scale industry, for the most part light industry, already constituted a steadily growing proportion of the total income of the Indian bourgeoisie.

A direct contradiction also became apparent between the transactions in which the Bombay bourgeoisie collaborated with the British and its own industrial activities. The bourgeoisie of Bombay often acted as intermediary in the sale of precisely those types of foreign commodities which it manufactured in its own enterprises (in the main textile), or it participated in the export of Indian raw material (cotton), which was used in the capitalist countries to produce commodities (cotton fabrics) that subsequently competed with the products of the Bombay industry on the markets of India. This contradiction became more acute during the second half of the 19th century as a result of the simultaneous growth of both the local output of cotton goods and the import of these commodities from Great Britain. For example, in the 1890s when the cotton industry was being set up in Bombay, the import of fabrics via Bombay almost quadrupled as compared with the 1850s. The local mills were forced to increase the sale of their goods, principally yarn, in the overseas markets while hundreds of millions of yards of Lancashire cottons were imported through Bombay. At the close of the 19th century the export of yarn made in Bombay caught up with, and at the beginning of the 20th century surpassed, the import of British cloth (in terms of value).[16]

Up to the close of the 19th century the contradictions between the local bourgeoisie and imperialism were mitigated by the fact that the national industry of Bombay maintained only limited relations to the home market, for the factory owners of Bombay were able to sell their goods on the Asian markets, especially those of China. But in the beginning of the 20th century Japanese fabrics and yarn ousted the products of the Bombay industry from the Far Eastern markets. Consequently, the industry of Bombay had no alternative but to endeavour to gain a foothold on the home market. The inevitable re-orientation of large-scale national industry towards the home market was one of the main reasons for the support the Swadeshi movement

16 *Gazetteer of Bombay City and Island*, I, 421.

received from the big bourgeoisie. Thus an intensification of the struggle for the national market waged by both the large-scale and small national industry against British industry marked the beginning of the imperialist epoch. The growing turnover of agricultural commodities within the country—in which not only the merchants were interested, but also the peasants—reduced the direct dependence of the Indian merchants on British capital.

The big bourgeoisie was associated with imperialism not only through the commercial operations in which it collaborated with the foreigners, but also by its active participation in the exploitation of the peasants by methods characteristic of feudal landlords and moneylenders. The conditions created by imperialism allowed merchant's capital over a long period of time to lead a parasitic existence in the sphere of developing small commodity production, thereby reducing the desire of the trading and moneylending strata to invest their accumulated resources in industry. But it would be wrong to assume that the possession of landed property did not lead to conflicts with the colonial regime. The heavy land tax deprived the landowners of a considerable part of the rent. A. I. Levkovsky quotes in his works data relating to the fight for a reduction in the land tax carried on during the Swadeshi movement by landlords who had risen from among the moneylenders by acquiring landed property. They even went as far as to refuse to comply with the decisions of the court. In 1905, for instance, two wealthy Parsis who stubbornly refused to pay their taxes were arrested in the Surat district.[17]

Finally there was a third economic factor that determined the mutual relations of the big bourgeoisie and the colonialists, namely the industrial interests of the former. The transformation of the merchants who collaborated with the British into factory owners led to contradictions between them and imperialism. These contradictions arose because British finance capital extracted from the Indian factory owners the super-profits created by severe exploitation of the proletariat. The colonial administration took a part of these profits by means of excise duties, taxation, railway charges and customs levied upon imported machinery, semi-finished products and raw materials. Another part of the profits was appropriated directly by British capital, which forced the Indian factory owners to pay high monopoly prices for industrial machinery, technical services, auxiliary materials (coal, petrol and lubricants), semi-finished products (yarn, metals, dyes), and raw materials (for instance, Egyptian long-staple cotton). It was to a considerable extent due to the extraction of profit in this way that representatives of British capital (agents of engineering firms, technical consultants and even foremen) were able, with the support of their banks, to build numerous factories in Bombay and elsewhere.

17 *See Natsional 'no-osvoboditel' noe dvizhenie Indii i deyatel 'nost' B.G. Tilaka,* 301-02.

One can get an idea of the heavy tribute the national industry was forced to pay because of its technical backwardness to British capital from so authoritative a witness as Sir Charles Wood, the Secretary of State for India, who declared in the House of Commons that in the sixties the prices of machinery were three times higher in India than in Britain, and of coal six times higher.[18] During the latter half of the 19th century it cost Rs 700-800 thousand to equip a cotton mill in Bombay with machinery.[19] A calculation shows that the machinery of one cotton mill enabled British engineering firms to extract an excess payment of up to half a million rupees from the Indian bourgeoisie, or approximately half the share capital (on the average, the share capital of a Bombay mill amounted to one million rupees).

One of the principal factors which caused the political subordination of the big Indian bourgeoisie to British imperialism was its dependence on the import of capital, i.e. machinery for its factories. Lenin stresses that "The colonies possess no capital, or practically none, of *their own* and while finance capital predominates cannot obtain any capital other than under conditions of political subordination".[20]

Because a considerable part of the surplus-value created by the proletariat in Indian-owned enterprises was appropriated by foreign capital, capital invested in the national industry had to extract additional surplus-value if it was to receive the average profit. In other words, since the national industry had to pay a heavy tribute to the British monopolies, Indian industrial capital could not operate unless it steeply raised the rate of exploitation of the working class. British capital, therefore, exploited the proletariat of India not only in its own enterprises, but also in the enterprises belonging to the national bourgeoisie. The working class of India was, in this way subjected to a two-fold capitalist oppression.

Colonialism, which did not allow India to create her own engineering industry and her own qualified engineers, forced the Indians to be contented with equipment discarded in Europe. We do not refer to agriculture, where the techniques were kept altogether at a medieval level. The production of relative surplus-value was extremely difficult under such conditions. The principal method used to increase surplus-value was, as we have seen, the lengthening of the working day, that is the production of absolute surplus-value. The extremely savage methods of exploitation were aggravated by the fact that the Indian worker was forced to sell his labour-power at a price that was considerably lower than the value of the physical minimum of the

18 *Hansard's Parliamentary Debates. Third Series*, Vol. 160, p. 495.

19 *Bombay Industries...* , 47.

20 V.I. Lenin, *Questions of National Policy and Proletarian Internationalism*, (Moscow, 1960), 173.

means of subsistence he needed. The severe worsening in the position of the working class of India which was caused by colonialism was the objective economic reason for the uncompromising struggle waged by the Indian proletariat against imperialism.

Two ways to increase industrial profits were open to the national bourgeoisie; it could either cut its expenditure on the purchase of labour power (which meant a further attack upon the living standard of the working class), or reduce the portion of the profit which imperialism extracted from the national industry. Whenever, therefore, imperialism started an attack against the profits of the national bourgeoisie, the latter almost immediately increased its pressure on the working class, and, on the contrary, the growing resistance of the working class forced the national bourgeoisie to defend its economic interests in a more resolute way against the onslaught of British capital and the colonial authorities. Therefore, even the purely economic struggle of the Indian proletariat in the national enterprises had objectively an anti-imperialist character, for it placed certain obstacles in the path of imperialist attacks on the national industry and intensified the contradictions between the Indian bourgeoisie and British imperialism.

British capital could extract the colonial profit only by taking advantage of the political, economic and technical dependence of India. To increase this dependence the colonial authorities hampered the development of the engineering, metallurgical and chemical industries, the construction of electric power stations and the progress of technical education.

One of the principal means used by the colonialists to slow down the industrial development of India was the intentional neglect of the national banking and credit system. The first Indian modern capitalist credit institutions appeared only in the beginning of the 20th century. We will merely mention the Bank of Baroda set up in 1908, the Central Bank of India in 1911, and the Bank of India in 1906. By 1913 there were altogether 18 big Indian banks; each with a capital of over Rs 500 thousand, the total capital and reserves of these banks amounted to Rs 5 million and deposits to Rs 15.1 million.[21] But these first national banks were far smaller than the British banks and their operations were restricted to the financing of trade. There were still no banking institutions to whom the Indian industrial enterprises could turn when they needed lont-term loans.

The policy of retarding industrial development gave rise to contradictions between the big bourgeoisie and imperialism, and at the same time made the Indian factory owners dependent on British

21 L. C. Jain, *Indigenous Banking in India* 153.

capital. The Indian capitalists were compelled to leave the administration even of enterprises the share capital of which belonged mainly to Indians (for instance in the jute industry) in the hands of British managing agents. The colonial conditions were, thus, compelling the various strata of the Indian middle class, not only commercial agents or landowners but also industrial capitalists to collaborate with British capital. It is obvious that in this so-called collaboration the Indians had to play the role of the dependent, junior partner. This collaboration did not remove the contradictions between British capital and the big Indian bourgeoisie, but merely aggravated the conditions that were most unfavourable to the Indian partner.

The deep-seated contradiction in the attitude of the big Indian bourgeoisie can only be grasped in the light of Lenin's proposition about the two historical tendencies in the national question found in developing capitalism: on the one hand, the awakening of national life and, therefore, the economic consolidation of the nation, and, on the contrary, the development and intensification of all kinds of intercourse between nations, and in particular, the creation of the international unity of capital in the economic life in general.[22]

At the close of the 19th century, on the eve of the imperialist epoch, when the evolving Indian bourgeoisie was making a stand for its own market, the colonial apparatus of British finance capital introduced restrictive measures against national enterprises, namely, the imposition of the excise duty on factory-made products and Curzon's finance reform. This action of colonialism which was manifestly against the national industry, accelerated the organisational and ideological development of the Indian national movement.

Almost from the very inception of Indian bourgeois nationalism two tendencies could be discerned. One was represented by the big bourgeoisie and the landlords associated with it; the other by the petty bourgeoisie together with the intelligentsia and the top strata of the village who sided with it. The Indian National Congress, which was founded in 1885 with a moderate leadership, expressed the interests of the rising big bourgeoisie and the landlords.

At the close of the 19th century and the beginning of the 20th a group of petty bourgeois patriots and revolutionaries took shape in the National Congress, the so-called 'Extremists' headed by Bal Gangadhar Tilak. In the early 20th century the group exerted a considerable influence in Bengal, Maharashtra and the Punjab, that is among those nationalities where the process of national consolidation had reached the furthest development at the time.

22 See Lenin, n. 20, 32.

The restricting measures of the colonialists were in the first place directed against Indian modern industry. But although contradictions continued to exist, the economic interests which the big Indian bourgeoisie had in common with the imperialists—through collaborating with them in commerce, in the exploitation of landed property and even in industry itself—and the fear of the rising struggle for liberation waged by the working class and peasantry, were bound to weaken its opposition to the colonial regime. This was the reason for the timorous behaviour of the big bourgeoisie and its readiness to compromise with and capitulate to imperialism.

Only with great difficulties could the petty bourgeoisie withstand the competition of British imports in its own market even without the introduction of the special restrictive measures. Moreover, unlike the big bourgeoisie—which was accumulating capital by means of commerce, in which it collaborated with the British and the semi-feudal exploitation of the peasants—the petty bourgeoisie was not tied to the British by common interests. On the contrary this type of commerce and landownership fettered its economic development in the town and countryside. The petty bourgeoisie was, therefore, from the outset intensely hostile to imperialism. Indeed in its fight against colonialism it expressed bourgeois democratic tendencies with the greatest force. But feudal, patriarchal and, particularly religious survivals were far more conspicuous in its tactics, and specially in its ideology, than in the tactics and ideology of the big bourgeoisie, whose development was strongly influenced by European liberalism.

Another feature which distinguished the nationalism of the rising bourgeoisie from petty bourgeois nationalism was that the latter assumed a specifically local (i.e. Maratha or Bengali) colouring from the very beginning. The struggle of the petty bourgeoisie for its own market was to a great extent a fight for the market of one particular nationality. The ideology of the big bourgeoisie, on the contrary, tended to ignore the special interests of the various Indian nationalities, for the big bourgeoisie—and especially its leading sections, the Gujaratis and Marwaris—could exploit the whole of India by means of their trading and moneylending operations and capital investments

At the close of the 19th century a competitive struggle began between the various national groups of the big bourgeoisie, primarily waged by the Gujarati and Marwari bourgeoisie, on the one hand, and the weaker bourgeoisie of the other nationalities and communities, on the other hand.

The Swadeshi movement, in particular—which was a manifestation of the fight of the Indian bourgeoisie for its own market and against British competition—was used chiefly by the big Gujarati bourgeoisie to strengthen its position in India, after having lost the Chinese market.

Its organ the *Indian Textile Journal* wrote in 1935 that, during the stormy days of the partition of Bengal, Bengali political leaders and journalists frequently blamed the Bombay factory owners for extracting fabulous dividends from the Swadeshi movement, which was just then coming into being.

The transformation process of the main strata of the Indian bourgeoisie into the national bourgeoisie was not yet completed when the First World War began. The term national bourgeoisie as we use it denotes the big and small industrial capitalists and also the representatives of merchant's capital concerned with the commodity exchange within the country, that is, the sections whose basic economic interests demand the independent development of the country along capitalist lines. Before the onset of the general crisis of capitalism it was usual for the factory owners to combine their industrial activities with commercial activities in which they collaborated with the British, and for the merchants to combine their independent commercial operations with transactions in which they acted as intermediaries of the British; this impeded the sharp opposition of their economic interests to the oppressive policy of the imperialists.

Only after the First World War, when the volume of the trade in which they acted as middlemen began slowly but steadily to shrink, both in absolute terms and relative to the total turnover of goods, did independent industrial enterprise become the only major, profitable sphere for new investments. It was precisely these developments which in the period between the two World Wars led to a certain disintegration of the strata of the bourgeoisie that collaborated with the British, and accelaerated the formation process of a national bourgeoisie comprising the various sections and strata of the middle class on the basis of their common anti-imperialist interests.

We have merely attempted to give a general outline of the economic pre-conditions on which the political attitude of the principal sections of the Indian bourgeoisie was based at the close of the 19th century and the beginning of the 20th. India's complicated political and economic situation introduced a number of important modifications into this attitude. The landlords who participated in the National Congress influenced the programme of the big bourgeoisie. This influence increased the inconsistency of the big bourgeoisie in its relations to colonialism and the feudal survivals. The political platform of the small industrialists and traders took shape under the direct influence of the petty bourgeoisie, i.e. the peasants and the intelligentsia.

Religious and communal prejudices and caste relations played a considerable part in the political life of the Indian bourgeoisie. It is well known that the British imperialists made use of the religious and communal prejudices to sow the seeds of discord among Indians belonging to different religious communities. Hardly any research has been carried out up to now to determine what influence the caste organisation exerted on the political attitude of wide sections of the petty bourgeoisie. The top strata of merchants and moneylenders utilised the caste solidarity and the idea that the interests of all members of the caste were identical to establish their control over the less wealthy members of their caste. It is no mere chance that the poorer strata of the castes of traders and moneylenders were politically the most inert section of the petty bourgeoisie, and remained for a long time isolated from the national liberation movement, the active participants of which regarded them with hostility if not hatred.

But the developing Indian capitalism gave rise not only to the bourgeoisie with its nationalistic ideology; the most important result of the capitalist development of the country was the creation of the industrial proletariat of India. At the close of the 19th century and during the early 20th century the forces of the Indian working class were growing in numbers. The workers at that time were still under the influence of the ideas of reformist trade union leaders and petty bourgeois revolutionaries. But it was precisely this growth of the Indian proletariat and its first actions in 1906-07 which prepared the ground for the union of the Indian working class movement and Marxism-Leninism which was to take place under the influence of the Great October Revolution.

The nature of the contradictions between imperialism and the big bourgeoisie differed fundamentally from the contradictions existing between imperialism and the Indian proletariat. The big bourgeoisie came into conflict with imperialism because of its struggle to expand the sphere of its capital investments and its fight for increased profits. For the proletariat the further advance of British capitalism endangered its reproduction as a class and constituted a threat to its very existence. Imperialist oppression and exploitation also imperilled the existence of the petty bourgeoisie. The anti-imperialist interests which the petty bourgeoisie had in common with the proletariat were conducive to the infiltration of petty bourgeois ideas into proletarian circles. Only a later period created the necessary conditions for the union of the working class movement and the theory of scientific socialism.

EPILOGUE

The principal events of modern Indian history represent stages in the development of either the inevitably increasing contradictions between imperialism and the people of India as a whole, including the bourgeoisie, or the growing class contradictions within the semi-feudal colonial society. Although at times these two processes came into conflict with one another, they had a common basis: the development of capitalist relations in the country.

The capitalist development of India in recent times has in fact led, on the one hand, to a rapid sharpening of the antagonism between the Indian bourgeoisie and imperialism, and on the other, to the ideological separation of the proletariat from the bourgeoisie and to a clash of their class interests. In other words, the dual character of the Indian bourgeoisie, which was earlier to a certain degree an economic potentiality, became a political reality. At the same time the transformation of the bourgeoisie into the national bourgeoisie was in the main completed.

The extremely limited progressive elements which were connected with the transplantation of capitalist relations into India, which occurred as a result of capital export were on the eve of the First World War completely exhausted. While investing a minimum of productive capital the British monopolies stepped up as far as possible the extraction of the colonial tribute. Their parasitic activity no longer merely retarded the development of the productive forces in India, but led to the direct curtailment of production in a number of important economic branches and, above all in agriculture. The increasing parasitism and decay of British finance capital did not result, however in the complete stagnation of the Indian economy. Colonalism hampered and retarded the development of capitalism in India, but could not stop it entirely.

During the First World War the British industry was fully occupied with war orders, and the British marine with military transport. The volume of British, and also other European, commodities reaching the Indian market was therefore greatly reduced. It seemed that the circumstances were favourable to the development of the Indian industry. But the war did not only reduce the import of consumer goods;

it deprived the Indian industry of foreign machinery at the same time. The Indian entrepreneurs could, therefore, expand their output only by using more labour-power, that is by a further intensification of labour and the employment of fresh sections of the proletariat. But they did not find it easy to do this either; for there was, in particular, a lack of semi-finished products and auxiliary materials. On the whole the First World War led to increased accumulation of money, but retarded its transformation into productive capital. The discrepancy between the accumulation of money capital and its productive utilisation grew during the war and as a result of the war. It was, in our opinion, the principal economic reason for the sharpening contradictions between the Indian bourgeoisie and imperialism in the postwar years.

The beginning of the crisis of the system of colonial exploitation and oppression in India was a manifestation of the general crisis of capitalism, which developed during the First World War and deepened after the October Revolution. National liberation was no longer a historical perspective but had become a concrete political objective of the Indian people. This objective could only be achieved by an anti-imperialist mass struggle. The historical problem that faced India was, which class—the proletariat or the national bourgeoisie—was to be at the head of the national liberation struggle. The methods and the development of the struggle depended on the answer to this question. More important still, the transition to the next stages of the national progress also depended on this answer.

The national bourgeoisie succeeded in gaining and maintaining the hegemony in the national liberation movement. As early as 1919-22, when the mass resistance to imperialism was rising, the Indian bourgeoisie devised such ideological and tactical principles for the struggle which would enable it to control the mass movement and determine its direction and scope in accordance with its own interests. Gandhi's policy was based on these principles. The national bourgeoisie advanced Gandhism not merely because of the necessity to gain the leadership of the national movement, but also as a result of the serious differences that existed between the bourgeoisie and colonialism.

The sharpening contradictions between the big bourgeoisie and imperialism after the First World War helped to unite the Indian national and petty bourgeoisie on the basis of a general anti-imperialist programme. This unification did not, of course, prevent the occurrence of various trends within the framework of the united bourgeois national movement, but these trends were neither ideologically nor organisationally separated from the Indian National Congress, as were the "Extremists" headed by Tilak in 1908. The section represented by Gandhi was able, despite frequently arising friction, to maintain the leadership of the revolutionary petty bourgeois trend in the Congress.

After the revolutionary wave of the early twenties receded, a period began during which a temporary stabilisation of imperialism took place accompanied by a certain adjustment of its relations with the Indian bourgeoisie. Although the British monopolies retained all the key positions in the economy of the country, they were, all the same, compelled to retreat a little. The import of British consumer goods, especially cloth remained far below the prewar level; this enabled the cotton industry to expand its capacity in Ahmedabad and other industrial centres. National capital took the first steps to build up the cement and sugar industries. The Tata Iron and Steel Company was able to avoid the threatening catastrophe.

After the bourgeoisie regularised its relations with imperialism, it began an attack on the living standard of the working class. But this was no longer the same working class. A union of Marxism-Leninism and the working-class movement of India had taken place towards the end of the twenties. The reply of the workers to the onslaught of the bourgeoisie was the famous Bombay strikes. The illusions about class peace in the Indian society collapsed in the fire of strike actions. The Indian bourgeoisie demonstrated with utmost clarity that the exploitation of the proletariat of its own country was inherent in its nature.

The evaluation of the role of the national bourgeoisie in the colonial and semi-colonial countries (and India in particular) which was given in a few publications during the period of the personality cult showed some sectarian traits. Although it rightly stressed the contradictory class interests of the proletariat and the national bourgeoisie, it did not sufficiently reveal the contradictions that existed between the latter and imperialism. The one-sided views put forward by Stalin were, unfortunately, also expressed by individual Soviet orientalists during the following years. In the altered contemporary conditions this dogmatic, sectarian method of approach to the national bourgeoisie seriously hampered the scientific analysis of a number of historical changes that were taking place in the countries of the East.

The world crisis of 1929-33 put an end to the comparatively peaceful relations existing between the Indian bourgeoisie and imperialism. The dissolution process of the whole complex of transactions associated with colonial exploitation in which the Indians acted as intermediaries, that began after the First World War, was accelerated by the world crisis. The destruction of productive forces in the peasant economy caused a catastrophic drop in the production of foodstuffs per head of the population. The export of provisions had, therefore, to be discontinued. The export of industrial crops was also reduced, partly for the same reason and partly because a processing industry was growing locally. In terms of volume, the export diminished even more than is apparent, for the foreign monopolies cut the prices of colonial raw materials as much as possible. This together with shrinking imports led to the absolute reduction of commerce in which the Indians collaborated with the British.[1] But the small volume of Indian foreign trade did not, of course, mean that the exploitation of the country as an agrarian and raw material appendage was diminishing. The point is, that during the war period and the years following it the disparity in the values exchanged between colonial India and the imperialist countries was growing. According to a British, source, the prices of commodities imported by India went up by 90 per cent between 1913 and 1923, while the prices of the raw materials she exported increased only by 45 per cent. The prices continued to diverge even more in the following years.

The ruin of the peasant economy also restricted the sphere in which the moneylender could invest his capital, for an essential condition of his activity is that the producer "is the owner, whether actual or nominal, of his conditions of labour".[2] The dissolution of the economy and the slump in the prices of agricultural products made it impossible for the peasants to pay interest regularly on the debts they contracted thus upsetting the normal course of the moneylender's business. The moneylenders, therefore, seized peasant holdings more and more frequently. After having acquired the land the moneylender rented it to the same peasants on enslaving conditions. The expropriation of the peasants by the moneylender was not accompanied by the transformation of the money which the latter had accumulated into agricultural productive capital, that is, by the flow of capital from the sphere of circulation into the sphere of production. A part of these accumulations was used, as before, to grant loans to the peasant; for the new landowners did not cease to conduct moneylending operations, especially among their tenants. But because the peasantry was ruined it was, on the whole, not profitable to lend the peasants additional sums of money. As it was the peasants were ground down with interest payments on the loans and up to the Second World War the total

1. The total amount of Indian foreign trade sank from Rs 4,270 million in 1913-14 to Rs 2,990 million in 1919-20. Then it slowly recovered reaching Rs 4,520 million in 1929-30, the highest point in the postwar period, after that it diminished rapidly during the crisis years; in 1932-33, for example, it amounted to Rs 3,380 million. Moreover the commodities which Great Britain and India traditionally exchanged suffered most; in 1913-14, 3,159 million yards of fabrics were imported into India; during the war, in 1917-18, 1,522 million yards; in 1922-23, 1,576; in 1932-33, 1,225; and in 1935-36, 947 million yards. In 1925-26 India exported 4,173 million bales of cotton; in 1932-33 2,063; and in 1935-36, 3,397 million bales. *Year-Book of India,* (Calcutta, 1925). 791; *Ibid.*, (1927) 750-51; *Ibid.*, 1934-35, 916, 926; *Ibid.*, 1937-38, 770, 775.
2. Karl Marx, *Capital*, III, 581.

agricultural debt was automatically growing at a rapid rate due to accumulating interest.

The decline of commerce in which they collaborated with the British and the restricted opportunities of investing moneylending capital in the peasant and handicraft economy, together with the growing competition of British commercial and banking companies, compelled the Indian bourgeoisie to look for new spheres to invest their large accumulations. In other words, the bourgeoisie was faced with the problem, which had grown more urgent than ever, of how to ensure the reproduction of its capital on an expanded scale. The only sphere where this could be done was large-scale industry. Thus the decay of agricultural production, caused by foreign finance capital and feudal relics, compelled the Indian bourgeoisie to invest in industry.

During the years of crisis and depression the special rate of interest obtaining in Indian industry remained on a fairly high level. The reasons were the increasing exploitation of the Indian proletariat and the relatively high prices of industrial commodities which the British monopolies maintained. The industrial branches developed during the thirties—i.e. the cotton, sugar and cement industries—belonged in the main to Indian capitalists and worked for the home market. This, however, did not change the colonial character of industry in India, for the engineering industry remained at a rudimentary stage while the growth of metallurgy and power supply was quite insignificant in comparison with the enormous size of the country. The transformation of large accumulations of money into productive capital made the procurement of machinery an even more acute problem, since the supply of machines still remained the monopoly of foreign finance capital.

The world crisis of 1929-33, therefore, destroyed the temporary stability of the preceding years. The antagonism between the national bourgeoisie and the foreign monopolies was clearly evident in commerce and finance, in agriculture and, principally, in industry. Therefore, when in 1930-32 the masses of the Indian people, whose shoulders had to bear the full weight of the crisis began the fight, the bourgeoisie participated in it and heated the movement. It was actuated not only by the desire to retain the leadership of the national struggle, but also by the necessity to win concessions from imperialism.

There is no need to describe here the subsequent stages in the national liberation struggle and the role played by the national bourgeoisie. We will merely mention that the bourgeoisie took advantage of the newly arising correlations of forces, which were continually becoming more favourable to the Indian people, to wring as many concessions as possible from imperialism. Imperialism made use of the tactical and ideological weakness of the bourgeois leadership to try to reduce to a minimum the concessions it was forced to make.

The door for the development of capitalism and the economic and political consolidation of the national forces was, to a certain extent, opened by the retreat of imperialism. The more, therefore, imperialism retreated at one stage of the struggle the stronger became its antagonism to the Indian people at the following stage. The crucial point of the objective dialectics inherent in the struggle was that the more complete an agreement the bourgeoisie, as the leading force of the movement, and imperialism reached,[3] the bigger an obstacle to the economic and political advance of the country did the compromise they achieved become during the next stage. While it is possible to criticise the inconsistency and class limitation of these agreements, it would, therefore be wrong and not dialectical to describe these agreements as final settlements.

During the Second World War imperialism was compelled to grant economic concessions to the Indian bourgeoisie, which made enormous profits thanks to military orders and the war boom in general. But the bourgeoisie was unable to renew and expand the productive capacity of its enterprises during the war years. Moreover, the wear and tear of machinery in the Indian industry—that is the consumption of fixed capital—was enormous. After the war, therefore, reproduction, which had always been an acute problem facing the national industry of India, became a question that affected the very ability of Indian industrial capital to operate. If one also takes into account that during the war years the decline of agricultural production persisted and grew even worse one must say that the direct destruction of the productive forces in India was not only a characteristic feature of the first stage of British rule but also of its last stage. Only by gaining its independence could the Indian people restore its economy and develop it further. The inevitably approaching economic catastrophe was indeed the principal objective cause that impelled the whole people of India, including the national bourgeoisie, to unite in a common decisive struggle against the colonial dictatorship.

India won her independence under the leadership of the national bourgeoisie. This class was able to retain the leading role in the movement chiefly because its own interests coincided in the main, with the interests of the whole Indian people at this stage of the revolution. When the bourgeoisie, its political organisations and its leaders defended their own interests in their fight against imperialism, they did at the same time also express the basic aspirations of the masses of the people, although they expressed them by no means fully or

3. We have in view not only the well-known agreements between the leaders of the Indian National Congress and the British authorities, but the total complex of economic and political concessions which the Indian bourgeoisie obtained from imperialism.

adequately. The political leaders of the Indian bourgeoisie could, therefore, speak in the name of the whole nation. Another contributing factor was that the political class differentiation within the Indian society was impeded because all classes had a common enemy—the open colonial dictatorship.[4]

Under these circumstances the working class of India, which invariably acted as the heroic vanguard of the national liberation movement, could not become its leading force. Against the background of the non-violent resistance to imperialism led by the bourgeoisie, the, actions of the workers, who used their proletarian methods of combat, and the peasant revolts—which were also headed by representatives of the working class—dealt especially heavy blows at the colonial regime. Had the British colonialists further delayed the recognition of India's independence they would have had to wage war against the whole people of India. It is possible that British imperialism might even have risked such an adventure. But after the Second World War great changes had taken place in the world: the correlation of forces of socialism and imperialism in the international arena was substantially altered, British imperialism itself had been weakened and could not risk its capital investments in India. After a number of evasive manoeuvres it was compelled to retreat and to hand over political power to the Indian national bourgeoisie. A new era in the history of India began, which impressed its own distinctive features on the fight against imperialism and the correlation of class forces within the Indian society.

---

4. A. M. D. 'Yakov and T. M. Reisner, *Rol' Gandi v natsional 'no-osvoboditel'noi borbe narodov Indii* (Gandhi's Role in the National Liberation Struggle of the Indian People), *Sovetskoe vostovedenie*, 1955, N. 4.

INDEX